An Introduction to the Philosophy of History

Michael Stanford

Copyright © Michael Stanford, 1998

The right of Michael Stanford to be identified as author of this work has been asserted in accordance with the Copyright, Designs and Patents Act 1988.

First published 1998

2 4 6 8 10 9 7 5 3 1

Blackwell Publishers Inc.
350 Main Street
Malden, Massachusetts 02148
USA

Blackwell Publishers Ltd
108 Cowley Road
Oxford OX4 1JF
UK

Library of Congress Cataloging-in-Publication Data

Stanford, Michael, 1923–
    An introduction to the philosophy of history / Michael Stanford.
        p.   cm.
    Includes bibliographical references and index.
    ISBN 0–631–19939–X (hbk.: alk. paper). — ISBN 0–631–19941–1 (pbk.: alk. paper)
    1. History—Philosophy.   I. Title.
D16.8.S717   1998
901—dc21   97–24619
                                                                            CIP

British Library Cataloguing-in-Publication Data

A CIP catalogue record for this book is available from the British Library.
Typeset by Pure Tech India Ltd, Pondicherry
Printed and bound in Great Britain by MPG Books Ltd, Bodmin, Cornwall

This book is printed on acid-free paper

An Introduction to the Philosophy of History

To my children:
Charlotte, Philippa, Julian and Richard –
together with
Martin, Lluis, Caroline and Marion –
with my love.

Contents

Preface

Until the publishers showed me good reasons for doing otherwise, I wanted to call this book 'The Continuing Conversation' or 'The Unending Debate'. For I am convinced that some such phrase truly expresses the nature of history as a study of the past. As we all know, the word 'history' can be used to describe either of two sequences – that of events or that of our accounts of those events. The term 'philosophy of history' has the same ambiguity. It can be a rational endeavour to arrive at general or critical notions about either the first sequence or the second: up to about the mid-twentieth century it usually meant the former; since then, usually the latter. Thus the philosophy of history itself has a history and we have four sequences in all. None of these four has reached a fixed conclusion, nor can it do so till the end of time. That this is true of the first sequence is obvious. Many people, especially those of a positivist cast of mind, have thought that the second, at least, should be determinate, thus narrowing the options for the third and fourth. This is not so.

A. C. Danto has pointed out that all historical descriptions are, and must be, temporary and provisional. No complete description of the past can be given till the end of the future – that is, until the sequence of events also comes to an end. If this is true of descriptions, it must also be true of historical explanations and interpretations. This consideration also brings out something often overlooked: that the first and second sequences are not separate but constantly interact, each helping to shape the other. Histories have their effect on current events, just as current events provoke particular histories.

It is sometimes complained of historians that they so often disagree. There may, of course, be technical reasons for this: one historian may be more neglectful than another of the skills of their craft. But over many a large question, like how to account for the fall of the Roman Empire or for the fifteenth-century Renaissance in Italy, there can be disagreement among the most competent historians. One must not use this undoubted fact to justify the claims, fashionable in certain quarters, that there was no historical past at all; or, if there was, that we can have no knowledge of it – which for men (if not for gods) must come to much the same thing. Events of the past were as real as events of the present are now and as events of the future will be. All are equally happenings located in time and space. Avoiding this error, we must not rush into its opposite and claim that we have a conclusive account of the past, one that cannot be questioned, added to or altered. All interpretations and explanations are, and must be, as temporary and provisional as the descriptions. It is therefore not a weakness of history that it generates unending debates. That is its function. History, like politics, is the activity of free peoples. Whenever we find unanimity among historians, that is as dangerous as unanimity of political opinions. Both are the recognizable properties of dictatorships, not of free states. Open and continuing discussion is of the essence for both history and politics.

Therefore history is to be seen not as a set of cast-iron facts, but rather as an ongoing conversation with one's fellows about affairs of importance or interest – past, present or future. The discussion can at times become debate, or fierce argument. But, as in any civilized exchange, it is as necessary to understand the views of others as to convey one's own.

Philosophy I take to be an attempt at a rational approach to the problems and puzzles, wonders and mysteries, that are encountered either in life in general or in one particular aspect of life. History (in either sense of the word) provides plenty of these.

As for the philosophy of history, its task is, first, to grasp the nature of the activity under study; and, second, to address those problems and puzzles that arise from that activity but that the techniques within that activity cannot handle. Thus the attempts made in the twentieth century to portray history either as a form of science or as a form of literature are equally mistaken. History is not a concept but an activity – an activity of a unique kind. The primary task of the philosopher is to grasp the particular nature of that activity, taken in the most comprehensive senses as I have suggested. History is, I believe, best understood as an endless debate, constituting an important part of the continuing conversation of mankind. As such it makes a significant contribution to our responses to the two ever-recurring questions about where we stand and how we act in the world presented to us: 'Where are we now?' and 'What should we be doing?' Neither question refers to the past, but past reality *and* what we make of it are both essential to effective answers.

Philosophy of history must be a rational discussion and critique of all these issues – a discussion which, like history itself, must never cease.

Now a word of thanks to my helpers. Andrew Pyle, of the Department of Philosophy of the University of Bristol, was kind enough to read the whole text in its first, rough, form. His comments were invaluable. The remaining errors are, of course, my own. My thanks are also due to the unfailing support and cheerful confidence of my commissioning editor, Nathalie Manners. My greatest thanks must, however, be to my wife, who has put in hundreds of hours on the word-processor, has rectified many of my mistakes, has given a quantity of sensible advice, and – above all – has cheerfully endured my all-too-frequent preoccupation or short temper. Without her this book would never have seen the light of day.

Michael Stanford

Introduction

'Philosophy . . . arises . . . from wonder.'
[Aristotle, *Metaphysics*]

1   The Importance and Fascination of History

1.1   The possibility of a philosophy of history

In a free society no limits are deliberately placed upon what a philosopher may wonder about. Yet there are limits *in fact* upon the scope of philosophy. These limits are placed by failure of imagination, neglect of the familiar or weakness of perception. The worth of a philosopher lies not in the problems she solves, but in the questions she asks. (If and when a problem is regarded as permanently solved it generally ceases to be of interest to philosophers.) Much of the greatness of Socrates lay in his ability to show that we do not understand the most familiar words we use – such as 'courage'. He taught us to wonder and to ask.

The science and philosophy of the modern world are based, to an amazing extent, on the thinking of the ancient Greeks, whose strong urge to know was (flatteringly) attributed by Aristotle to all men (Aristotle, 1961, p. 51). However, their urge to know seems not to have extended very much to history. Certainly there were great historians – Herodotus, Thucydides, Polybius – among the Greeks, and certainly some of their past played a central part in their thinking. But it was the past as portrayed in legend, poetry and drama rather than in historiography. Most significantly, the problems presented by attempts to know how the past actually was, to understand it, to find its meaning, to come to terms with how it relates to us and we to it – these problems were rarely (if ever) the concern of Greek philosophers. In short, the Greeks had history but not the philosophy of history.

When we turn to the world of today we find that the study of history has become a widespread industry in our institutions of learning, plays a large part in the education of the young and affords a good deal of leisure interest to thinking people. An awareness of the past bulks large in our lives, whether it comes to us in works of historiography, whether it is mediated through works of art, literature and architecture, or whether it is presented in TV, film, or other popular media. But although our historical consciousness today appears to be much greater than that of the Greeks, the philosophy of history is still comparatively neglected. This seems strange, for surely so large a concern with the past and its meanings cannot fail to throw up problems of interest to the philosopher (as this books tries to show). Is there not scope for wonder in this field, as there is in science, language, the mind, mathematics or morals?

1.2   The popularity of history

What, then, is our engagement with history? Why is it so widely studied, taught and read? There is no lack of historians who, in prefaces, speeches, articles or even whole books, urge its study and claim to show why it is important. Briefly put, such study can satisfy sheer curiosity (about what our predecessors were like and what they did); it can stimulate our imaginations through the strange and the exotic; it can tell how people have lived in other states and societies and so, by comparison, help us to understand our contemporary problems. It can increase our patriotism or our sense of corporate identity. It can trace the origins and causes of present states of affairs. It can make us broader-minded and more tolerant by showing that it has been possible for people and societies to behave very differently and yet be equally human, no better and no worse than we are. In all of these there is present Aristotle's 'urge to know', particularly the urge to know about other people.

Most of us have felt, at some time or other, the truth of the old adage: 'I am a man; I count nothing human indifferent to me – *Homo sum; humani nil a me alienum puto*' (Terence). The novel, the soap opera, the tabloid all bear witness today to our inexhaustible interest in the doings of other people, whether real or fictitious. History has always fed upon it. But for two thousand years or more the narratives of historians were largely confined to the important few – kings, generals, prophets, saints. Some history is still written like this, but now only exceptionally. The last two hundred years have seen an explosion of historical subject matter. In the nineteenth century a few historians pushed beyond the confines of politics and religion; they turned to the activities of 'ordinary' people and wrote economic and social history. Today there is almost no society or social group, no human activity, that has not become the object of historical study.

1.3   Extension of the historical field

A further, and more subtle, development is writing the history not of what people did but of what they thought; hence the history of ideas. But not all ideas were clearly articulated in historical texts. Therefore historians have extended their researches beyond ideas consciously held and clearly expressed. Now they seek out the semi-conscious assumptions that we take for granted and rarely examine, but which are yet so powerful in our lives. This is the history of *mentalités* or mentalities. A recent book will furnish an example. Robert Wohl's *A Passion for Wings: Aviation and the Western Imagination, 1908–1918* (1994), with its many illustrations of early aircraft, would appear at first sight to be a history of aviation – of what people did. In fact, it tells a story even stranger and more fascinating – of what men and women thought about the conquest of the air. It relates in word and (perhaps more forcefully) in picture their perceptions and reactions, the fantasies, hopes and fears stimulated by these extraordinary events. Similarly Lynn Hunt's *The Family Romance of the French Revolution* (1992) shows how in France things so commonplace and unquestioned as beliefs about the family were changed by the events of that revolution. Equally it tells how these changing concepts in their turn affected the course of the revolution. (As one might guess from this and from the word itself, the study of *mentalités* was pioneered by French historians, particularly but not exclusively by those of the so-called 'Annales school'.) The idea of examining historical shifts in fundamental assumptions was not altogether new to philosophy. It is found in Nietzsche's *The Genealogy of Morals*, in Collingwood's *Essay on Metaphysics*, in Kuhn's *The Structure of Scientific Revolutions*, and in Foucault's, *The Archaeology of Knowledge* and *The Order of Things*. Thus history is seen today not merely as the story of what men and women have done, but also of what they have thought. Hence a well-written historical narrative must combine the two and show how actions and ideas acted upon one another.

Moreover, man's search for his past has gone further. Since the eighteenth century the science of archaeology has been developed and the notion of prehistory has arisen. Today a very great deal is known about how people lived in preliterate societies of the thirty thousand (or even three hundred thousand) years that preceded the 'dawn of history' – which occurred about 3000 BC. After that date there grew up the great civilizations of Egypt, the Near East, China and eventually America. Little was known about them, however, until the excavations of the nineteenth century. Even more surprising was the discovery of wholly unknown civilizations, such as those of Minoan Crete and the Indus Valley in the early and mid-twentieth century respectively. The movements and settlements and inter-minglings of ancient peoples have been further explored by scholars of language, of blood groups and of genes. Knowledge of the human past has seen an explosion almost comparable to that of the physical sciences.

2 Philosophical Peculiarities of History

Where does philosophy come in? First, (as we noted), it would be surprising if so vigorous and widespread an enterprise did not generate some interesting problems for the philosopher. As a modern philosopher of history has said, 'It is only because history is a distinctive and rich field of intellectual endeavour – because it is clearly valuable in itself – that it is worth philosophising about' (R. F. Atkinson, 1978, pp. ix–x). Indeed, when we come to examine the subject we find these expectations more than fulfilled. For history (i.e. the study of history) has several peculiarities. One is that, although it claims to relate empirical facts about the objective world, those facts do not belong to what is present, observable, to be confronted, but to phenomena that are past, unobservable and (in any normal sense) non-existent. Another is that unlike most other academic pursuits, history has little or no jargon of its own (See Körner, 1970, p. 48). It is conducted largely in everyday language, and where jargon does intrude it is the jargon of specialized sciences. A third, not unconnected, is that history concerns and is concerned with virtually every other human activity. In this respect it resembles philosophy itself. Perhaps history and philosophy are not so much different subjects (as might be botany and geology), but two different ways of confronting the world.

Yet another peculiarity (again unlike most other academic pursuits) is that history lacks theories and laws; it has no nomological structure, (from the Greek 'nomos' – a law). This goes far to account for its lack of jargon. Any structures that historians may use are almost always derived from elsewhere, generally from more theory-based sciences. Nevertheless, though it lacks a theoretical structure, history has its own methodology – or perhaps several methodologies. Fifth, history is a discipline where the researcher is at one with her material – at least in belonging to the same realm of things. Like psychology and sociology, history (if a science at all) is one of the human sciences – those that, as Anthony Giddens has said, stand in a subject–subject relation (rather than a subject–object relation) to their field of study (Giddens, 1976, p. 146).

Sixth, while most academic disciplines study how things are, history (like geology, astronomy and evolutionary biology) is concerned with how things were. But the subjects that it studies (men and women, actions, states of affairs, ideas) did not long remain as they were; they underwent change or even disappeared altogether. History, therefore, is about the impermanent. It must study not only the natures of those things that form its subject matter; it must also ask how, why and when they changed. 'When' turns out to be particularly important; indeed, chronology is almost the only inherent structure that history possesses.

Seventh, and lastly, our fourth and fifth points come together in the realization that both the student and his study belong not only to the same world, but to the same temporal order. Being in history and knowing that you do is called 'historicity' – a characteristic that is not shared by other animals nor, indeed, by all the human race. But for those who know history at all, an awareness of their own place in history, their historicity, is very important. As Pascal put it, 'History is a book which we write and in which we are written.'

So what, you ask, does this mean? And here we have our finger upon one of the key concepts of history – meaning. Not only the student, but also the reader of history, indeed anyone who is aware of the past in any way, must continually be asking the same question: What does this mean? What did historical events mean to the agent or the observer – the execution of Louis XVI to the people of Paris? What did they mean to the journalist, the diarist, the memoirist, who each gave their own, subsequent, interpretation? What did they mean to the twentieth-century professor who writes books in an attempt to understand and explain these events? Most important, what do all these taken together mean to you? They make up part of what life means to you. The search for meaning and the questioning of other people's meanings is central to any human study – to history above all.

3   Contemporary Neglect of the Philosophy of History

3.1   The scarcity of publications on the subject

Once a year, at least, the major academic publishers produce a catalogue of their publications of philosophy. (I have three before me now.) The books are listed under such divisions as Metaphysics, Ethics, Logic, Philosophy of Science, Philosophy of Mathematics, Philosophy of Mind, Environmental Philosophy, Philosophy of Social Science, Feminist Philosophy, Philosophy of Literature, Political Philosophy, Philosophy of Education, Aesthetics and Philosophy of Religion. Rarely do we find a section labelled 'Philosophy of History'. It is clear that for the majority of our contemporaries who read, write and teach the subject, there is little attraction in *that* sort of philosophy.

The contrast with the flow of books on other aspects of philosophy is striking. Why is this? It cannot simply be that so large an intellectual enterprise as the study of history offers nothing of philosophical interest. How, then, are we to account for its current neglect by philosophers?

3.2   Two kinds of philosophy of history

Before we attempt this question it is necessary to make clear the distinction between the two kinds of philosophy of history; these are known as substantive, or speculative, on the one hand, and analytical, or critical, on the other. This distinction is related to another one – that of the two meanings of the word 'history'. This may refer either to the course of events, what actually happened, (history 1), or to what is believed and written about those events (history 2). Sometimes they are distinguished as 'history-as-event' and 'history-as-account'. Before the twentieth century the term 'philosophy of history' usually referred to speculations about the whole course of events (history 1). This was the work of great system-builders, of whom Hegel, Marx, Spengler and Toynbee are probably the most familiar. These might be described as theories of all the (known) facts. Such is substantive or speculative philosophy of history. During the twentieth century both philosophers and historians have rejected these grand schemes for the good reason that the evidence is insufficient to justify such ambitious pretensions. Instead philosophers have turned to the 'second-order' activity of questioning and criticizing the ways in which historians work. This is philosophy of history with all the facts left out. It is concerned not with what actually happened but with how we think and talk and write about what happened – in short, with history 2. This is analytical or critical philosophy of history and is what is generally meant today by 'philosophy of history'.

Yet it is worth asking whether the older kind of philosophy of history has been too readily dismissed. For the speculative philosophies of writers like Hegel and Marx did at least attempt to grapple with some of the big questions of history-as-event. Not all philosophical problems are about history 2. History 1 leads us to ask, for example, whether the course of history is a process, and, if so, what its nature, what it can mean. Since all history 2 involves some sort of interpretation, it is not trivial to ask what is being interpreted. We shall say more about these questions later.

However, even if philosophers were right to reject speculative philosophy of history, that would meet only half the case. The other question still remains: why do they largely ignore the analytical kind, the critical study of the work of historians – history 2?

3.3 The search for reliable knowledge

I suspect that a concern with knowledge has much to do with it. Modern philosophy is generally held to start with René Descartes, who in the early seventeenth-century wrestled with the questions of knowledge and truth. He resolved 'never to accept anything as true if I had not evident knowledge of its being so' (Descartes, 1970, p. 20). Exactly what sort of evidence guarantees knowledge has been the subject of long debate, but John Locke, towards the end of that same century, had few doubts: for him all knowledge is based on experience. If Descartes is the founder of modern philosophy, Locke is the father of British empiricism. (The word comes from the Greek *peira* = trial, hence also experiment or experience.) This has been the dominant, though by no means the only, trend in twentieth-century British philosophy – a concern with knowledge and truth, and a tendency to answer questions by reference to experience. Another characteristic of modern philosophy in Britain and the US is its analytical approach. More than one philosophical method can be described as analytical, but the basic notion of increasing our understanding by breaking something down to its constituent parts is common to them all. One way of doing this is to search for the smallest meaningful parts and then to build up an artificial system – the approach of Frege, Russell and the early Wittgenstein; another is by seeking to clarify meanings by observing the concrete, everyday use of words and sentences – the approach of the later Wittgenstein, J. L. Austin and Gilbert Ryle.

In this dominant mode of empiricist philosophy we note three things: a concern with the facts about ourselves and the world, a concern with language by which we think and speak about ourselves and the world, and a concern with meaning – a concept basic to communication between sentient beings, but which also extends beyond that. Noteworthy here is the empiricists' admiration for science. Of the three traditional branches of philosophy – metaphysics, logic and epistemology – the tendency of analytical philosophers has been to reject the first, to pay some attention to the second and to concentrate on the third. Questions of knowledge and truth have bulked large, and science appears to them to have afforded the best sort of answers. The true empiricist, they feel, is the natural scientist. So for most analytical philosophers, few of whom have actually engaged in scientific research, science has seemed the very paradigm of logically ordered empirical knowledge.[1] As Wittgenstein put it, 'The totality of true propositions is the whole of natural science...Philosophy aims at the logical clarification of thoughts. [It] is not a body of doctrines, but an activity' (Wittgenstein, 1974, p. 25, sections 4.11 and 4.112). These words, written by an officer of the Austro-Hungarian army serving in the First World War, can be taken as, roughly, the basic attitude of many analytical philosophers for the rest of the twentieth century.

Now it is clear that to such a cast of mind the study of history can have no great appeal. It is not very amenable to the empirical approach, at least, not in its positivist form (but see below, chapter 2, 4.4). Historical facts are not certain; historical judgements are frequently disputed; historical statements do not mirror reality in any obvious 'cat-on-the-mat' mode. As we have seen, history is peculiar in a number of ways. With no single methodology either of research or of explanation, no artificial language of its own to give it the precision of scientific terms, lacking the mathematical base of the more advanced sciences and, above all, with no theoretical structure, no hierarchy of laws of increasing generality, history simply fails to qualify as a science. Judged by such criteria it seems epistemologically inadequate.

3.4   Are history and philosophy rival but complementary?

Such a suspected inadequacy may be the strongest reason for the comparative neglect of the philosophy of history, but it is not likely to be the only one. Rather than speculate further at this stage I will confine myself to the suggestion that history and philosophy are two different ways of looking at the world. Each is autonomous and each has enormous scope, leaving virtually nothing outside. Each locates us in society and in the universe. 'Neither, from its point of view, can be placed on the map of human thought and activity: each is a way of drawing the map though, of course, each occupies a definite area on the other's map' (Atkinson, 1978, p. 8).

4 Present State of Philosophy of History

4.1 A slow rapprochement

Very many of the issues and problems that a contemporary philosopher of history might wish to deal with have been raised in the past. There is nothing very new in the problems of objectivity, of causality, of relativism, of explanation or of laws in history. Indeed, one editor, presenting in 1959 an anthology of twentieth-century writings on history, thought that 'the philosophical reflections about history during the eighteenth and nineteenth centuries are still, in their total impact, superior to what has been produced in our own age' (Meyerhoff, 1959, p. v). Whether he would say this today is debatable. It is more profitable to note some changes in approach to these topics in the second half of the twentieth century.[2]

First, I should note that philosophical remarks about history, at least in the English-speaking world, have usually been made by historians rather than philosophers. This was not the case on the Continent where Kant, Fichte, Hegel, Marx, Dilthey, Croce and other philosophers made significant contributions. Unfortunately the historians' contributions were often somewhat hasty and ill-informed; most tended to think that history was their own business and philosophical thinking could be left to the philosophers. The distinguished medieval historian, Bishop Stubbs, roundly declared, 'I am no believer in what is called the philosophy of history' (Stubbs, 1906, p. 194). It is a pity that he had no philosophical critic to point out to him the prejudices that sometimes underlay his historical judgements; e.g. 'Northern Europe owes its civilisation to the church, and Southern Europe owes everything that is vital, sound, and good to the influence of the North one way or another exerted upon it' (Stubbs, 1906, p. 237). It can only be of benefit to the work of historians (in spite of sceptical remarks made by such as J. H. Hexter or G. R. Elton) that philosophers sometimes turn a critical eye to it. Stubbs was not the only historian of distinction to offer somewhat jejune opinions. 'I have read nothing by Wittgenstein and only a few pages about him' wrote J. H. Hexter (Hexter, 1972, p. 20, n. 9). 'The typical mental processes of the philosopher or the critic or the social scientist, no matter to what school they may belong, are essentially hostile to the typical (and necessary) mental processes of the historian.' And 'we can leave the philosophers and critics to play their games' was the sneer of Sir Geoffrey Elton (Elton, 1991, pp. 61–2 and 31). Second, we should notice that the now familiar distinction made between the two meanings of history (history-as-event and history-as-account) has greatly clarified writing and thinking on the subject. Almost equally useful is that between speculative philosophy of history, dealing with the former, and critical philosophy of history, dealing with the latter. And, third, we may remark that the concern (noted above) of recent philosophy with knowledge and truth and with language and meaning has been of particular benefit to the philosophy of history. The related tendency to examine history as if it were a form of science has been, perhaps, less helpful.

4.2 The impact of Collingwood

This question, as well as the wider question of the relations of history and philosophy to each other, brings us to 'one of the most lucid and penetrating writers on philosophy of history in the language, R. G. Collingwood' (Walsh, 1967, p. 48). His life's work, he wrote, 'has been in the main an attempt to bring about a *rapprochement* between philosophy and history' (Collingwood, 1944, p. 54). As a student at the beginning of the twentieth century he was surprised at Oxford philosophy's 'total neglect of history, as an example of knowledge' (p. 59). He discovered that 'the thing they called theory of knowledge had been devised with special reference to the methodology of natural science; and that anyone who attempted the "application" of it to history found, if he knew what historical thinking was like, that no such application was possible' (p. 60). Is this the situation today? I take up a well-regarded modern textbook on the theory of knowledge (Dancy, 1985). Neither 'history' nor 'historical' appears in its index.

Yet it was not the inadequacies of fashionable epistemology that moved Collingwood. It was rather his perception that, roughly in the half-century preceding the Second World War, 'historical thought had been achieving an acceleration in the velocity of its progress and an enlargement in its outlook comparable to those which natural science had achieved about the beginning of the seventeenth century' (Collingwood, 1944, p. 61). He was certainly correct about the progress in history 2. The discipline has continued to expand at the same remarkable speed since he wrote. If philosophy of history has not advanced at the same rate that is not the fault of Collingwood. He did more than any other, at least in the English-speaking world, to galvanize critical thinking about history. His arguments are discussed below. Here it is sufficient to state his views thus: instead of the hypothetico-deductive methods of the sciences, historical understanding depends on a grasp of purpose and meaning. Such concepts are not susceptible to scientific method.

4.3 Philosophical challenges

After the posthumous publication of Collingwood's last books in the 1940s there was a revival of interest in some of the philosophical questions of history, particularly about historical knowledge – how obtained, how validated, how organized. We may note two other influences here. One was the impact of logical positivism, which had a striking, if brief, success after the publication in 1936 of A. J. Ayer's *Language, Truth and Logic*. The other was the argument (first appearing in an article in 1942) of an American philosopher of science, C. G.

Hempel, that all explanation, in history as much as in the natural sciences, depends upon general laws. Without mentioning his name, Hempel was clearly contradicting Collingwood. For the next two decades the philosophy of history excited more general attention than in pre-war years. As the literature of this period (roughly mid-1940s to mid-1960s) reveals, the arguments centred almost exclusively around questions of knowledge and explanation. As one philosopher noted in 1965, the recent 'renaissance of interest in the philosophy of history' in the guise of theory of knowledge was really two revivals: one represented by professional historians, the other by professional philosophers. Yet these groups wrote and worked entirely independently of each other: 'the fact seems to be that there is an absence of either agreement or controversy between philosophers and historians who devote some thought to problems of historical knowledge' (see Mink, 1965, in Dray (ed.), 1966, p. 160). This unfortunate state of affairs was eased by the founding of the journal, *History and Theory: Studies in the Philosophy of History* in the United States in 1961. Here both philosophers and historians can find a common meeting place. The journal has done much to bridge the gap between the two disciplines.[3] Nevertheless, both on the editorial board and among the contributors professional philosophers easily outweigh the historians. The journal is to this day little read by historians, if we may judge by the lack of references.

Closely linked to questions of knowledge and explanation in history are those of causation and free will, of the objectivity of historical accounts, of action theory and methodological individualism, of relativism and the place of values and value judgements. Such were the stock-in-trade of most writers on the philosophy of history up to the late 1970s. And all these have implications for philosophy in general; they are not confined to history. In one important respect the debate continues much as it did in Collingwood's day: is history basically a science, however inadequate (that is, perhaps an immature or proto-science like psychology or geography), or is it something quite different, so different that it can never become or be mistaken for a science? Wherein does this difference (if there is one) lie? Is it to be found elsewhere than in the rather worn questions I have just cited?

4.4   The importance of meaning

More recently the answer (or, more accurately, several part-answers) have been emerging. It is hinted at by Mink in the article referred to above. He concludes that both parties to this debate have omitted something of importance. This is that they have treated history as if it dealt exclusively with discrete facts or events. One side argue that such facts need to be explained by means of general laws – the scientific type of explanation. The other side argue that they can be explained in the commonsense way, just as one explains single events (a fire, a road accident, a quarrel) today. Historical facts are no different from today's except that they are past. But history is not always (or even chiefly) about single phenomena. Mink points out that historical judgements are often 'synoptic'; that is, that they are single judgements about a large number of facts or events taken together. He suggests 'interpretive history' as a name for this.

Central to the philosophy of history today is the concept of meaning. This was already present in Collingwood. He stressed meaning in the sense of purpose – something that he saw as fundamental to historical understanding, for it was a necessary part of the activity both of the historical agent and of the historian. As he works, the historian must understand his own purposes as well as those of the agents he is studying. Since, by definition, an action (as distinct from instinctive behaviour) is informed by purpose, the historian cannot understand the action unless he understands the purpose. If, says Collingwood, the historian 'is such a kind of man that he cannot do this, he had better leave that problem alone' (Collingwood, 1944, p. 76).

But meaning was, as we have remarked, a matter of concern to analytical philosophers also. Among some it tended to be a concern with the meaning of words or phrases. This was the line of the earlier Wittgenstein. In his later work, however, Wittgenstein urged us to look not for the meaning but for the use.[4] And use had to be considered in various 'forms of life'. Hence context, not only textual context but also living context (*Sitz-in-Leben*), was seen to be essential to understanding. Nor was meaning a matter only for philosophers. A revolution has been occurring in linguistic and literary studies in recent decades. This revolution, which has had a major impact on literary theory and criticism, stemmed largely from the new disciplines of Semantics (the study of meanings) and of Semiotics (the study of signs). It is discussed below, chapter 7, 1.

5 How Philosophy of History Relates to Other Disciplines

We have seen that Mink was struck by the synoptic judgements of historians. These judgements are made when a historian sees a number of disparate elements coming together to make a single historical phenomenon – a market collapse, a revolt, or the passing of a piece of legislation. In doing this he is putting his data together in a particular way. This way is not the hypothetico–deductive method of scientific convention. Rather it is formed on the basis of the historian's grasp of the *meaning* or *significance* of the phenomenon – a significance to which each constitutent part makes its own single contribution. Hence Mink calls such synoptic judgements 'interpretive history'.[5] This is a good name, though it is perhaps difficult to think of any kind of history that is not ultimately interpretative.

We have here put our finger on the thing that (as we have seen) links the philosophy of history with contemporary thinking in other spheres – literary theory, sociology and philosophy. This connecting factor is the concept of meaning, together with its related concept of interpretation.

Indeed, the key to all human studies – literature, sociology and history especially – is a grasp of meaning. For 'meaning' is a concept that links mind, language and society. But among so many disciplines there is variation and disagreement about the exact nature of the concept to which the metaphor of 'grasp' applies.

6 Philosophy of History and Contemporary Concerns

6.1 Groups marginalized in history

Many people nowadays are much concerned with questions of feminism, racism or homosexuality. It is (rightly) felt that certain groups, because of their race, their poverty, their gender or their sexual orientation have been marginalized in our society. This tendency to push some people to the margins not only deprives them of their fair share of power and of material goods, but also denies them the proper degree of respect that human dignity everywhere demands. To right these wrongs will involve not only restoring a just proportion of society's material goods, but also, and importantly, changing the ways in which we speak and think. What difference do words make? one might ask. Is it not enough to give these people their due place in society? No, because we now realise (after reading linguists like von Humboldt, Sapir, Saussure and Whorf) that the language we use shapes the way we think. It is not easy (some would say, not possible) to correct our thoughts, and hence our attitudes and our actions, without correcting our speech.

If it is asked where history comes in, let us turn first to the course of events (history 1). History 2 is notoriously told by the winners. But if we look more carefully, do we not see that the Celtic peoples (Irish, Scots, Welsh) played an important part in the history of Great Britain? Did not the labouring poor both actually perform the Industrial Revolution and suffer its most painful consequences? Have not the subject peoples of the British Empire their own tale to tell of what used to be celebrated as its glories? Are not the peoples of the Third World today being harshly exploited by the triumphant capitalism of the First World? Were not some of the greatest creators of modern civilization homosexual, like Leonardo da Vinci, Michelangelo or Marcel Proust? And who can say that women did not play as necessary a role as men in the long march from the Palaeolithic Era to the twenty-first century?

6.2 Altering historical perspectives

When we discern the parts they played in history 1, must we not rewrite our history 2 in order to acknowledge their roles? But we must go further. We must not only add new facts. We have to bring new understandings to the facts. And not only this: the whole perspective of history must be altered by these changes.

History 1 (the course of events) is made up of people: of groups, of communities, of organizations, of nations, of races, of civilizations. Constituent of the latter are not only the human beings, but also the human products, like ideas and their material expressions – notably books, music, pictures, buildings, trading companies, legal systems and governments. The problems these raise concern one branch of the philosophy of history – the substantive part. The questions asked in the last paragraph but one indicate that new problems thence arise for such philosophy: for example, how far can the needs and purposes (hence the very nature) of a community be identified with those who make the decisions if over half the members of that community are incapable of making known *their* needs and wishes?

6.3 The impact on philosophical questions

History 2 (accounts of history 1) is concerned with how we know, interpret, understand and assimilate past happenings. It is the task of critical philosophy of history to examine, question and evaluate the performances that make up history 2. From the history of women, black peoples, etc. new problems arise. Epistemological questions are to be addressed in respect of the comparatively scanty evidence available and the different nature of these sources from more conventional history.[6] Equally, the interpretation and understanding of the evidence calls for different viewpoints and wider imagination. While it is not entirely true that only women can understand the history of women (or only blacks black history), it is not entirely false either. But the greater task is that of assimilation. If we 'take on board' these new histories, we may find new answers to our philosophical questions. Metaphysical problems about the nature of humanity as a whole, or of what it is to be human – for example, the 'Dasein' of Heidegger or the 'existential being' of Sartre; problems about how groups, societies, institutions, cultures are constituted, and what degree of reality is to be attributed to them; problems about the nature of the historical process (if there is such a process) – all these will take on new shapes and will require other than traditional answers. It is even more obvious that fresh problems will arise for moral and political philosophy – for example, questions of 'reverse discrimination' in compensation for the past. Finally, all the really big problems about meaning will be altered: problems such as 'How do we make sense of the whole continuum of time and history in which we are all placed?' Thus there is no doubt that contemporary concerns can be very important to history, and hence to the philosophy of history.

6.4 Postmodernism and postmodernity

Less profound, but of some interest, are the implications of another contemporary concern – postmodernism. Postmodernists claim that now, as the second millennium gives place to the third, we find ourselves in the condition of 'postmodernity'.

This condition is not easy to define, but it certainly involves a recognition (so they claim) that we have lost our bearings. The theological and metaphysical bases of our culture have given way, our 'meta-narratives' no longer make sense, our values have been disvalued, and our lives (including our common life in history) have meaning no longer.[7] The whole situation is visually summed up by the eclecticism of contemporary architecture. There can also be little doubt that the condition of postmodernity has been rendered even more puzzling and uncertain by the claims to attention of the hitherto marginalized groups that we have been discussing. Feminism, for example, is a major phenomenon of postmodernity. But apart from these and a number of other particular issues, postmodernism is of particular relevance to the philosophy of history. For, first, its claims (strictly, the claims of postmodernists) about the characteristics peculiar to a given era entail certain philosophical positions about history as a process and the possibility of an era or age actually existing as such. Second, they entail the notion that any given era is identifiable by a set, peculiar to itself, of certain characteristics; and, third, that such an era with its defining qualities can be recognized by those actually living in it. All these are philosophically debatable (and indeed debated) questions. Paradoxically, some postmodernists also put forward arguments that claim to invalidate (or 'deconstruct') our beliefs in truth, reason and objectivity. This puts into question not only the 'white, male, bourgeois' history nowadays so frequently challenged, but also many of the claims of marginalized groups just referred to. Indeed it questions the very possibility of history at all – including the claim that we can recognize that we live in a particular historical period, that of postmodernity.

7   Future Possibilities of the Philosophy of History

It is, of course, impossible to forecast the future. All that I can do here is to draw attention to what I regard as suggestive trends in contemporary thinking. There is no guarantee that philosophy of history will go these ways, but I think it will be healthy if it does.

7.1   Philosophers of history to give more weight to history

First, there is the (increasingly recognized) need for philosophy of history to be a little more modest. The tendency for theologians and philosophers to legislate (on the basis of their own disciplines) for the course of history is now quite discredited. Probably the greatest philosopher to give attention to history was Hegel. Yet even he, in spite of several disclaimers, imposed upon it the axiom of his own subject: 'The only thought which philosophy brings with it to the contemplation of history is the simple conception of reason; that reason is the sovereign of the world; that the history of the world therefore presents us with a rational process.'[8]

Voltaire, who invented the term 'philosophy of history', wrote '*Il faut écrire l'histoire en philosophe* – You have to write history like a philosopher.' (But perhaps he meant 'like a scientist' since philosophy and science were barely distinguished in those days.) Less discredited, but still erroneous, is the tendency of some modern philosophers to force history to comply with what they believe to be the precepts of science. One example is the attempt of the philosopher of science C. G. Hempel (referred to above) to identify historical with scientific explanation: 'But there is no difference, in this respect, between history and the natural sciences: both can give an account of their subject matter only in terms of general concepts', for 'general laws have quite analogous functions in history and in the natural sciences' (see Hempel, 1942, in Gardiner, 1959, pp. 346, 345). It is to be hoped that future philosophers of history will be guided more by the concerns of history 1 and history 2 than by notions drawn from outside them.

7.2   Substantive philosophy of history not to be neglected

Second, there has been too wide a gulf between the substantive and the critical branches of the subject. The latter has concentrated on broadly epistemological concerns of history 2. But there are important metaphysical and existential problems arising from history 1 – the domain of the neglected substantive branch. Indeed, one may question whether the two branches are completely separate. Just as there is some interplay between history 1 and history 2 (between history-as-event and history-as-account), so there must be some relation between the corresponding branches of the philosophy of history. (For example, the questions raised above about the possibility that we are in an era of postmodernity is about history 1, and hence belongs to the substantive branch. Yet the resulting questions about how such an era is to be known and thus differentiated from others is an epistemological question for the critical branch.)

7.3   A greater recognition of continuity

Third, I would suggest that the key concepts to history 1 are change and continuity – indeed, change in continuity. That we live in the dimension of time and that all temporal existents (ourselves included) are subject to unceasing change is a commonplace truth too obvious to need arguing. It is less often remembered that the continuity of history continues – into our presents and on into our futures. In an important sense we are one with our pasts. Just as there is no break between now and five seconds ago, so there is none between now and the age of the pharaohs. How are we linked? In three ways: first, by memory; second, by generations; third, by culture. Personal memory as a link with the past needs no explanation here – though it is not without its problems. The second linkage consists of the interactions between parents and children, teachers and pupils, older and younger colleagues. The third linkage (culture) consists of belief and ritual, of legal, social and political institutions, of art and music, architecture and philosophy, but above all, perhaps, by literature. In this way Homer and Dante and Donne are our contemporaries, along with Jane Austen and Charles Dickens. It may be that 'the past is a foreign country', but it is not a strange country. We belong to it as well as to our own. It is, I believe, healthy to have a sense of the past around us – a sense of our own past, in houses, furniture, family traditions, books and pictures and mementoes, as well as in the familiar man-made environment of country and town. It is these things that make real history for us, not the remote and artificial images of the heritage industry which serve only to create a gulf between us and the past, our past. Our lives are continuous with those of our forebears, as I hope our children's will be with ours.[9]

7.4 Meaning recognized as the key

Fourth, I believe that the key concept to history 2 is meaning. All human actions embody intention. (This is so by definition: unintentional deeds count as behaviour.) History 2 involves knowing and understanding as much as possible of the human past. The most important part of the latter consists of human actions. To understand them means grasping the intentions that they embody. Such grasping of intentions is part of the function of interpretation. Hence it is only right that philosophy of history is turning more and more to interpretative questions, rather than those of knowledge and explanation which tended to preoccupy earlier generations. But interpretation has an application wider than that of grasping intentions. It also involves meaning in another sense – that of significance. This can mean determining what events and concatenations of events are significant – in what ways significant, and significant for whom. Another aspect of this approach to history involves a third application of the concept of interpretation. This is 'making sense' of something. We use it when we interpret a document or an inscription. We can also use it in Mink's sense (see Introduction, 4,4) of the synoptic judgement of a number of events or states of affairs. Such judgements may be said to 'make sense' of something – in this case, a cluster of phenomena like the attack on the Bastille or the anti-Corn Law agitation. Sometimes we find it possible to make sense of even wider clusters, like the civilization of ancient Egypt, the Roman Empire or the twentieth-century Cold War. We can also make sense (as I suggested above) of our personal past and of our place in the continuum of history.

It may be objected that 'making sense' is a rather subjective concept, for, notoriously, what makes sense to you may not make sense (or the same sense) to me. This is unavoidable. When we discuss signification (in chapter 6, 1, below) in connection with Peirce and Saussure we shall note that there has to be a third element to provide the link between the sign and its object or referent. This third element, an idea or concept ('*interpretant*' or '*signifié*'), must

be mental – that is, it must occur in a mind. Saussure insists on this p\
is in nature no necessary connection between, say, the word 'STO\
we should do at the road junction. It always takes a mind to make\
connection we call 'meaning'. Thus interpretation in any of the abov\
a mental activity. While most people's thoughts are not too dissin\
neither language nor society would work if they were), yet it is neithᴜ ᴜkely
nor desirable that everybody should think the same at all times on all subjects.
Thus there is, and must be, some variation in how different people 'make sense' of
things – whether it be a word like 'democracy' or a phenomenon like a general
election. Historical judgements, like political, moral and aesthetic judgements, are
essentially interpretative. This is our lot. We are, thank God, human beings
not robots. Fortunately the interpretative nature of history 2 is increasingly
recognized.

7.5   Understanding objectivity

Fifth and last, there is the problem of objectivity. At first sight it may seem that
embracing the interpretative approach requires a rejection of the search for
objectivity. But not so. Historians, like their academic colleagues, are under a
moral obligation to seek the truth wherever it is to be found. In his essay of 1784,
'An Answer to the Question: "What Is Enlightenment?" ' Kant gave the answer in
two words 'Sapere aude – Dare to know' (see Kant, 1977, p. 54). The obligation
binds historians, scientists and philosophers alike. But sometimes the quest for
objectivity has been thought to require an abandonment of all awareness of values
– the so-called 'value-free' approach. This is impossible for the human sciences.
Since we are men and women, not gods, Martians, robots or insects, we cannot fail
to recognize human good when we see it. No one can be blind to the fact that
peace is better than strife, food than famine, or neighbourly understanding than
indiscriminate massacre. Since historians are men and women writing for men and
women about men and women, they cannot, or should not, pretend to be blind to
human needs and human good. Not even the fundamental obligation to truth is
value-free. Such 'freedom' may be possible in mathematics and logic (though even
here rationality is necessary), but it is neither possible nor desirable in human
affairs. Objectivity offers real problems, which will be discussed below in chapter
2, 1 and 2. Any discussion, however, should recognize two simple facts. One that
past events, though no longer present to the senses did nevertheless take place and
were then as real as are the events of the present moment. The other is that we can
have no bird's-eye (still less a God's-eye) view of the past. That must always be
regarded from one or more particular perspectives. Moreover, it is increasingly
and rightly recognized that objectivity is not to be identified with an abandonment
of values.

   Such (on an optimistic view) are the directions in which the philosophy of
history would appear to be moving.

Notes

A word about the short bibliographies at the end of each chapter. They are intended to be no more than guides to some easy approaches to the topics of the chapter. Those interested in following up particular points can be guided both by other references in this text and by the bibliographies of the works suggested. Students will, of course, have the guidance of their tutors. In view of the broad range of topics covered in this book, a full reading list would be unmanageably large.

1 Paradoxically the aim of science is to produce testable hypotheses of a high degree of generality – which are abstract entities, not empirical at all. Does the admiration of the empiricists for so Platonic a scenario betray the effect of an education in the classics rather than in history?
2 Some notion of these earlier ideas about history may be gleaned from Gardiner (1959), Stern (1970) and Iggers (1983).
3 Regrettably there is as yet no comparable publication in the UK, though certain proposals are now in place.
4 Such a phrase as 'It's all hunky-dory' illustrates the difference between its use (we know how and when to use it) and its meaning (which is obscure).
5 He uses the American form 'interpretive'. I prefer 'interpretative'.
6 For the fortuitous, contingent and disproportioned nature of historical evidence, see Vincent (1995, pp. 8–16).
7 This is not as new as it sounds; it is all pretty familiar to readers of Nietzsche (1844–1900).
8 Hegel (1956, p. 9). Compare Elton's remark: 'The historian cannot but work on the assumption that whatever happened is capable of a rational explanation and that evidence is the product of an act discoverable by reason.' See Elton (1969, p. 105).
9 For more on this, see Raphael Samuel, *Theatres of Memory* (1994) and Walsh, K. (1992).
10 'les termes impliqués dans le signe linguistique sont tous deux psychiques et sont unis dans notre cerveau – the terms involved in the linguistic sign are both mental and are joined in our brain'. Saussure (1980, p. 98).

Suggested Reading

Perhaps the best introduction to the philosophy of history is still Walsh, W. H. (1967). Also good for beginners are Dray (1964), Tosh, (1984), and Atkinson (1978). Valuable, but rather more sophisticated, are Aron (1961), Oakeshott (1983), Veyne (1984), and Callinicos (1995) – the last-named is the latest and probably the best. Though idiosyncratic, R. G. Collingwood is the most rewarding of the few English philosophers to pay serious attention to history. Since his writings are both clear and relatively brief, you should not fail to read his *Autobiography* (1944) and 'Part V – Epilegomena' of *The Idea of History* (1961). The arguments may become clearer if you read the short, earlier essays in Collingwood (1965).

The opinions (again, mercifully short) of three great Germans open up important but unfamiliar perspectives. These are Kant (1784a) and (1784b), Hegel (1980) and Nietzsche (1957).

Useful selections of readings are to be found in Meyerhoff (1959), Gardiner (1959) and Stern (1970).

Finally one must not ignore what the historians themselves have had to say about their discipline. Apart from Collingwood (himself both philosopher and historian), among the most notable are Appleby et al. (1994), Bloch (1954), Braudel (1980), E. H. Carr (1964), Cipolla (1991), Kitson Clark (1967), Elton (1969) and (1970), Hexter (1971) and (1972), Marwick (1990), Renier (1965) and Vincent (1995).

1

History, Philosophy and the Social Sciences

'At the present time there is virtually no rapport between history, philosophy and the social studies.' So wrote a scholar in 1968 (Leff, 1969, p. 1). If this described the state of things in Britain, it was perhaps less applicable to the Continent, or even the United States – but let it stand. By contrast, today there is a good deal of interplay between history and 'the social studies', as well as between them and philosophy; there is much less between history and philosophy, a defect that this book aims to rectify. In considering these interrelations it may be helpful to envisage them in the shape of a triangle thus:

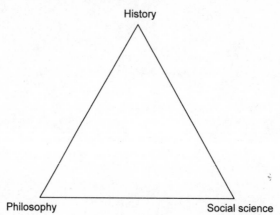

We shall look first at the corners of the triangle, then at the three sides.

1   Corners

1.1   Definitions

First, what are they? For history (at one corner) we may accept Pirenne's definition: 'History is the story of the deeds and achievements of men living in societies'

(Renier, 1965, p. 35). Or we may prefer Elton's enlargement: 'The study of history comprehends everything that men have said, thought, done or suffered' (Elton, 1969, p. 20). Referring to a distinction made earlier, we note that both men are speaking of the study of history, i.e. history 2, not the past itself, history 1.

Next, what is philosophy (at another corner)? One of the neatest answers is that 'philosophy is thinking about thinking'.[1] Another is Hilary Putnam's: Philosophy is 'education for grown-ups'.[2]

At the third corner are the social sciences. (Leff's phrase, 'social studies', is now little used.) What are they? Perhaps the simplest definition is 'the study of society and human relationships'.[3] This sounds remarkably like Pirenne's definition of history, but history is not identical with sociology. The differences, then, cannot lie in their subject-matter (for both are concerned with human beings in society), but must lie elsewhere. This we shall discuss a little later. But what *are* included. The main social sciences are economics, political science, sociology and anthropology. Linguistics, social psychology, international relations, geography and even religious studies can be included, as well as history.

1.2 How scientific are social sciences?

Our definitions have referred to 'study' and 'studies', but how should one study? The accepted answer is 'by scientific method'. Hence the normal title of 'social sciences'. Now there are two ways of looking at this. One way is to assume that the natural sciences have set the correct pattern of scientific study. It follows that the social sciences are only sciences in so far as they conform to the standards and procedures of the natural sciences. The other way is to recognize that the social sciences have standards and procedures peculiar to themselves and that these necessarily differ in some respects from natural science. Holders of this view are then at pains to show that the social sciences are still sciences, though of a different kind. Their philosophical basis is just as sound; it is simply that, dealing with a different subject matter from the natural sciences, they must to some extent differ in standards and procedures. They are, however, equally rational.

Whichever view we take, it is not to be denied that the social sciences do claim to be true sciences. This has been apparent from their birth in the eighteenth-century Enlightenment, when what we should now call economics and sociology first took shape; economics with Quesnay and the Physiocrats in France, sociology with Adam Ferguson, John Millar and Sir John Sinclair in Scotland. It would not be far from the truth to say that these and other men of the Enlightenment saw themselves as attempting to do for the study of mankind what Newton, Boyle, Huygens and others had done for the study of nature. The consequence is that social scientists often claim their science to be objective, empirical, and law-based – that is, resting upon the supposed laws of human nature and of society. However, not all practitioners have been able to sustain this claim, and many nowadays do not try. It is a far cry from the 'social statics' and 'social dynamics' of a positivist like Auguste Comte with his search for 'invariable natural laws' to an anthropologist like Clifford Geertz who asserts his discipline to be 'not an experimental science in search of law but an interpretive one in search of meaning'.[4]

1.3 Weber and the role of subjectivity

How has this come about? What has gone wrong with the ambitions and intentions of the founding fathers of social science? That social science cannot be the same as natural science becomes clear in the work of the great German sociologist, Max Weber (1864–1920). His thinking turns around three points: the first is that in studying beings like ourselves we have an internal understanding of what it is to be human (in contrast with merely external acquaintance with natural objects); the second is that human actions (whether individual or corporate) are the units of sociology and that actions are defined as intentional behaviour in which meaning is central; the third is that all human life is lived in a particular social and historical environment and has to be understood in relation to these impermanent settings. It is clear that each of these three notions is at variance with the positivism of Comte who believed in universal laws of human behaviour that are as certain, as objective, and as unchanging as the laws of the natural sciences. Of course, Weber was not the first to make any of his three points, nor did they remain undisputed after him, but he is perhaps the greatest social scientist to recognize and to wrestle with the dilemma of all the social sciences: how to reconcile the inevitable subjectivity of all human actions with the demands of objective science. The difficulties are compounded by the fact that to practice a social science is itself a human action; as such it is suitable matter for a social science. Thus one can have a sociology of sociology, an economic analysis of economics, an anthropological study of the customs and beliefs of the 'tribe' of anthropologists. (One can also have a philosophy of philosophy and a history of history, but hardly a chemical analysis of chemistry.) Nevertheless, subjecting a science to a critical analysis by its own methods is not always well received. To suggest that the thinking of sociologists, historians or philosophers, for example, is often guided by considerations other than the pure, disinterested pursuit of truth can provoke indignant rebuttals. It seems to impugn both their professional integrity and the validity of their conclusions. Yet it should be obvious to social scientists above all that economists must be influenced by economic factors, anthropologists by sociological ones, or sociology by politics, and so on. Some would go further and claim that for such reasons the social sciences are essentially reflexive; that is, that the existence of the sciences influences their data, and that their findings, in turn, shape the sciences. This creates problems for the concept of objectivity. (Quantum theory, of course, creates similar problems for physics.) All this adds to the problems of social scientists. In general, we can say that almost every social scientist today lives and works somewhere between the two poles of positivistic objectivity and insightful subjectivity. While a stand at either pole is unconvincing, for neither scientific rigour nor empathetic understanding can be totally rejected, yet there is a large number of possible intermediate positions allowing more or less weight to either consideration.

Now that we have identified the three disciplines (philosophy, history and social science) at the corners of our triangle, we can proceed to the relations between the pairs, symbolized by the sides of the figure. We shall first look at the history–social science side, and then see what relevance it has for the other two sides.

2   History and Social Science: the Right-hand Side

It will be convenient to see first what they have in common, and then how they differ.

SIMILARITIES

2.1   Structure and action

As we have already noted, they both study people in society, and thus are both quite clearly distinct from the sciences of nature. With a common subject matter, we might suppose that they could be distinguished by different methods. In fact, there is some common ground here too. This is found in the twin concepts of structure and action. Every society has a structure, itself composed of a number of lesser structures. Without pressing the definition, let us assume that the structure of a society consists of those more or less enduring elements that form the setting within which human action takes place. (The metaphor of stage and actors will do here.) These elements may be formal (like governments, traffic systems, educational systems) or informal (like customs, beliefs, modes of speech). Distinct from the structure are the motivated and (usually brief) actions of men and women in that society, acting individually or collectively. In 1789 and again in 1989 some apparently very stable societies abruptly came to an end. Why? The answer may be given in terms either of structure or of action. Various parts of the systems of government and of society suddenly failed. The people, who had been steadily losing faith in these systems, suddenly rose in protest and the upholders of the systems promptly ceased to sustain them. To continue the metaphor: did the stage and scenery collapse? Or did the actors abandon their usual roles and radically change the drama?

I have taken my example from a textbook of social science (Hollis, 1994, Introduction). But the same examples (of the end of the French monarchy and the endings of Communist regimes in Eastern Europe) could have been taken from history books. Almost any historian's account of these events will describe *both* the changes in and the weakenings of the structures *and* the strongly motivated actions of the people taking part in these momentous events. Sociology is slightly less accommodating (or more rigorous). Some thinkers, like Marx or Durkheim, believed that there are laws of, and facts about human affairs which are distinct from the humans themselves. This is called 'holism'. Others like John Stuart Mill believe that society is made up of the actions and interactions of human beings – hence human consciousness and human intentions are fundamental to society. This is 'individualism'. As Mill put it, 'Men are not, when brought together, converted into another kind of substance, with different properties' (quoted in Ryan, 1973, p. 119, n. 4). Marx, by contrast, asserted that 'it is not the consciousness of men that determines their being, but, on the contrary, their social being that determines their consciousness'.[5]

2.2 Forces and structures of history

It is important here to distinguish structures of society from the so-called forces of history. In the first preface to vol. 1 of *Capital* Marx warns his German readers not to be smug about the superior conditions that German workers enjoy over the English. They will not avoid 'the natural laws of capitalist production. It is a question of these laws themselves, of these tendencies working with iron necessity towards inevitable results. The country that is more developed industrially only shows, to the less developed, the image of its own future' (Marx, 1977, p. 416). Few non-Marxist historians now believe in such laws of development. However, the social structures of the social scientist and the Marxist laws of development through time can be seen roughly to correspond to Comte's 'social statics' and 'social dynamics' respectively. Most social sciences have worked out some account of 'social statics', i.e. of the systems and structures of society, but few have given a convincing account of 'social dynamics', that is of the laws of the changes in human society over time.[6] One notable exception was W. W. Rostow's attempt to do so for economic change in *The Stages of Economic Growth: a Non-Communist Manifesto*. This work, published in 1960, is (like the similar theories of Gerschenkron) now not much esteemed. A more useful work is Robert Nisbet's study of the Western theory of social development (see Nisbet, 1970). Among historians, though few subscribe to developmental theories of history, most acknowledge the place of social, political and economic structures. Few, perhaps, would agree with Christopher Lloyd that their approach and methods are inadequate, but Lloyd makes a strong case. Like Marx, he believes that history is driven by hidden forces. He begins with the assertion that 'The macro structures of economies and societies and the causal mechanisms of their formation and history are beyond common-sense understanding' (Lloyd, 1993, p. 1). What is hidden from the ordinary man-in-the-street and from many historians ('who believe that no special general concepts, methods ... apart from ... "common sense", are required'), is revealed to social science. 'Only a form of analysis and a mode of understanding that penetrates to the obscured structural relations and imperatives of economies and societies can begin to reveal and explain the real history and powers of the organizational basis of social life' (Lloyd, 1993). The whole book is a well-argued plea for a structural approach to history.

2.3   The 'Annales' school

A similar approach has already become familiar in the French Annales school of historians. Indeed, Lloyd explicitly states the need to go beyond Annales (1993, p. 2.) These French historians attempt a 'total history' (by which is meant not world history, but an integration of all kinds, methods and aspects of history), a serial history (i.e. surveying the same phenomenon over a long period, as in the Chaunus' *Séville et l'Atlantique 1504–1650*, employing available statistics), and a structural-functional approach which concentrates on the continuities and systems of society.[7] Certainly Braudel himself was at pains to include history among the social (in his words, human) sciences.

2.4.   Other areas of common ground

Thus we see that structural approaches are common ground to social science and to many historians.[8] Other areas of common ground are the debates over hermeneutics (i.e. the importance of meaning in history and the social sciences), over holism and individualism, over action or behaviour, over explanation or understanding, over causes or reasons, over values, and over the need for a technical language (or jargon).[9] All these debates we find in both social science and history. Above all, both disciplines increasingly recognize the importance of the concept of meaning in their studies.

DIFFERENCES

2.5   Concepts in social science and in history

In spite of the efforts by numerous historians, social scientists and theorists of both camps to assimilate history to the social sciences, there remain marked differences. One is that the social sciences tend to create their own objects. Money markets, kinship structures, social equilibria, anomie, reference groups, or signifiers are not the familiar objects of everyday life; they are constructs of various social theories. This fact helps to reinforce the argument (referred to above) that social sciences are reflexive. History, on the other hand, has few concepts peculiar to itself; that is largely because it has no theory peculiar to itself. Oakeshott suggests that history has a few words 'with given specialized meaning': namely, ' "past", "happening", "event", "cause", "change" and so on' (see Oakeshott, 1983, p. 6). More plausibly, there are at least two concepts initiated by historians that have been widely taken up by social scientists: namely, E. P. Thompson's 'moral economy' and Eric Hobsbawm's 'invention of tradition' (see P. Burke, 1992, pp. 1–2). Historians normally use either the words and concepts of everyday life (i.e. no special jargon), or they use the words and concepts of other institutions or disciplines: law, administration, geography, the Church, the armed forces, the arts, as well as sometimes of the social sciences – in particular, of economics, sociology and demography. One philosopher, Stephan Körner, has drawn attention to the 'double-layered' nature of the natural and social sciences.

> Any branch of inquiry in which predictions are made by identifying theoretical concepts and statements with corresponding commonsense ones might be called 'double-layered'. All quantitative natural and social sciences are double-layered... Even seemingly descriptive and taxonomical sciences may be double-layered... History, on the other hand, is single-layered. In its traditional form, it tries to describe sequences of events as they have occurred, and has no use for a simplified ideal world as described by an axiomatic or less strictly organized theory. (Körner, 1970, p. 48)

Historians, on the whole, do not interpret the world via a screen of theory; they try to see it and understand it directly.

2.6 History inclusive: science exclusive

A second difference is that the social, like the natural, sciences select data of a certain kind and thus make an abstraction from reality. In the real world everything is mixed up with everything else. Take a horse. To the physicist it is of a certain size and weight and can exert so much force (horse-power) in work. To the economist it represents so much capital outlay by its owner, who will perhaps use it to generate so much income. To the zoologist it is a specimen of the genus *Equus*. To the chemist it is an apparatus for metabolizing oats into muscular power, and so on. None of these pay much attention to the other, and all fail to recognize my friendly old Dobbin. History, however, embraces the totality of human experience, while at the same time trying to give full value to the individual.[10] The reason for this inclusive approach is not unconnected with the previous point – that science often creates its own objects while history favours the ordinary and unspecialized.

2.7 Sciences and theory

A third difference, then, is that as sciences abstract from reality, so they construct a network of theory from these abstractions. Positivists used to believe (some still do) that their generalizations from observed facts were identical with the laws of nature, including human nature. Most scientists today are more cautious; they distinguish degrees of certainty between a hypothesis, a theory and a law. Never-

theless, the tendency is still there – to find the truth in wider and wider generalizations of increasing degrees of certainty, objectivity and reliability. This movement takes us further and further away from the individual and from Blake's
words: 'To Generalize is to be an Idiot. To Particularize is the Alone Distinction
of Merit.' (This was written on the margin of Sir Joshua Reynolds' discourses on
art, and in the context of the arts I think we have to side with Blake against
Reynolds.) An emphasis on the individual and particular in history is, of course,
fundamental to historicism, except in Karl Popper's idiosyncratic definition of
'historicism'.[11]

All sciences, social as well as natural, are orientated towards the discovery of
laws (or at least the establishment of general truths). However, some social
sciences are more 'law-seeking' than others. Perhaps the extremes are occupied
by the heavily theoretical science of economics at one end and cultural anthropology, with its emphasis on 'thick description' and the understanding of meaning, at the other.

2.8   Mathematization

This law-seeking tendency is reinforced by the use of mathematics. Many people
consider that any science becomes more 'scientific' (i.e. rigorous, objective, valid
and reliable) just in so far as it has a mathematical structure – that is, in so far as it
is 'mathematized' (see Körner, 1970, pp. 44–7). Mathematization has not yet
advanced far into history in its traditional form, though some important steps
have been taken – particularly in economic history and demography (see, for
example, Le Roy Ladurie, 1979 and 1981; Floud, 1974 and 1979; Temin 1973;
Fogel and Elton, 1983). To be really effective in a scientific discipline, mathematics
has to be part of the basic theories of that discipline as it is in physics and biology.
Stephen Hawking puts the point very clearly: 'I therefore take the view . . . that a
theory of physics is just a mathematical model that we use to describe the results
of observations . . . Beyond that, it makes no sense to ask if it corresponds to
reality, because we do not know what reality is independent of a theory' (Hawking,
1993, p. 44). No historian could utter those last eleven words) We should also note
that almost all scientists (except perhaps some advanced theoretical physicists) use
nothing but algorithms – that is, mathematics that can be performed on a
calculating machine. Yet Roger Penrose (a collaborator of Hawking) points out
that 'algorithmic things constitute a very narrow and limited part of mathematics'.
Indeed, he believes that mathematics exceeds all formal mathematical systems:
'The notion of mathematical truth goes beyond the whole concept of formalism.
There is something absolute and "God-given" about mathematical truth.' It 'goes
beyond mere man-made constructions' (Penrose, 1990, pp. 128, 146). The theories of the social sciences are not easily mathematized, we must conclude. As for
history, mathematics may be useful (as in demography) but, in consideration of
the above, must remain marginal.

2.9　History studies the unobservable

Yet another distinction between history and the social sciences lies in the nature of the evidence. Experimentation and observation have essential roles in science, though the social sciences have little opportunity for the former. History has almost no opportunity of either, for its subject matter is the past and, by that very fact, unobservable. Economists, sociologists, anthropologists, political theorists can study the phenomena of their disciplines in the world around them. Not so the historian; he can only study the evidence left behind by the phenomena of *his* discipline. The phenomena themselves, the events and the people, have vanished.

2.10　Can human actions be universalized?

This leads us on to an important problem that has by no means been solved: What is the place, if any, of time in the social sciences? On one side of the question is the fact that the natural sciences have always sought, and largely do still seek, to find laws of nature that apply equally in all times and places; they are universal. On the other hand, the social sciences deal with human actions. Human actions are expressions of consciousness and will; values and meanings are central to them. They can be observed objectively, but they have to be understood subjectively. How can universal laws be established about such things?

TIME AND THE SOCIAL SCIENCES

2.11　Can the social sciences ignore time?

We have seen that many scientists believe that time has no place in the laws of nature. Such laws are timeless and eternal – if oxygen and hydrogen combine to form water, then they always have and they always will. Yet time cannot be excluded from every natural science (see below, chapter 1, 2.16). With the social sciences it seems even more doubtful. For human beings not only perceive meanings; they also remember and record experiences. When atoms of oxygen and hydrogen combine into water they do not remember that they did it last time; they just do it. But humans are not like that. Their memories and records often influence them not to repeat former actions exactly. Moreover, humans change their environments – not only by movement, but more significantly by construction – of agriculture, crafts, buildings, associations, organizations and institutions, and of bodies of knowledge. Thus similar actions occur in different environments and then are not so similar after all. Above all, people have languages and they talk to one another. This changes both the outer situation and the inner dispositions of the actors. Things are by no means the same in different circumstances. In short, allowances have to be made for the passage of time and the changes (inner and outer) that it brings with it.

2.12 Social theory as a cause of social change

More confusingly, some of these changes result from the very descriptions of society. As one social scientist has pointed out,

> social life is in part the product of social theory. For in a way that is not generally true in the natural sciences, the social description of social reality can be self-validating. If people come to believe, for whatever reason, that they are acting from a given motive, there is a sense in which they are bound to be right, and thus a perfectly good sense in which a description of their actions in such terms is quite correct. (Ryan, 1970, pp. 18–19)

This is another example of the reflexivity of social science referred to above. It is, of course, equally true that people often deceive themselves about their motives. Then we should want to give a different account of their actions.

2.13 Do social sciences need theories of development?

The social sciences face similar problems with respect to time as the natural sciences. Their practitioners may make the assumption that human nature is roughly the same in all ages. If so, then they may draw their data indifferently from the past as from the present. (Economists and sociologists of religion are often among these). This leaves them open to charges of anachronism. On the other hand they attend to the historian's claim that time does matter, because earlier states of affairs influence later ones (by foreclosing certain options) and in later ones men may learn from earlier ones. For these and other reasons people and economies undergo change. This means that social scientists have to work out theories of development; they are dealing with continuing processes, not with simple 'nuggets' of data to which time is irrelevant (as it is with atoms of hydrogen and oxygen). This is particularly necessary for those economists, sociologists and anthropologists who deal with developing countries, where change in all these spheres is so rapid as to force itself upon the scientists. The problem for them is that, although they are dealing with material from the past – material that has often only been made available by historians, yet they cannot treat their material like historians. The latter are quite happy to tell what happened without excogitating any over-arching theories. The social scientist, however, cannot forget that he is a scientist; he frequently feels the necessity of making law-like generalizations and sometimes even of constructing theories of change and development applicable to all his material on the model of the natural sciences.

2.14 Three lines for sociology: Wright Mills

What is the social scientist to do? The far-seeing American sociologist, C. Wright Mills, identified in 1959 three attitudes in contemporary sociology. One was a theory of history, concerned with 'stages' in history as well as the regularities of social life. Marx, Toynbee and Spengler are among the creators of what he calls 'a trans-historical strait-jacket into which the mateials of human history are forced'. A second was the elaboration of a systematic theory of the nature of man and society. This aimed at 'classifying all social relations and providing insight into their supposedly invariant features'. This he calls 'Grand Theory'. The third looks 'towards empirical studies of contemporary social facts and problems' (Mills, 1970, pp. 30–1). What is the social scientist to do (for the problem is not confined to sociology)? Must he try to deal with the problem of time and the changes that it brings to any society? Or are his theories based on present and past data indifferently? One economic historian insists on the latter: 'To qualify as economic history a piece of research must employ the conceptual instruments, the analytical categories and the type of logic forged by economic theory.' To think otherwise, to believe that different mental tools must be applied to very remote and different societies, 'is fundamentally incorrect, or at least is in need of substantial qualification' (Cipolla, 1991, p. 7). It is unlikely that many economic historians would disagree. Economists and most anthropologists and social psychologists work on the same lines. And yet...

2.15   None of the three solves the problem of time for the social scientist

To come back to the sociologist: which of Mills's three paths should she choose? The first seems at first sight the obvious one, for this does explicitly tackle the problem of time and change. The difficulty is that it is a daunting task, and even the best attempts (whether by the sociologist Spencer, the economist Marx, or the historian Toynbee) have been notably unsuccessful. Most critics agree with Mills that the result is 'a trans-historical strait-jacket'. (We shall return to this topic.) The second would work if we could be as certain as the economic historians that we possess concepts, categories and methods that are valid for all times and places. Any such system (or set of theories) would have to include a theory of social development (the counterpart to theories of economic growth). Mills criticizes one of the best of the grand theories of his day (that of Talcott Parsons) for failing in just this respect: 'Any systematic ideas of how history itself occurs, of its mechanics and processes, are unavailable to grand theory, and accordingly, Parsons believes, unavailable to social science' (Mills, 1970, p. 52). Nevertheless, grand theory has returned to popularity, as is recorded in the title of Quentin Skinner's collection: *The Return of Grand Theory in the Human Sciences* (1985). Yet among the thinkers discussed there we find little explicit theory of the 'mechanics and processes' of social change. They concentrate on a more modern concern – that of meaning. To be sure, they are reacting 'against the assumption that the natural sciences offer an adequate or even a relevant model for the practice of the social disciplines'. They acknowledge the need for 'a hermeneutic approach to the human sciences' (Skinner, 1990, p. 6). (Hermeneutics is the science of interpretation, hence of the discovery of meaning. It derives from Hermes, the ancient Greek messenger of the gods.) But as for taking account of time, it seems that grand theory is still open to Mills's criticism. The third possible approach, the empirical, is the least likely of the three to produce any such theory. None of its various methods is intended to account for change and development. Indeed, unlike grand theory, its concentration on narrow issues and on methodological experiment causes it to eliminate 'the great social problems and human issues of our time from inquiry' (Mills, 1970, p. 84). Perhaps it is worth considering what may be gathered from John Stuart Mill's theory of ethology. He thought it possible to work out a science of human nature in its varying circumstances and occasions.

> The laws of the formation of character are, in short, derivative laws, resulting from the general laws of mind, and are to be obtained by deducing them from those general laws by supposing any given set of circumstances, and then considering what, according to the laws of mind, will be the influence of those circumstances on the formation of character. (Mill, 1988, p. 54)

Certainly such a science would have its problems, but possibly no greater ones than those the social sciences and history have today in trying to explain the behaviour of people in past (or even present) societies. Mill's 'ethology' or laws of the formation of character, are not too remote from the 'mentalities' of the Annales school.

2.16   The problem for the sociologist

Let us look at Wright Mills' second path. The phenomena of the social sciences not only vary (often quite unpredictably) from place to place, but they also change continually and often very rapidly. Let us suppose that a sociologist is making a detailed study of a city. It will make a great deal of difference whether his study is being made in 1900, 1925, 1950, 1975 or 2000. Not only will the facts be very different, but the assumptions and working methods will not be the same. To establish really satisfactory results he will have to look at all the data for each of these dates and find a methodology that embraces all of the methods used. This would certainly be possible, but it cannot be done before the year 2000, since in no earlier year could he predict the results of the fifth survey. He is thus, willy-nilly, drawn into history; his five sociological surveys become a history of the city. Inevitably he will find himself faced with all the problems with which the historian is familiar, but for which the normal sociologist is not trained. As Mills observed, most sociological surveys are empirical and so are assumed to deal with one point in time – that is, the three or so years preceding the present when the researcher was gathering his materials. Since the researcher knows perfectly well (though he may forget) that the city he is describing was not always like that nor will long remain so, he should include a date in his title: not, say, 'An Industrial Community in the Mid-West', but 'A Mid-West Industrial Community in the 1990s'. One may then ask him which of his conclusions are valid only for the 1990s, which of them are valid for a longer period (and for how long), and which, if any, may be taken to have universal and permanent validity. He can hardly answer such questions without reference to change over time and hence to history. This shows the weakness of the 'second path'. The chemist analysing a substance or the biologist tracing the mechanism of inheritance does not have to face such questions. His conclusions, once established, are taken to be true for all time. If they do not remain for all time, it will not be because acetic acid or genomes have changed, but because the sciences of chemistry and genetics have changed – and presumably have progressed.

2.17   Some attempts at theories of change by social scientists

It would be quite wrong, however, to conclude that sociologists, economists and anthropologists ignore the problems of social change. There is quite a large literature on change (often called 'development') in all three areas.[12] As true scientists, they do not limit themselves to a detailed study of one change (as historians tend to do), but try to formulate theories of change by collecting and comparing several examples, as Barrington Moore did with dictatorship and democracy or Theda Skocpol with revolutions. The example of Rostow in economics has already been mentioned (p. 24). Beyond these comparative works it may be possible to develop typologies of social change. As Bottomore points out, this would be highly advantageous (if successful) for many reasons (see Bottomore, 1971, p. 308). This is Mills's first path. The difficulties are formidable, however, as Mills points out, and few have attempted it. Some of the difficulties would arise from the problem of finding a methodology equally applicable to all historical times and places. Many more difficulties would be presented by the paucity of data for many past societies, as well as of the interpretation of what we have. Not surprisingly, most sociological theory is based on the sort of societies that produce sociologists. (The same is true of historians, except that they do not theorize nearly so much, for theory-building is not their *raison d'être*.)

We may conclude that the role played by time (or rather, by temporal change) is a very real problem for the social sciences – a problem from which many natural sciences are largely though not entirely free. Geology, evolutionary biology, archaeology and cosmology are sciences where temporal change is a central concern. There is much debate in each of these about theories of change. Difficult as are the problems they face, historical sociology faces greater ones. For example, rocks do not remember the past or hope for the future.

2.18   Historiography an individual product

Most scientists work in teams. The individual is rarely known to the public unless he or she makes some spectacular discovery. By comparison the historian is quite a star. She performs alone. Rarely does the name of a collaborator appear on the spine of her books, in contrast with scientific articles, which usually have several signatories. 'What worthwhile book after the Pentateuch has been written by a committee?' asks George Steiner (Steiner, 1989, p. 36). In this respect social scientists are more like historians than natural scientists. Even so, the subject matter of history is, perhaps, less determinate than that of social sciences and interpretation may play a larger part. As a consequence a work of history usually offers a more personal view than one of economics or sociology. Perhaps it is for this reason that there is a good deal of discussion about the literary qualities of historians' works, while the literary merits of social science works are rarely noticed. Their authors would say this is as it should be: science should be written in a plain, no-nonsense style – as has been the custom in England since the Royal Society established the tradition of scientific style in the seventeenth century. Indeed the merits of scientific prose have recently been recognized in an excellent anthology, *The Faber Book of Science* (1995), edited and introduced by a literary scholar, John Carey. Few social scientists appear in this work; their writing is not, on the whole, notable for literary merit. Literary considerations aside, the writings of historians seem to embody a personal perspective more than those of scientists. Partly this is because they work as individuals and partly because they see themselves as continuing a tradition. 'The historian writes as much in response to other historians, past and present, as he does to his own circumstances' (Leff, 1969, p. 14). This is surely less true of the scientist. Fernand Braudel argues for team work in the human sciences (which for him includes history), but social science sees, perhaps, less team work than the natural sciences (see Braudel, 1980, pp. 55–62).

MUTUAL ASSISTANCE

Finally, before leaving the topic of the relations between history and the social sciences we should glance at some of the ways in which they can assist each other.

2.19   The scientific approach: non-personal elements

The two primary questions for historians (as we have already noted) are 'What exactly happened?' and 'Why did it happen?' Traditional historians wrote narratives which told of the actions of important persons or of personified institutions like states, trading companies, or other formal organizations. Both the 'What?' and the 'Why?' were answered in personal or quasi-personal terms. Since the

Enlightenment the importance of non-personal factors in history has been increasingly recognized: in different ways Voltaire, Montesquieu, Vico, Rousseau, Adam Smith and Kant all contributed to this. Hegel, with his emphasis on the advance of Spirit in history, and Marx, with his class conflicts and class interests, reinforced the tendency of historians to look for the collective and impersonal elements in history, as well as (sometimes instead of) the parts played by individuals. Such elements are distinguished by having no consciousness, no will, and no apprehension of meaning. Now it is typical of all sciences to pay little attention to the individual, but rather to seek generalizations leading to theories and laws from which deductions, predictions and explanations can be made. Individual cases are seen less as interesting in themselves than as confirming or disconfirming instances of generalizations. In order to do this scientists concentrate on selected features of reality and ignore others, which they leave to other scientists. Thus the economist may be concerned with rates of exchange, leaving questions of the chemical analysis of the coinage to a chemist and the weight of the bullion to a physicist. Both the tendencies to abstraction from concrete reality and to generalization from examples are contrary to the traditional outlook of historians. However, as, in the last two or three hundred years, historians have become more aware of the non-personal elements in the life of men and societies, so the social sciences have developed to explore just these elements which older historians either took for granted and ignored, or simply did not know of. Romans of the Empire were not unaware of the depreciation of the coinage, but they had no economic theories to explain either the causes or the effects of the phenomenon. Yet even historians have to make comparisons, or they could never tell what was significant. The Italian Renaissance or French Revolution would have secured much less attention had they not been virtually unique. But once into the business of making comparisons between societies, some attempt at social theory is almost unavoidable.

2.20 The benefits brought by social sciences to history

To put it shortly, the social sciences have had a greatly beneficial effect upon history in a number of ways: they have brought a knowledge of the social settings and structures within which historical actions have taken place; they have supplied knowledge which fills up the gaps in the historian's evidence; they have refined and improved the thinking and the methods of historians about societies of the past; and – this is formidable – have offered accounts of the course of history, accounts in terms of large elements and impersonal forces, that challenge the traditional view of history as the story of the actions and passions of particular men and women.[13] Historians themselves disagree widely as to whether this last consideration is beneficial to historiography or not, but it is certainly not to be ignored. Above all, because the social sciences are so theoretical they involve a good deal of criticism and argument. The historian who is aware of these debates is likely to be more nimble, more rational, and more critical (especially self-critical) in his thinking.

2.21   The historian helps social science

2.21.1   The historian's warnings for social science: irregular and unpredictable change   Now we reverse the question and ask what the historian can do for the social scientist. It was once supposed that the chief (or only) function of the historian in this respect was to provide hard data for the hypotheses of the scientist. Few hold this view today, if only because hard (that is, uninterpreted) data are not easy to come by. The main functions of the historian *vis-à-vis* her social scientist colleagues is to comment and criticize from her own rather different experience and outlook. The central features of her outlook are likely to be the past (with its concomitants of time and change), the individual (person, action, place or event), and the seamless web of human affairs, woven through the weft of inter-laced societies and along the warp of time. The first types of warning come from her dealings with the past. She can warn her colleagues that things were not everywhere as they are now; distances and time and space can produce social elements that are not those of contemporary Western societies. Since it is in these societies that the social sciences have chiefly developed the danger of neglecting such differences is obvious and most scientists acknowledge it, yet it is not always sufficiently guarded against. Again, as we have seen, time is important in its aspect of change. Because the social sceinces have grown up in the shadow of the physical sciences, many writers have (as we remarked) tended too easily to assume the static or changeless outlook of physics or chemistry. On the other hand, in so far as social scientists are successful in establishing laws that are quasi-independent of time (like Gresham's law of depreciation of coinage), then the historian of every age has a useful tool. Functionalists tend to view a society as a machine that works unceasingly and regularly – like a clock or the engine of a car. It might be better to view it as a tree or an animal or a man that grows and changes in often unpredictable ways. Again, the social scientist will protest that he is well aware of this. Indeed it is true that a number have attempted to develop theories of societal change, though perhaps with no great success.[14] It may be that more social scientists should have some explicit hypothesis of change woven into their theoretical structures. The difficulty is that societal change appears to be even less predictable than changes in trees or men (as historians are well aware), so it is very tempting for many social scientists to forget or ignore change altogether. Most historians are quite content to admit that there are no laws of history, though many are willing to see whether and where the laws of the social sciences may apply to history.

2.21.2   Importance of the individual   The second type of warning comes from the historian's emphasis on individuals of various kinds. This in itself gives history a rootedness and an empiricism that is often absent from the theoretically constructed sciences where, as we have said, a particular is only an instance of a generalization. The whole point about the individual (person or event) is that it is concrete. For example, if we know only that 90 per cent of the children in a certain area regularly attend Catholic schools, then the prediction that Mary Smith (a child of that area) had a Catholic education has a 90 per cent chance of being right. But we need historical (not sociological) evidence about Mary to know precisely whether she had that upbringing or not. And Mary is a real person with whom a man might fall in love (with all that that implies); he would not give his heart to a sociological statistic. The many-sidedness of the real Mary Smith brings us to another warning. Science abstracts; history looks to the totality. If we wish to explain a particular action of Mary Smith, we are likely as historians not to seek that explanation solely within the theories of social science, but to look at her natural circumstances – where she lives, the climate, her state of health and medical history, for example. We also need to know her past, her personal relations and, in particular, the events preceding the action in question. There is almost no kind of fact or phenomenon that is inadmissible as part of the explanation – fairies and astrology excepted. A sociologist may look for sociological explanation (or part thereof) almost anywhere. Another way of putting this is to say that the individual (person or event) is best seen as the point of intersection of innumerable systems. All systems are woven together to make up Maitland's 'seamless web'. Finally we must not forget that, whereas for the scientist, meaning inheres primarily in ideas and theories, for the historian (as, in different ways, for the lover and the poet), meaning can be most powerful in the concrete individual person or place or happening.

2.21.3   Values and objectivity   A third type of warning relates to the vexed question of values. Among both social scientists and historians there has been a long debate as to whether it is possible to describe human behaviour in language that is 'value-free'. Can either sociologists or historians be as coldly, clinically objective about their subject-matter as mathematicians and physicists are about theirs? As Weber pointed out, values largely constitute a culture. It may be possible for the sociologist or anthropologist to give an objective account of the values of the alien cultures she is studying. But the scientist is herself part of a culture; her very research is a social activity within her own society – a society that would not exist at all (as has often been pointed out by functionalists) without a large consensus of values. How can her activity be free from her own and her society's values? The assumption among most historians and social scientists in the nineteenth century that value-free objectivity was attainable has largely given way in the late twentieth century to the reluctant admission that it may be quite impossible after all.[15] The contribution that the historian can make to the debate is to point out that there are more than two stages in doubt (the values of the group under study and the values of the scientist). It is clear in history that there are three; not only do the values of the historical agent and those of the historian have to be taken into account, but also the values of all those who have supplied information (i.e. evidence) about that agent. If we look at a national hero or heroine, like King Alfred or El Cid or Joan of Arc, we find that they are represented to us by story-tellers, poets, painters, politicians, priests and propagandists of various kinds. In such accounts it is *their* values that predominate – values that are likely to be quite different either from the values informing the actions of the historical agent or from those of the modern student striving for an objective understanding of that agent. The scientist must be reminded that the values of any intermediary must be taken into account. This is true even when the scientist is conducting his research in face-to-face interviews, which in the nature of things cannot often be the case. For reporters even from within the community under study will be tempted to give their version of the values of that community; indeed, even individuals questioned about their own personal values are tempted to report that values they feel they ought to hold rather than the ones upon which they act.

2.22   Summary: the historian warns of time, meaning and value

We can sum up by saying that the problems of time, of meaning and of value are problems with which the historian is more familiar than the average social scientist. This is largely because the former, whatever help he receives from scientists and their theories, is much more committed to the individual and the concrete.

3   Philosophy and Social Science: the Base

We now turn to another side of the triangle and look briefly at the relations between the disciplines at two other corners.

3.1   What is a social science?

Philosophical questions about the social sciences often start with an examination of whether or not they are properly called sciences – something for which the standard is set by the natural sciences.[16] There is no reason, apart from primogeniture, why all sciences should be expected to conform to the model of the natural sciences. Any science, we may agree, is aimed at the extension of our knowledge. Surely the two fundamental questions to be asked within the boundaries of a particular science are 'What is there to be known?' and 'How do we know it?' The first question is ontological and belongs to metaphysics; the second is methodological and belongs to epistemology. Can we give general answers to these questions on behalf of all the social sciences? Let us at least try.

3.2   Matter

3.2.1   Actions and integrations   We gave an answer to the first question when we accepted the definition of social science as 'the study of society and human relationships' (see chapter 1, 1.1, above.) It is possible to be a little more explicit. Life in society may be divided between *social interaction* and *social aggregation*. The first establishes relationships between people – relationships of care, affection, co-operation, exchange and so on. The second establishes institutions: languages, churches, political parties, businesses, clubs, markets, as well as groups united only by common qualities of class or gender or by access to common resources, like a well or a library or a hospital. The distinction is clear in theory; in practice less so. For example, a peasant who comes to town to sell a few chickens or rabbits will choose to do so in an open space rather than a narrow lane. Thus a market grows up in the square and comes to be established there, first by custom and then by municipal regulations. In this way individual relationships create social institutions; interactions make aggregations. An interesting ontological question is 'What degree of reality is to be granted to these entities – interactions and aggregations?' For although they involve material things like chickens and market-stalls and piepowder courts, it is human relations, together with certain words, feelings, customs and prescriptions (all non-material), which constitute the social realities that are the subject-matter of the social sciences.

3.2.2   Individuals   A second ontological problem relates to the individuals themselves. Each of them has certain qualities and capacities that make him or her a recognizable individual. How far are such qualities and capacities (in particular the abilities to think and speak rationally) inherent in the individual and how far are they dependent on social interaction? Of course, we are all more or less capable of adapting our behaviour to our environment; in a new situation we can accept a new currency, a new set of customs, a new diet, and learn a new language. But these are intentional actions. The question is: how far is each one of us, willy-nilly, a social product – a product not of this or that society, but of society at all? It is clear that any one who grew up in solitary confinement would not exhibit the powers of speech and of rational thought. Yet this does not prove the capacities to be lacking, but only the opportunity of exercising and developing those powers, just as one who never got out of bed would be unable to walk. Such questions may appear purely speculative, but the answer one gives can radically affect one's views not only on the upbringing of children but of moral responsibility, of justice and of politics. The question might thus be put: 'What am I, and why am I that?'

3.2.3   Pseudo-persons   This brings us on to the key question about social aggregation. Such aggregations, it will be recalled, include clubs, governments, corporations, unions, and other groupings. The question about all these is 'How far and in what sense, can they be regarded as persons?' We understand (from thousands of years of experience) how and why our fellow humans think and act. This understanding is a sort of commonsense psychology. But increasingly in the contemporary world we find that actions in society are not personal interactions but are performed by this or that corporate body – as it may be General Motors or the French Ministry of Foreign Affairs or the Lawn Tennis Association. Most of these are recognized at law and are capable of suing and being used in the courts as if they were individuals. What sort of reality do they possess? – again the ontological question. Their legal reality is established. But what sort of rules govern their behaviour? Can we apply commonsense psychology about desires and motives and reasons and intentions to them? If so, we can readily grasp why they acted in such a way in the past and how they are likely to act and react in the future. In practice, we frequently treat corporations as individual persons – sometimes successfully, sometimes not. But our questions still stand.[17] It may be helpful here to note that our understanding of individual human behaviour is much increased by fiction, whether in literary or dramatic form. Books and films and plays are subtle educators in humanity. But when corporate bodies appear as characters in fiction they are nearly always represented by their human agents. It is easier to dramatize Stalin than the Communist Party of the Soviet Union. The point is crudely put in the adage about corporations and public bodies – that they have neither a butt to kick nor a soul to save. Can the actions of such institutions be interpreted in terms of the ambitions, desires, hopes, fears, intentions of their human agents (presidents, secretaries, representatives and so on) or are there non-human, non-psychological forces which determine their behaviour in ways remote from commonsense psychology? This in addition to the legal and constitutional functions and restraints? It is clear that whichever way we answer these questions the answers are going to affect our understanding, our theories, our explanations in both history and the social sciences.

3.3 What is a social science? – Method

Having looked briefly at the question 'What is there to be known?', we now turn to the second question: 'How do we know it?' The major debate here turns on how we understand the phrase 'social science'. Does the adjective imply that we have a quite different kind of science, or does it merely indicate the subject matter to which science is applied – that is, society? Do the phrases 'natural science' and 'social science' indicate one science with different objects or two different modes of working and understanding? In the first case the word 'science' has the same meaning in both phrases; in the second the word has two different meanings.

3.3.1 Positivist or interpretative? Those thinkers of positivist inclinations (like Comte, or Hempel or Popper) hold that a social science either follows the methods and procedures of the natural sciences (roughly, the hypothetico-deductive

method) or it is not a science at all, but something else. (History, psycho-analysis, cultural anthropology are often seen as instances.) On the opposite side are those who take the second view: namely, that the methods and procedures of the social sciences are justifiably different from those of the natural sciences, but they nevertheless constitute equally valid sciences. The key distinction here goes back at least as far as Vico (1668–1744). We can come to understand human things (laws, languages, customs and so on – the subject matter of what later came to be recognized as the social sciences) because 'we' made them – that is, they were brought about by men and women like ourselves. On the other hand, we cannot fully understand the world of nature (the subject matter of the natural sciences) 'which, since God made it, He alone knows'; that is, we have no instinctive understanding of how a crystal or a nebula or a butterfly comes about (Vico, 1970, # 331, pp. 52–3). We have to rely on external observation, with all its shortcomings, instead of enjoying (as with human affairs) the inside view. This sort of insistence on the inner perspective in the human or social sciences is to be found in the hermeneutic approach of Continental philosophers, like Dilthey and Gadamer. It is also found in that tradition in the English-speaking world which stems from the writings of the later Wittgenstein and is briefly and clearly set out in Winch's *The Idea of a Social Science* (1958).

3.3.2   Three issues: universality, empathy, value   There are, however, other considerations. These turn around three concepts: universality, empathy, value. Let us take them in that order.

(1)   *Universality.* We all come to an understanding of society from the particular one in which we grow up. Can we then proceed to study other societies (rather as a naturalist collects beetles or butterflies) and find sufficient common features to be able to work out a theory of society in general which is applicable to any and all particular societies? Marx, Durkheim, Pareto, and, to some extent, Weber, all attempted this. Later the practice went out of fashion, but there are some indications of its revival (see especially Skinner, 1990). It is obvious that any success which can be achieved in this reinforces (by reason of its objectivity and universality) the claim to be a 'real' science. It is not agreed on all sides, however, that it has yet been done.

(2)   *Empathy.* This insight into human affairs which the social scientist enjoys simply by virtue of being human is regarded by some as essential and by others as negligible. The former claim that social scientists can say little of importance about human affairs unless they can understand (from the inside, as it were) the thoughts and behaviour of the human agents. In particular, can they describe the social phenomena in the same terms as the participating agents would have used? The latter claim that this empathy or insight (often designated by the German word *Verstehen*) may be useful but not essential. They believe it is possible to give

an objective explanation of social behaviour without any regard to how the agents themselves saw their actions. Again, this would make theories more 'scientific', but such attempts at a general social psychology have been much criticized.

(3) *Values*. As we have seen, the values held by individuals, groups, or whole societies are an important part of social phenomena; few studies in any of the social sciences can ignore them. But science should, almost by definition, be objective, unbiased, completely neutral in respect of values and preferences. One might rather have a cat than a skunk about the house, but the creatures are equal to the zoologist. One of the apparent achievements of Weber was to demonstrate both the importance of values for the sociologist and that it is possible for him to take full account of the values of his subjects while remaining totally value-free (neutral, impartial) in his studies. But is it possible? Every social scientist is part of a society. As such he can hardly fail to have certain feelings about his own society and others like it. It is difficult not to feel either satisfaction or dissatisfaction with the social arrangements around one. The former sensation leads to a conservative outlook, the latter to a reformist one – at least with respect to some if not all aspects of society. It is also almost impossible to believe that any piece of social study will not have some impact upon the society in which it is made. There is some evidence, for example, that entrepreneurs in nineteenth-century Europe and America ran their businesses with ruthless disregard for human considerations because they had read the early economists like Ricardo and believed that this was how capitalists just had to behave. Can one believe then in the possibility of a fully objective social science if, as in this case, even the most neutral and objective statement about society can bring about changes? It seems that, at least sometimes, to study society is to change it. (Reflexivity again.)

3.3.3 Critical theory and value-free social science   Almost any social scientist who has been influenced by Marx will tend to the second position. Of interest in this respect are the exponents of what is known as 'critical theory'. These come from the Frankfurt School of Social Research, founded in 1923. The leading thinkers were Adorno, Horkheimer and Marcuse. With the coming of Nazism the group moved to America. After the Second World War the School was re-established in Germany. The most distinguished member at the moment is the German philosopher, Jürgen Habermas. Inspired by Kant, Hegel and Marx, critical theory can be seen as an attempt to bring philosophy to the critique of society and thus to make a social world that is more in accordance with the requirements of reason. It is interesting in view of the recent growth in the importance of language for philosophy, that the most distinguished proponent of the School bases his theories for a better society on the theory of 'communicative action'. Put crudely and over-simply, we might say that for him speech and conversation are the necessary foundations of a good society: that is, we can find in communicative action a set of norms which we can recognize as binding in moral and political contexts.[18] Habermas is to be respected not only as a philosopher, but also as a participant in political debate in matters of serious public concern, as we shall see below. All that we note at the moment is that in the continuing tradition of the Frankfurt School and Critical Theory we have a philosophico-social project which aims to show not merely what society *is*, but what it ought to be; and not only what it ought to be, but what we can make it. In this project both philosophy and science are brought into the service of action. Is this a violation of the sanctity of academic studies? Or is it their justification? Do we live in order to think better? Or do we think in order that we may live better? (Aristotle had no doubt of the answer.)

In the light of what we have said about social science we can now see that since history and social science have a common subject matter (i.e. human beings in society) they have a good deal to share with each other. They should see themselves as complementary ways of dealing with the same sort of phenomena, rather than as rivals. It seems that nothing but good can come of their co-operation, though one might make the caveat that they should take care that attempts to be good social scientists do not make for worse historians, and vice versa.

4   Philosophy and History: the Left-hand Side

We now turn to the third side of the triangle and look at the relations between philosophy and history. It is, of course, the subject of this whole book, but in the light of the three-fold comparison that we have been making round the triangle, it is worth considering how the three concerns came together. For it is difficult to discuss either history or its philosophy in total isolation from the concepts of the social sciences.

Let us ask again of history, as we asked of social science, the two key philosophical questions: 'What is there to know?' and 'How do we know it?'

4.1   Does social realism raise questions for both philosophers and historians?

It has become more clear that, in answer to the first question, the social sciences are offering an increasing range of possible entities. They include such things as Krondatieff long waves or rites of passage or interest groups or *mentalités* or norms or carnivals or epistemes. As the historian's field has expanded, says Peter Burke, 'historians are having to concern themselves with questions which have long interested sociologists and other social scientists' (P. Burke, 1991, p. 16). We have already asked about the structures of social science: are they an essential part of society? Or are they only the theories that social scientists employ in order to understand society, rather as the meteorologist draws weather fronts on his maps? (The highly coloured and complex diagrams represent nothing more than air and water in motion.) On the other hand, there is a not implausible answer for the reality of social structures: the theory of 'sociological realism'. As a proponent of this theory puts it, 'A policy of sociological realism presupposes that society and culture are independently real entities that are neither artefacts of the theorist's or actor's creation nor reducible to characteristics of individuals or patterns or individual behaviour. Although social structures and cultures cannot be sensed they are deemed to exist in virtue of their causal powers to influence the behaviour, beliefs, and understandings of persons, and they are knowable through the behaviour, products, and utterances of persons' (Lloyd, 1993, p. 39). Does this establish the degree of their reality? There is some analogy with sub-atomic particles, which are known rather as the causes of observed effects than by any observable features of their own.

4.2   How we know: both methods required

It might be supposed that the historian's traditional emphasis on persons and events is inconsistent with the scientist's emphasis on theory. In fact, many good historians and social scientists (e.g. Charles Tilly, Ernest Gellner, Emmanuel Le Roy Ladurie, Natalie Zemon Davis and so on) make equal deployment of both fact and theory. Lloyd argues that 'structures and events are not somehow ontologically separate things'. The relation between them is not a dichotomy but a 'symbiotic duality'. (This might be defined as a relationship in which each owes its existence to the other) (Lloyd 1993, p. 48). The ontological question is then easily answered: 'We know what there is by employing both the methods of the historian and those of the social scientist.' Emphases may vary, but even the most positivist of social theories cannot ignore the people who are its subject, nor can the most individual of histories (say, a biography) altogether ignore the society in which that individual has lived and which has largely shaped that very character that the biographer is studying. 'Structure and agency,' says Alex Callinicos, 'are so closely interwoven that to separate either and give it primacy over the other is a fundamental error' (Callinicos, 1989, pp. 6–7). This is a thoughtful study of the complementarity of the twin approaches of social science and history. Callinicos is convinced 'that Marxist theory can develop only in the closest dialogue with historical research' (p. 7).

In short, now that we have been round the whole triangle we can see some of the ways in which history, philosophy and social science relate to, and often feed off, each other. Let us pull them all together by taking a look at the interesting concept of tradition.

4.3   Tradition is a concept for our whole triangle

The tendency of people, groups and societies to revere and imitate their predecessors is, I suppose, as old as mankind. There is a very good reason for it: a good job well done need not be done again. We have no need to spend time and energy in re-inventing the wheel. On the other hand, there has to be change and progress or we should still be using tools of flint and living in caves. Hence there is rarely ever agreement either within a society or among social theorists of the correct place of tradition in social life. Historians have thrown up few social concepts of their own, and of these few two stand out: E. P. Thompson's 'moral economy' and Eric Hobsbawm,'s 'invention of tradition'. Thompson used his phrase to account for the nature of food riots in eighteenth-century England. 'It is possible to detect in almost every eighteenth-century crowd action some legitimising notion,' he says. 'By the notion of legitimation I mean that the men and women in the crowd were informed by the belief that they were defending traditional rights or customs; and, in general, that they were supported by the wider consensus of the community' (E. P. Thompson, 1993, p. 188). The power of tradition to legitimize a political or social practice has never been better recognized than in the invention of tradition. Hobsbawm writes: ' "Invented tradition" is taken to mean a set of practices ... which automatically implies continuity with the past.' He goes on to explain that 'the peculiarity of "invented" traditions is that the continuity with it [i.e. the historic past] is largely factitious' (Hobsbawm and Ranger, 1984, pp. 1–2). A third Marxist historian, Christopher Hill, has made us familiar with the concept of the 'Norman Yoke' employed in seventeenth-century England to protect supposed Anglo-Saxon liberties – another largely bogus tradition employed in a good cause.[19] As we shall see, tradition has a particular importance for Gadamer and his hermeneutic theories of thought and society.

4.4   Tradition in literature

In a justly famous essay a great poet attempted to define the place of tradition in literature. Tradition, he insists, requires a sense of history. 'And the historical sense,' continues Eliot, 'involves a perception, not only of the pastness of the past, but of its presence ... This historical sense, which is a sense of the timeless as well as of the temporal and of the timeless and of the temporal together, is what makes a writer traditional.'[20] This absorption of both the timeless and the temporal, together with the problem of distinguishing them, was never greater than in early modern times. It was a pressing concern for every humanist in the Renaissance (see, for example, Peter Burke, 1972; T. M. Greene, 1982).

4.5   Tradition in religion

Again, we can see that tradition has played, and still plays, an important part in religion. The Reformation was largely, though by no means entirely, a conflict between concepts of 'the Church' as the embodiment of tradition and 'the Word of God' as ever-new inspiration. The conflict is to be seen today between established churches and the new churches or sects based on 'movement of the spirit'. It is also seen, as Weber points out, in the constant blunting and assimilation of charisma by the forces of convention, though there remains a continuing interrelationship between the two (Weber, 1978, p. 237). Perhaps nowhere is the power of tradition so massively experienced as in matters of religion – and this is true of all religions, not just Christianity.

4.6   Tradition in society

Social scientists, too, are well aware of the problems of tradition. Weber cites traditional behaviour as one of his four categories of social action. He defines traditional behaviour as 'the expression of a settled custom' (Weber, 1978, p. 28). Sociologists and anthropologists find custom everywhere, and it plays a large part in their studies. Perhaps, though, it would be useful to make a distinction between custom and tradition – that is, between on the one hand acting according to custom because to the agent that mode of action is the only way (or the only sensible way) of doing something, and on the other hand choosing to act according to precedent or tradition in preference to a possible alternative. The conflict appears again in economics. Orthodox economists start from the axiom that human beings act from the rational motive of making the greatest gain for the least expense – the behaviour of the so-called *homo economicus*. It is obvious to almost all other social sciences that people are frequently moved by non-economic considerations – frequently by traditional ones which conflict with economic interest. This is particularly clear in developing countries. In jurisprudence there is the interesting anomaly of English common law, based on precedent, which never properly came to terms with Roman law (the basis of law on the Continent), which is based rather on reason. The Anglo-American legal tradition is still markedly different from the European. This constitutes another problem for European union.

4.7   Tradition in political thought

Lastly, the role of tradition in political thought is well explored in the writings of Michael Oakeshott and J. G. A. Pocock, as well as in the *Festschrift* on Oakeshott's retirement, which concentrates largely on tradition. 'Michael Oakeshott,' say the editors, 'attempts to define the logic of tradition or history; and to indicate the historicity or traditional character of logic.' In the realm of practical experience he had the common sense to wish never to see them separated.[21] The roles of tradition and history in moral philosophy have been forcefully argued by Alasdair MacIntyre (MacIntyre, 1985 and 1988).

4.8   The Historikerstreit: tradition as national self-image

All these issues come together in an important debate that took place in Germany a few years ago. It is known as the *Historikerstreit* – the conflict of historians – a conflict in which Jürgen Habermas played a leading part. Pocock, in fact, has made the relevant points here:

The consciousness of time acquired by the individual as a social animal is in large measure consciousness of his society's continuity and of the image of its continuity which that society possesses; and the understanding of time, and of human life experienced in time, disseminated in a society, is an important part of that society's understanding of itself – of its structure and what legitimates it, of the modes of action which are possible to it and in it. (Pocock in King and Parekh, 1968, p. 209)

The questions of a society's 'image of its continuity' and of its 'understanding of itself', and hence of certain possible ways of acting – all these have pressed hard upon the German people since the fall of National Socialism at the end of the Second World War. They then became fully aware of the nature of that system and, in particular, the deliberate massacre of millions of Jews – 'the Holocaust'. How is a people to retain its self-respect, to feel its historical identity, to retain its links with predecessors like Goethe and Kant, Bach and Beethoven, when the same national tradition must include Adolf Hitler (not a German till 1932) and Heinrich Himmler? This is no idle question. A nation without self-respect, without a comfortable sense of identity, a nation that is not at ease with itself can be as dangerously unpredictable on the international scene as a similarly afflicted individual on the social scene – 'a loose cannon on the deck'. This is what the *Historikerstreit* was all about. It is a conflict that has quietened down, but has not been resolved.

4.9   The Holocaust in German history

Essentially, the argument was about guilt for the Holocaust – a guilt, by the way, which the German government has handsomely acknowledged. Among many questions, the central one was whether the Jewish Holocaust was a unique crime, or whether it was only one of several examples of mass murder and genocide. In particular, it was asked whether Stalin's political murders of the citizens of the USSR exceeded Hitler's murder of the Jews and other German citizens. The answer is, Yes: Hitler's victims amounted to seven or eight million, Stalin's to some twenty million (Maier, 1988, pp. 74–5). Apart from the question of uniqueness there is that of the relation of the twelve terrible years of National Socialism to the rest of German history. Can we show that it was the (organic) outcome of what went before it? Has it left residues in subsequent years? Or was it, as some have claimed, a phenomenon, an accident – terrible but almost unique (like a man struck by lightning) – that could not have been predicted beforehand nor rationally accounted for afterwards? If so, it could be 'bracketed out' of the otherwise 'seamless web' of German history.

4.10 Does social science trivialize evil?

A third question is particularly relevant to the social sciences. What are the methodological implications of including the Nazi regime under the category of 'totalitarianism' or 'fascism' – as has often been done? Does it then become just one instance of a type? If so, is it then trivialized? Moreover, suppose the social scientist follows the Weberian line of seeking understanding, of trying to empathize with the agents, of grasping what *they* saw as the meaning of their actions. 'Tout comprendre, c'est tout pardonner.' Is it possible to achieve understanding without at least a tendency to pardon some things? After all, the guards at the extermination camps were made of human flesh and blood, however much the contrary may have appeared to be the case.

4.11 Do historians trivialize evil?

When German politics swung to the right in the 1980s some so-called 'revisionist' historians put forward views on these questions which seemed to soften the guilt of the German people. To them came a vigorous response from Habermas. He asserted, first, that the Federal Republic of post-war Germany had benefited from its adoption of American political culture: 'We adopted the political theory of the Enlightenment, we grasped the pluralism which, first carried by religious sects, molded the political mentality, and we became acquainted with the radical democratic spirit of the American pragmatism of Peirce, Mead, and Dewey' (see Maier, 1988, p. 40). Already, some years before, Habermas had had a major debate with Gadamer over the implications of hermeneutic theory – too conservative, in Habermas's view. Now his suspicions of too much emphasis on tradition came to the fore with the revisionism of what he saw as neo-conservative historians. Like Gadamer, they felt the importance of endowing the past with meaning. But in doing so were they not, thought Habermas, nurturing a dangerous myth?

4.12 How must we come to terms with our past?

How then should the Germans relate to their traditions. Only, said Habermas, by facing up to and criticizing their past in the light of Western values and admitting how wrong it was. The revisionists, he felt, in their anxiety to put Germans at ease with their past, were actually making the evils of that past in some way acceptable. Habermas summed it up:

> Can one claim to be the legal heir of the German Reich, can one continue the traditions of German culture, without taking historical responsibility for the form of life in which Auschwitz was possible? Can one take responsibility for the interconnected origins of those crimes with which our own existence is historically woven in any other way than by means of a solidaristic memory of

what is now irreparable, in any other way than by means of a reflective, critical attitude vis-à-vis the traditions that endow our identity? (Maier, 1988, p. 59)

The whole story with its implications for philosophy, for politics, for the social sciences and, above all, for history can be read in Maier's excellent account.[22] Here we may end by underlining two words of Habermas: – meaning and responsibility. These are the watchwords of the good historian who is also a good citizen. They remind us that philosophers, historians and social scientists alike are not only students of, but also participants in, the life of humanity. They face also the third of the key questions put by Socrates and Kant: How should we live?

Notes

1 See *Oxford Companion to Philosophy* (1995, p. 666).
2 *Cogito*, (1989), vol. 3, no. 2, p. 90.
3 *Concise Oxford Dictionary of Sociology* (1994), p. 493.
4 See Comte in Gardiner (1959, pp. 77–9); Geertz (1975, p. 5). For further discussion of meaning and science see chapter 5, 2.5).
5 Marx, Preface to *A Critique of Political Economy* in Marx (1977, p. 389).
6 See Wright Mills's discussion, chapter 1, 2.14–17.
7 There is a large literature on the Annales school, but perhaps the simplest approach is via Stoianovich (1976) and Braudel (1980). See also the important article by Lynn Hunt, 'French History in the Last Twenty Years: the Rise and Fall of the *Annales* Paradigm', *Journal of Contemporary History*, (1986), vol. 21.
8 For a discussion of structure in historiography, as distinct from the supposed structures of history, see Stanford (1986).
9 See remarks by Körner, chapter 1, 2.5.
10 The first of European historians, Herodotus, already exhibits a regard for this totality while foregrounding the individual.
11 For historicism see chapter 5, 3.
12 Many are cited in Bottomore (1971, p. 311–12); p. Burke (1992, pp. 17–19); Callinicos (1995, pp. 6–8).
13 For a fuller discussion, see Burke (1992); also Stone (1987); C. Lloyd (1993); Stanford (1994); Callinicos (1995).
14 See Mills's remarks and the discussion above. Also see P. Burke (1992, pp. 14–20).
15 For history, see Novick (1988); for social science, see, for example, Giddens (1976) and (1984).
16 See, for example, Ryan (1970, chapter 1, 'The Questions that Philosophers Ask').
17 Thomas Hobbes has a theory of 'Feigned Persons' in chapter 16 of the *Leviathan* that is well worth pondering on in this context.
18 For the Frankfurt School, see Jay (1973); Connerton (1976); Hoy and McCarthy (1994). For Habermas, see Habermas (1972), (1979), (1987); also Bernstein (1985), (1991); Jay (1989).
19 See Hill, *Puritanism and Revolution* (1962).
20 'Tradition and the Individual Talent', in Eliot (1934, p. 49).

21 See King and Parekh (1968, p. 2). For his writings, see Oakeshott (1933), (1962) and (1983). For Pocock, see Pocock (1957), (1972), (1975) and (1985), as well as his contribution to King and Parekh, 'Time, Institutions and Actions: an Essay on Traditions and Their Understanding'.

22 Two books furnish an interesting exploration of how Germany and Japan have tried to come to terms with their parts in the Second World War. They are Buruma (1994) and Bosworth (1994). Both illustrate the vital necessity for any society to arrive at the truth about its past – however difficult that may be. The same, of course, applies to Britain and Ireland or to the British Empire. To discover the truth is surely the first duty of the historian. In many debates about meaning that duty must never be forgotten.

Suggested Reading

History and the Social Sciences

The basic texts are probably Weber: Weber (1964, pp. 87–155), or Weber (1978, pp. 3–13). Burke (1992) is very useful. You may also look at Nisbet (1970), Stone (1987) and Skocpol (1984).

Philosophy and the Social Sciences

Good modern texts are Hollis and Lukes (1982) and Hollis (1987) and (1994), Elster (1989). Ryan (1970) and (1973) and Winch (1958) are not to be overlooked. Rex (1970) gives a useful summary of points. Dunn in Hookway and Pettit (1980) is worth reading, as is the Introduction to Skinner (1990).

Philosophy and History

The leading works have already been cited in the suggested reading to the Introduction. A very useful survey up to 1981 is Bann (1981).

2

Main Themes

1 The Problem of Objectivity

1.1 History is important – but reliable?

'*La historia es muy importante*,' said the waiter. My wife and I, lunching in a small Spanish town, were discussing an exhibition in the local museum. It showed the life of that town over the years 1936 to 1975 and the impact upon it of the civil war and the subsequent rule of General Franco and the Falangists. The waiter was echoing the words of the curator who had been telling us of the purpose of the exhibition – to keep memories alive and to instruct the young. All Spaniards agree that civil war must never be repeated and the great majority believe that democracy must continue rather than dictatorship. Hence the need for all to be aware of the past: '*La historia es muy importante*.'

But what did the waiter mean by 'history'? As we went round the museum we strove to imagine civil war and near-starvation in those same streets. Was 'history' those imaginings? Or was it the beliefs (somewhat hostile to Franco) of the curator and his colleagues in mounting the exhibition? Or was it 'the truth' somehow distilled from the hundreds of histories of those years? Or was it the sad events themselves – now long gone, but not to be forgotten?

It could be said that the whole study of history centres around this problem. In a way, though it has peculiarities of its own, history faces the question common to all sciences: Is the world always as we believe it to be? Or is there sometimes a gap between how things seem to us and how they are in themselves? Can we always distinguish appearance from reality? This evokes questions about truth and objectivity – which, by the way, are not the same. It is ironic that the natural sciences are among the most widely recognized repositories of the truth today and yet offer in their history some of the most striking examples of error – such as beliefs in geocentrism, the fixity of species, phlogiston, ether, the indivisible atom and so on. History can hardly hope to do better in this respect and can count itself lucky if it does no worse.

It may seem strange, but it is the case, that in history argument often turns on questions of objectivity, rather than on truth. For example, few visitors to that museum in Sant Feliù could argue that the objects were not real, that the photographs were not genuine, or that the captions did not correctly state the time, place and subject. But a Falangist sympathizer might well protest that the whole was slanted to give an unfavourable picture of the Franco years. It was objectivity, rather than truth, that could be called in question. And this applies to the work of historians as a whole. They are trained to be thorough in their searches, accurate in their note-taking and conscientious in their citation of references. As A. E. Housman said, for the scholar accuracy is not a virtue; it is a duty. Nevertheless, few historians have satisfied every reader of their unquestionable objectivity. So let us bite the bullet and examine the question of historical objectivity. With luck we shall find that it opens up many of the problems of interest to the philosopher of history.

1.2   Objectivity: the problem stated

What we mean by 'objectivity' is that our ideas, judgements and statements should be formed wholly from the object (whatever it may be) under consideration. Their truth or falsity should be independent of what anyone thinks or feels. By contrast, subjective ideas, judgements and statements arise from the nature of the knowing subject; their truth or falsity is not independent of what he or she thinks or feels. If we follow the old adage, 'In all things let experience be your guide', then we use the methods of empiricism. But is it always possible to confine ourselves to the object, or (as it may be put) the facts? Let us consider the three closely related topics of the last chapter; namely, philosophy, social science and history. Nowadays (it was not always so) philosophy is largely a 'second-order' subject. First-order subjects like chemistry or engineering deal with the world; second-order subjects deal not directly with the world but with those that do – that is, with the first-order subjects. Although some philosophy (metaphysics and perhaps logic) deals with very general and abstract features of the world, most deals with the modes and structures of our thinking. Thus philosophy is only to a very small extent to be reckoned as an empirical subject. The social sciences, however, appear to deal with the world and hence to rest on an empirical base. There is a catch, however. The ideal of objectivity is to know, or to state, how the world is, quite independently of the knower. But with the study of society the possibility has been questioned. After all, the state of mind of a person fully aware of her own actions is not the same as that of a sleep-walker. Similarly, a society that contains economists, sociologists, psychologists and so on, all busily analysing that society, is not the same as one that lacks them. Economic facts and theories, for example, influence economic behaviour. When a bank runs into difficulties share prices and deposits fall, and it runs rapidly into greater difficulties. With the social sciences, unlike the natural sciences, it is not clear that their objects of knowledge do exist in a state entirely independent of any knower (see above, chapter 1, 4).

1.3   Objectivity in history?

History, however, seems to be on safer ground. Admittedly its subject of study is roughly the same as that of the social sciences – the world of men and women living in societies. But surely there is one important difference: the historical world cannot be affected by our knowledge of it. Like the natural world of the scientists, the world of the past is (or was) quite independent of the present knower. This is guaranteed by the fact that causes cannot operate retrospectively: nothing that happens today can alter what happened yesterday. Thus in history we have the possibility of a degree of objectivity that is not found in either philosophy or the social sciences.

But is history capable of the objectivity found in the natural sciences? When scientists discuss the possibility of making contact with other civilizations elsewhere in the universe, they assume that the laws of nature provide the common factor from which mutual understanding could develop. A highly intelligent denizen of Alpha Centauri (say) should be familiar with mathematics, atomic structures, Planck's constant, etc. But would this hypothetical extra-terrestrial be capable of knowing, of understanding and, finally, of writing our terrestrial histories? Can our histories ever be written in a form so objective that they would be equally comprehensible to both terrestrial and extra-terrestrial readers – something quite possible for at least some of our science? A moment's consideration of this question will reveal the difficulties that a demand for a purely objective history faces. Yet the task has been attempted. When Lord Acton set about compiling the volumes of the *Cambridge Modern History* (1902–12) he wrote in 1896: 'Contributors will understand that . . . our Waterloo must be one that satisfies French and English, Germans and Dutch alike; that nobody can tell, without examining the list of authors, where the Bishop of Oxford laid down the pen, and whether Fairbairn or Gasquet, Liebermann or Harrison took it up' (quoted in Stern, F., 1970, p. 249). Clearly he wanted them to write with complete impartiality. Impressive as those twelve volumes were, few would now regard them as models of historiography. What degree of objectivity they achieved was purchased at the high price of a crushing dullness of style, a narrow range of topic, a lack of illuminating connections and the neglect of most of the interesting questions. They have now sunk into deserved neglect.

1.4   Doubts about historical objectivity

So what are the difficulties that lie in the way of purely impartial and reliable history? One is that history, like the social sciences, is a reflexive activity: that is, it consists of society thinking and writing about itself. Admittedly, as we have just seen, no historian can affect the particular events he is writing about; they have already happened and are beyond change. But, like the sociologist or economist, what he says can bring about changes within his society. The Germany of 1871 to 1919 (sometimes known as 'the Second Reich') owed both its construction and its aggressive policies in large part to the writings of German historians. A century later a number of writers, lamenting Britain's decline from earlier greatness, have attributed this to a neglect of science and technology. In fact, until the last two decades of the century, Britain's performance in these spheres compared well with all but the two superpowers. A possible effect of these erroneous histories is the discouragement of talented youngsters from entering upon scientific careers.

A second consideration is that history is set in the midst of change. The historian not only writes *about* the constant flow of events; she also writes from *within* the flow. History, like science, must always be written from a given point in time or place. The difference is that for the scientist (or so he would claim) the laws of nature are the same for all times and places, so that it does not matter where he works. The historian can hardly claim as much. If there are laws of history that have the same reliability and universality as the laws of nature, we have yet to find them. Thus the position (in time and place) from which a historian writes gives a certain perspective to the work. It may be that all perspectives on atomic structures or the force of gravity are the same, so that perspective is negligible. This is far from the case with history.

A third consideration is that history is written from within societies about societies – whether the same or other. 'Society' here need not refer to large units like 'twentieth-century Britain'. The American historian, J. H. Hexter, has given an illuminating account of the importance to him and his work of a much narrower society – that of his professional colleagues (see Hexter, 1971, chapter 3). Most historians working today can record a similar experience. Now it is characteristic of any society, large or small, that its members share at least some agreement about values. Even galley slaves or prisoners, though in conflict with the values of the ship or the prison, yet share certain values among themselves. Thus historians face a double difficulty – though one not necessarily quite insurmountable. They have the problem of imagining what it is like to live in another society dominated by values different from theirs. They also have the problem of trying to stand sufficiently free from their own society's values to enable them to write objectively for a wider audience.[1] For example, Hexter's 'society' of professional historians set a very high value on truthfulness. Machiavelli and his fellows did not. On the other hand, an American historian would probably have more instant rapport with Machiavelli's republicanism than would a British or German historian (see, for example, Pocock, 1975, chapter 15). Yet that very republican inheritance which makes it easier for an American historian to understand Machiavelli could give a tinge to her writing that would make it unacceptable to a reader with monarchist, communist or fascist beliefs.

Finally, we have the weighty consideration of language. All of what the historian writes and most of the evidence that she reads is couched in words. For the great part, these words (whether in primary source or in finished work) consist of attempts to record, describe and explain concrete happenings in the real world. Hence the whole tangle of problems – problems that historians and others have wrestled with since Socrates – about the relations between language and the world. We shall have more to say about these.

After these introductory remarks, let us take a closer look at objectivity.

2   Objectivity in History

What has been, cannot not have been: and so Agathon is right in saying,
  'Of this alone is Deity bereft,
  To make undone whatever hath been done.'

                       Aristotle, *Nicomachean Ethics* (1139b)

2.1   What do we mean by that expression?

The past is solid, unchangeable. Is it beyond the powers of Man to give an account of it that is equally solid and unchanging? This was the ambition of the first of modern historians, Leopold von Ranke, when he wrote in 1824 that he intended to tell of the past '*wie es eigentlich gewesen* – as it actually was'. This was the ambition of the Positivist historians of the nineteenth century. It was still, as we have seen, the ambition of the editor of the *Cambridge Modern History* in 1896 (see above, chapter 2, 1.3).

In the twentieth century historians think themselves less naïve and some ridicule Acton's hopes of complete objectivity. But we should remember that these words were written by a sincere Christian, a great historian and an intellectual giant of unimpeachable liberal ideals. His intention was not merely that the proposed history should be accurate. His greater aim was to put an end to the religious and political prejudices that had brought so many wars and massacres in the past. Was he wrong to want this? Or to believe that biased history was partly to blame? To desire toleration and mutual understanding? The twentieth century, in which political and ideological hatreds have cost tens of millions of lives and traumatized as many more, cannot afford to laugh at Acton; it must respect his intentions.

But was he attempting the impossible? Is objectivity a will-o'-the-wisp, leading historians ever deeper into the mire? Let us see what we mean by 'objectivity'. An American scholar, Peter Novick, defines it as including:

a commitment to the reality of the past, and to truth as correspondence to that reality; a sharp separation between knower and known, between fact and value, and, above all, between history and fiction. Historical facts are seen as prior to and independent of interpretation... Truth is one, not perspectival. Whatever patterns exist in history are 'found', not 'made'. (Novick, 1988, pp. 1–2)

Most of these issues are dealt with elsewhere in this book. They are so numerous and varied that one can sympathize with Novick's exasperation: 'I don't think that the idea of historical objectivity is true or false, right or wrong: I find it not just essentially contested, but essentially confused' (1988, p. 6). Formally, historical objectivity, as we have said, requires an account or description of a set of events or states of affairs written solely in terms of the object, uninfluenced in any way by the subject – the latter being one who relates, writes, reads or believes the account. (This conforms to the usual epistemological picture of a knowing subject who knows the known object.) In practice, when we speak of objectivity we have in mind one or both of two related meanings: one is empirical, that of conforming to reality; the other is rational, that of acceptability to any reasonable person. The first appeals largely to common experience; the second appeals more to theory as in mathematics or advanced science. (The justification of Einsteinian Relativity, for example, is more a matter of reason than of common experience.) Historians may seek objectivity in either sense, or both.

2.2   Is objectivity possible in history?

The next question is to ask whether historical objectivity in any sense is, in principle, a possibility. It is often taken for granted that disagreement among historians proves the contrary. But, of course, it does nothing of the sort. The fact that none of the arrows have hitherto hit the bull's-eye does not mean that there is no bull's-eye. (And, of course, it is possible, though less likely, that one arrow has already found the centre of the target and we have not realised it.) If we want to establish that objectivity is, in principle, impossible we shall have to find better arguments.

To those who believe it is possible, one may put the next question: Has it ever been achieved? They may answer, Yes, and point to an example. It is then up to the critic to examine that example to see whether it does indeed meet the requirements of objectivity. If she (the critic) agrees that it does, then we should do well to examine it so that we may know in other cases how to achieve objectivity. On the other hand, they may answer, yes, but be unable to point to any example. In that case we must press them for convincing reasons to accept what seems a matter of faith.

But even for those who believe objectivity is not possible in history (and this is the prevalent opinion nowadays), it is not an end to the matter. We might do well to admit objectivity as a 'regulative ideal', so that it may guide us as nearly as possible to the impossible goal. This useful notion is like that point that draws the compass needle to the north. Long before they could ever arrive there sailors found that the magnetic pole gave them an invaluable sense of direction. Similarly, Kant pointed out the value of some transcendental ideas (i.e. ideas that extend beyond our knowledge of the world). We must beware of their 'supplying concepts of certain objects'. But they 'have an excellent, indeed indispensably necessary, regulative employment'. This is to direct 'the understanding towards a certain goal'. Such a goal, though a mere idea, serves to unite and direct the concepts of reason.[2]

2.3   Is objectivity desirable in history?

Before we go any further we should stop and ask one more question: is historical objectivity always desirable? Thomas Nagel has pointed out that the objective standpoint is not the best for every kind of understanding: 'An objective standpoint is created,' he says, 'by leaving a more subjective, individual, or even just human perspective behind; but there are things about the world and life and ourselves that cannot be adequately understood from a maximally objective standpoint... A great deal is essentially connected to a particular point of view, or type of point of view, and the attempt to give a complete account of the world in objective terms detached from these perspectives' brings us into error (Nagel, 1989, p. 7). The question for us is whether history is to be counted among those things that cannot be adequately understood from an objective standpoint. It is necessary to add that what is in mind here is not a matter of totally rejecting objectivity, but rather of seeing that in many cases adequate understanding is achieved only by combining both subjective and objective standpoints. The obvious case is love and friendship. Of course we must be capable – from time to time – of taking an objective view of our family, our friends, our dogs, our teddy bears; but our love for them springs from subjective sources.

Nagel suggests three areas where it is necessary to combine subjectivity with objectivity. One is consciousness and the mind–body problem; another is ethics; a third is the problem of the meaning of life. One can see that in all these cases 'the view from nowhere' (to use Nagel's book title) may be necessary but is certainly not sufficient or adequate for a full understanding of these problems. In each case one must also take into account 'the view from here'.

2.4   Is there a place for subjectivity in history?

Is history, to repeat the question, one of those areas where the subjective view must be taken into account? There are several reasons to suppose that it is. First, we should remember that history is about people – their actions and sufferings. Fully to understand their doings and their predicaments it is necessary to enter, as far as possible, into their perceptions, their reactions, their calculations, their emotions. These insights are necessary not only to understand what is recorded of past actions but also to understand why and in what circumstances these very records (the primary sources for the historian) were made. The problem was neatly illustrated once in a TV programme where a historian put the case that Britain should have negotiated a peace with Hitler early in 1941. The subsequent studio discussion was divided between comparatively young historians, who worked rationally and objectively from the records, and elderly people who had lived and fought in 1941. The latter were highly indignant at what they thought was a preposterous suggestion – quite unthinkable. Not only ought it not to have been done; it could not have been done, they said, for public opinion would not have permitted it. The young historians, taking a rational and objective view of the situation in 1941, were baffled. Of course, powerful emotions have played a decisive part in many another episode in history, but it is doubtful whether any such occasion can be properly understood without a considerable degree of empathy. No external description, no view from nowhere, it may be argued, does justice to the reality of the human situation. We must also have 'the view from here'.

A second consideration is that history does not come to an end when the books are written. Historiography, the product of working historians, is designed to be read (or received through some other medium of word and image.) While it is certainly possible to read history in quite a detached way, either as a well-told story or as a fascinating exercise of the intellect, many (perhaps most) people read or view it with some feeling that it concerns them and their interests. This is readily apparent when they read the history of their own town or nation, religious or political grouping. (Books on the Second World War were remarkably popular in Britain over the subsequent half-century, but in almost every case the reader wanted history from the British point of view; few demanded an Italian or Japanese history of the war.) Now this betrays a human weakness which may or may not be desirable. To be sure, a history of one's own people strengthens one's feeling of belonging, one's sense of identity. Right-thinking people tend to disapprove of such chauvinism nowadays. But what of the insistent and largely successful demands for black history, women's history and so on? Is it not clear that the capacity of history to give a sense of solidarity (much disapproved of in one context) is, not unreasonably, the very thing that gives it value in the eyes of those groups who feel disadvantaged? Their demands, from which one can scarcely withhold sympathy, is not for objective history, but for history from their point of view. Do Nagel's arguments not have some application here? Furthermore, should one recognize that most historiography has been distorted by a white, male bias? If so, we then need black history and women's history to restore the balance and thus to ensure a greater degree of objectivity. (see also Chapter 7.3.)

2.5 Seeking objectivity in history: the map analogy

However, faced with our two questions about the possibility and the desirability of objective history, most people, I guess, would answer impatiently, 'Yes, it is desirable and one should try to be as objective as possible.' So, keeping in mind the notion of objectivity as a regulative ideal, let us see how we should set about it and what practical difficulties might lie in our path.

It may be helpful here to appeal to a neighbouring discipline, geography. An objective account of some stretch of the past would be in many ways like the map of a stretch of country. First we should notice that a fully historical account would omit nothing. But that is impossible; just as to plot everything on the terrain would require a map as big as the area it portrays. Therefore, in history as in cartography, there has to be a reduction in scale. The historian needs to summarize, to capture in a few words or sentences, complicated states of affairs and a tangle of intertwined events. In history, as in map-making, this should be done without any loss of proportion; the balances must be kept and the shapes preserved. This is particularly difficult when dealing with collectives (nations, churches) or with complex characters – as great men and women usually are. What single statement can give an adequate description of Bismarck?

As the scale is steadily reduced, more and more has to be omitted; selection is essential. But on what principles do we select? Part of the answer is simple – as in mapping. We have different maps – road maps, geological maps, vegetation maps – to demonstrate different kinds of information. Similarly, as well as general histories, we have specialized histories of technology, art, religion, administration, law, and so on. This helps, but it by no means solves the problem of selection. Within each of such histories, however specialized, there have to be decisions about what can be left out and what must be kept in. What determines the choice of features to be 'mapped' in historiography? I think it is historical importance.

2.6   Historical significance

But how do we estimate the relative importance of the various historical elements (events, characters, states of affairs and so on)? Perhaps the commonest criterion is the size of impact upon other events, people and so on. This is by no means the only criterion. For example, an art historian might seize upon a particular style that had no predecessors and few successors and yet consider it very important for other reasons – ethical, metaphysical, religious, aesthetic, feminist and so on. Minoan art is a possible example. In reading any work of history it is rewarding to note the particular historian's criteria, not so much for evaluating what he has put in as for recognizing what he has left out – and then, acknowledging that there must be omissions, asking why these particular ones. As E. H. Carr said, it is always worth knowing what bees are buzzing in the historian's bonnet (Carr, 1961, p. 23).

Nevertheless, the criterion most frequently adopted is that of consequences. It would be difficult to omit the Norman Conquest from any history of England because it changed so much, its effects were so far-reaching. Yet we must be careful not to make either of two risky assumptions here. One is the familiar problem of counter-factuals. We think we know that an event 'changed the course of history'. But, as Oakeshott has pointed out, that event and its successors *were* the course of history. How things would have been without that event we can never know, we can only guess. The second doubtful assumption is that historical importance is only to be measured by subsequent effects. This leads to the notorious 'Whig interpretation of history': the approach that evaluates any past event by its relation to the present. Leopold von Ranke (1795–1886) long ago registered his protest against this: 'Every epoch is immediate to God and ... its value rests in no way upon what emerges from it, but upon the very fact of its own existence.' The Conquest bulks large in the history of England because of the long-lasting changes made in administration, law, land-holding, taxation and the Church. To us, that was its importance. Yet to the people of England at the time what was most important may have been something quite other – perhaps that the ruling classes were not native Englishmen and spoke an alien tongue.

2.7   Causation

Putting all these objections to one side, let us suppose that selection *is* made on grounds of historical significance, and that significance is measured by the extent of its effects. This immediately brings us face to face with the problems of causation in history.[3] There are many difficulties involved here, particularly in the complexity produced by the many-sidedness of human life. An event in military history may have fiscal, religious and psychological effects; a technological innovation may have significant consequences in demography, morality and the price of houses. The barriers carefully erected between one type of history and another are overleapt at every turn. Is there nothing, as some of the Annales school maintain, but total history?

2.8   The chances of evidence

So far we have been pursuing the implications for historiography of the model of cartography. This graphically illustrates many of the difficulties of attaining objectivity in historical accounts. But there are others. Perhaps the chief enemy of the balanced, well-proportioned account is the chanciness of evidence. It so often happens that the remaining evidence for a particular episode in history is not only insufficient (which is bad enough), but is hopelessly one-sided (which is worse). Sir Steven Runciman, the historian of the Crusades, drew upon a surprisingly wide range of sources, not only from the Latin West, but also Byzantine, Hebrew, Syriac, Armenian, Arabic and Persian histories. Nevertheless, it is manifest that the evidence from the Islamic side of these wars is very scanty compared to that from the Christian side. Whether more exists I do not know; clearly it was not available to Runciman. In the absence of a balance of information it seems almost hopeless to seek for objectivity. Another example is that of the

A good example

1798 rebellion in Ireland. Of this there remain 10,000 documents on the government side, about 100 on the rebels' side[4] Probably no one is to blame here; it is just bad luck – a factor often under-estimated by popular opinion, which prefers to find someone to blame for unfortunate states of affairs.

2.9   Bias

Lastly we turn to the more familiar enemies of objectivity in history. These are the various biases of the historians themselves. Some stem from the personality of the writer, others from prevailing schools of historical thought and method, others again from national, religious, metaphysical or ethical prejudices, and still others from publishers and their estimates of 'what the market will bear'. These kinds of bias are well known. Indeed, they have been very thoroughly explored in an entertaining but scholarly work, Peter Novick's *That Noble Dream: the 'Objectivity Question' and the American Historical Profession* (1988).

2.10   Language: public opinion

Finally, two other enemies of objectivity should not escape our notice. One is the limitations and distortions that language imposes upon any kind of thought. The other is the limitations and distortions imposed upon history by the understanding of its recipients, the public. It is not enough that objective history should lie in the printed page. Printed pages are not actors in history; the actors are men and women. What historians write and think is often less important than what people make of their writings. So we return to our original questions: What is objectivity in history? Is it desirable? Is it possible? Can it even be a regulative ideal? How may we set about attaining it? An essential part of these considerations is, as we have seen, the question of evidence, a subject to which we now turn. The other issues mentioned – that is, causation, bias, language, public reactions – we shall deal with in their turn.

3   Evidence

'You must not tell us what the soldier, or any other man, said, sir,' interposed the judge; 'it's not evidence.'

Charles Dickens, *Pickwick Papers*

I may command where I adore. Why, she may command me: I serve her; she is my lady. Why, this is evident to any formal capacity.

William Shakespeare, *Twelfth Night*

3.1   The acquisition of knowledge

We suggested above that there must always be some gap, small or large, between how things really are and how we think they are: the belief/reality problem. Knowledge is the name given to our human attempts to bridge this gap. Sometimes we may have succeeded and are in possession of certain knowledge. Unfortunately we can rarely, if ever, be sure when this occurs. To know is one thing; to know that we know is another. If such certainty is ever achieved in any of the realms of human knowledge, history is rarely among them. Nevertheless, we can be reasonably sure of a good deal of what historians tell us, so it is worthwhile spending a little time on seeing how historical knowledge is acquired.

Historians seek to know the world of the past. That world is in principle no different from the world of the present except for one thing – its displacement in time. How we come to know the world about us and how accurate is our knowledge are enduring problems for philosophers and scientists alike. The historian is distinguished only by the fact that his knowledge has also to transcend the temporal break between past and present. Leaving epistemologists, neurologists and others to explore human knowledge of the present world, we will concentrate on how historians acquire knowledge of the world of the past.

3.2   Knowing the past: evidence and interpretation

Let us take by way of example our knowledge of the Second World War. Over half a century later a good many people are still alive who remember it. In another half-century no one will remember it, but for the time being those memories are a rich source of knowledge, though always incomplete and often questionable. A great deal of material has also survived from those days – weapons, uniforms, gas masks, ration books and so on. There is also indirect or negative evidence – like bombed sites or repaired buildings; things that ought to have remained but have not – Hiroshima, for example. There is also a good deal of pictorial evidence – sketches, paintings, photographs, films. But the overwhelming amount of evidence is none of these things, but consists of words – diaries, letters, official documents – in short, private and public papers of every kind, not to mention books, journals, newspapers, pamphlets. There remain also a few recordings of the spoken word. All these, and other things that originated between 1 September 1939 and 14 August 1945 constitute what is called primary evidence of the war. Since 1945 a large number of books and articles have been published about the war; these constitute secondary evidence.

On this subject there is so much evidence, both primary and secondary, that it might be supposed that we know all, or nearly all, that we need to know. But this is far from the case. Memories are often unreliable, much material evidence has disappeared, documents have been lost or deliberately destroyed, tens of millions of witnesses have died. The resulting gaps in knowledge mean that many important issues remain undecided. The trials of alleged war criminals at Nuremburg in 1946 assembled truckloads of documents and hundreds of witnesses, but not every case could be decided with certainty. Since then historians still debate such questions as the degree of the German people's responsibility for the Holocaust; whether France surrendered unnecessarily in 1940; why Hitler declared war on the US in December 1941; why the US was taken by surprise at Pearl Harbor; whether Hitler's Balkan campaign of spring 1941 contributed to the failure of the Russian campaign later that year . . . and so on.

These, like most other historical problems, turn on the interpretation of available evidence. Many would be brought nearer solution if there were more evidence, but often nothing can be done about this. It is important to remember that truth in history is partly at the mercy of the evidence that survives. That is why serious historians are always searching for more evidence. The finding of evidence and its interpretation proceed together; the one does not wait for the other. Nevertheless, only when all available evidence has been brought under consideration can the task of interpretation be completed. Evidence and interpretation are the twin pillars of historical knowledge.

3.3   Evidence for what is not evident

It is important to realize that evidence is essential in history, as in science and law, precisely because the desired truth is *not* evident. It is not evident in law; if it were there would no trial, no case to be disputed, only a penalty or damages to be fixed. To settle a case at law, evidence (that is, things that *are* evident) have to be brought into court. In science evidence is required to support or falsify theories. It is evident that heavy objects fall. It is not evident that, other things being equal, all bodies fall with equal acceleration. And in history evidence is required most of all, because history is about the past – none of which is now evident. In each of these spheres we have to advance by means of what is evident to attain truths that are not evident.

In law, science or history one piece of evidence is rarely conclusive. Not even the whole body of evidence puts the matter absolutely beyond question. All that English law requires is that the case be established beyond reasonable doubt. If more were demanded most cases would be like *Jarndyce* v. *Jarndyce* – everlasting. Again in science every theory is strictly provisional; it holds only until it can be replaced by a better. No scientist believes we have arrived at ultimate truth. No historian would claim ultimate truth either. Evidence only *tends* to prove or disprove. In both science and history many things are so well established as to be beyond reasonable doubt. Nevertheless, we should not forget how often in the history of science things that were supposed to be beyond doubt have been effectively questioned – geocentricity, phlogiston, ether, absolute time, for example. Since history is, by its very nature, a less exact discipline than the physical sciences, we must not expect its conclusions to be any less open to doubt. As

Aristotle said, we must not expect more exactitude from a science than the nature of it will bear.[5] There is always a delicate balance to be maintained between reasonable doubt and reasonable conviction; neither the dogmatist nor the total sceptic has any place in the study of history. For its more thoughtful students this delicate balance has endless fascination.

'Faith,' said St Paul, 'is evidence of things unseen.' But not only faith. Muddy footprints in the hall and pop music blaring from the bedrooms tell that the children are home from school though they are still unseen. There is nothing recondite about using evidence for things unseen. Familiar sequences of events repeat themselves so often that we can deduce the whole sequence from the last stage. The ripe corn in the field (seen) is good evidence for previous ploughing and sowing (unseen). Thus in the vast majority of occasions of using present evidence for past events there is no problem. History and archaeology deal with the more problematic and usually more remote cases.

3.4   Evidence from relics

Some of these cases will not admit of any solution beyond reasonable doubt, usually for lack of evidence. Yet we may confidently hope to know more in the future than we do at present. Surprisingly, all the evidence for that future knowledge exists now. Indeed, we can go further and remind ourselves that all the evidence for the whole of our knowledge of the past, whether geological, archaeological or historical, is now in existence. It can never increase, though we may confidently expect to discover more of it. If that thought is depressing, we can cheer ourselves a little by its counterpart: everything that now exists furnishes some evidence for the past. The challenge is to know how to use it. Much of the most interesting progress in the study of history in the twentieth century has been learning how to use previously neglected evidence – field marks, place names, hedgerows, popular songs, blood groups, for example. To these we can now add mitochondrial DNA, with the opportunity it offers to trace human ancestry in the female line.

The breakthrough comes when it dawns on us that things that have been in existence for some time (for example, place names or blood groups) are relics of the past. But a relic, though evident, does not constitute evidence unless someone perceives how it can be used as evidence. 'History is all around us,' it is often said. If by 'history' is meant 'the past', it is manifestly untrue. If 'relics of the past' is meant, then this is true everywhere and at all times. Everything that has existed for more than a few moments is likely to have undergone some change, and is a relic of its former, slightly different self. (The clothes you are wearing are relics, in this sense, of the brand-new garments you bought weeks, months or years ago. You yourself are a relic of the child you once were.) The skill lies in deducing the earlier state of an object from its present state. When that is done, the present object (the relic) becomes evidence for the earlier state. The past, which is history's domain, was constituted by things in their earlier not their present states.

This applies to people, to documents, to institutions, to hedgerows, to landscapes or to nations. It is essential to understand the processes through which such things pass.

3.5   Reconstructing the past

The major skill of the historian (for historians also possess a number of minor skills) lies in his ability to discover what was from what is. Of course archaeologists, palaeontologists, geologists, philologists, art- and book-restorers, detectives, and indeed anyone whose task it is to 'reconstruct' some part of the past, also possess various aspects of this skill. Walking through a wood you see a few feathers on the ground and wonder how they came there. The warden or gamekeeper will tell you at a glance not only what bird died there, but also what beast or bird killed it, and roughly how long ago. The relics are clear to both of you, but they constitute evidence only for him. It is often claimed that one thing is evidence of another; formally that X is evidence of Y. But this claims only that X contains potential information about Y. It is not enough. We must ask, evidence for whom? For relics themselves do not speak. It is humans who 'make them speak', turning evidence-as-relic into evidence-as-argument. Strictly, we must say that X is evidence of Y for Z. Thus it is clear that evidence is not a two-term relation (between X and Y), but a three-term relation, linking X, Y and Z. In all this, Z is the most important factor. It is her intelligence and experience that enable her to make the link (imperceptible to most of us) between the evident relic (seen) and the past occurrence or condition (unseen). It is the trained skill of the expert (historian, gamekeeper, palaeontologist) that makes for us the connection between the present and the past. History, like hunting, geology, detection, and so on, rests on judgements. In all these cases the judgements, even of the experts, are not infallible. (Strictly their conclusions do not constitute 'facts'.) In many cases they are not beyond dispute. Nevertheless, the judgements of the experts are the best we have. (Not even in the Bible were history and palaeontology written directly by a divine hand.) Only in law and politics do apparent exceptions appear. Trials are decided by juries of ordinary men and women, presumably on the grounds that they are the experts on ordinary life. Similarly, in democracies governments are elected by the people, presumably not on the grounds that they are experts in governing (like politicians and civil servants), but because they are experienced in being governed.

3.6   How to use evidence: three steps

In using evidence (in history, as in these other spheres) three stages have to be considered. The first task is to examine the relic and be quite sure that it is what it seems to be – not what it was (that comes later), but what it is now – stone not concrete, vellum not paper, gold not brass, and so on. The second is to attempt to trace its history – how it came here, what changes it has undergone, by what means. (Think of a derelict, dilapidated house.) This stage is often a matter of tracing processes backwards – as in the cornfield example. In the case of a small object (a document, an ornament) we must trace what the art historians call its 'provenance' – through whose hands it has passed and what they may have done to it. Only in the third stage do we come to consider its origins. Here the important questions are to ask how and why it was produced, by whom and with what intention, in what context (prevailing styles and methods) and in what circumstances. The key concept is that of meaning, a concept of several dimensions. What did the producer (for example, the goldsmith who made the brooch or the writer of the letter) intend by it? What meaning did it have for the recipient or public of the day? (Think of a song, for example). What is its significance for us? All these are implied when we ask the *meaning* of the relic. It is particularly important in history to try to arrive at the intention of the author of a document. Is he writing for other eyes – his superiors, his opponents, posterity? Or for his own eyes only, as in a diary or account book? If the historian knows or suspects the former he must be more sceptical. Many writers (from Herodotus and Thucydides downwards) have actually intended to provide evidence for future ages.

3.7   Conflicts of evidence

In many cases the historian (like the other experts) will find a conflict of evidence. Some interpretations of the relics before him will suggest one conclusion, others a different one. There is a clash of interpretations. In trying to make up his mind he will consult books and colleagues. He may even suspend judgement until he is possessed of further evidence. But the past, not being before our eyes, is so uncertain that conclusions about important matters must perforce rest on finely balanced judgements. T. H. Huxley spoke of 'The great tragedy of Science – the slaying of a beautiful hypothesis by an ugly fact.' The same happens in history, though, of course, the assassin is new evidence, not a new fact.

3.8   History founded on evidence?

Evidence, therefore, is the foundation of history, for (taken in the broad sense to include memory) it forms the the only bridge between the past and the present. Nevertheless, relics cannot speak for themselves. The connection that they make has to be perceived by a human mind. Sometimes this is very simple, as when burnt cakes show the housewife that she has left them too long in the oven. Sometimes it is complex and difficult, as when historians try to account for the destruction of Minoan Crete or the decline of the Roman Empire.

Historical evidence, it must be remembered, consists largely (though by no means entirely) of written sources. Where these are absent (either never written or later destroyed), we can have little knowledge. This consideration has become particularly important in the twentieth century when almost universal written communication has been replaced by telegraph, telephone, radio and other electronic methods.

The discipline of history (to vary the earlier metaphor) advances on two legs: one of them is evidence, the other is interpretation. Each leg has to be used with great caution. Evidence, before any interpretation takes place, is itself a great cause of bias in history. We must not overlook this in our eagerness to discuss questions of interpretation. Bias in evidence must be considered before bias in interpretation. One source of bias in evidence is sheer chance. It is quite fortuitous what happens to have been written and what not. It is even more fortuitous what happens to have survived – whether we want the lost books of Livy, the records of the city of Paris before 1871, or the papers of British cabinet ministers of the early twentieth century.[6] A greater bias results from the fact that the winners not the losers write history. Hence we know what the Normans did in England in the century after 1066 but little of what the English did. In general we know more of the deeds of men than of women, of slavers than of slaves, of imperialists than of subject peoples, of police than of prisoners, of old than of young, of landlords than of peasants, of bourgeois than of proletarian, of Christian than of pagan Romans, of governments than of rebels, and so on. Beyond all this we have to be wary of the intentions of the 'winners', of the efforts they make either to censor or to pervert the record.[7] Indeed, many documents, not only the memoirs of public men and women, are written 'for the record'. The intention is not to reveal the truth to posterity but to distort or to conceal it (see also Bloch, 1954, pp. 60–1).

So much for evidence. Interpretation is a large question to be dealt with later (see chapters 4, 2, and 7, 2 below).

4   Truth

4.1   What do we mean by it?

We have introduced the notions of objectivity and truth. Having said something about the former, a few words about the latter will be appropriate. Since it is often demanded of historical accounts that they say without bias or prejudice exactly how things were, it is easy to confuse the two; the demand seems to be calling for both, objectivity and truth. But they are not identical. The truth or falsity of an objective statement is independent of anyone's thoughts or feelings: thus 'Birds have wings' and 'The Sun goes round the Earth' are both objective statements. On the other hand, 'I feel elated' and 'I feel depressed' are both subjective, though (if spoken by the same person) they cannot both be true at the same time.

There is no need here to discuss philosophical theories of truth. We shall not go far wrong if we accept the old saying: '*Veritas est adaequatio rei et intellectus* – Truth is the correspondence between fact and mind.' Exactly what is understood by '*adaequatio*' and 'correspondence' is not our concern here. Nor need we now bother about whether 'correspondence' is a definition, a criterion, or even something else. We should, however, pay attention to the fact that, whereas this ancient adage speaks of 'intellectus' – 'mind' or 'understanding', modern philosophers prefer to discuss truth in relation to statements. Occasionally they prefer sentences or propositions to statements, but rarely do they see truth as a property of a judgement or an understanding. To do this avoids a good deal of argument: it is easier to see the truth or falsity of what people say or write than of what they think. Nevertheless, there can be a distinction between what someone judges to be the case and what they put into words. Often one's judgement (for example, that water is the quickest way to put that fire out) is acted upon but never actually uttered. It is important not to forget this in history, for sometimes a historian's work is guided by judgements that he never puts into words. For example, most nineteenth-century historians believed that the white races were intrinsically superior to all others and this was implicit in many of their judgements, but it was not always stated explicitly.

4.2   The word–world problem

To come back to statements, we should remember that true or false statements inevitably raise the vexed question of how words relate to the world. How do they describe the world? How may they describe it accurately (or inaccurately)? Again, these are philosophical questions that are not here to be explored. Yet they cannot be totally forgotten in any philosophical discussion of history for the simple reason that most of history, whether primary evidence or finished work, takes the form of words – usually written words. The word–world relationship is brought out in a useful remark by the Oxford philosopher, J. L. Austin:

> When a statement is true, there is, *of course*, a state of affairs which makes it true and which is *toto mundo* distinct from the true statement about it: but equally of course, we can only *describe* that state of affairs *in words* (either the same or, with luck, others). (Austin, 1970, p. 123)

Put simply, it is the task of the historian to describe, as accurately as possible, former states of the world. In this we might suppose that the same empirical methods employed by the journalist or travel writer or naturalist or field anthropologist would serve his aims. But there is one big difficulty. Empirical methods are the methods of experience; how can the historian, if his subject is earlier than the twentieth century, have had experience of that subject? Can the study of history then be an empirical exercise? And if not, can it be truthful? If the criterion of truth is a satisfactory relationship (an '*adaequatio*') between statements and the world they describe, how do we get at the second term of the relationship to see whether the description fits? These are searching questions, and one must not assume that there is any one simple answer. Indeed, when faced with philosophical puzzlement, it is often advisable, before attempting an answer, to look critically at the questions to see if they have been properly put. Presently we shall see that these searching questions may be, at the least, misleading.

4.3   Going astray

One misapprehension of the problem is to be found in the words of a French thinker, Roland Barthes. In an otherwise discerning essay 'Historical Discourse', he affirmed: 'Historical discourse is presumably the only kind which aims at a referent "outside" itself that can in fact never be reached' (Barthes, 1962, in Lane, 1970, pp. 153–4). This belief (that the referent can be reached only through discourse) has been widely adopted by postmodernist writers on history. One claims, for example, 'That the world/the past comes to us always already as stories and that we cannot get out of these stories (narratives) to check if they correspond to the real world/past, because these "always already" narratives constitute "reality"' (Jenkins, 1991, p. 9). It is, of course, true that one cannot directly observe the past, but that fact does not imply that the historian is entirely confined within narratives and other discourses. There are available many kinds of non-discursive information about the past: memories, artefacts, pictures, to name a few. We shall have more to say about this in chapter 9, 3, below.

The same consideration – that we can make no direct observation of the past – has led one or two philosophers to put forward 'constructionist' or 'constructivist' theories of history. They deny that knowledge is possible of an independently real past and conclude that 'the past' is what historians construct in their narratives and descriptions. (Knowledge of a 'past' so defined is, of course, easily possible) (see J. W. Meiland, 1965; Leon J. Goldstein, 1976). Such theories depend on one of two assumptions: either that the past has no reality and therefore cannot be known; or that all knowledge is equivalent to direct observation, and since past events cannot be directly observed, the same conclusion follows: that the past cannot be known. The first assumption is quite implausible. Since no limitation is placed on the word, 'the past' must include events of five minutes or five seconds ago. Can it be argued that the breath I drew a few seconds past and have not yet expelled is not real? Is reality confined to the present minute, second, nano-second? Then what is the present? How long is it? The theory is reduced to absurdity. Nor can we escape by suggesting that the assumption applies only to the historical past, for then we must ask at what point the historical past ceased and the present began. At which point did unreality suddenly give place to reality?

4.4   Can historical knowledge be empirical?

If the first assumption leads to absurdity, what can we say of the second? This does not deny the reality of the past, but only the possibility of knowing it. This argument rests on the assumption that we can know only what is directly observed. Let us concentrate on that phrase. Does it confine each of us to personal observation? Must I be totally ignorant of America because I am not there now? No; I know something of America because I have been there, and also because others who have been there have told me of their experiences. Is this not empirical knowledge? True, I cannot now observe what is going on in Fifth Avenue, but I could do if I happened to be there. I was not in Dallas when Kennedy was shot, but I could have been. If, to avoid these difficulties, we define empirical knowledge not as what I am observing now but as what, in principle, could be observed, then knowledge of the death of Kennedy or of Napoleon's crossing of the Beresina is genuine empirical knowledge. You and I *could* have been there, and other people were.

This is not to say that experiences may not sometimes be misdescribed – deliberately, carelessly or in ignorance. Care has to be taken; reports have to be checked wherever practicable; photographs have to be tested. But these considerations do not invalidate empirical enquiry. They are normal procedure in science, medicine and law, for example, as they are in history. No one suggests that geology and palaeontology are not genuine sciences on the grounds that past happenings are no longer directly observable. History is an empirical discipline after all. We may say of history what Thomas Nagel says of knowledge in general:

> The role played by particular experience and by the action of the world on us through our individual perspectives can be only selective – though this is a very important factor, which makes the acquisition of such knowledge as we may have importantly subject to luck: the luck of the observations and data to which we are exposed and the age in which we live. (T. Nagel, 1989, p. 83)

Careful, painstaking work in performance of the duty of accuracy does not guarantee either truth or objectivity, but it is surely the indispensable groundwork for either.

4.5   The ethical dimension of truth

Another aspect of truth is not to be overlooked – its connection with what is right, straight, reliable. This reminds us that the notion of truth can have strong moral overtones. Let us consider two beliefs: (1) grass is green; (2) it is wrong to torture children for fun. Most people, we may take it, hold both. If asked, we would say that (1) is true because it fits the facts. But where are the facts that fit (2)? Does the universe possess a moral order that justifies belief in (2), as there is a physical order that justifies belief in (1)? Or should we say that (2) is a social convention that has developed in the interests of a continuing community? In either case, it seems to be more than a linguistic accident that both (1) and (2) are true statements – even if we concede that they are not quite the same kind of truth.

It is worth bearing this in mind when we ask of a historical account, 'Is it true?' We should consider not just whether each statement fits the facts (ignoring for the purpose what 'fits' and 'facts' can mean). It is proper also to ask whether the whole piece is right, honest, straight, reliable, and even honourable. Does it play fair with its readers? Does it do justice to its subjects? Voltaire said, cynically, that history is but a pack of tricks we play on the dead. A modern historian reminds us that 'One of the most important obligations of the historian is to keep good faith with the dead and not to score cheap points off them' (Cannon, 1980, pp. 10–11). Sometimes the attempts of journalists, publicists, politicians, social scientists or historians to represent in words the complexities of human affairs may be true in a narrow sense, yet remain as a whole neither right nor honourable. The concept of truth has an ethical dimension, and the duties of the historian are moral as well as epistemological.

5 Social Processes and Frameworks

5.1 Continuity and change

Those remarks about the dead remind us that the historian is concerned (morally and epistemologically) with her fellow humans, and that her obligations are not confined to the living members, but extend both to the dead and to the as-yet-unborn. The continuity of the human race, and therefore the continuity of its history, is never to be overlooked. On the other hand, change is as characteristic of history as continuity. We live in an expanding universe. As biological beings we are in a process of evolution that is likely to continue as long as life lasts on the planet. Third, each generation learns both from its parents and from its own experience. Social and historical situations are never exactly repeated, if only because men know something of what has gone before. For all these reasons it can be said that every situation in which men find themselves has no identical predecessor and will never be exactly repeated. Change is the order of the day. And this is true in spite of the fact that there are societies that live quite unaware of historical change. Carlo Levi thus described the peasants of a remote Italian village in the 1930s 'They cannot have even an awareness of themselves as individuals, here where all things are held together by acting upon one another ... They live submerged in a world that rolls on independent of their will' (Carlo Levi, 1982, p. 79).

Change would be baffling did the changes occur purely at random. Fortunately the world is full of regular processes. Although we now learn that the movements of the heavens are not completely regular, yet for thousands of years these movements have been used to measure time; the Sun and the Moon are regular enough for most practical purposes. Other regular and roughly predictable processes are biological. Creatures begin as seeds or spores or eggs, grow, reproduce and die, while the next generation takes their place. Sexual union of plants or animals ensures a combination of genes so that the next generation never exactly reproduces the one before. Careful observation of plant and animal growth has been a vital study for farmers ever since the Neolithic age began some ten thousand years ago – and perhaps for hunters before that. It was the widespread experience of breeding livestock that gave Darwin one clue to the origin of species – a theory that has been described as the biggest single idea ever. As the sciences of geology and chemistry developed in the nineteenth century alongside that of evolutionary biology we came to a new understanding of our natural environment and how it came about. A century later we are seriously concerned lest it be fatally damaged. The key notion is understanding the processes.

5.2 The processes of society

Important as the natural processes are, they are of only minor concern to most historians. Their chief preoccupation is with the processes of society. Our relations with the natural world are essential bases of life; we have to be fed, clothed and warmed. But on these simple foundations have been built all economies, all social interactions, all cultures, whose symbols and imaginations and creativities give value to our lives. As Aristotle insisted so long ago, man is a '*zoon politikon* – a creature of the ordered community (or state)'. To live in solitude, he added, is for a beast or a god, not for a man. The human race as a whole exhibits a diversity of physical types, but this is nothing to the variety of social and cultural products. Languages alone run into several thousands. Dress, manufactures, customs, economic, social and political relations are multifarious and have been even more numerous. The same may be said of psychologies; have any two minds ever been exactly alike? Laws and customs, governments and trading companies, farms and factories, fashions in the arts and dress, in music and literature, clubs, societies, institutions and organizations all have their effects upon human activities: they make them possible, but they also restrict and control them. They provide our 'second nature', which is added to our 'first nature' of genetic inheritance. All these manifestations of society and culture provide the framework within which men and women have pursued, and still pursue, power, wealth and status, as well as the more worthy ends of the intellect and the spirit. Historians and social scientists alike have to juggle with three sources of any human action: namely the genetic inheritance; the social framework and fashioning; and the individual decision.

This intricate social framework is made up of numerous processes. To live in civil society we require at least a rough working knowledge of the functions of a shop, a school, a bank, a transport system and so on. The historian, being himself a citizen, has such a working knowledge of his own society, as well as of the intimate and important experience of personal relationships. On the basis of this knowledge he can extrapolate to some comprehension of the (more or less) different processes that form the framework of the society under study, that within which lived and worked the characters of his history, Here, again, the key notion is the understanding of processes.

5.3 Individual lives

Finally we come to the doings of individual men and women in the past. Many lives have been recorded, but most have passed without record. How have the comparatively few been selected for history? One obvious explanation is that they were seen as important in their own day. The actions of rulers and conquerors affected thousands of other lives. Another is that many saints and heroes have been remembered because they were so untypical. Most people are neither saintly nor heroic. Where these qualities are admired, outstanding manifestations of faith, charity or courage will be valued for their very rarity. There is more difficulty with people whose importance seems greater in retrospect than it did to their contemporaries. This is especially the case in the arts and sciences, where recognition is often delayed: think of Giotto and Vermeer, Copernicus and Mendel. Therefore the historian usually has greater difficulty in finding out about such people than about those whose importance was seen at the time and details of their lives remembered. Finally, we must remember that in many cases sheer chance determines whether or not evidence remains. This is particularly true of the ancient world. The bulk of Greek and Roman writing has not survived.

The interpretation and understanding of individual lives has several interesting aspects. It is often claimed that historians have an inbuilt advantage over natural scientists in that they are themselves the very same sort of creatures that are under study. Admittedly the modest and blameless life of the historical researcher hardly resembles the colourful days of a Tamburlane or a Messalina, but still the historian is a man or woman like them, and has more in common than a crystallographer has with a crystal or an entomologist with a beetle. One of the best of philosophers of history, R. G. Collingwood, stressed this fact when he argued for his theory of recapitulation: namely, that the historian must re-enact past thoughts in his own mind. A human artefact (tool, painting, text) embodies the thought of its maker. 'To discover what this thought was, the historian must think it again for himself' (Collingwood, 1961, pp. 282–3). Since we cannot see or hear the past, our only direct contact with our predecessors is to think their thoughts.

Whether it is possible to do what Collingwood requires is, perhaps, debatable; to *know* that one has recapitulated the thought is more problematic. Nevertheless, Collingwood is right to point out that we can understand other people – inwardly, so to speak – largely because we are ourselves human. Greek and Roman historians confined themselves almost entirely to political history, and tended to explain all human actions in moral terms. Thus they omit much that we should wish to know about the ancient world. There is the advantage, however, that it is easy to follow their accounts – largely because the moral values of civilized people do not differ very much. For a long time (perhaps since the Renaissance) we have been able to recognize our contemporaries in the writings of Thucydides or Plato, Cicero or Tacitus. Hume was exaggerating, but not very much, when he said: 'Would you know... the Greeks and Romans? Study well... the French and English.'[8] (Presumably Collingwood shared this belief when he used as example the thoughts of the Emperor Theodosius.)

5.4 Social and cultural variation

Human nature, Hume claimed, does not change. Whatever truth may be in this, it is certain that societies and cultures change – and some change rapidly. In the twentieth century they have been doing so before our very eyes. Now, as we have already remarked, it seems that there are two parts to human nature: what one inherits in one's genes, and how one is shaped by one's upbringing and life-experiences. In the long vista of multi-cellular life on Earth (over half a billion years) the genetic inheritance of men and women two thousand years ago cannot have been very different from our own. But their technologies, their economic systems, their political machinery and their social arrangements differed considerably. It is a fascinating task (and all the more fascinating because almost impossible) to try to estimate, first, what these social and cultural systems were at any particular time or place in ancient Greece or Rome; and, secondly, to estimate how large a part they played in forming the character of any particular Greek or Roman. Cato could claim an ancestry socially far superior to that of Horace, but which was the better writer, which the greater man? And why?

Part of the attraction of ancient history is that we are dealing with highly civilized men and women, in many ways so like ourselves, who yet lived long ago in social and physical environments very different from own own. Nevertheless the problems just outlined – about both the exact nature of the social and cultural environment and the extent to which any one person's character is due to that environment and how much to genes – remain almost as challenging for the history of the nineteenth century as for that of the first century. There is not a lot that the historian can do about unravelling the genetic inheritance – any progress here must be left largely to the scientists – but he can investigate the social and cultural environment and try to guess how much that shaped the character, the thoughts and the actions of historical agents. This is why the history of modern historiography has moved from political history to economic, to social, and to cultural systems – first, to formal systems (religion, science, philosophy, education and the arts); and later to informal systems (customs, habits, folk-lore, mentalités). By the end of the twentieth century historians realize that there is no department of human life so trivial that it can be ignored, no activity so pointless that it may not modify, and hence make more explicable, other aspects of history. This is amply illustrated by Peter Burke, Richard Cobb, Robert Darnton, Natalie Zemon

Davis, Lynn Hunt, Ronald Hutton, Emmanuel Le Roy Ladurie, Lawrence Stone, Keith Thomas, E. P. Thompson, Michel Vovelle and many others.

6 Teleology

6.1 When am I me?

The discussion of social processes brings up the problems of continuing identity: what is it that continues through historical change? Do you and I remain the same during our lifetime? Was the Gladstone of the Home Rule Bills the same person as the conservative supporter of Peel some forty years earlier? Was the aged Louis XIV, sitting by the fire in domestic intimacy with Madame de Maintenon, the same man who had fallen romantically for Marie Mancini in 1658 and had sought to marry that engaging niece of Mazarin? Physically, perhaps. In terms of continuing consciousness, certainly. But politically or pragmatically? That is doubtful. The point is of interest to the historian, for she often has to understand the interplay of personalities much as a critic views the contrasting characters in a drama, or even as a chess-player estimates the relative and conflicting powers of the pieces as they stand in the game. In such situations it is the energies, the knowledge and the interests of each character *at the time* that is relevant. It would be wrong to assign to a long-lived player in the political scene the same qualities in old age as in youth. As pieces on the political chessboard, Gladstone and Elizabeth I and Bismarck could hardly be regarded as always possessing the same political identity and power.

If the argument holds for human continuities, it is much stronger for other characters in the dramas of history: institutions, organizations, political parties, churches, nation-states. In what sense is the Germany of 1996 the Germany of 1936 or of 1896?[9] A little thought must bring us to the conclusion that continuity of role or of title may conceal considerable differences of character.

6.2 Lines or circles?

Then there is the question of cyclical or linear views of history. For us it seems natural to see our lives, and indeed the course of history, as extended along a one-dimensional line. The line may bend and even at times seem to turn back on itself like a train winding through hills, but no more than with a train do the later parts touch the earlier. Peoples that did not have a strong sense of the past, largely because they were in any case ignorant of the past, saw time as a series of repetitions, very much like the recurrent seasons. This ignorance did not prevent some early peoples from making ambitious calendrical calculations. Among these was the so-called 'Long Count' of the Mayas of Central America, which consisted of 1,872,000 days (approximately 5,100 years). Plato was impressed by the fact that the Earth and the seven heavenly bodies (Sun, Moon and the five then known planets) revert to the same relative positions once every 36,000 years. This would afford ample time for a repetition, even if the Egyptians did have a historical record of nine thousand years (as Plato alleged in the *Timaeus*), going back to the legendary Atlantis (Plato, 1965, pp. 34–8, ## 22–5). Thucydides wrote (in the fifth century BC) for 'those who want to understand clearly the events which happened in the past and which (human nature being what it is) will, at some time or other and in much the same ways, be repeated in the future'. (Thucydides (1954), p. 24; Book 1 #22). The author of the Biblical book of *Ecclesiastes* is well known for his pessimism: 'Is there any thing whereof it may be said, See, this is new? It hath been already of old time, which was before us.'[10] What is perhaps less often realized is that this man was a very untypical Jew. He was a great sceptic, much influenced by Hellenistic culture of the third century BC. The true tone of the Hebrew religion was expressed in an emphasis on the acts of God in the life of that people – pre-eminently, of course, their salvation from Egyptian slavery in the Exodus. Unlike most ancient peoples the Jews had a strong tradition of linear history. This attitude was continued and reinforced in Christian tradition.

6.3 Continuities or chasms?

If we have settled the question between linear and cyclical history, we have not yet determined a related question. Do present events grow out of every stage of past events, or are there great chasms and discontinuities? Is our past like a tree, which at every stage shows the traces of its earlier growth, or is it like a path? A path is certainly linear, but there is no way of deducing its nature in one part (damp and boggy,) from another part (rough and stony). In the late nineteenth century, after Darwin, it was tempting to see the human past on the model of biological evolution, where traces of even the earliest forms of life are to be found in the latest. Recent advances in palaeontology have thrown doubt on this. There are many discontinued lines (see Gould 1991, pp. 46 and 288). But whatever the truths about biological evolution, there is no reason (apart from economy of thought) to suppose that they apply to human history. Equally there is no justification for a full-blooded teleological approach to history: the belief that it is all leading up to a destined end. For some this is a matter of religious faith, and so it must remain. There is not, as Hegel and Marx thought, historical support for the idea. At least, there is not yet much support. Our question must be settled empirically from a careful study of the facts if and when there are enough in our possession for a decision.

The notion of teleology is, however, worth a little more consideration. Derived from the Greek 'telos = an end or conclusion', the word indicates that a phenomenon is to be explained or understood in terms of its consequences rather than its causes. (Aristotle's 'final cause' is that for the sake of which something else is or acts.) The study of the end or purpose of things is usually taken to involve a mind that has such intentions or purposes. Before Darwin the whole of nature was seen as an illustration of purposive creation. Fishes have gills in order to live under water; bees collect pollen so that flowers may be fertilized, and so on. Nowadays biologists have almost entirely rejected such purposive explanations. They prefer to describe gills, pollination, and so on as *functions*. Functions are phenomena that enable fish, bees, flowers and so on, to live as they do, but they come about not by the purposive action of a creator, but by preceding occurrences in the course of natural evolution. The question for us is whether the notion of teleology, in any form, is helpful in understanding history.

6.4 A plan for history?

When Kant confronted the problem of making sense of human history, he wrote:

> The only way out for the philosopher, since he cannot assume that mankind follows any rational purpose of its own in its collective actions, is for him to attempt to discover a purpose in nature behind this senseless course of human events, and decide whether it is after all possible to formulate in terms of a definite plan of nature a history of creatures who act without a plan of their own. (Kant, 1784a, in Reiss, 1977, p. 42.)

Although Kant's suggestion of a non-divine purposive power behind history was to be taken up in various ways by such other Germans as Herder, Hegel and Marx, the idea now finds as little favour with historians as the corresponding notion does with biologists. But this is not the end of the matter. For although we do not readily accept that there is one over-riding plan to shape the whole course of history, yet we have to recognize that man, unlike nature, is capable of purposive action. Our lives look forward to the future; our thoughts are filled with hopes and fears, and almost all our conscious actions have some purpose. Moreover, many of our actions have a generalized purpose without any particular consequence being intended. I may save my money for the future without any particular purchase in mind, or I may not even spend it at all. Yet saving is a purposive action. Other actions are not intended to bring something about, but to prevent its occurrence. Such are all manner of health or safety precautions. The fact that our intentions are often frustrated by chance or by the intentions of others does not alter the fact that our lives are largely purposeful.

6.5 Purpose as explanation

How does this affect history? It does so in one way by accounting for major historical occurrences, like the post-Hegira spread of Islam, the Crusades, the Renaissance, the Reformation, the Enlightenment, the abolition of the slave trade.

In none of these cases did things turn out exactly as intended, yet they would never have happened at all had not many people at the same time had a common intention. It seems that there is at least some room for teleological explanation in history. We can never hope fully to account for the human past if we do not take into account the importance of human intentions – whether or not some of these (as is inevitable) were doomed to frustration.

There is another point. Popper fiercely attacked Hegel and other theorists who believed they had found the fixed pattern of past, present and future history. But may we not point out that the past can only be fully understood (if at all) in complete retrospect; that is, we have to stand where we are and contemplate the full picture of the whole human past in order properly to understand where we are. Moreover, since our perspective is constantly changing, this overview is in need of constant revision. Nor should we forget that our interpretation of this total past is always likely to be coloured by our hopes and fears for the future – for even historians are like other men and women in being much preoccupied with the future – with what is likely to happen and what they intend to do. A full understanding of the past, we may venture to say, is necessary for a full understanding of the present, for both past and present, together with expectations of the future, are all part of the same picture. This may sound like a counsel of perfection, but if we compare our present knowledge of the total historical past with the knowledge available to Herder or Hegel we can see how much progress has already been made. We shall never, before the end of time, attain a complete understanding of history (as Danto points out), but that is no reason for not trying for a steady improvement (see Danto, 1965, chapter 8).

7   Pattern, Structure and Colligation

7.1   Dangers of analogy

Yet such a total overview is awe-inspiring. How many intellects are capable of encompassing it? Most people need some degree of simplification. This can often be done by analogy – a comparison with something simpler and more familiar. Yet analogies can always be dangerous – never more so than when ideas are drawn from one area and unquestioningly applied to another. The human race goes on from age to age. We are born small and helpless, grow strong, gain experience, then die. In spite of common phrases like 'a mature people' or 'the childhood of the race', there is no reason to think that the model of a human life has any application either to a nation or to the human race as a whole. Again, history exhibits many changes, some of which are undoubted improvements. Yet how much justification is there for a belief in perpetual or inevitable progress? 'If a man were called to fix the period in the history of the world, during which the condition of the human race was most happy and prosperous,' wrote Gibbon, 'he would, without hesitation, name that which elapsed from the death of Domitian to the accession of Commodus.'[11] Regress is horrifyingly possible, as the scientifically organized extermination camps of Nazi Germany testified. There seems no good reason to suppose that history has any predetermined shape or inevitable end. Words like Fate, Fortune and Destiny are empty air. The great German historian Leopold von Ranke was right to declare that every age is equally near to God, and that the worth of an epoch is to be found in itself, not in anything that derives from it (Ranke, 1973, p. 53). Karl Popper attacked the abuse of such analogies in his *Poverty of Historicism* which he dedicated to the memory 'of the countless men and women of all creeds or nations or races who fell victims to the fascist and communist belief in Inexorable Laws of Historical Destiny'. Ranke and Popper were right. The course of history is not determined; there is no necessity about it. History is largely what we make it, though we cannot choose the circumstances – as Marx pointed out (Marx, 1973b, p. 146). That is why our every act matters; it may make a difference, how great we can never know. The course of history is shaped by every one of our actions; indeed, in a fundamental sense, it *is* every one of our actions.

7.2   Interpretation

The tendency to impose patterns upon history is not, however, confined to the great theorists – Herder, Hegel, Comte, Marx and others. There is something to be learned here from the psychology of perception. Workers in that field have observed that 'normally our percepts always possess some kind of form or arrangement' (Vernon, 1962, p. 52). This form is an interpretation of the data, usually favouring either what is familiar to us (e.g. a circular shape) or is important (e.g. the outline of a hawk to a young bird). This tendency to impose form (or *Gestalt*) is amusingly illustrated in familiar optical illusions. In these cases we make incorrect interpretations, we infer the wrong conclusions. The work of the historian resembles that of the archaeologist, the medical diagnostician or the detective. They all interpret the data, or clues, presented to them in a way that 'makes sense'. This is surely an extension of the role of interpretation in perception – provided we give a broad meaning to 'making sense'. Optical illusions, like faulty diagnoses or discarded scientific theories, show that our best interpretations are sometimes erroneous. The solution, of course, is not to give up interpreting (which in perception is anyway hardly possible), but to do it better – which means, initially at least, more carefully.

7.3   Patterns

So now let us look at the patterns that historians impose upon, or detect in, history. Was there really a Renaissance, a Reformation, an Enlightenment? Or an English revolution in the seventeenth century and a democratic one at the end of the eighteenth? Or are these merely convenient labels invented by historians to make sense of disparate events?[12] Indeed, the very concept of 'event' is open to question. If, as seems likely, the universe is in a continuous flow of fundamental forces, and if, as seems certain, time is continuous because it is infinitely divisible, then any division we make either of time or of this flow is purely artificial. Days, months and years roughly correspond to celestial movements, but hours and minutes are mere divisions – like a metre of cloth that a draper cuts from a roll. Similarly, what we call an event or a happening is something that we have carved out of the flow of things to suit our purposes. Moreover, the concept of event can be challenged from another direction. The French historian, Fernand Braudel, rejected events in favour of '*la longue durée*' – the long stretch'. His great work on the Mediterranean in the age of Philip II was constructed around three time scales: the structural (or long timespan), the conjunctural (trends or series over shorter periods of 20–50 years) and the event-based. He was very dismissive of the last of these; he called events 'the ephemera of history', like fire-flies (Braudel, 1975, p. 901). For Braudel, history is not a kaleidoscope of brief events, but a pattern of long continuities.

We have spoken of the political, economic, social and cultural systems within which people live and act out their lives. We have also suggested that this 'framework' provides an individual's 'second nature' – the 'first nature' being genetic inheritance. It is noteworthy that most writing of history has moved from the classical mode of history as the story of great individuals to a study of these non-personal frameworks. (Braudel's *Mediterranean* set the pattern for such historiography; he condemns not only individuals but even particular events to comparative insignificance.) There are several reasons for this alternative. One is a growing realization of the importance of the framework in providing a second nature and hence a fuller explanation for the actions of individuals. For example, if an Ottoman vizier behaved differently from a Victorian prime minister, the explanation lies more in the different social and political settings than in individual characters. The second is the growth of the social sciences, from which historians have drawn a better understanding of economic and social processes. (Macaulay's famous third chapter of his *History of England*, written in 1848, is perhaps the first recognition in English historiography of the importance of such processes.) A third conjecture is that most of those lives that have been recorded are now known – certainly the most significant ones. The lives of great men and women have become an increasingly well harvested field; the ambitious historian needs to exploit other terrains with different crops. Hence the increasing turn first to economic, then to social, now to cultural history and, least but not last, the nebulous area of popular beliefs and manners known as the history of *mentalités*. The exploitation of these new fields offers to aspiring historians new challenges, the need for new methods and fresh assumptions, and the satisfaction of throwing new light from unprecedented angles upon familiar themes. The enormous expansion in width and range of historical studies in the twentieth century brings us much nearer to an adequate representation and understanding of our whole history (or histories).

Former generations of historians saw the political, economic and social frameworks of society as the backcloths for the drama enacted by a few significant individuals of the day – rather like a performance of Shakespeare's *Julius Caesar*. Some historians now share the hope that various histories can be woven together into one total history (or *'histoire globale'*). The analogy of a patterned cloth emerging from the loom is useful here. One can identify the many different themes or types of history – political, constitutional, jurisdictional, legal, fiscal, and so on to histories of customs, manners and superstitions. The movement of the web reminds us that the pattern is not fixed, but is rather a network of dynamic relationships. The actors are now no longer set in front of the framework like characters in a drama, but form part of the threads and are involved in the pattern. Events are no longer isolated historical atoms, but nodes where several threads briefly come together. This view of a possible history may be an unattainable ideal, but at least it succeeds in combining the notions of history as pattern and history as process.

7.4   Metaphors

It is worth pausing to take a closer look at the metaphors that are often used about history: process, structure and pattern. The field of history is that extended period of time (up to five thousand years) and that region of space (mostly the surface of the Earth) in which the actions of men and women have taken place and have left sufficient vestiges for us to form some notion of what they were. As we have seen, this field is in a continual state of flux, never the same for more than a few moments. Nevertheless, there is a continuity within this flux. Natural objects (hills and seas), man-made artefacts (Pyramids, poems and paintings), ideas and systems, laws, customs and practices, institutions, and, finally, human beings themselves all endure for shorter or longer periods of time. Thirdly, we have to remember that all these units are not isolated but are in constant and necessary interaction with each other. (A suitable metaphor here might be the ecology of a tropical forest.) Fortunately these interactions – a man ploughing and sowing a field, buyers and sellers in a market, kings waging war, and so on – tend to follow the same pattern over long periods of time. This not only enables the actors to have a pretty good general idea of what is going on around them; it also permits the same understanding (within limits) to the historian.

Thus we can define 'pattern' as 'an arrangement of elements or units which, through repetition, becomes identifiable and recognizable'. A tune or the shape of the figure three are examples. This ability to recognize shapes or patterns plays an important part in perception by people and animals, as we have already remarked. Often we think we can perceive a repeated pattern in events: as it might be, in general elections, in *coups d'état*, in monopolies, in food riots. The more frequently a pattern is repeated the more easily and promptly it is recognized. Now here is a stumbling block. We are all familiar with puzzle or joke drawings, where the trick turns on the eye's readiness to supply a missing detail in the drawing. For example, two almost identical scenes are drawn and placed side by side; the reader is challenged to find the difference. It may be long before, say, it is observed that in one case a finger or ear is missing. With familiar patterns the mind can easily overlook small differences. This can have serious consequences in history, as in practical life. If we assume that this situation has the same pattern as a preceding situation, we shall respond in the same way. But if they are *not* the same, then our reaction may be quite, even disastrously, inappropriate. It is like missing the bottom step on a staircase. The rising in Paris of 13 Vendémaire (5 October) 1795 was expected by its organizers and participants to bring one more revolutionary victory to mob violence. On this occasion a young artillery officer was called in. Bonaparte had no scruples about firing on the people, three hundred of whom fell dead or wounded. Popular power ended in a 'whiff of grapeshot', and the army entered upon French politics – with still unended consequences for France and the world. An old pattern was broken and a new one emerged.

7.5 Structures

How do structures differ from patterns? In this way: a structure is that arrangement of parts or elements which determines the nature of the whole. A pattern is merely an arrangement of elements. Let us suppose a palaeontologist unearths a number of fossils of the same creature, but in each specimen the head is lacking. He would soon become familiar with the pattern of the skeleton, and would thus be able to assemble the bones if they had been separated, but he would know that he had not secured the structure of the animal. The bones without the head would not determine the character of the whole.[13] Here it is necessary to note only two things: one, how pattern and structure differ, and, two, the necessity of distinguishing an imposed from an inherent pattern or structure. The inherent ones are really there in the historical events; the imposed patterns or structures exist only in the mind of the historian. It is vitally important not to mistake the latter kind for the former. Patterns in history should be found, not made (Novick, 1988, p. 2).

This is particularly necessary for so-called 'structural' historians. They tend to emphasize the continuing patterns of historical processes and lay less stress on disparate events. They maintain that the patterns they identify are indeed the true structures of history; that is, that these political, economic and social patterns do, indeed, determine the nature of history. A structural historian writes: 'I persist in holding that the structural histories of economies and societies... proceed largely independently of beliefs... about them... Theorists and philosophers,' he goes on, 'only try to conceptualize the world... the point is to *explain* the origins and nature of the real structures of the world and their transformations' (Lloyd, 1933, p. 4). Structural history is a valid, if ambitious, enterprise, but its success wholly depends upon a correct identification of the 'real structures of the world'. Otherwise, and just because it gives more hostages to Fortune, it is in greater danger of disaster than a more cautious, event-based and empirical style of historiography. Two well-known instances exemplify the point. Hegel believed that history was the march of Absolute Spirit in the world, a march that proceeded by dialectical steps of thesis, antithesis and synthesis. Marx also believed in a dialectical process, but substituted material relations for Absolute Spirit. If either of these should turn out not to be real structures of the world, then Hegelian structural history or Marxist structural history must be fundamentally flawed. The difficulty in these, as in all other cases of structural history, lies in the question whether the structures are 'real structures of the world' or structures existing in the brain of the historian and imposed upon the world.

7.6 Colligation

A similar question arises in connection with the related idea of historical colligation. In an excellent introduction to the philosophy of history some years ago, W. H. Walsh put forward the idea of 'colligation'. This is a mode of explanation much used by historians and characteristic of their approach. It is 'the procedure of explaining an event by tracing its intrinsic relations to other events and locating it in its historical context'. This sort of explanation depends on the belief that 'the event in question is to be seen as part of a general movement which was going on at the time' (Walsh, 1967, p. 59). By way of example, he suggests that Hitler's reoccupation of the Rhineland in 1936 be seen as part of his policy of German self-assertion and expansion. The connection is one of policy. As Walsh explains: 'Because actions are, broadly speaking, the realisation of purposes, and because a single purpose or policy can find expression in a whole series of actions ... we can say in an intelligible sense that some historical events are intrinsically related' (pp. 59–60). In such cases, he goes on, we can say that not only are later events in the series determined by earlier ones, but also (surprisingly) that earlier ones are themselves 'affected by the fact that the later ones were envisaged'. Hence historical thinking, because of its subject matter, 'often proceeds in teleological terms'.[14]

This idea of colligation raises a number of other questions. For instance: Does colligation lie at the core of narrative? Does colligation give us a legitimate mode of explanation? Since historians cannot write about everything they must necessarily make selections for their chosen theme or topic. Must details of a theme always be 'colligated' in this way? Is colligation a form of interpretation?

Let us reiterate the one important question: Is the pattern, structure or colligation found in the events themselves, in the field of historical reality? Or is it a product of the historian's mind and so imposed upon reality. The point is exemplified in the familiar detective story. A crime is committed; the police produce an explanation and arrest an innocent person. The detective hero steps in to correct this blunder and to solve the mystery. About two-thirds of the way through the story he, in his turn, produces a better explanation. Later his convincing explanation turns out to be wrong, and the mystery deepens until the hero finally solves the problem and discovers the true criminal. All three explanations have arranged the supposed events in a particular pattern, a pattern that seems to explain the mystery. The first two patterns, however, prove to be no more than products of the thinking of the police or the detective. Only the third pattern (also, of course, the result of thought) offers the correct solution, for that is the pattern of historical reality. That was the pattern inherent in the events; the two false patterns were not inherent, but merely imposed. Contrary to what may be popularly supposed, the fundamental challenge to the historian lies not so much in hitting upon a correct description of this or that happening as in finding the correct arrangement of events, together with the connections between them. It is these assemblages – whether patterns, structures or colligations – that constitute the heart of history. There is a parallel in science. A century or more ago biologists would make collections of shells, eggs, butterflies and so on, and examine them in isolation. Nowadays they find it more revealing to study the animals in the context of other creatures in their natural environment; they prefer the animal alive in the forest to dead in the laboratory. Thus 'natural history' yields place to 'ecology'. In biology as in history the holistic approach often proves the more revealing. It is the connections that matter.

Notes

1 This may lead to Gadamer's 'fusion of horizons' – see below, chapter 7, 2.6–2.8. See also the useful remarks on Gadamer in Callinicos (1995, pp. 84–6, 90).

2 Kant (1963, p. 533, B 672). For a full exploration of regulative ideals, see Emmet (1994).

3 Causation is discussed in chapter 3, 1.

4 See Vincent (1995, p. 12). Vincent's chapter on historical evidence is well worth reading.

5 *Nicomachean Ethics*, 1094b.

6 For this last, see Vincent (1995, p. 13).

7 See, for example, the British falsifications of First World War history discussed in Denis Winter, *Haig's Command* (1991).

8 In *An Enquiry Concerning Human Understanding* (1975), section VIII, #65, p. 83.

9 This question provoked the *Historikerstreit* of the 1980s – see chapter 1, 4.

10 *Eccles*, I, 10.

11 Gibbon, *Decline and Fall* (1910), chapter III, p. 78. He was referring to the years AD 96–180.

12 For more discussion see Stanford (1986, pp. 36 and 108).

13 A further discussion of structure follows in chapter 4, 1.5 and 1.6.

14 Walsh (1967, p. 60). We discussed 'teleology' in the preceding section.

Suggested Reading

Objectivity

The classic statement on this is Acton (1970). Nagel's essay 'Subjective and Objective' in Nagel (1991) raises philosophical issues, dealt with at greater length in Nagel (1989). Both E. H. Carr (1964) and Vincent (1995) discuss some of the difficulties for historians. The masterpiece in this field, however, is undoubtedly Novick (1988).

Evidence

Several thoughtful historians discuss this. One may, with profit, refer to Elton (1969) and (1970) or to Kitson Clark (1967) or to Marwick (1990). Both Bloch (1954) and Vincent (1995) make interesting and original points. The provocative views of E. H. Carr (1964) on this subject have, perhaps, been given too much credence.

Truth

Historians are more concerned with the application of terms 'true' and 'false' than with their analysis. Most would go along with Austin (1970) in adhering to the correspondence theory. The discussions in Pitcher (1964) are clear and useful. Abandoning that approach can lead via coherence theories to relativism and total historical scepticism of the kind found in Goldstein (1976) and Meiland (1965). The pragmatic theory of truth, see William James (1907), is coming back into fashion in some quarters. See, for example, Rorty (1982) and (1989). It can hardly fail to appeal to some philosophically minded historians. More conventional views are well expressed in Kitson Clark (1967), Elton (1969) and McCullagh (1984).

Social processes and frameworks

The way in which society enframes, structures or informs historical actions is nowadays such a commonplace that one could begin with almost any modern historian. Histories like those of Keith Thomas (1978), Peter Brown (1991) and Le Roy Ladurie (1978) and (1980) provide good examples. For a more theoretical discussion, not altogether neglecting Hegel (1980) and Marx (1973a), (1973b) and (1975), see Mandelbaum (1977), Peter Burke (1992), Lloyd (1993) and Callinicos (1995).

Teleology

On this theme we may find points of interest in Plato (1965), Kant (1784a), Wilcox (1987), Popper (1961) and Le Poidevin and MacBeath (1993).

Patterns

I can recommend only Walsh (1967), Stanford (1990) and Lloyd (1993).

3

Causes and Explanations

1 Causes

1.1 What is a cause?

The notion of cause and effect is used in everyday life, in science and in history. We may think of a cause as something that produces or brings about something else (its effect).[1] Our concern here is, primarily, how it is used in history: for it is the recognized duty of the historian not merely to *recount* the events of the past but to *account for* them. Usually, though not invariably, this means citing supposed causes. There is often a good deal of historical argument about what caused particular important events, like the French Revolution or the American Civil War. We ask a different, and more fundamental question, if we want to know exactly what the historian means by 'cause'.

1.2 Everyday causes: four features

First let us look at everyday usage, where we are familiar with cause–effect sequences, like pressing the switch to make the light come on. Philosophers point out several characteristics of such experiences:

1   The sequences occur so frequently that we take them for granted. Nevertheless, if we had known nothing like them before we could not have predicted the second event from the first. In philosophical terms, there is no a priori knowledge of the sequence.
2   We tend to call the first event the cause because we believe that without it the second event would not have occurred. (This is not to say that the second event *had* to follow – the light doesn't always come on; only that if the first doesn't happen, then neither does the second.)
3   While there may be a number of preceding events or circumstances that affect the outcome (e.g. the wiring from switch to light), we tend to single out one of them as *the* cause.

4   This selection of 'the cause' from a number of relevant events or circumstances is fairly arbitrary. What is selected depends on the purpose of the investigation or the interests of the investigator rather than anything intrinsic to the events themselves.

1.3   Selection of cause

This last point may be expanded. Why do people choose this rather than that as *the* cause? Personal interest may be one reason. A man is mugged. Why? 'Because he foolishly walked down unfrequented streets late at night', says his friend. 'Because he wasn't carrying a gun', says his sensation-loving son. 'Because of the depravity of human nature', says the priest. 'Because of the high rate of unemployment', says the sociologist. 'Because I had to get more drugs', says the robber. Another reason for picking out a cause is that it offers a point of control. Collingwood defines it thus: 'A cause is an event or state of things which it is in our power to produce or prevent, and by producing or preventing which we can produce or prevent that whose cause it is said to be' (Collingwood, 1940, pp. 296–7). In this case a cause is seen as a point of intervention. 'Why cannot the bus get down this road?' 'Because the council has not put yellow lines along the kerbs.' Other causes might be given: because people park their cars there; because the bus is too wide; because the houses are too close together; because too many people drive into the town every day. Collingwood's argument is that we select as the cause that factor in the situation which we can most easily control or manipulate. This is true, also, of the many cases where the human link in the chain is easiest to control. A third criterion for the selection of a cause is the variation from the norm. In the investigation of a railway accident the inspectors will disregard the speed and load and weight of the train, but pick out the bent rail as the cause of the accident. It is not that the other factors were irrelevant to the crash, but they were present in normal running of the trains. It was the abnormal condition (the bent rail) that they selected as the cause (see Hart and Honoré in Dray, 1966, pp. 216–17).

1.4   Causes and conditions

As soon as a multiplicity of causes is postulated new problems arise, for we now have to consider conditions as well as causes. Which is which? A condition may have to be present for the effect to occur. For example, the successful striking of a match requires a dry match, a dry rough surface, the presence of oxygen and a certain dexterous motion of the hand. In the absence of any one of these the match will not light. Are they all causes? Or are they only necessary conditions?

Various scenarios will show that there is no intrinsic difference between a cause and a condition. In practice, if it is asked why the match was lit, the most likely answer is something on the lines of 'Because Mary wanted to light the fire'. Where people are concerned, causes are frequently attributed to human volition. In this case we should say that Mary's wish was the cause and the other things (oxygen, rough surface and so on) were necessary conditions. But the case might be otherwise. Let us suppose that an ignorant child picks up the match and goes round the room rubbing it on various surfaces. On the sixth occasion the match surprisingly bursts into flame. Then we shall be inclined to answer the question by 'Because it was rubbed on a dry rough surface'. Now the surface, once a condition, has become a cause. Or imagine several clumsy people trying to light the match, but failing to move their hands in the right way. At last one of them succeeds. What was the cause? A certain motion of the hand – which in the case of Mary was seen as a mere condition. Of course, we might name all the conditions and say that together they constitute the cause. But how tedious that would be. And could we ever be sure of citing *all* the possibly relevant conditions?

All this shows two things: one, that what calls for explanation is generally the exceptional and unexpected; and, two, that what we call a cause and what a condition depends on what needs explaining. There can, therefore, be no *inherent* difference between a cause and a condition.

In everyday life we are less concerned with explaining past occurrences than in bringing about future ones. When we set out on a course of action (cooking a meal, going on holiday), we consider how our aims can best be achieved. We choose the means appropriate to the desired end – for example, we break the eggs into a basin, whisk them with a fork and fry them in butter to make an omelette. Let us note that here we are seeking a *sufficient* cause or set of conditions, rather than the necessary cause or set of conditions that we tend to use in accounting for a past event. Instead of looking for 'that without which E does not occur', we now want 'that with which E does occur'. A necessary condition (as we have seen) is determinate; it is what must be present, though it may have many constituents. A sufficient condition is not determinate; there may be several alternatives (the eggs may be whisked by a blender, fried in oil and so on), but it must guarantee the result. A necessary condition does not guarantee the result; it only guarantees that the result cannot occur without it.

A word of warning here: a necessary condition is so called because we believe *this particular* condition is necessary for that particular result. It makes no assumptions about the necessity of *any* causal relationship whatever. Whether causality is a necessary relation – like logical implication – remains a matter of debate (see Hospers, 1967, pp. 308 ff; Hume, 1975, p. 75; Kant, 1963, p. 125; Ayer, 1964, pp. 194–8).

1.5 Causes in history

Now let us turn to history. Historians rarely think in the mode of single-cause/single-effect. Affairs are more complicated. Let us ask why the Nazis came to power in Germany in 1933. The common man might answer by naming a necessary condition – that without which the event in question would not have occurred. There are, as it turns out, quite a number of possible answers. 'Hitler would not have been made chancellor – if he had not had a great deal of electoral support, – if he had not been backed by a strong force of storm troopers, – if he had not been pushed into power by a group of right-wing politicians who hoped to manipulate him, – if Germany had not been suffering an economic crisis.' Probably each of these is a necessary condition. Any one could be identified as the 'real cause'.

The historian's typical answer to this objection is to say (as we said above about the match) that not one condition but all taken together were the cause of the Nazi triumph. But can we then be certain that we have listed all the necessary conditions? It was hard enough in the case of the match. Here it is much more difficult. Might we not have to add the Treaty of Versailles, the failure of Ludendorff's 1918 offensive, the murder of the Archduke Franz Ferdinand, the nature of Bismarck's government, and so on through German history right back to Arminius and the defeat of the Roman legions in AD 9? To define the 'real cause' as the sum of the necessary conditions makes the question 'Why?' unanswerable.

Is it better with sufficient conditions? In the winter of 1940–1 Hitler's generals were planning an attack on their official ally, the USSR. A well organized sudden assault by what was then the finest army in the world would surely be sufficient to capture the enemy's capital and compel his surrender. As we know, the German armies narrowly failed to take Moscow in December 1941 – and indeed never did. Clearly the splendid army, the suddenness of the attack and the efficient organization did not constitute a sufficient condition for victory. What was missing? The time available. The German army's assault was delayed by the Balkan campaign of spring 1941, which lasted longer than had been expected. As a result the attack on the USSR did not take place until 22 June, and by October the Russian winter was slowing the invaders before their 'blitzkrieg' could reach Moscow. It is often alleged that it was the Balkan diversion that proved fatal to Hitler's plans. (However, other historians argue that the Balkan campaign did not delay Operation Barbarossa.) So are we to conclude that a sufficient condition would have been the aforesaid army, suddenness and organization plus a longer timescale? Perhaps, but no one can be sure. It may be that Hitler would also have needed the co-operation of the Russian peasants, supposedly 'liberated' by the invaders. Perhaps other conditions would have been needed. Again there is no obvious limit.

It seems that to identify the cause of X with a sufficient condition or set of sufficient conditions for X is little more feasible than with necessary conditions. Without knowing what would have happened otherwise (the counter-factual situation), we can never be sure that we have properly identified the complete set of events that were sufficient to produce the result.

1.6 Counter-factuals: or What didn't happen

The common view of historical causation has been put like this:

> We may suppose that the notion of cause was introduced into history from everyday life, which means that a cause in history was, originally, an event, action or omission but for which the whole subsequent course of events would have been significantly different. (Walsh, 1967, p. 190)

Thus we find one of the great historians of the French Revolution saying, 'There would have been no French Revolution – such as actually took place – if the king, "handing in his resignation", had not convoked the Estates-General' (Lefebvre, 1947, p. 2). Lefebvre's identification of the cause rests on the assumption that he knows what would have happened otherwise – no revolution. But how can anyone know what did not occur?

This is hardly a problem in daily life, where we find regular sequences of events: we press a switch and the light comes on; we turn the tap and water flows. Hence we can argue back from the effects: if the light is on someone must have pressed the switch; if the water is running, then the tap must have been turned on. (Clearly these arguments are not totally reliable – there may be a leak in the pipe, for example – but the first approximation is good enough in the majority of cases.) The point is that we are so accustomed to such regular sequences of cause and effect that we take it for granted that we know what would have happened otherwise. (No pressing the switch, no light; no turning the tap, no water). The more regular are such sequences (that is, the fewer the exceptions), the surer we feel of what would have happened. Suppositions of this kind, about what would have happened but did not, are said to be 'counter-factual'.

In history the commonest method of identifying a cause is to make counter-factual suppositions. It will be clear at once that in doing so we can be less sure than in matters of daily life. The reason is simple: we experience hundreds or thousands of sequences of the 'switch–light' kind; we have comparatively few examples of the sort of thing we want to explain in history – cultural renascences, religious reformations, democratic revolutions. We can compare so many cases of familiar sequences ('switch – light; no switch – no light') that we can be pretty sure of our counter-factual suppositions, and hence of the cause. Abraham Lincoln in his second inaugural address (1865) said that slavery was 'somehow the cause of the war'. But did he have experience of many instances of 'slavery – war; no slavery – no war' to justify his belief? Of course not. Yet this is the sort of thing that historians often say.

Did Lefebvre have many experiences of 'Estates-General – revolution; no Estates-General – no revolution'? Again, no. It seems likely that he was following a different tack. He was probably using the method of Hart and Honore (discussed above) of identifying the abnormal factor in the situation. But, of course, summoning the Estates was not the only abnormal element of the situation in 1788. Might not other abnormal factors (like the high cost of bread in Paris) have led to a revolution even if the king had *not* called the Estates? So why pick on this one?

We must note that Lefebvre labelled the king's action as 'the immediate cause'. He distinguished this from the 'ultimate cause', which he identified as the rise of the bourgeoisie. Such distinctions are not uncommon. Later that king died on the scaffold. Why? Because the blade cut his head off. But is that a sufficient explanation of regicide? Certainly the fall of the blade was the immediate cause, but do we not need to seek other 'deeper' causes? Why bother about the immediate cause in the case of the Estates? I think it is because the historian often wants to attach the cause as closely as possible to the effect, so that there is no room for any alternative effect. If the cause is immediately followed by the effect, there is an appearance of inevitability about it. Generally, citing the immediate cause explains why the event occurred at that moment rather than at another, but not why it happened at all. This latter is usually answered by citing some 'deep' or 'fundamental' or 'ultimate' cause. The fundamental cause is held to be something that, sooner or later, would bring about the effect (war, revolution and so on), but not at any particular time. (That is fixed by the immediate cause.)[2]

It is likely that Lincoln saw slavery as a deeper cause of this kind. Probably he did not feel it necessary to trace out the exact chain of causes leading up to the war as historians do. The main point for us is that in history, as in daily life, causal judgements frequently rest on counter-factual assumptions. That means that the validity of the judgement is no greater than the validity of the assumption about what did not happen. To do it successfully, the historian has to have a sort of sixth sense, an apparently instinctive 'feel' for the way things flow. But, of course, it is not an instinct at all, it is the result of experience. Strictly, we are here dealing not with certainty but with probability – a topic to be discussed later.

1.7   Responsibility

The alleged cause of an event may be either human or natural. In and after the American Civil War both Northerners and Southerners tended to blame each other for that national disaster. Nearly all believed that the cause of the war lay in human volition (see Pressly, 1965, passim). A similar controversy arose after 1918 about the responsibility of the Germans for the First World War. In 1919 the new republican government of Germany had to sign a peace treaty at Versailles that included the notorious Article 231 – a 'war-guilt' clause that fixed upon Germany the sole responsibility for the conflict and which was used to justify the heavy reparations demanded. In this clause many historians find the 'seeds' (or part-cause) of the Second World War of 1939–45. Thus the search for a cause often becomes a search for human responsibility. (For another dispute about re-sponsibility see the *Historikerstreit* in chapter 1, 4, above.) To human actions a moral quality inevitably attaches which is absent from occurrences in nature. Significantly, historians have been known occasionally to try to cool angry passions by lessening human responsibility and finding the cause in nature. One Northern scientist tried to do this by explaining that the ultimate cause of the American Civil War was the climate (see Pressly, 1965, p. 60). We may note that there is a parallel between historians' search for moral responsibility and the methods of a law court (see Hart and Honoré, 1959, pp. 213–37).

1.8 Collingwood's causes

Whether or not human volition is to be regarded as distinct from natural causation or merely another kind of cause is still a matter of debate. It depends largely on how you understand such concepts as 'cause' and 'motive'. Collingwood distinguishes between three kinds of cause: cause in history 'that which is "caused" is the free and deliberate act of a conscious and responsible agent, and "causing" him to do it means affording him a motive for doing it'); cause in practical life (like the examples of 'switch – light', 'tap – water', discussed above); and cause in science (like 'clouds cause rain'). The first is the person-to-person causation of human relations; the second is the person-to-thing causation of technology; and the third is the thing-to-thing causation of the natural sciences (Collingwood, 1940, pp. 285–7). Others argue that, since a cause is that which brings about an effect, the cause may be indifferently human or natural or frequently (especially in history) a combination of both.

1.9 Context-dependency

An important point is that the identification of cause is 'context-dependent'. Since the actual state of the world is so complex, we must ignore most of it and concentrate on what concerns our present interests and purposes. Thus the cause of Mr X dying of poison may be given either as the intentions of the murderer or the nature of the poison or both, the judge is likely to be concerned with the first cause given, a chemist with the second. Was the battle won by the superior skill of the winning general or by his superior armaments? A scrupulous historian will consider both and try to weigh them up. It is a disadvantage of the division of history among various expertises – military, scientific, religious, economic and so on – that historians are tempted to find the cause in their own speciality.

All this lends some support to a sceptical position about cause in history. While one would not deny that earlier events bring about some later events but not others (thus that *post hoc, sed non propter hoc* is not vacuous), yet human affairs are so complex that it may legitimately be doubted whether causes in history can ever be identified completely or accurately related to their effects or (even if not certainly) at least with a degree of practical and useful probability. There is something to be said for the view of Oakeshott that the concept of cause is superfluous for the historian:

> It is a presupposition of history that every event is related and that every change is but a moment in a world which contains no absolute *hiatus*...History accounts *for* change by means of a full account *of* change...The conception of cause is thus replaced by the exhibition of a world of events intrinsically related to one another in which no *lacuna* is tolerated. (Oakeshott, 1933, p. 143)

Should we, perhaps, admit that our identification of causes rests on our own interests, tells us little about why things really occurred, and says more about the historian than about history?

1.10   Four conclusions

We may now draw our conclusions about causation in history.

(1) Any attribution of causation may be partly subjective. What we designate as 'cause' depends on where our interests lie. The notion of cause can be a tool to fix moral or legal responsibility; it is helpful in other affairs (such as car mechanics) to see where repair or alteration or amendment would be useful.

(2) Though partly subjective, the attribution of cause in historiography is not arbitrary. It rests, as we have seen, on counter-factual judgements – on estimates of what would have happened if...or, sometimes, if not...These counter-factuals have to be guessed at. They can never be known because they never happened.

(3) The counter-factual judgements of a historian are not wild guesses. They rest on her estimates of probability. If she decides, for example, that the victory of the colonies in the American War of Independence was due to the strength of character of George Washington, this is because she judges that the probable course of events without him would have been the victory of the greater military power. Another historian might opt for the probability of British victory in the absence of French intervention.

(4) Estimates of historical probability are far from mathematical probability. They rest, rather, on an understanding of human affairs. This means knowing how people generally act, or, more sophisticatedly, how people of that period and society generally acted. But this was always true of historians. A comparatively recent development has been the study of the various systems of human society: political, juristic, fiscal, commercial, industrial, ecclesiastical, educational and so on. (Each has now its own academic discipline). To estimate the probable course of events (that is, what would have happened had some element been absent from

the situation, like George Washington or French naval power in the North Atlantic), the historians needs a pretty clear idea of the working of the various systems in the societies of that time – in this case, especially diplomatic, naval, logistic, military, social and socio-psychological systems. It is hard enough to write a history within a system – say, a history of French jurisprudence in the eighteenth century. Even here the story is never completely enclosed; other events, systems and people intervene and have to be understood on different terms. For the historian of a nation at war the task is much more daunting, for here a number of systems operate within and between the warring societies. They all have to be understood sufficiently well for the historian to be able to say with some assurance: 'This event was particularly important, for if it had not occurred things would have taken a very different course.' In many cases, then, the historian has not only to understand a variety of different (and usually now outdated) systems; he has also to comprehend how they interact. He has to have a grasp of the flow of events. Without such knowledge his counter-factual judgements lose validity.

We may conclude that the notion of cause in history can lead to some very tangled arguments. Writers who want to use it should first be clear (and make their readers clear) what they understand by it. Finally, we should stress the importance of counter-factuals in historical judgements. Historians have to account for what happened. This is largely done, we now see, by means of what did not happen.

2   Explanation in General

2.1   What is explanation?

'Explain – to unfold, to make plain or intelligible'. So reads the dictionary definition. Few would disagree with this. But to proceed to actually explaining things raises more than one question. First, how do we approach the task? Should we start from the problem, the *explicandum*, that which is to be explained? Or should we consider first the person to whom it has to be explained, and start from his or her state of mind? The former view might be thought to imply that there is one correct explanation to be given of any phenomenon, but this is not so. Dr Johnson once answered Boswell's query with an explanation. When the latter protested that he did not understand, Johnson growled, 'Sir, I have found you a reason. I am not obliged to find you an understanding.' Some people hold that this is the right method. 'If you ask me for an explanation I will give you the proper one; whether you understand it or not is your problem.' This somewhat brusque attitude is justified by those who believe that the explanation must show the logical link between the *explanandum* and the *explanans* (that which does the explaining). For example, the explanation of why my glass fell to the floor when it slipped from my fingers (the *explanandum*) is the law of gravity plus the statement of the initial conditions (the *explanans*). The explanation consists in showing the logical link between the falling and the law: the event to be explained was 'covered' by that law (or instantiated the law). This sort of explanation is often referred to as the 'covering law' type.

Now let us start at the other end. If the question about the falling glass is asked by a young child, then citing the *explanans* (in this case, the law of gravity plus initial conditions) may well fail to explain. Newtonian dynamics is beyond him. The explanation is not an explanation in this case, because the phenomenon has not been made plain or intelligible to the enquirer. We have to find some other psychologically more helpful way of explaining, such as 'the glass fell because the Earth attracted it'. So the first question is: on which end of the problem should we concentrate, the phenomenon or the enquirer? The paradox is that the proper explanation on some occasions can fail to be any explanation at all, for it makes nothing 'plain or intelligible'. This difficulty arises especially with explanations in science.

2.2   Must explanation be scientific?

Let us take a closer look, then, at where explanations belong. Sometimes philosophers discuss them as if they belonged only in the philosophy of science. The example just given certainly belongs there, but is that the only place for explanation? The second part of our discussion (about the child) suggests that explanation may also be a part of family life. More formally, it belongs to the discipline of pedagogics, where (as we have suggested) rather different considerations rule. Of course, it also belongs to everyday life, which is where we mostly encounter it, but since everyday life is not a theory-governed enterprise (like science, philosophy or pedagogics) it is not easy to take a clear view of the issues. In philosophy, explanation belongs not just to the philosophy of the sciences, whether natural or social, but rather to the wider sphere of epistemology – the theory of knowledge in general. This raises the question of whether explanation takes on a different form in other areas of knowledge than the natural sciences. Some philosophers (notably C. G. Hempel and Ernest Nagel) answer 'No' to this; for them explanation is the same in all areas of knowledge. We must not foreclose the question, however. The role of explanation in the social sciences and history will be discussed in the next chapter. If explanation has a place in so many different human activities, the question must be asked whether it is the same thing in every case or whether it varies. We shall see.

Let us start with the natural sciences. The common view is that they investigate the external (or natural) world and formulate hypotheses or theories to account for what has been observed. A good theory is one that, when tested against the world, not only explains what has happened but also predicts what will happen. One distinguished philosopher of science, Karl Popper, has argued that by bringing single phenomena under general laws we can do three things at once.

> The use of a theory for the purpose of *predicting* some specific event is just another aspect of its use for the purpose of *explaining* such an event. And since we test a theory by comparing the events predicted with those actually observed, our analysis also shows how theories can be *tested*. Whether we use a theory for the purpose of explanation, or prediction, or of testing, depends on our interest, and on what propositions we take as given or assumed. (Popper, 1962, Vol. 2, pp. 262–3)

This may be considered an over-simplification of scientific procedures, but at least we have a clear picture as a basis for further discussion. However, in *A Brief History of Time* Stephen Hawking discusses the problem of why electrons circle the nucleus in fixed orbits within atoms. The solution, begun by Niels Bohr and completed by Richard Feynman, both explained the phenomenon and made possible predictions which on testing appear to confirm the theory – a theory which is based on the assumption of wave/particle duality. This seems to be how Popper saw it when he wrote the above in 1943 some forty-five years before (see Hawking, 1990, pp. 59–60). In physics then it appears that prediction and explanation can be two sides of the same coin; the 'coin' being the subsumption of single phenomena under general 'laws' or hypotheses.

This is not always the case. In the biological sciences the position is rather different. Darwin's theory, for example, is strongly explanatory but weakly pre-dictive. This is perhaps also true of geological theories. What of human actions? To take a relevant if trivial example, if I am asked why I am writing this book, I reply that I have a contract with the publishers. Although my actions could be explained by a general law (for example, 'Honest men keep their contracts' – the method favoured by Hempel), that seems unnecessary here. The realms of every-day life, like those of the social sciences and history, on the whole neither admit of nor require law-based explanations of the type that Popper and Hawking are talking about.

2.3   Must explanation be caused?

There is another thing to notice in the scientific example. It is assumed by both the scientist (Hawking) and the philosopher (Popper) that explanations are causal: that is, that to explain is to show the cause, and vice versa. Not all philosophers agree. David-Hillel Ruben argues thus: No contingent thing or event causes itself. Therefore causation must be a relation between two distinct existences. But in some cases the *explanandum* and the *explanans* are the same thing. Thus in these cases the explanation is non-causal (Ruben, 1990, p. 218). What are such cases?

Perhaps the simplest example is found in ordinary life:

'It's bed-time, Johnny!'
  'Why is it bed-time?'
  'Because it is eight o' clock.'

Or a less probable conversation:

'What is this hard stuff on the water?'
  'That is water, too – frozen water.'
  'It doesn't seem to be water. Please explain.'
  'Analysis shows it to consist of H_2O . . .'
  'Oh, then it *is* water.'

In these and similar cases the explanation is done not by citing causes, but by showing that two apparently different things are one and the same thing under different descriptions. An explanation by re-description can start from either side of the identity, depending on what is known and what needs explaining. ('Why is he celibate? Because he is unmarried.' Or 'Why is he unmarried? Because he is celibate.') Put simply, it is sometimes a matter of 'explaining what' rather than 'explaining why'.[3] It seems doubtful whether 'explaining what' can ever be done on Hempelian lines.

Ruben has a more important point, however. We have seen that the 'proper' or 'correct' explanation may not actually explain anything – as in the case of a child or ignorant person. To effect explanation we have to offer something that the enquirer can understand: explanations should be 'audience- relative'. Admitting that point, we must not run off to extremes and suppose that any explanation will do that satisfies the enquirer. The explanation must be true, or at least so grounded in truth that it conveys truth to the enquirer. This is not always easy. How much truth can one convey to an ignorant or stupid enquirer? Nevertheless, Ruben insists that 'explanantia' (that is, things that explain) 'fully explain explananda' (that is, things to be explained) 'only in virtue of how things really are. Explanations work', he goes on, 'only because things make things happen or make things have some feature'. Explanation, therefore, is not basically psychological, even though it tries (or should try) to meet the enquirer's mental needs. It is rather a matter of knowledge, resting firmly upon reality. As Ruben puts it, 'explanation is epistemic, but with a solid metaphysical basis' (Ruben, 1990, p. 232). The importance of this point will be seen when we come (in chapter 4) to explanation in the social sciences and in history. For there what exactly *is* reality becomes more debatable.

2.4 Good explanations and full explanations

The distinction between explanation that is psychologically satisfying and explanation that is epistemologically and metaphysically sound has other ramifications.

Hilary Putnam is right to say that 'explanation is an interest-relative notion' and 'explanation has to be partly a pragmatic concept' (Putnam, 1979, pp. 41–2; quoted in Ruben, 1990, p. 21). For we should not be seeking an explanation if we had no interest in the question. And we stop seeking when the explanation works; that is a pragmatic consideration. Such explanations are 'audience-variant'. But there is a distinction between a *good* explanation (that is, one that works) and a *full* explanation (that is, one that rests on 'how things really are'). Philosophers, as distinct from teachers and other everyday explainers, must not rest content with good explanations; they must, as Ruben insists, ask what would be a *full* explanation. A full explanation leaves no more to be asked; it meets every logical (though not psychological) question. Its information content enables it to be audience-invariant. There may be scientific explanations or everyday explanations; there may be audience-variant or audience-invariant ones; there may be good explanations and adequate explanations; there may be partial explanations and complete ones. Important for the philosopher is the full explanation. All other types depend on that one; in principle, every incomplete explanation should be capable of being expanded into a full one.

Now a full explanation is rarely possible in practice. It is rather of the nature of Platonic ideas or at least of Kantian regulative ideals. The latter are 'concepts not realisable in particular instances but which have a role in setting standards for practical reason'.[4] 'Full explanations . . . may well be close to ideal things; if almost no one ever gives one, that tells us a lot about the practical circumstances of explanation-giving, but provides no argument whatsoever against such an account of full explanation' (Ruben, 1990, p. 202). In practice explanations are nearly always incomplete, some parts being omitted for one or more of three reasons – ignorance, lack of time or space, or the assumption that much is known to the enquirer already. As suggested above, a good explanation often requires a rough approximation to the truth, rather than a meticulously accurate, but lengthy, account. The latter may well confuse and weary the enquirer, so that a *full* explanation then becomes a *bad* explanation. Ignorance is a frequent obstacle; we can rarely be sure that we are in possession of all the relevant points (facts, generalizations and deductions) and that all these desiderata are correct. Nevertheless, full explanations *can* be given. Consider the following:

'Why has this fish-like creature four vestigial limbs?'
   'Because (a) it is a whale; (b) all whales are mammals; and (c) all mammals have four limbs.'

Provided that the fact (a) is correct, that the law-like statements (b) and (c) are true without exception, and that the deduction is valid, then we may claim to have given a full explanation. However, even this can be almost endlessly expanded in terms of genetics, embryology and evolution. In offering explanations we cannot often be certain of every constituent part. Nevertheless, it is important to have a clear idea of what a proper (i.e. full or complete) explanation would be like. In passing we note that the 'whale' example is a non-causal explanation. It answers 'Why?' by explaining 'What'. When we come to explanations in history we shall see that we often have to explain 'Who', 'What' and 'How' as well as 'Why', and sometimes even 'When' and 'Where'.

2.5   Causes and explanations are different kinds of things

Non-causal explanations remind us that cause and explanation are not merely different things, but different *kinds* of things. Strangely, this distinction is often overlooked. Strawson puts it neatly:

> But if causality is a relation which holds in the natural world, explanation is a different matter . . . it is not a natural relation . . . It is an intellectual or rational . . . relation. It does not hold between things in the natural world, things to which we can assign places and times in nature. It holds between facts or truths. (see Strawson in Vermazen and Hintikka, 1985, p. 115)

Causes happen, whether we understand them or not. The black rat brought plague to Europe in the fourteenth century, though no one at the time could offer what we believe to be the correct explanation. (It is an interesting exercise to see where the contemporary explanations failed to satisfy the criteria laid down in the previous paragraph. Did they or did they not establish a 'rational relation'?)

Another logical point arises from the 'whale' example in that both deduction and induction seem to be required. The deduction is fairly simple, but the cogency of the whole explanation rests on the validity of the two generalizations (b) and (c). Are these inductive? As a mode of reasoning induction is notoriously imperfect. Are these 'facts' empirical? Are they contingent truths? Or are they necessary truths, because they are part of our definitions of whales and mammals? In any case we can never be sure that our generalization has covered all possible whales and all possible mammals, past, present and future. Definitions, especially in the biological sciences, are often fuzzy at the edges. Yet in the empirical fields of the sciences and history we have to find satisfactory ways to classify and to account for phenomena. Avoiding sheer speculation, we try to make inferences based securely on the evidence. One way of doing this is by Inference to the Best Explanation – 'the core notion in epistemology' (see Harman, 1973, pp. 130–5; also Hanson, 1972, chapter 4). Surveying the evidence before us, we infer what, if true, would give the best explanation of that evidence. The method is, of course, very similar to the procedure of the detective in a crime novel. (What would best explain the corpse in the library, the locked door, the overturned decanter, the footprint in the flower-bed and so on?)

2.6   Inference to the Best Explanation

The method of Inference to the Best Explanation enables scientists and historians to use our practised skills in explaining things to arrive at the best account of how the world is. All empirical studies are inevitably incomplete; whether we are concerned with black holes or sub-atomic particles, with suicide rates or revolutions, we strive for the truth but can never attain unquestionable certainty. (How boring if we could!) The big question is – What is the best explanation? The one that best fits the evidence, of course. But there is more than one way of 'fitting'. One philosopher suggests that we distinguish a 'lovely' from a 'likely' explanation. The former covers a wide range; it accounts for a lot of things. The latter appeals to our sense of probability (see Lipton, 1991, p. 61). The clause in insurance policies that excludes 'acts of God' is lovely in the sense that almost any kind of inexplicable disaster can be attributed to the Deity. It covers many cases. Yet such an explanation does not seem likely at all; Christians and atheists are at one on that. Again, during the Cold War it was the policy of many governments to blame social unrest upon Communism. This was lovely, for it covered many occurrences. But it was not very likely in the case of ignorant and illiterate peasants who had never heard of Marx or Lenin. On the other hand it is likely that bad dreams are due to an indigestible meal eaten late, or that a chill is due to standing around in wet clothes. These likely explanations are 'unlovely', for they have narrow ranges of application. I cite such rather extreme cases for the sake of clarity. In practice, the two qualities are usually more nearly balanced and the choice becomes more difficult. Even when the advantage of one or the other seems clear, there can still ensue heated arguments: some people prefer lovely solutions, others the more likely. Some explanations can be audience-relative and of more psychological than rational value (as in dealing with young children), but other explanations are yoked in to the serious work of scientists and historians pursuing the truth about the world.

2.7   Explanation in the pursuit of wisdom

Finally it is worth considering that not all explanation occurs between the learned and the ignorant. Explanation is often valuable when two people (of equal epistemological weight, so to speak) explain themselves to each other. This may rectify misunderstandings of many kinds – from 'I did not intend to be personally offensive' to 'I was not putting forward a Marxist thesis when I suggested a link between unemployment and crime'. This mutual explanation enlarges our horizons (by fusing them, as Gadamer would say) and increases our wisdom. Similarly, explanation can be interpretation (as the dictionary reminds us), for it is often helpful to find different ways of expressing the same meaning. But the last word on explanation may be left to Robert Nozick in his aptly named *Philosophical Explanations*. Just as Lipton has shown the benefits of explanation for empirical studies, so Nozick argues that that is a very good way of doing philosophy – though not the only good way. Although 'the major philosophical theories of continuing interest are ... possible readings of the actual world', yet it is a better strategy to aim 'for the true explanation' (Nozick, 1981, p. 21). 'Moreover, my desire is to explain how knowledge is possible, how free will is possible, how there can be ethical truths, how life can have meaning. That is what I want to know' (p. 21).

3　Statistical Explanation

3.1　General laws and deductive-nomological arguments

Many people wish to stress the scientific nature of the social sciences. Since statistics has become a hand-maid of almost all sciences, we should first look at statistical explanation. Historians, too, have been making increasing use of statistics, so the following remarks concern them also. A scientific approach involves, among other things, an empirical approach to the data, and a claim that all observable phenomena, whether natural or social, are subject to general laws. Such laws have several characteristics: (1) that they are predictive; (2) that they are explanatory; (3) that they can themselves be derived from more fundamental laws, the whole arranged in a hierarchy of generality. (Thus the law that water turns to ice at 0°C. is itself a special instance of more fundamental laws of crystalline structures, and of the structure of the constituent atoms of oxygen and hydrogen). Given such general laws all that is needed on this account for the explanation of any particular event is a statement of initial conditions plus a statement of the relative general law (or laws). For example, asked to account for the ice on a step that caused a man to fall and break his leg, it will be sufficient to state the general law about the freezing of water and to point to the two facts that the step was wet and that the air temperature had fallen below 0°C (initial conditions). Arguments of this type are called deductive-nomological, or D-N, arguments.

3.2　Probability and inductive-statistical arguments

Such explanations are logically sound arguments of the deductive kind. Unfortunately not all explanations have such logical force, for the simple reason that many laws are not universal. We should accept a bullet in the brain as sufficient explanation of a man's death, but that a bullet in the brain is fatal is not a universal law: people sometimes survive such an injury.[5] In practice we tend to accept 'what generally happens' rather than 'what universally happens without exception' as a basis for explanation. We look rather for a convincing degree of probability. But explanations or predictions that rest on probability rather than certainty lack the logical force of D-N arguments. Statistics will often show that the event to be explained (the *explanandum*) has a very high inductive probability. There is a clear logical distinction between a deduction that *must* follow from the premises and an induction that is arrived at from a large number of instances, but not all possible instances. If we know that all the people in this room are married, then we can legitimately deduce that any one person must be either a husband or a wife. But if every dog I have ever met had four legs, that does not prove that all dogs have four legs, nor can I predict with certainty that the next dog will have four legs; three-legged dogs are not unknown. If empirical matters rarely yield universal truths, we have to rely on general truths of the form: 'Nearly all As are Bs' or 'All hitherto observed As are Bs,' but never 'All As are Bs without possible exception'. So we have to abandon certainty in favour of probability. In the previous example, the probability is that the next dog will have four legs, but it is not certain.

But how probable? That is the business of statistics to tell us, as far as may be done. That is why there is another argument to set beside the D-N one. It is called the inductive-statistical type (I-S). This offers an explanation that consists of a statement of initial conditions together with a statement of the statistical prob-ability of the occurrence. It will be noticed that here 'statistical probability' has been substituted for 'general law' in the D-N type. If the statistical probability is very high, then we are likely to accept an I-S type argument as sufficient explanation. For example, a victory is held to be explained if it can be shown that the battle was won by an army that outnumbered its opponents by twenty to one. A very large superiority of numbers is almost always decisive; but not quite always, as the campaigns of Pizarro in Peru or Clive in India demonstrated. What is known as the Hempel–Popper theory of explanation accepts that scientific explanations are of either the D-N type or of the I-S type (see Hempel, 1942, in Gardiner, 1959).

3.3   Objections to inductive-statistical arguments

There are some objections, however, to placing I-S arguments on a par with D-N arguments.[6] The first objection is that one philosopher, Rudolf Carnap (on whom Hempel explicitly relied for his concept of I-S explanation), firmly denied the possibility of inductive inference. For him the I-S argument is not an argument at all (see Salmon, 1971, pp. 8–9). We need not here go into Carnap's logical arguments, but rather note that there is also a serious practical objection to explanation of the I-S type. If the *explanandum* is held to be explained by a high degree of probability, just how high is high? If we toss a coin once there is an equal probability of its coming down either heads or tails. But if we toss it ten times the probability of all heads is quite small. (It is equivalent to odds of 1 to 1,023). In ten tosses there is a high probability that there will be a mixture of heads and tails in the result. We can, indeed, calculate the probability of all heads from evens (one toss) to very long odds indeed (ten tosses). The 'high statistical probability' of the I-S argument may be held satisfactorily to explain the outcome of a mixture of heads and tails. But suppose the improbable occurs and we get the perfectly possible result of ten heads. How does the I-S argument account for that? Clearly it does not. If the I-S argument works for a high degree of statistical probability, where, between one toss and ten tosses, do we say that it ceases to work because the probability is not high enough? Perhaps it may be objected that the line cannot be drawn at any point between one and ten, but that it is all a matter of chance. In that case, no explanation is forthcoming and the so-called I-S argument is seen to be no argument at all. It is not an acceptable substitute for strict D-N explanatory arguments after all.

The objection to Hempel's theory turns on the question; 'How high is high enough?' That theory fails to explain events of middling or low probability. Yet such things are known to occur. For example, a degree of radioactivity is a genuine causal explanation of a series of clicks on a Geiger counter. Yet the connection might appear extremely improbable in the light of other known sources of sound. We may say that rare events are inexplicable. And that for one of two reasons: *either* that they cannot yet be explained in our present state of knowledge, but that they really are determinate and will one day be explained when our knowledge is greater; *or* they are intrinsically inexplicable because they are strictly indeterminate – they just have no cause at all. Which of these two we accept must remain a matter of opinion or of faith. The fact remains that with the Hempel theory there is no valid explanation for anything that lacks a high degree of probability. Yet these are not normally the events that call for explanation: it is the three-legged dog, not the hound with four legs; it is the black not the white swan; it is the survivor of the bullet in the head; it is the victory of the weaker side that call for explanation. As Popper says: 'a statement with a high probability will be scientifically uninteresting, because it says little and has no explanatory power ... as scientists we do not seek highly probable theories but explanations; that is to say, powerful and improbable theories' (Popper, 1969, p. 58).

3.4　Other ways to use statistics

We may be tempted at this point to abandon statistics and to look elsewhere. But there are yet two possibilities for statistical explanation. One is to abandon any attempt at either predicting or explaining any particular event and instead to concentrate on the observed phenomena. With a fountain we cannot tell exactly where the next drop will fall (alternatively, where the last drop fell) and in a thunderstorm we cannot tell where lightning will strike next (or why it has just struck where it did). But in both cases we can bring a lot of understanding to the phenomenon, including its general causes and its limits. We can even make an estimate of the greater or lesser probability of a drop falling or lightning striking at any particular point. And this in spite of the fact that the processes are strictly stochastic. Chaos theory, with its 'strange attractors', offers a good example of the understanding of process rather than of the single event.

Another possibility is to look for statistical relevance rather than statistical explanation. If, for example, we notice that more drops fall from the fountain on the west side of the basin than on the east, we may surmise that a wind from the east has something to do with it. This does not, of course, provide either the exact explanation or prediction that we might like, but at least it increases the probability on one side of the basin and decreases it on the other. An examination of the circumstances of any phenomenon is likely to suggest present factors that are statistically relevant, though perhaps not statistically countable or measurable. We may define 'statistical relevance' thus: a certain factor is statistically relevant to the occurrence of an event if it makes a difference to the probability of that occurrence (see Salmon, 1971, p. 11). Although we may not be able to give any numerical value to this difference, it is possible to indicate the limits of relevance and to indicate the direction of influence. A valid explanation of the D-N type brings *all* the relevant factors in. We may give this the value of 1. (For example, given the laws of the movements of the Earth, the Sun and the Moon, and given their present relative positions, we can equally and correctly predict the next eclipse of the Moon and explain the last one. The relevance of the factors is unity.) An apparently similar argument runs thus: 'Birth control pills prevent conception. This man has been taking such pills for years. Hence he has never become pregnant.' For obvious reasons this argument has relevance value of zero. This is the limit at the other end of the scale. Most assemblies of relevant factors fall between one and zero.

3.5   Statistical relevance: the statistical-relevance model

The advantage of bringing statistical relevance into explanation is that our explanations are then not confined (as with the I-S model) to high degrees of probability. For statistical relevance (the S-R model) an explanation is 'an assembly of facts statistically relevant to the explanandum, regardless of the degree of probability that results' (Salmon, 1971, p. 11). The S-R model thus has the advantage over the I-S model that it can offer some explanation for events of middling and low probability, as with the example of the Geiger counter. Its disadvantage is that it cannot offer a watertight explanation of the D-N kind, or even one (I-S) like it.

3.6   Probability and practice

Statistics begins with very simple cases, like tossing of coins, where the possibilities are confined to two and where the process is perfectly stochastic uninfluenced by other factors. When we come to most practical situations, however, especially in the context of humans in society – the realm of history and the social sciences – then we are dealing with very complex situations indeed. It is rarely possible to separate with certainty the possibly relevant from the totally irrelevant. Although the mathematics of normal distribution, binomial and Poisson distributions and so on is not easy, yet most of the difficulties lie elsewhere. One problem is of giving numerical values to qualities. (How does one measure the degree of charity in a medieval monastery?) Decisions have to be made about what is quantifiable and what is not. Secondly, for purposes of comparison, measures have to be made in the same (or numerically related) units. (Goldsmith's village parson was 'passing rich with forty pounds a year'.) Above all, much statistical explanation depends on a correct analysis of what is to be measured against what.

We need to measure one thing against a set of other things in order to arrive at some estimate of the probability of its occurrence. What is the thinking behind this? Strictly the future is always unknown, but in practice we can, and need, to plan ahead. This is possible because we have some knowledge of the past which we can apply to our intentions for the future. When we have acquired a skill (typing, driving, speaking) we do it almost unthinkingly. But sometimes we have little or no clue to what will happen (as in playing cards or dice), yet it will be helpful to calculate probabilities. How do we calculate? Strictly (at least on one line of thought) it is impossible to assign probability to a single event; probability can only be assigned to relative frequency in an unending series. If I toss four coins, will they come down in the order heads, tails, tails, heads? It is impossible to answer either 'Yes' or 'No'. What one can say is: 'If you toss them a large number of times, the desired sequence will tend to occur one time in sixteen.' Is it or is it not legitimate to transfer this probability value of one in sixteen (or 1/16) from the series to the single instant? The assumption that it is legitimate is what lies behind the success of insurance firms, bookmakers, casinos, and so on. In strict logic, the probability value tells us nothing by way of predicting the next single event or explaining the last. Yet it is undeniably useful to be able to assign a probability value to a single event, whether as prediction in the planning of future actions, or as explanation of past events.

3.7   Reference classes

How then do we transfer a numerical value from occurrence in a series to the probability of a single instance or event? This may be done by assigning the single instance to a reference class, and transferring the probability from that class to the single event. In the above example, what we sought (the desired *attribute*) was the sequence HTTH. The *reference class* was an unending series of tosses. We transferred the frequency of occurrence in the reference class to the probability of the single event and thus gave that event a probability value of 1/16. It is important to notice here that the reference class should be *homogenous*; that is, every member should be a random member, for if any member has a characteristic that differentiates it from other members (in relevant respects) then the class is not homogenous. For example, it is important that every coin should have a head and a tail, and it is important that they should be fairly spun. It does not matter what is the monetary value of each coin, nor whether it is spun by a man or a woman.

In most cases, however, probability is not so easy to calculate. What, for example, is the probability that the next president of the United States will be black? We could take as the reference class all the inhabitants of the US. We know with what frequency the attribute (black) occurs in the total population. Let us call that frequency n per cent. Then n per cent (or $n/100$) would be the value that we seek: the probability of the next president being black is $n/100$. If, however, we took as our reference class all the presidents in the world (of whom a good many are black), then the required attribute would be more frequent and we should have a different and higher probability value. But supposing we took as our reference class all the presidents of the US. Of these none have been black. Then the probability value would come out as $0/100$ or zero. This seems almost certainly wrong when we recall that General Colin Powell was offered (and refused) the Republican nomination in 1996 – though of course he might still have stood and lost.

3.8 Choosing a reference class

How, then, do we select the correct reference class for the calculation of probability? In such selection there are two conflicting requirements. One requirement is that the reference class should be wide, as wide as possible, in order to give maximum statistical validity. The selection of a small reference class, in our examples the presidents of genuine democracies, would be statistically invalid. The other requirement is that the reference class should be narrow, as narrow as possible, in order to exclude irrelevant factors.

It is at this point that we see the importance of statistical relevance. If, for our question about a black US president, we took for reference the class of people at present in the US, we should get an unrealistically low probability, for it is a condition of the Constitution that the president must be a US citizen. All non-citizens of the US are statistically irrelevant and must be excluded from the reference class; hence the percentage of black residents can be assumed to be smaller than that of black citizens. Considerations of relevance can reduce the size of the reference class and so increase the probability value. (Remember that the higher the probability the more useful it is for both prediction and explanation.)

We can now see that the desired estimate of probability is the ratio of two numbers: the occurrence of the attribute and the members of the homogenous reference class. It may be expressed thus: attribute/reference class.

Since the higher the value the more useful it is, we may seek to increase the value either by enlarging the numerator (the top figure) or by reducing the denominator (the bottom one). In what ways, in our example, might we increase the probability value? If we were interested in the question of white supremacy in the US government we might also ask the probability of a president of Asian or Native American descent. What is the probability of the next president of the US not being white? Clearly it is greater than the probability of a black president. This is the result of widening the attribute (or numerator). On the other hand, if we are also calling male supremacy into question, we may ask the probability of a black woman as president. Here, of course, the probability is smaller because we have reduced the numerator by approximately half. (Again we note that, since there have been no female presidents, the reference class of US presidents would give us an unrealistic zero probability).

Another way of increasing the value is by reducing the reference class (the denominator). We may remember that the president must, by constitutional law, be thirty-five years old at least. Thus the next president must now be at least thirty-one. (The next presidential election is never more than four years away). If we then take as the reference class all US citizens over thirty-one, we have just about halved the denominator. Unfortunately, since about the same proportion of black citizens are over thirty-one we have effectively halved the numerator also. The probability has not changed.

Other factors might be considered, such as having two parents still alive, owning a car whose number plate ends in an even number, having a taste for jelly babies. None of these seems relevant to the probability of becoming president. Introduction of any such factor would indeed reduce the reference class and increase the probability value, but they must all be ruled out as irrelevant. They must not come into the statistical calculation.

3.9 Conclusion: 'covering laws' of little use to the historian

By now the theoretical form of statistical explanation and prediction (for it is the same form) should be clear. In practice the difficulties come not only in the counting (which in history is often a great problem) but also in choice of reference class. Equally important is the modification (reduction or enlargement) of either attribute or reference class by the consideration of factors of statistical relevance. The latter, as we have said, goes some way to account for events of middling or low probability – always a problem for Hempel's theory of explanation which relies on high probability. Popper himself (unlike Hempel in this) denied the explanatory usefulness of probability.[7] 'The probability of a statement (or set of statements) is always the greater the less the statement says ... Accordingly every interesting and powerful statement must have a low probability' (Popper, 1969, p. 58). As we have already pointed out, it is the rare and strange that calls for explanation, not the customary and the normal. Yet this is just what statistical probability fails to explain. Statistical relevance, however, can be a help, even though not in itself a solution. Unlike the scientist, the historian need not formulate theories of any kind. He may (and usually does) look for explanations that do not depend on theory – not even 'powerful and improbable theories'. Unsatisfactory as it may be, it is of more practical use to the historian than the Hempel theory – famous in the long dispute over 'covering laws' in the philosophy of history. Covering laws are of little use to the historian, because so often they cannot explain the abnormal or unexpected, which is just what calls for explanation.

After this general survey, we now turn to those kinds of explanation more nearly concerned with the philosophy of history. In doing so, however, we must not lose sight of the criteria for explanation, and the several types, methods and uses of explanation, that we have discussed in this chapter.

Notes

1 See *The Oxford Companion to Philosophy*, p. 126.
2 For further discussion of immediate and fundamental causes, see Gardiner (1952, pp. 66 ff); Stone (1972, chapter 3); Stanford (1994, pp. 194–203).
3 For further discussion, see Ruben (1990, pp. 209–32).
4 Emmet (1994, p. 2). Like the concepts of a frictionless plane or a perfect vacuum, they are guides, not attainments. Kant discusses them under the heading of 'The Regulative Employment of the Ideas of Pure Reason' in the *Critique of Pure Reason* (1963), B 671–96, pp. 532–49.
5 Of course, such observations may sometimes be guides to a more basic law.
6 See Popper's remarks about the captain of *HMS Pinafore* in Popper (1962, vol. 2, pp. 264–5).
7 Cf. Hempel's 'it seems possible and justifiable to construe certain explanations offered in history as based on the assumption of probability hypotheses rather than of general "deterministic" laws, i.e., laws in the form of universal conditions' (Hempel, 1942, in Gardiner, 1959, p. 350).

Suggested Reading

Cause

For the general notion of causation a good philosophy text, such as Hospers (1967), will state the main issues. Hume's argument against causality must not be neglected – see Hume (1975), section vii). Nor should J. S. Mill's arguments in A System of Logic (1973, Book III). For a good modern study, see J. L. Mackie (1974).

Historical causation is a special and difficult case. The argument is always vitiated by our necessary ignorance of counter-factuals: we can never say what would have happened next if a particular event had turned out otherwise. However, some clear discussion is to be found in Atkinson (1978) and in Dray (1964) and (1980). The legal slant on the question can be found in Hart and Honoré in Dray (ed.) (1966), which also contains useful pieces by Oakeshott (taken from Oakeshott (1933)) and by Scriven (1966). G. R. Elton (1970) contains a lively attack on non-historians' attempts to understand historians' use of causation, which is worth reading. Collingwood's attempt to differentiate types of causation (in Collingwood 1940, part III C), has much to be said for it. One historian's attempt to grapple seriously with the concept of causation (Stone, 1972, chapter 3) was not wholly successful. The article on causes of the American Civil War that begins 'A specter haunts American historians – the concept of causality' demands to be read. It is by Cushing Strout (1960) in Nadel (1965). Two other articles in the same collection, by Benson (1960) and by Eckstein (1965), also deal with causation in history.

Explanation

Again, the general approach to explanation is a commonplace of philosophy textbooks. Here we need only mention Hospers (1967). One may also cite the Introduction to Nozick (1981), McCullagh (1984), chapter 2), Ruben (1990) and (1993), Lipton (1991), and Achinstein (1983). One book, however, should not be overlooked: *von Wright (1971)* makes very clear the two philosophical traditions of explanation.

4

Explanations in the Social Sciences and in History

1 Explanation in the Social Sciences

1.1 A science of society?

The idea of social science arose in the eighteenth century as part of the Enlightenment. Seventeenth-century scientists (Kepler, Galileo, Harvey, Boyle, Huyghens and, above all, Newton) had been amazingly successful in demonstrating the laws (as they saw it) that nature obeyed. Put over-simply, the following century wanted to find laws of man in society to parallel those of nature. As Hume put it: 'It is at least worth while to try if the science of *man* will not admit of the same accuracy which several parts of natural philosophy are found susceptible of.' (By 'natural philosophy' he meant what we call 'natural science'.) (Quoted in Hampson, 1968, p. 98.) Established and more or less unquestioned forms of society and social ideas were upset by the almost simultaneous French and Industrial Revolutions. Some deeper understanding of what was going on seemed imperative. And that understanding, most practitioners agreed, should be empirical, methodical and objective. Perhaps the clearest statement was to be found in the Positivist philosophy of Auguste Comte (1798–1857). The first principle of his philosophy was 'that it regards all phenomena as subjected to invariable natural *Laws*' (Comte in Gardiner, 1959, p. 76). Another assumption was that a Positivist social science was needed to supplement the existing natural sciences:

> Now that the human mind has grasped celestial and terrestrial physics – mechanical and chemical; organic physics, both vegetable and animal, – there remains one science, to fill up the series of sciences of observation, – Social physics. This is what men have now most need of: and this it is the principal aim of the present work to establish. (p. 77)

One may speculate how this intellectual assurance would be deflated by the tremendous advances in the physical and biological sciences since then (the

1830s). Far from being already grasped, they had hardly begun. However, the problems of explaining the mysteries of nature or of society were equally simple to Comte: 'What is now understood when we speak of an explanation of facts is simply the establishment of a connection between single phenomena and some general facts, the number of which continually diminishes with the progress of science' (p. 75).

1.2   The main points of positivism

It is worth pausing to consider what is taken for granted here, for Comte's description of a social science is still adhered to by some thinkers. First, it is assumed that a single social phenomenon is a concrete, indisputably objective entity – like a gold nugget or a beetle. Comte does not see that such phenomena – a handshake, a debt, a revolt – may be susceptible of different interpretations. Thus the objectivity of his 'facts' may be called into question – not the physical object or event, of course, but its description. Social phenomena can have more than one meaning and hence many descriptions. Second, he identifies 'general facts' (presumably what we would call generalizations) with laws. But a fact is not the same kind of thing as the laws that scientists formulate and test. The term 'fact' implies an indisputable truth, while scientific 'laws' in practice are law-like statements – that is, continually improved theories that approximate (ever more closely, we hope) to the truth.[1] Moreover, Comte's notion of a general fact is weakened by the shortcomings of induction. 'Socrates is mortal' is an indisputable truth that most people would accept as a fact. 'All men are mortal' is a generalization or 'general fact' that cannot be substantiated because it involves untold future generations. Third, he assumes that these generalizations (or 'general facts') are capable of reduction without remainder to other generalizations of greater range. Such reductions are often useful in the natural sciences (where the behaviour of water can be explained in terms of its constituent atoms, for example – atoms that form parts of other substances also). Whether reductions are useful or even possible in any one social science is questionable. Fourth, he assumes that explanation is achieved by showing that a phenomenon is one of a number of similar phenomena collected in a generalization. 'Why did he kill himself?' 'This phenomenon occurred because statistics show that a fairly constant proportion of the population commit suicide every year'. (Kant had seen this statistical fact as a natural law in 1784; Durkheim was to see it as social law in 1897.) Such an answer is hardly insightful; nor is it satisfactory in law or of comfort to the bereaved. Are not other modes of explanation required, both in science and in law? Fifth (and this is the weightiest objection), Comte assumes that social scientists are as detached from their subject matter as natural scientists are. Natural scientists are not themselves chemicals or insects. But society itself is made up of men and women, including social scientists and their students and readers. Is it possible for society to stand outside itself and look at itself, any more than the eye can see itself? The latter is done only indirectly: we look at each other's eyes or our own in a mirror. That is why the social sciences are sometimes said to be 'reflexive' activities. Pursuing this analogy, we could say that the equivalent of looking at each other's eyes is the comparative method in the social sciences, while the 'mirror' in which we see ourselves is social theory. Neither the method nor the theory is without big problems.

1.3   The debate opened by Comte

The foregoing five points indicate where modern understandings of the social sciences find more room for uncertainty and debate than did a didactic positivist like Comte. Nevertheless, it must be remembered that positivism (only slightly modified from Comte's outline) has survived for at least a century and a half. His views are certainly not unrecognizable and some find them still acceptable.

My parody of a law-like explanation of suicide was, like all parodies, slightly unfair. The enquirer clearly was asking for a cause. It is unfair to Comte to imply that he was not aware of the importance of causation as a means of explanation. It comes in with his division of Social Physics into Social Statics and Social Dynamics. The former viewed society as a steady state (much as structuralists and functionalists in the twentieth century were to do), while the latter looked to societies in movement – the concern now of theorists of social change. As he said:

> The true general spirit of social dynamics then consists in conceiving of each of these consecutive social states as the necessary result of the preceding, and the indispensable mover of the following...In this view, the object of science is to discover the laws which govern this continuity, and the aggregate of which determines the course of human development. (Comte in Gardiner, 1959, p. 79)

How Comte saw the 'course of human development' was illustrated in an essay he wrote a few years earlier on reorganizing society. He opposed the tendency of historians to praise great men for their achievements, and rather attributed improvements to the 'preponderating influence of Civilization'.

> Generally speaking, when the individual appears to exert a great influence, it is not due to his own forces, since these are extremely small. Forces external to him act in his favour, according to laws over which he has no control.

Therefore, he sees no point in discussing the merits or demerits of his proposed 'New System' for social progress. It must follow natural trends. 'The principal, indeed the only question, should be: What is that Social System indicated by observation of the Past, which the progress of Civilization must establish' (p. 81). It is clear that Comte's answer to the question of why things happen as they do, is to attribute them to the impersonal and advancing forces of civilization, helped or hindered only to a minute extent by the efforts of humanity. This seems a rather inadequate account of historical causation. Nevertheless we should be grateful to Comte for introducing many of the issues of social science so clearly. It is important to have fixed points for the beginnings of our debates.

1.4 Laws of society?

So what are we to say about explanation in the social sciences?

The first thing we have to say is that there is more than one way of seeing the social sciences. Are they, or are they not, like the natural sciences? This is the big question. The second, smaller but inevitable question (common to all explanations) is: What sort of explanation do you want? Not what exactly do you want explained (though we always have to be clear about this), but which of several kinds of explanation would you regard as satisfactory? At least, this is the polite question. There are those coarser souls who assert that theirs is the only correct explanation and you can take it or leave it.

To return to the social sciences: the simplest approach to the problem is to ask whether we emphasize the first or the second word in that phrase. If we concentrate on 'social' we are led to consider how we men and women behave with each other – moved by hopes, desires, fears, hatreds, affections, calculations and emotional reactions. We understand these things 'from the inside', as it were; that is, from experience rather than observation. If, on the other hand, we concentrate on 'science' we are led to considerations of observations of phenomena, of data, of method and of theory construction or, alternatively, of the discovery of natural laws. An emphasis on the first word, then, suggests that the social sciences are not at all the same as the natural sciences; emphasis on the second suggests that they are. Each approach has its vigorous defenders, just as they both have numerous ramifications.

As we have already observed, when the social sciences first came on the scene in the eighteenth and early nineteenth centuries the stress was on science. Natural scientists still believed, like their seventeenth-century predecessors, that the laws of nature existed independently of mankind (like rocks hidden deep in the Earth) and only awaited discovery. As Alexander Pope put it: 'Nature and Nature's laws lay hid in night: / God said, Let Newton be! and all was light.'

In the 1840s the German physicist Helmholtz could write: 'To understand a phenomenon means nothing else than to reduce it to the Newtonian laws. Then the necessity for explanation has been satisfied in a palpable way.' (quoted in Hanson, 1965, p. 91). One can see how well this chimes with Comte's views on science, both natural and social. This belief in laws of nature that are hidden but can be discovered is equally to be found in the nearly contemporary writings of Marx. For him, too, in order to understand what is going on around us we have to grasp the causative laws of society – Comte's 'Social Dynamics'. As we have noted

Marx attributed social antagonisms to 'the natural laws of capitalist production' (see above, chapter 1, 2.2). In the late twentieth century, however, natural scientists are less certain that they have discovered such laws; they compare and criticize theories. As we have seen, there is a distinction between objective laws of nature waiting to be discovered and our corrigible theories (law-like statements) which approximate to them. The whole of Popper's well-known theory of falsification assumes a gradualist approach towards the truth rather than an instant grasping of it. The remarks of a modern physicist are revealing:

> Physical theories provide patterns within which data appear intelligible . . . A theory is not pieced together from observed phenomena; it is rather what makes it possible to observe phenomena as being of a certain sort, and as related to other phenomena . . . From the observed properties of phenomena the physicist reasons his way towards a keystone idea from which the properties are explicable as a matter of course. The physicist seeks . . . a set of possible explanations. (Hanson, 1965, p. 90)

This is similar to the practice of 'inference to the best explanation' described above. Unlike Comte's rather facile positivism, contemporary science is prepared to criticize even established tenets. What were long taken to be laws of nature are now sometimes revealed as corrigible theories.[2] The progress of science, notoriously, is made over the corpses of dead theories. Nevertheless, it is possible for a Realist to have faith in the hidden, incorrigible laws of nature, even if we cannot be sure that we have found any. As we remarked, the problem lies in the being certain in any particular case.

1.5   Structures

As the natural sciences have become more critical of theories, so the social sciences have largely abandoned the belief (so strongly held by people like Comte and Marx) in the 'iron laws' of society. But wide differences remain within the social sciences. The concept of law has been partly replaced by that of structure. Now what is meant by 'structure'?

The term is too widely and loosely used to be capable of exact definition. Roughly, it is the relationship between parts and wholes. Yet not any relationship, but that relationship which determines the character of the whole. To take a simple example, it is not just that the three sides are parts of a triangle; it is that the relationships among the three (that they meet at their ends, that no one is longer than the sum of the other two and so on) determine that there is a triangle – that is, a three-sided plane figure that encloses a space, that contains three angles, that each is less than 180°, that the sum of the angles equals two right angles and so on) The relationships among the parts determine the nature of the whole.[3] Sometimes the term is used to refer to the relationship; sometimes it is used to refer to the whole. Thus the ties of blood and marriage within a society are called a kinship structure.

Two further points are to be remembered. One is that a pattern is often mistaken for a structure. But a pattern is merely a shape or arrangement; it need not determine the nature of the whole. If it does, it is more than a pattern, it is a structure. People sometimes loosely refer to an arrangement of parts as a structure when they should speak of a pattern. The second point is that in society structures emerge by repetition. If one man leaves all his property to his eldest son that is a matter of little remark. When most men in a given society do this, generation after generation, then we give the practice a name ('primogeniture') and it becomes a structure of family relationships and part of the structure (social and economic) of that society. The anomaly is that a recurring pattern of relationships in a society *becomes* a social structure. (Just how much repetition is needed to transform a pattern into a structure is a question rarely asked. But when that repetition is seen as sufficiently important to give a discernible character to the family or the society, then it can be called a structure.)

There is also a distinction to be made between concrete and analytical structures. The former include organizations – farms, schools, trade unions, trading or manufacturing companies. The latter are largely unseen – like kinship structures or the flows of capital. What makes the notion of structures difficult to grasp is that they are, in a way, self-shaping: repetitions of behaviour constitute a social structure, and (as every sociologist knows) structures influence, even sometimes determine, behaviour. Is there a 'chicken-and-egg' problem? For this reason it is occasionally suggested that 'structure' is not a concept at all, but a metaphor.

1.6 Are structures like laws?

The modern widespread use of the term probably stems from the great French sociologist, Emile Durkheim (1858–1917) with his insistence that 'The first and most fundamental rule is: *Consider social facts as things*' – the opening words of his *The Rules of Sociological Method* (1895) (Durkheim, 1964, p. 14). 'The unique data of the sociologist', he maintains, are 'all that is given, all that is subject to observation . . . To treat phenomena as things is to treat them as data' (p. 27). Therefore, the sociologist need have no truck with ideas. What people think about value is unimportant; the sociologist need look only at values in economic exchanges; not moral ideals but rules of conduct; not dreams of love, but facts of marriage and divorce. This approach is not intended to denigrate ideas; it is simply to say that they are not the business of the social scientist.

One can now see how the notion of structure in the social sciences is analogous to that of law in the natural sciences. Both designate 'that which regularly occurs'. Just as there seems to be a law that bodies attract one another in inverse proportion to the square of the distance between them, so there might appear to be a law that a given percentage of the population commit suicide every year or that a rise in the bank rate reduces inflation. But it would be dangerous to assume that structures are the same sort of thing as natural laws. One difference is that we generally demand a higher level of consistency for laws. We do not posit a natural law unless things always behave in the same way; for the sort of recurrent behaviour that makes a structure we are usually content that most people behave like that. Thus structures, unlike laws, are not predictive of individual behaviour. A more important distinction is that most (so-called) laws of nature are reducible to wider laws of greater range. Thus it is a law that water always freezes at a certain temperature. But this law can be explained by showing it to depend on the underlying molecular and atomic make-up of water. (However, there is a limit to these reductions; the law of gravitation quoted above seems to be one of the ultimates of the universe – at least, until physicists discover the 'grand, unifying theory' that many of them hope for) (see Hawking, 1990, pp. 155–75). It is a question how far social generalizations can be reduced to wider, more fundamental ones. Thus both laws and structures are based on patterns of recurrence, but they are not to be confused.

1.7   What kind of explanation?

So what about explanation? Is the 'covering-law' type adequate? 'Why did this butterfly come out of a chrysalis?' 'Because all butterflies do.' This is not really good enough in the natural sciences; it needs to be under-pinned by a more fundamental reason. The social sciences ask no less. Thus 'Why was this parlia-mentary candidate successful in that constituency?' 'Because she was of the left and she stood in an inner-city area, and left-wing candidates are usually returned in such areas.' Now at first this looks like a simple 'covering-law' type of explanation – 'All (or most) As are Bs. This is an A. Therefore this is (or is very likely to be) a B.' But does the explanation rest solely on the observed recurrence of left-wing electoral successes in inner-city areas? Does it not appeal to our wider knowledge: namely, that left-wing politicians tend to promote policies to help the poor, that inner-city areas tend to be inhabited by poorer people, and that electors tend to vote for those likely to help them? Here we have an explanation based entirely on observed social facts, just as an entomologist might be explaining one beetle's movements by generalizations about observed beetle behaviour, and this, in turn, supported by a wider generalization. This is the scientific approach that Durkheim desired.

The question now arises as to whether we should go beyond Durkheim. After all, the logic of the argument is not rigorous; there are too many 'tends to', too many uncertainties. Can our understanding penetrate more deeply? Of course it can. We can 'get inside' these people's minds as we cannot 'get inside' the brains of beetles. We know, or can guess at, the motives of both the politicians and the electors – though we may not all make the same guesses. Now as soon as we mention minds and motives we are in a different ball-game altogether from

Durkheim's. He held that we should concentrate on the external observable phenomena of society, not upon ideas. For these are 'not immediately given. They cannot be perceived or known directly, but only through the phenomenal reality expressing them' (Durkheim, 1964, p. 27). He is right: we can see what the politicians and electors do; we can only guess at their motives. But as social scientists should we, or should we not, ignore the unseen parts of human behaviour? Should we treat our fellows (and ourselves) as phenomena of nature, to be studied in the same way? Or do we make use of the special insights that we (being humans as well as scientists) have into the subject matter of the social sciences – which is, of course, the behaviour of men and women in society and also the behaviour of those societies themselves? The question is fundamental. Our choice of explanation (as well as many other things of importance) turns on how we answer it.

1.8 Causal explanation

Let us return to Durkheim. His principle was in effect 'Treat social facts as things, and don't get tangled up in ideas for they are too indeterminate'. Human behaviour is thus observed behaviour; as with chemicals and insects the scientist restricts himself to what he can see. His explanations are of the same kind, whether they refer to observations of beetles, men and women, or acids. His explanations are causal: 'E happened because C caused it to happen.' To the question 'What do you mean by "caused"?', he will reply, 'I mean that if C had not happened, then E would not have happened.' If pressed further, 'How do you know what would or would not occur without C?', he will reply, 'Because I have tested the situation both with and without C. Whenever C is present, then so is E; whenever C is absent, then E does not occur. Thus I can say with confidence that C is the cause of E, or at least one cause, of E'. We may press him further, and ask him to justify the term 'whenever'; for surely he has made only a limited number of observations. How can he be sure that what he has observed in some cases must apply in all cases? (This is the notorious problem of induction.) He will then have to acknowledge the logical point and agree that he has not established complete certainty, but will fall back on one or both of two positions. The first is to appeal to statistics. He can claim that he has made enough observations for the chances of error to be calculated as so small as to be, in practice, negligible. The other way is to use the principle of reduction and demonstrate that his particular generalization is supported by a more fundamental law of wider application. If, for example, he is studying the breeding habits of chaffinches and finds that all the females lay eggs, he need not fall back on statistics to justify his belief in the behaviour of future generations of chaffinches. He can simply point to the fact that all (female) birds lay eggs and chaffinches are undoubtedly birds. Causal explanation in the natural sciences thus rests upon well established generalizations – generalizations that are sometimes so strong that they are called laws.[4] This is how the social scientist, too, will explain social phenomena if he follows Durkheim's recommendations. And indeed many do just this.

1.9   Insightful explanation

Now let us disobey Durkheim and see what happens. Taking ideas into account will bring us to quite a different kind of causal explanation. 'Why did you do C?' 'Because I wanted to bring about E' – 'Why did you give her flowers?' 'Because I wanted to please her'. In this case. also, C can be called the cause of E: her pleasure – or rather my expectation of her pleasure (E) – is why the gift (C) occurred. An interesting point of logic is that her pleasure is an explanation. Or should we say that the explanation is the *idea* of her pleasure? Anyway, we we did not arrive at that explanation by observing a number of similar cases and then inferring a generalization from them. Our method was much simpler: we asked him why he did it. 'Ah!' interjects the Durkheimian scientist, 'But your causal explanation rests on two ideas: his desire to please her and his expectation that flowers would do so. Ideas are not social facts; they cannot be observed. Their nature is difficult to determine; it is easy to be wrong about them. True scientists prefer not to make unsupported guesses, but to rest their conclusions upon objective, readily observable facts'. To this we may protest that, being human ourselves, we have an insight into the behaviour of other humans – an insight that is lacking in the case of natural objects. Why adopt the lengthy and roundabout methods of the natural scientist (which, after all, can never guarantee more than very high probability), when we can go straight to the point? Human insight is a key that can unlock many doors; it seems perverse to ignore it.

That, in essence, is the great divide in the social sciences. There are modifications and ramifications of both positions, but the basic question remains: Are the social sciences essentially different from, or essentially the same as, the natural sciences? Is there just science (scientific knowledge, scientific method, scientific explanation), or do all these terms have different meanings according to whether humanity is, or is not, the subject of study? The debate continues.

1.10   The behaviour of societies

The social sciences, however, are not restricted to the explanation of a single occurrence, like the gift of flowers. They are concerned with individuals in relation with others, with the varieties of those interpersonal relations, and with the groupings and organizations that are made up of human beings in those various relations – societies and society. Robinson Crusoe alone on his island can hardly be a subject for social study, but as soon as he is joined by Man Friday the sciences of politics, economics, sociology, anthropology and linguistics get a toe-hold. Questions of communication, of customs and beliefs, of deference and control, of the distribution of goods and of power all now appear on that little island. The various ways in which these and similar questions are answered about human relations constitute the structures of any society. But let us notice that while the human behaviour that exhibits these relations is observable, the relations themselves are not: they are mental constructs. Hence social structures of these kinds (called 'analytic') belong to the realm of ideas, not of material observable facts. Other social structures – tribes, nations, clubs, businesses, governments, and so on – are called 'concrete', though they are only partly material; they are also ideal. It is not possible to see or touch General Motors or the University of Cambridge or the state of Pennsylvania or the Royal and Ancient golf club of St Andrews, but only their members and certain material objects pertaining to them. These are strictly ontological questions (concerned with the modes of being), but they are not entirely irrelevant to questions of explanation.

1.11 Structures in explanation

Once upon a time, we may suppose, one or two people found themselves by the sea – perhaps by accident or in the pursuit of food. Having a little time on their hands they sat and contemplated it, bathed in it and then lay in the sun. Feeling refreshed they went back and told their friends. More came down to the sea to savour these pleasures. In a short time, paths and roads were made, followed by railways and airlines; towns grew up to meet the needs of the visitors. Before long a billion-dollar tourist industry had developed. This industry is a social structure. It includes both 'concrete' structures – shops, offices, hotels, sports clubs, airports and so on – and 'analytic' structures: of investment, local government, conformity of dress, honeymooning and other celebratory rituals, beliefs in the restorative qualities of sea and salt water, aesthetic preferences for a tanned skin, and so on. All these structures depend upon repeated patterns of behaviour – behaviour that is connected in one way or another with going on holiday.

Now going on holiday is a voluntary activity. The phenomenon, we may say, is brought about in every instance by the intention of gaining pleasure or health. Since each individual has a reason for going on holiday, a causal explanation in these cases consists of giving the reason. If we turn from one holiday- maker to the millions that make up the industry we find large numbers of people doing much the same things. These repeated patterns of behaviour constitute the structures of tourism outlined above. And let us notice that many of the structures – airlines, banks, hotels, restaurants – facilitate holiday-making, but they also channel it. By making some things easy, they make other things harder, and so people are induced to follow the easy paths. The concrete structures help to fashion the unseen analytic structures of behaviour – advertising is a good example of the concrete shaping the abstract. To return to the question of explanation: if we are asked to explain any phenomenon of the holiday industry, do we answer in terms of the hopes, wishes, calculations of the individual, or in terms of the structures of holiday-making? Do you want an explanation 'from the bottom up', so to speak, or 'from the top down'? Partly this depends on whether the question is individual or statistical: 'Why did Smith go to Spain?' or 'Why do so many Britons go to Spain?' But only partly; either question could be answered from the top down or from the bottom up, though it is clear that the first suggests an individual answer, the second a structural one. Probably the best explanation would combine both types.

1.12   Grand theories

It is possible to go further. After all, the banks, hotels, shops at the seaside are only parts of a larger economic structure that spreads over the whole nation and extends to other nations as well. The analytic structures are also parts of wider structures of custom, belief, preference, dress, etc. They all go to make up civilized society. And when society is viewed as a whole, one realizes that the complex is too vast and intricate to be taken in by any one mind. Yet it holds together, it preserves much the same shape, it proceeds fairly predictably; in short, the whole thing works – at least, most of the time. Why is this? Are there hidden laws of society that make it work: Economists have long believed that there are for economics. But more ambitious than the economists have been those thinkers who formulated 'grand theories' of society – theories that purport to explain how the whole thing hangs together. We have already seen that Comte believed in 'invariable natural laws' and in 'the preponderating influence of Civilization'. We have seen Marx in *Capital* speaking of the 'natural laws of capitalist production' working themselves out with iron necessity (see above, chapter 1, 2). Other comprehensive theories were put forward by Herbert Spencer, Max Weber and Talcott Parsons. After falling into disrepute for a generation or two, attempts to comprehend all social phenomena in one theory have been recently revived, as Quentin Skinner notes in his introduction to *The Return of Grand Theory in the Human Sciences*.[5]

1.13   Functionalism, for example

We need not here go into the various grand theories. It is sufficient to note that they are not apparent to the eye. One may observe human behaviour and assemble those observations into a generalization – 'Brides wear white and carry flowers', for example. But the sort of laws that the grand theorists postulate are more like the laws of nature – that is, deducible from the facts, but not themselves observable. Newton's three laws of motion were necessary to his whole theory but not themselves evident. We are accustomed to hidden laws in physics and chemistry (gravitation, valency); why not in the social sciences? Once they have been discovered, they can be used for purposes of explanation. For example, theories of functionalism liken a society to an organism. In this every individual and lesser group has a part to play in maintaining the functioning whole. A functional explanation accounts for a phenomenon in terms of its consequences; that is, in the contribution it makes to the stability of society as a whole. However, such an explanation rests on several questionable assumptions. One is that society has an existence over and above the individuals in it; this assumes an analogy with the human body, where one may explain the function of the pancreas not in terms of the needs of the liver or the heart, but in terms of the whole. But is it certain that societies have needs as human beings do? And if they do, what guarantees that they will be satisfied? Another assumption is that social phenomena all somehow contribute to the requirements of the whole. How, then, do societies ever break down? We have fairly clear ideas about what sorts of injuries and diseases are fatal or non-fatal to a particular type of organism. Have functionalists worked out a pathology of societies? How are anti-social phenomena to be accounted for or evaluated? A third assumption is that we are all clear about what is a society. But they vary widely in size, in composition, in density and in boundaries. What differentiates a society from a non-society? What line separates a society from its environment, human or natural? These are some of the criticisms to be made of functionalism as a basis for explanation.

1.14 Distinctions of theory

Thus we need not trace out each over-arching theory that social scientists use for explanation. It is sufficient to note the main distinctions, one of which is that between those theories that treat human beings as primary or fundamental and societies as secondary, and those that allot primacy to societies (like functionalism) and explain individual human behaviour in terms of social wholes. The distinction is between collectivism or holism on the one hand and individualism on the other. Comte put the first case by stating that a society is 'no more decomposable into individuals than a geometric surface is into lines'; while Mill put the opposite case: 'the Laws of the phenomena of society are, and can be, nothing but the actions and passions of human beings' (both quoted by Lukes in Ryan, 1973, p. 119). A second distinction has already been referred to: it is that between using the methods of natural science for the study of human behaviour and using our insight (often called by the German term *Verstehen*) for our privileged knowledge of human beings. Thus the functionalist posits hidden laws (which he believes deducible from the phenomena) to account for regularities in human behaviour. The altern- ative theory often put forward by individualists is to point out that humans know what rules are and how to follow them.[6] Rule-following, therefore, can account for a good deal of the observed regularities in society without the need to postulate impersonal forces. Whether to follow a rule or not is my decision; it is intentional action, not compulsion by a hidden force. Thus a stream of traffic may look like water flowing under the impulse of natural forces (mostly gravity), but in fact the 'stream' is composed of many purposeful and rational actions by numerous drivers. Theories that rest on human decisions of this kind are called 'action' theories. These are generally opposed to functional and structural theories which (following Durkheim) attribute reality to societies and their constituent structures. When the emphasis is on both structures and functions we have a more powerful theory – 'structural-functionalism'. Talcott Parsons gave such an account of society as a system of systems (based on structures *and* functions) in *The Social System* (1951) and *The System of Modern Societies* (1971). His was a splendid example of 'grand theory', as Wright Mills pointed out (see Mills 1970, pp. 33–59).

A third distinction to be observed among social theories rests on the fact of change. This (both as fact and as concept) is familiar and indeed fundamental to historians. But social scientists do not always regard it. As we have seen, functional theories find it hard to account for change.[7] Hard, though not impossible. Theorists of society can postulate timeless structural constants that are built into the system and so bring about predictable changes according to the pattern. This is true equally of the theories of Talcott Parsons and of Karl Marx. Action theorists find it easier to explain change. They need merely to point to change as the result of deliberate decisions. It is, of course, true that changes rarely turn out quite as intended. Sometimes change can result (as in a bank crash) from men's attempts to maintain the *status quo*. Nevertheless the cause of the bank crash was human actions (though mutually frustrating ones), not hidden, impersonal forces.

1.15   Accounting for change

Accounting for change may be done either on the small scale – say in families or clubs or villages over a few years, or on the large scale – dealing with the rise and fall of civilizations (Spengler and Toynbee), or even of the development of the entire human race – Hegel, for example. The essential difference between a social theory of change at any level and a history of changes is that one claims the ability to predict; the other does not. A historian tells what happened in the past and tries to account for it; a social theorist tries to explain all changes – past, present and future. He knows not merely what *does* happen but what *must* happen. Any scientific theory that validates causation must also justify prediction (see Popper, 1962, vol. 2, pp. 262–3). But are there any successful candidates for the role of social prophet? Do social theorists nowadays claim to predict? If not, are their causal accounts valid?[8]

Many people have been tempted by the obvious analogy of growth. We talk of young nations, mature nations, developed and developing nations – of the birth, the growth, the maturity, the decline, and even the death of societies – kingdoms, states, empires. Does this metaphor have any basis in reality? Are social collectives organic beings? Many people have thought so in the past, but few, I believe, do so today (see Nisbet, 1969, pp. 3–11). Even less in favour is the belief in the cycles of history, though it had strong adherents in the past (see Trompf 1979). One social scientist who believed that regular patterns of change are and will be followed by all societies was W. W. Rostow, who published *The Stages of Economic Growth: a Non-Communist Manifesto* in 1960. His theories are largely discredited today. Much more common are social scientists who bring social science theories to an understanding of the past. Among these may be mentioned Barrington Moore, Theda Skocpol, Reinhard Bendix, Seymour Martin Lipset, Charles Tilly, S. N. Eisenstadt, and Immanuel Wallerstein (see Skocpol, 1984, pp. 20–1; P. Burke 1992, p. 18). Such theories are of explanatory value in relation to the past, but unless they also claim to predict the future they hardly differ from the explanations offered by many (though not all) historians. We may leave these to be discussed in the next section. There is a logical difference between theories of all known societies and theories of all societies, known or unknown. The latter is vulnerable to disproof by any fresh instance – the problem of induction. The former is not so vulnerable. Most social scientists, like most historians, prefer to confine themselves to explaining what is already known and forbear to speculate about what is as yet unknown. But of course such theories are comparatively weak; if they do not claim the ability to predict can they be truly scientific?[9]

This discussion has brought us to explanations of the past. Here the activities of some social scientists overlap with those of historians.[10] There is no need for overt hostility or prickly defensiveness in a common area of interest. E. H. Carr was surely right that 'the more sociological history becomes, and the more historical sociology becomes, the better for both. Let the frontier between them', he continues, 'be kept wide open for two-way traffic' (Carr, 1964, p. 66). To this it is only necessary to add that this desirable *rapprochement* depends on a full understanding of each by the other. So let us proceed to explanation in history.

2   Explanation in History

2.1   History a science?

Is history one of the social sciences (as many institutions assume) or is it not? Partly this is no more than a matter of definition. If by 'history' we mean only an organized study of the past, then it may well, though not necessarily, be a science (if it uses regular assumptions and procedures). On the other hand, most historians deny that they are scientists or that they follow scientific procedures or make scientific assumptions. And surely they are correct in this. The great figures of nineteenth-century historiography who made history a discipline of repute – Ranke, Michelet, Macaulay, de Tocqueville, Prescott – were not, and did not claim to be scientists. Those who did try to write history as a science – Taine, Buckle, and (in some ways) Bury – by general consent belong to the second or third rank, conspicuously less successful as historians. But is there a third possibility? Can it be that there is such a thing as a 'science of history' comparable to, but distinct from, the natural and social sciences? Do we find here, as in the natural sciences, an organized and coherent structure of knowledge, with methods and assumptions common to workers all over the world? At the moment, the answer must be 'No'. Opinion in the profession is divided as to whether history is, and should be, on the way to becoming such a science (as Braudel and most of the Annales school believe), or not (as most English-speaking historians believe).

2.2   Criteria of explanation

It is obvious that our views on explanation in history depend to some extent upon our views of the discipline, upon our answers to the questions, 'Is history in any sense a science?' and 'If so, in what sense?' Many people, however, think it fruitless to ask such questions, insisting that we should concentrate simply on what historians actually do. Yet 'what historians do' is not always beyond criticism. Are we to accept that 'anything goes' by way of historical explanation? Should we not recall the criteria already discussed? One thing we noted was that explanation is not peculiar to any kind of science; it is an epistemological matter, belonging to the theory of knowledge in general (see chapter 3, 2, above). More important is Ruben's insistence that explanations should be grounded in truth and reality; they need 'a solid metaphysical basis' (see chapter 3, 2.3, above). We also note Putnam's point that explanation is interest-relative. Since any explanation should address the interest of the enquirer (for why else should any one enquire?), explanations are also pragmatic in part. It is important also to remember Strawson's point that, although causation is very frequently used in explanation, yet the two are very different kinds of things, belonging to different ontological realms: causation lies in the natural or 'real' world, explanation in the intellectual or mental world, (see chapter 3, 2.6). Finally we note that explanation itself can be a useful tool in establishing our knowledge of how the world really is. This is done by inference to the best explanation – the typical method of the fictional detective. And, in choosing the best explanation, we have to decide between 'lovely' explanations – powerful, of wide range and explaining a lot – and 'likely' ones – those that fall in with our preconceptions of probability based on how we already believe the world is (see chapter 3, 2.7).

2.3   The action–meaning gap

The basic need for explanation in history is similar to the need in science; we want it because the world is actually different from the way we customarily think it is. A modern scientist, writing a book under the title: *The Unnatural Nature of Science*, begins:

> In fact, both the ideas that science generates and the way in which science is carried out are entirely counter-intuitive and against common sense – by which

I mean that scientific ideas cannot be acquired by simple inspection of phenomena and that they are very often outside everyday experience. Science does not fit with our natural expectations. (Wolpert, 1993, p. 1)

Many people, including historians, have believed that writing history is just a simple matter of writing down what actually happened – '*wie es eigenlich gewesen*' to quote the famous words of Ranke. This can be very different from what people at the time thought was happening. Thus historians, alert to irony, have been struck by the gap yawning between what historical agents are actually doing and what they think they are doing. We have already considered this ignorance of agents in relation to Danto's point about incomplete descriptions – Martin Luther did not know, when he nailed the theses to the door of Wittenberg cathedral, that he was starting the Reformation. François Furet argues that for too long the history of the French Revolution has been written in terms of the agents' own views. He praises de Tocqueville's work on the Revolution for avoiding 'the tyranny of the historical actors' own conception of their experience...' Furet considers *L'Ancien Régime et la Revolution* to be 'the most important book of the entire historiography of the French Revolution'. And this because de Tocqueville perceived 'the nearly unbridgeable gap between human action and its real meaning that characterised the French Revolution' (Furet 1981, p. 16). It is always important to know of any event just what the participants thought was happening, just as we should know (if we can) the motives for their actions. Nevertheless, Furet is right to remind us that we must not stop there. However much insight we have into the minds of the agents themselves, this by no means explains all that happened. Events always have more than one meaning: some meanings for the participants, others for posterity. The corollary is that any one event calls for at least two different explanations. The gap is likely to be particularly wide in times of stress and turmoil (like the Protestant Reformation or the French Revolution), for historical actors are then likely to have even less grasp than usual of what is happening around them. This was as true of 1917 or 1989 as it was of 1517 and 1789.

2.4   The atemporal mode of explanation

There are two main modes of explanation – that is, of accounting for some particular event or grouping of events. They may be characterized as the atemporal and the temporal. The first is, roughly, the conventional scientific method. It is based on the observed repetition of events – say, that salt dissolves in water but oil does not. We may take Hempel's view of scientific explanation – not because it is up to date (it was written in 1942 and now secures the agreement of few philosophers of science – working scientists still fewer), but because it is the basis of a long debate about explanation in history. He claims that 'general laws have quite analogous functions in history and in the natural sciences'. A general law or universal hypothesis 'may be assumed to assert a regularity of the following type: In every case where any event of a specified kind C occurs at a certain place and time, an event of a specified kind E will occur at a place and time which is related in a specified manner to the place and time of the occurrence of the first event'. He goes on to assert (as Popper does) that 'the main function of general laws in the natural sciences is to connect events in patterns which are usually referred to as *explanation* and *prediction*' (Hempel, 1942, in Gardiner, 1959, p. 345). It is worth repeating here Popper's words: 'The use of a theory for the purpose of *predicting* some specific event is just another aspect of its use for the purpose of *explaining* such an event' (Popper, 1962, vol. 2, pp. 262–3). In this account (often known as the 'covering-law' or 'Hempel–Popper' theory) prediction and explanation are two sides of the same coin.

There is an important but unspoken assumption in the Hempel–Popper account. It is that events of exactly the same kind occur again and again. This being so, there is no point in fixing a chronological date to the occurrence. The laws of classical physics and of chemistry assume a regularity at all times. Now this assumption is justifiable within limits, but it is not difficult to think of cases where this is not so. Cosmology suggests one. We inhabit an expanding universe; Hubble's Law states that the recession velocity of a distant galaxy is directly proportional to its distance from the observer. At one time matter in the universe consisted only of hydrogen and helium; the other atoms developed later. The first forms of life on Earth developed without oxygen; now almost all living matter depends on it. Oxygen was a product of life before it became an essential ingredient (see, for example, J. Z. Young, 1971, p. 370). Thus the universe is not in the same state at all times. Or one can look at biological evolution. A Darwinian can explain the emergence of a particular life form – a trilobite or a triceratops, but it could not be predicted beforehand. Chance plays a large part in biological evolution: Gould has argued that 'general patterns of evolution imply the unpredictability of specific outcomes'. Each step in evolution is caused, 'but no finale can be specified at the start, and none would ever occur a second time in the same way, because any pathway proceeds through thousands of improbable stages. Alter any early event . . . and evolution cascades into a radically different channel' (Gould 1991, pp. 308, 51). This is a state of affairs ignored by Hempel but very familiar to historians: single events can be causally explained but cannot be predicted. Thus in cosmology, biology and history explanation and prediction are emphatically not two sides of the same coin. It would therefore be improper to call the atemporal covering-law theory of Hempel and Popper the 'scientific' approach.[11] Many defenders of historical explanation have resisted Hempel's claim that the scientific method of explanation is universally applicable by showing that it is *not* applicable to history – the claim is successfully resisted by W. H. Dray in *Laws and Explanation in History* (1957). They have been, perhaps, too ready to accept Hempel's claim for science.

It turns out that, far from being universal, his theory has only a restricted application even in science. There are large areas of great importance to science where it does not apply, for here time (that is, chronological date) cannot be omitted from the theory.

2.5　The temporal mode of explanation

We now turn to the other mode of explanation – the temporal mode. In this one the situation of the event in a chronological sequence *is* relevant. In some areas of knowledge – for example, chemistry – what has gone before is irrelevant: water is always a combination of hydrogen and oxygen. On the other hand geology, for example, is a study of a sequence of events. Carboniferous limestone today cannot be understood without a knowledge of multitudinous earlier events that made it what it is – water, plants, sunlight, decay and collapse, compression, uplift and so on. It is 220–75 million years old. Between then and now it has been slowly changing; at no two points in time was it exactly the same. This is a very different perspective on science from Hempel's with his examples of lunar eclipses. (Not even these have always happened as they do now, though they have been constant over long ages.) Indeed we are calling into question Comte's belief that every state of society is 'the necessary result of the preceding, and the indispensable mover of the following'[12] This belief rests on the assumption that social change is governed by immutable laws and that the 'aggregate' of these laws 'determines the course of human development' (Comte in Gardiner (1959), p. 79). Although few people today, I imagine, would admit to a belief in a rigidly determined course of human development, yet the conviction is not illogical. Those who believe that nature is governed by universal, immutable laws which only await our discovery of them, may also be disposed to believe that these laws leave little scope for alteration in human affairs. Men and women have always been much the same; weather and the natural environment may vary but cannot fundamentally alter; the fortunes of mankind may oscillate within limits, but can never be essentially different: these were the conclusions of many philosophers and scientists. For them the possibilities of history are confined within strict limits.

In cosmological time, as in geological or evolutionary time, things alter so slowly that the almost invisible pace of change can easily be mistaken for permanence. Among the triumphs of modern science are the researches that demonstrate great alterations in places where it was never before suspected. Darwin's discovery that biological species are not eternally fixed; the discovery by twentieth-century astronomers that the heavens do not move in repeated courses, but that the universe is expanding; the theories of Lyell in the nineteenth and Wegener in the twentieth to demonstrate the constant alterations and movements of the Earth's surface; all these show how time has entered into what was once the timeless. It is tempting to speculate what implications this has for the philosophy of science. How many of the supposedly immutable laws of nature (like gravitation), how many of the basic axioms (like the speed of light as the upper limit of velocity or the conservation of energy) may now have to be reconsidered? Can it be that the universe is much less law-like in structure and much more a field of contingencies than we had ever supposed? Probably we ought to pay more attention to the problems of initial conditions as well as those of laws. 'It is important to realize that laws do not by themselves completely describe the world' (see Davies, 1993, p. 87). One can only say at the moment that both quantum physics and chaos theory suggest that the laws of nature are looser constraints than was thought.

2.6 Implications for history

What implications have these thoughts for explanation in history? The first thing that strikes one is that the situation is much more familiar to historians, who are used to contingency and therefore less likely to seek general laws to account for their phenomena than are scientists. The second thought follows from that: if nature is not such a tight structure of immutable laws as used to be thought, there is less a priori obligation to account for historical phenomena in this way. It may be that Hempel's covering laws are the best way to explain history, but that now seems less probable in the light of the considerations in the previous paragraph. The contemporary situation of science (just outlined) is familiar to historians because in the historical sphere change is commonplace, indeed fundamental. The good and ill fortunes of men and women, as of parties or nations, are notoriously unstable. Many a grey beard has wagged on that theme for the last three thousand years at the least. 'Fortune is but a fickle jade' – and so on. This is not to deny that we make useful generalizations and nourish strong expectations about the behaviour of our fellows; social life would be impossible without them. Few traits of character are so exasperating as unreliability and unpredictability. But our general expectations, whether of one person or of people at large, do not have, and are not believed to have, the certainty of natural laws. The 'structures' – political, economic, social, cultural, linguistic – that are the bases of the social sciences fall in respect of certainty and reliability somewhere between natural laws and such general expectations. The old debate about whether history is or is not a science used to rest on the unquestioned assumption that we know what science is. The only question was whether history does, or should, conform to scientific requirements. Now something of the instability and contingency so familiar in the history of humankind is appearing in the history of the Earth and of the universe – that is, in the history of nature. If the history of nature is in these respects more like a process, and a chancy and continuous one at that, then it is more like human history than people supposed. We then have to reverse our former assumptions. Instead of asking whether history is or should be like science we should question whether science should not be more like history?

So let us continue our consideration of historical explanation.

2.7   Questions to answer

'Explanation' is a rather loose term with a wide denotation. Since virtually every aspect of human life comes into the field of history somewhere, there is a wide variety of things to be explained. Let us see if we can narrow the field a little. We may use Kipling's 'six honest serving men'.[13]

Explaining when and explaining where present few problems. They are usually a matter of relating the spatial or temporal location of one thing to another. 'Where did she choose to sit and meditate?' 'There – for that is her mother's grave.' 'Can you explain when military campaigns usually began in the Middle Ages?' 'In the spring, as soon as there was enough new grass to feed the horses'. Such questions, however, are more commonly asked thus: 'When did medieval campaigns start?' 'In the spring.' 'Why then?' 'Because not until then was there enough grass to feed the horses.' (Although the question asked 'Why?', the response explains the 'When'.)

A similar case holds with explaining who and explaining what. The question is often asked in the form of 'Why', though the response explains not a cause but an identity. Thus when he asked why a certain Edinburgh lawyer was so favoured in literary circles, George IV was told that Walter Scott was the author of *Waverley*. The king, who was familiar with both the book (published anonymously) and the man, was incredulous. The explanation is said never to have convinced him.

2.8   Explaining what

Explaining what has a rather more significant role in history. In addition to the case of Louis XVI on Bastille Day, who was told that the events were not a revolt but a revolution, there is the nature of that revolution itself. The revolutionaries believed that they were making a complete break with the past; most historians have unquestioningly accepted that. In 1865, however, Alexis de Tocqueville argued a strong case, in *L'Ancien Régime et la Revolution*. to the contrary. As a modern French historian re-phrases de Tocqueville:

> In reality it is the fruition of our past. It has completed the work of the monarchy. Far from being a break, it can be understood only within and by historical continuity. It is the objective achievement of that continuity, even though it was experienced subjectively as a radical break. (Furet, 1981, p. 15)

Although some of de Tocqueville's case is open to question, it is hardly to be doubted that the centralized 'administrative State ruling a society informed by an egalitarian ideology' of the Jacobins and the Napoleonic Empire was largely a continuation of the Bourbon monarchy. In short, it stemmed from Richelieu, not Robespierre. Thus the work of the historian often lies not in seeking causes but in establishing and explaining just *what* a given phenomenon *is*. Nor is this just a matter of description or nomenclature. Was Charles Edward Stuart the king or the pretender? Was the English Civil War just that? Or was it the Great Rebellion of the Royalist Clarendon, or the English Revolution of modern sympathizers? The title adopted for these and other contested movements indicates not only a historical interpretation, but also a political or religious allegiance. Did the sixteenth century witness a Counter-Reformation or a Catholic Reformation?

Partisanship apart and seeking to be as objective as possible, it is still never easy at the time to know how to characterize what is going on. The Italian Renaissance was only fully recognized by Giorgio Vasari (1511–74) nearly two hundred years after its beginning.[14] When I was in Moscow in September 1988 the total collapse and disappearance of the USSR was hardly dreamt of. Yet it was already occurring. What is happening in Europe today? Are we part of a great movement of integration, the birth of a United States of Europe? Or not? We must conclude that in history to explain *what* is as important and difficult as explaining *why*.

2.9   Explaining why and explaining how

It is to explaining why and explaining how that we now turn. It will be seen that what is involved in both of them is some understanding of the course of events. Indeed, one philosopher, Michael Oakeshott, has gone so far as to declare them the same. 'The only explanation of change relevant or possible in history is simply a complete account of change. History accounts *for* change by means of a full account *of* change'[15] Thus, for him, explaining why merges into explaining how. But for most of us the two things are not the same. Explaining how seems to call for no more than a narrative of succeeding events. The Bayeux Tapestry does this admirably, explaining, by showing, how the Normans won in 1066. It makes no attempt to explain *why* this occurred. It makes no reference, for example, to tactics and strategy, superiority of weapons, comparative numbers, morale or quality of men; all of these would form part of a military explanation.

Indeed explanation of the victory is a much more complex task. It involves at least three types of historical explanation. One is based on generalizations of human behaviour. These are rather like Hempel's covering laws, but with less certainty; the second is based on human intentions; the third rests on the role of sheer chance. All these can be illustrated in explaining why William won the Battle of Hastings, without going into wider questions of why he invaded England before that or how he reduced the country to submission afterwards. The generalizations are largely of a military nature. One can opine from what is known of other battles that the English had an advantage in their position on the ridge of a hill: the Normans in the flexibility of three divisions, each with three types of soldiers – archers, infantry and horsemen. The English had the psychological advantage of defending hearth and home; the Normans that they were fighting in a sort of crusade blessed by the Pope. These depend on the sort of 'trivial universal laws' that Popper says historians take for granted, (Popper, 1962, vol. 2,

p. 264). He is right that historical explanation can and often does rest on general-izations based on other similar historical phenomena. He is wrong to call them 'universal laws', however, for they are neither. Nor are they always trivial; each of the four cases cited above is an important part of the explanation, yet is not trivially obvious. Human intentions have largely to explain the orders given by the commanders in the course of the battle: why Duke William ordered a feigned retreat of some of his men; why Harold kept his men on the hill-top and did not advance his whole army when he should. These parts of the explanation are particular; they do not rest on generalizations, but on understanding individual actions. Roughly, they rest on what Popper calls 'the logic of the situation' (ibid. pp. 265 and 97.) Third, we have the role of chance in explanation. This is most apparent in the incident of the arrow in Harold's eye or in the fact that he heard of the Pope's decision against him on the eve of the battle. Historians are sometimes misled by the 'wisdom of hindsight' and see battles as foregone conclusions. Most commanders are aware that battles rarely proceed as planned; chance can always play a decisive role, and victory can never be taken for granted until the last minutes. The role of chance, luck or fortune is seen not only in particular incidents (like the arrow in the eye), but also in the whole concatenation of events, where a slight alteration in time or place or order of occurrence can be decisive of quite a different result. That is why Napoleon's first question about any general was, 'Is he lucky?' Chance should never be overlooked in explaining a battle or a war.

2.10   The role of chance

At this point we should make clear the part that chance plays in explanation. I have argued elsewhere that Chance is not a force in history, not one of the dynamics that bring things about (Stanford 1994, p. 204). This is to make the metaphysical point that Chance, Luck, Fortune, Fate and so on are not existent entities – as the Romans believed who worshipped the goddess Fortuna. In explanation this notion is largely irrelevant. By citing chance as part of an explanation all that it is necessary to mean is that the event or conjunction of events was quite unpredictable. This is a question of epistemology, not of metaphysics; a question not of reality but of our knowledge of reality. The one kind of question can be mistaken for the other. The onset of dysentery in the camp of a medieval army was then unpredictable: it was seen as a matter of bad luck or a divine punishment. A modern scientist, looking at the sanitary arrangements, could predict with near certainty the occurrence of the disease. Whether or not sheer randomness actually occurs in nature (and people are more inclined to think so in this century than in the last), events that we have no way of predicting may just as well be random for the purpose of explanation. The physicist's inability to predict the movement of a single sub-atomic particle may be due either to the sheer randomness of nature or to his present state of ignorance. The same is true of apparently chance occurrences in history.

It is important to note that it is not only single events that seem to be due to chance; it is rather the simultaneous conjunction of several. Herbert Butterfield raised the point when discussing God in history. J. B. Bury, one of the few Regius Professors of the subject to take an interest in philosophical questions of history,

> became greatly puzzled by the fact that he could explain why a Prime Minister happened to be walking down a street, and he could explain the scientific laws which loosened a tile on a roof so that it fell down at a particular moment; but he could not explain the conjuncture of the two – the fact that the Prime Minister should just be there to be killed by the falling tile – and yet it was just this *conjuncture* of the two things which was the most important feature of the story. What was more significant still – he found that all history was packed with these conjunctures – you can hardly consider anything in history without coming across them – so that this rigid believer in the firmness of scientific laws in history turned into the archprophet of the theory that Chance counted most of all.

Butterfield goes on to conclude that 'Chance itself, or some equivalent of it, seems to have its part to play in historical explanation, therefore. And the historical process is much more subtle and flexible than most people seem to understand' (Butterfield in McIntire (ed.) (1977, p. 198).

The discussion of coincidence goes back to Aristotle. He declared that 'there can be no theory of the accidental', and that 'there is no science of accidental being...there can be no systematic account of the extraordinary'. (Aristotle (1952), pp. 125, 127; *Metaphysics* E, 1026b–1027a). On this, a modern scholar remarks:

> But it seems clear enough that Aristotle's primary concern is with explanation; and that he claims, among other things, that chance happenings are those for which there is no proper explanation. But it is equally clear that this does not mean that we cannot in some sense give an account of them. (Barnes, 1995, p. 117)

Much of the argument turns on the definition of 'cause'; but on the question of explanation there is considerable support for the view that coincidences are inexplicable. Of course, whether or not they have causes, they certainly have effects.

2.11   Is the unpredictable at all explicable?

True as this may be, we must not exaggerate the role of chance. If the unpredictable plays its part, what of the predictable? We may be confident about predictions in accordance with the laws of natural science. When, on 21 May 1618, Slavata and Martinitz were flung from the castle windows in Prague it is not difficult to explain why they fell. Second, we may still be fairly confident about using the structures of the social sciences in explanation. After the Great Wall Street crash in October 1929 an economist could easily explain why many banks in Europe closed their doors. This, like the fall from the castle, could be as easily predicted beforehand (given the statement of initial conditions) as explained afterwards. The lesser certainty that we may have in the second case is because we are dealing with human actions, not natural phenomena. There is another possibility of explanation (already glanced at) – the role of chance. When the two ministers were flung from the window, one cried 'Jesu Mary, save me!' One of the defenestrators leaned out and gasped, 'By God, she has.' Indeed, against all likelihood, both men survived their fall. Whether their salvation was due to the intercession of the Virgin Mary (as their friends claimed), or to their falling upon the castle dung-heap (their opponents' story), the historian cannot say. Clearly it was not predictable, so in the absence of further information the historian has to put it down to chance. A fourth type of explanation is much less certain than the first two, but is characteristic of historians. This is something of a hunch based on experience – though, in the nature of things, upon second-hand experience. It is a sort of sixth sense of how the world runs, essential (as I pointed out in the discussion of causation) to attributing cause. An event, C, can be said to be the cause of another event, E, if we can say that if C had not occurred, then nor would E. In the natural sciences, and to a lesser extent in the social sciences, we have numerous repetitions of the conjunction of C and E; these, as Hume pointed out, give us at least the confident expectation of their happening together on future occasions. The problem in history, as many people have observed, is that C and E never repeat themselves in quite the same way. Indeed, we are in a dilemma. If we give a reasonably exact description of each phenomenon, then future occurrences are too unlike for any conclusion to be drawn, for there is too little repetition. If we interpret C and E so loosely that there are many instances, enough to make a fairly reliable generalization, then it can be denied that it is the same things being repeated. Which do we choose?

2.12   How historians face problems

In the face of this logical difficulty historians have developed a sixth (but by no means always reliable) sense of how things run, so that they can make at least tentative counter-factual predictions. Towards the end of his *History of the French Revolution* William Doyle suggests a number of them by guessing how the world would have turned out without the Revolution: 'After it, nothing in the European world remained the same, and we are all heirs to its influence. And yet, it can be argued, much that was attributed to it would in all probability have come about in any case.' These more or less inevitable phenomena include, he thinks, the social domination of property, various reforms in government and the growth in power of the state, as well as changes in religion and economics. Yet Doyle is compelled to acknowledge the role of what at least appears to be chance. 'Against all this', he goes on, 'it is equally hard to believe that the specifically anti-aristocratic, anti-feudal revolutionary ideology of the Rights of Man would have emerged as it did without the jumble of accident, miscalculation, and misunderstanding which coalesced into a revolution in specifically French circumstances'. He goes on to suggest other examples of apparent fortuity (Doyle, 1989, pp. 423–5). Perhaps all we can say is that sometimes probability overrides contingency, which is the assumption underlying counter-factual judgements, but that at other times it does not. On these occasions the chance event is like a fall of rocks at the top of a watershed which can divert a whole river into a different valley. There seem to be no rules for deciding whether it is probability or contingency that would have triumphed. Our judgements can be no better than educated guesses. Nevertheless, certain assumptions are basic to the modern historian's way of thinking. Among these are the assumptions that people and events have a definite location in time and space; that, so located, they have effects upon subsequent people and events; that everything has, therefore, a cause or a set of causes without which subsequent affairs would have turned out differently and that causes can be traced. He or she assumes that for these reasons exact repetitions in history rarely if ever occur; that, nevertheless, common elements may be abstracted from many similar events to constitute generalizations, and that some of the theories of the social sciences (and probably all of the theories of the natural sciences) may be employed in explana-tion. It is assumed that generalizations are, in principle, capable of being broken down into individual actions or events; that history is primarily concerned with human beings but must also take account of whatever in the non-human world affects them; that actions and events, therefore, have to be understood in context and that there are virtually no limits to what may be taken as context. Lastly, most modern historians take it for granted that every action or occurrence ought to be capable of rational explanation and that chance should be used only when rational explanation fails; that explanation in history is not governed by rigid precepts but that the historian may use any manner of explanation that seems convincing to her and is likely to convince her audience or readers. However, there is an important caveat to all this: it is that every one of the foregoing assumptions should be qualified by the phrase 'as far as present knowledge extends'.

2.13   Examples of explanation in history

The phrase 'present knowledge' opens up epistemological questions. What are the criteria for knowledge? Is there one set of universally recognized criteria, or are there many? If the latter, which should one adopt? The debate, begun by Socrates nearly two and a half thousand years ago, continues today. Here we are concerned only with what counts as historical knowledge.[16] Without going into either the philosophical problems of theory of knowledge or the methodological problems of how the historian acquires his knowledge and presents it to others, the situation at present is this: what counts as historical knowledge is what is recognized as such by historians of repute. Most of these are, or have been, in various institutions of learning. A historian's reputation rests largely on the judgements of her colleagues, and her colleagues are those reputable historians who accept roughly the same standards and criteria – including most, if not all, of those assumptions outlined above. This way of validating knowledge may seem rather precarious. (It reminds one of how survivors of a shipwreck, by holding hands in a ring, manage to keep everyone afloat.) Nevertheless, the predicament is not confined to historical knowledge; it is much the same with legal, medical, military, or scientific knowledge. In all these areas judgments must rest on the reliability of evidence and the efficacy of method. The alternatives of having resort to sacred texts or infallible authorities hold little appeal for lively intelligences.

At this point we may take a look at a few examples of explanation offered by modern historians of repute. We begin, very briefly, with Sir Lewis Namier's masterpiece of 1929, *The Structure of Politics at the Accession of George III*. By 'politics' he understands parliamentary politics, so the first chapter is 'Why men went into Parliament' – in this case the House of Commons, for motives are irrelevant to a hereditary seat in the Upper House. He tries to analyse the composition of the Commons 'from the angle of purpose'. His explanation is simple: 'Men went there "to make a figure"' (Namier, 1957, pp. xi, 2). He accounts for the phenomenon by a simple appeal to the common motive of pride. This is both the strength and the weakness of the book.

A more careful analysis of personal motive is found in Ronald Hutton's *The Restoration* (1987). The key move in putting an end to the English republic and in restoring the monarchy was General Monck's declaration in 1659 for Parliament against the rule of the army. The destruction of the latter soon brought Charles to his father's throne. But why did Monck take this fateful step? Hutton says that the sequence of events 'begs, resoundingly, the question of Monck's motives'. (Many historians, as we have remarked, have been tempted to read back invisible motives from an agent's visible actions; Hutton is not so naïve.) Was Monck beginning a long project which would eventually restore the king? Was he opposed to, or fearful of, the power of the army? Did he fear the consequences of the recent rise of religious fanaticism? As Hutton points out, every one of these explanations fits the facts, yet none of them is without objections. His solution is to treat the reader fairly by laying out each of the three possible candidates for the explanation, together with the pros and cons of each (Hutton, 1985, pp. 70–1). It may be remarked that these theories are not incompatible: Monck may have been influenced by all three motives.

Now let us move to a less individual sphere. Sir Richard Southern, in *The Making of the Middle Ages* (1953) explains why the practice of trial by ordeal was abandoned in Europe in the twelfth century:

The study of Roman Law opened men's eyes to the existence of an elaborate system of purely human proof; and the growth of a uniform Canon Law, which applied the methods of Roman Law, carried the lessons of the lawyers far and wide. Moreover, with the greater abundance of written evidence...disputed facts about ownership...became amenable to the test of human testimony. Above all, men came more and more to doubt the efficiency of judgement by ordeal...The effect, so far as the regular administration of justice was concerned, was immediate. Men were forced to prefer the probability arrived at by human agencies to the certainties of divine judgement. (Southern, 1967, p. 95)

What we see here is an important advance in administrative and legal procedure (part of the realm of the social sciences) explained by widespread change in mental attitudes. What connection is Southern tracing between causes and effect? He is not using the so-called 'scientific' method, recommended by Hempel and Popper, of stating a general law and an initial situation and then deducing a conclusion that may serve as either prediction or explanation. (One could, of course, cite some general law to the effect that 'People will abandon a practice that they come to see as unreasonable'. But the question is, 'Why did they come to see *this* practice as unreasonable?). Nor is he citing any of the generalizations or theories of the social sciences. He is supposing that when men's minds were opened to certain influences, their attitudes to certainty and probability, their acknowledgement of what constituted acceptable proof, and their views of the role of God in society underwent a profound alteration. Why should we accept this? Because it seems reasonable; because it falls in with the ways in which we think. But this method would hardly convince us if the historian were explaining a reverse move – from rationality to superstition, the abandonment of our legal practices in favour of trial by ordeal. Can it always be assumed that people move from superstition to rationality, and never the reverse? The proliferation of religious cults today casts some doubt. Do these considerations weaken Southern's argument?

2.14   Context

The question of how historians connect cause and effect brings up the problems of 'What is the relevant context?' and 'How far back do we have to go to trace the causes?' In 1974 A. G. Dickens opened his masterly little work on *The German Nation and Martin Luther* thus:

The Protestant Reformation has not infrequently been 'explained' by reference to movements of thought, politics and public opinion apparent only on the very eve of Luther's revolt. Such short-term analysis betrays not merely a weak grasp of historical causation but also a singular lack of feeling for the power of tradition over the German mind. (Dickens, 1976, p. 1)

Dickens finds it necessary to go back two hundred years to the early fourteenth century for his explanation, with some reference to the Investiture Contest which carried him back a further two centuries. This is a perfectly valid argument of Dickens. One might take it as almost axiomatic that great changes in human affairs not only have far-reaching effects; they also have deep-rooted causes. They are two sides of the same coin. Unfortunately, if historical causation is largely a matter of tracing necessary causes (those without which not...), then the causal chain of every event must be traced back to the creation of the world. One must stop somewhere, but where? The limits of historical explanation are the same as those we have noted in explanation in general. Full explanations are only envisaged in principle, rarely laid out completely. The limits are the prior knowledge and continuing interest of the enquirer; in practice logic often has to yield to the weariness of the flesh.

2.15   Comparison

Explanations are often required in history as questions arise from comparison. In late eighteenth-and early nineteenth-century England people of property were alarmed by the rapidly increasing urban masses of the Industrial Revolution. The latter were seen as potential 'sans-culottes' of a British 'Terror'. Their fears, however, were groundless. No 'French Revolution' ever occurred in England. Why not? One of the most ingenious answers to this question was given by a French historian, Élie Halévy, who published in 1913 A History of the English People in 1815. 'Why was it,' he asked, 'that of all the countries of Europe England has been the most free from revolutions...?...a system of economic production that was in fact totally without organization of any kind would have plunged the kingdom into violent revolution had the working classes found...leaders...But the elite of the working class...had been imbued by the Evangelical movement with a spirit from which the established order had nothing to fear.' When the great trade union movement arose it was led by men whose 'spiritual ancestors were the founders of Methodism'. The ruling classes, he said, saw with fear the growth of the free, or non-conformist, churches with their self-government and organization. 'So they called to mind the French Revolution and the American War of Independence and feared "Methodism" almost equally with Jacobinism. Had they understood the situation better, they would have realized that Methodism was the antidote to Jacobinism' (Halévy, Book III, 1938, pp. 47, 219). It is scarcely an exaggeration to say that Halévy answered the question: 'Why was there no "French Revolution" in England?' with the one name: 'John Wesley'.

Halévy's answer, that the behaviour of the masses was an effect of religious belief, is in contradiction to Marxist theories of material substructure and ideal superstructure. But if the answer is unexpected, the question is of a very common type: how do we explain different features in two very similar entities: (Or, occasionally, how do we explain the similar features of two very different historical entities?) We seem to have here a situation suited to the logic of John Stuart Mill. His rule for experimental procedure was: 'Vary one factor at a time and observe the result.' Thus if a phenomenon composed of three factors A, B, C is regularly followed by another of a, b, c; and if B, C (without A) are followed by b, c (without a), then A is the cause of a. Similarly,

$$
\begin{aligned}
&\text{if} \quad A, \ B, \ C \text{------}a, \ b, \ c \\
&\text{and} \ A, \ D, \ E \text{------} a, \ d, \ e \\
&\text{then} \ A \text{------} a.
\end{aligned}
$$

It is very tempting to apply this simple method to historical causation.

In particular, historians and social scientists have been attracted to the comparison of revolutions.[17] But in all comparisons in history we have first to ask whether the similarities on which the comparisons are based really existed or whether they are due merely to applying the same descriptions. The American, the French and the Industrial Revolutions occurred almost simultaneously and bear the same name. But were these historical phenomena three examples of the same thing? Or were they as different as an oak tree, a family tree and an axle-tree?

So there are at least four obvious disadvantages in applying Mill's method to historical causation. The first is that there are not many instances to compare – nothing like enough to give the regular occurrences of the natural sciences. The second is that the instances that *are* available for comparison may not be strictly comparable. This applies both to the total phenomena, like revolutions, and to the constituent factors, like the presence of a suitable ideology or a shortage of food. The third is that the analysis of either cause or effect into constituent parts (the As, Bs, Cs and a's, b's and c's) may be inaccurate; in particular, it is difficult to be sure that *all* the relevant causal factors have been included. A fourth difficulty is that the elements are not, as in the diagram, independent of each other. In practice they can react upon each other, so that the presence of one can strengthen or weaken the effect of another. For example, the presence of revolutionary propaganda may increase the virulence of food riots, as in Paris 1789 or Petrograd 1917; on the other hand, the fact that opposition to absolutism was drawn from almost all classes of French society at the beginning of the Revolution led later to social conflicts within the Revolution that ultimately frustrated it and prevented the fulfilment of pre-Revolutionary ideals. Nor do causes always have the same effects. Bible-based Protestantism, a major revolutionary force in Britain in the seventeenth century, was seen by both Marx and Halévy (in quite different ways) as a preventative of revolution in the early nineteenth.

2.16 Causal and interpretative explanation

Explanation in history, therefore, takes two main forms: causal and interpretative. The one explains why, the other what. Let us see how we meet these in the

French Revolution. A causal explanation refers to antecedent events and states of affairs: the dominance of the nobility, the ideas of the Encyclopaedists, the bankruptcy of the monarchy, the political theories of Rousseau, the price of bread, the recent growth of Paris, the example of the American Revolution, and so on. Discussion on these lines has filled many books and articles.[18] An interpretative approach explains *what* the Revolution was. Was it the triumph of representative government (Mme de Staël and other nineteenth-century Liberals); was it the triumph of the bourgeoisie (Marx) or of the people (Michelet); was it the death of feudalism, or of absolutism; was it the continuity of the *ancien régime* (de Tocqueville), or was it (as its participants believed) the birth of a new age? Part of the difficulty of interpreting the Revolution lies in the fact that it had many and various meanings not only to subsequent generations but to the people of France at the time. As Lynn Hunt remarks, 'There is no shortage of scholarly work showing that the Revolution meant different things to different people'[19] Indeed, as Furet has shown, the French Revolution is a peculiarly rich source of meaning, not only for France, but also for Europe in general both then and throughout the subsequent century. Together with Russia in 1917 it has been the mainstay of revolutionary tradition in the twentieth century, and its bicentenary in 1989 produced many books on its meaning – or, rather, meanings.[20]

It should be pointed out here that causal and interpretative kinds of explanation are not mutually exclusive but complementary. Before attempting to explain why, it is sensible fully to understand what it is that has to be explained. Which type of explanation we choose to concentrate on depends partly on what the question is and partly on what we take for granted. In one case, we know what it is but not how to account for it; in the other, we are not sure what it is, but once we know we can readily explain it.

2.17 Summary

2.17.1 Causal explanation
Let us conclude with a summary of what is involved in explanations of cause and of meaning in history. First, causal explanation.

We may begin by distinguishing *what* we explain from *how* we justify our explanations. It has often been remarked that in a causal explanation not every cause needs to be cited. One of the necessary causes of your reading this is that you were born, another is that you learned to read, a third is that you learned English. The number of these that could be cited is almost infinite and they are almost all trivial. In most cases it is the irregular, the unexpected, the break in the sequence that puzzles us. This is where explanation is called for. European monarchs, once crowned, reigned until their deaths. There is one exception; the Emperor Charles V, who abdicated in 1556 and retired to a monastery until his death in 1558. How do we account for this rarity? A long string of necessary causes (the institution of the Holy Roman Empire, his birth, his coronation and so on) are little help. Should we seek the sufficient cause? (C is a sufficient cause of E if E inevitably follows: a bullet in the heart is a sufficient but not a necessary cause of death.) Unfortunately a number of these could be suggested: the size of his empire, his long struggle for religious unity, his weariness and so on. Which is the right one? Must the abdication be the inevitable effect of any of these? Historians often fudge this by saying that the sufficient cause is not any one but many causes taken together. One logical difficulty here is that we cannot easily be assured that some relevant cause has not been omitted or that one not relevant has been included. Another problem is that if the sufficient cause is a bundle of causes, then such a bundle is probably unique, unlike any other. Scientifically, it is almost impossible to make a useful inference from a single instance. Mill's method of inclusion and exclusion (explained above) becomes inoperable in the unique cases. Nevertheless, Mill does suggest what is perhaps the least unsatisfactory route to a satisfactory historical explanation: that is, to try to match the exceptional effect (which is what usually calls for explanation) with an exceptional cause. In the case of Charles V one can say that other emperors (Chinese, Roman) had ruled empires of comparable size; other monarchs had been weary, and so on. My own choice of explanation would be his despair over his failure to mend the shattered unity of Christendom, for he was a man of faith and conscience. At least this seems a fair example of explaining an exceptional effect by an exceptional cause. It must not be forgotten, however, that this method (though the least unsatisfactory) depends largely on the validity of comparisons. And making comparisons in history is always a shaky enterprise. No two occasions or persons are exactly the same. One can only hope that, in stating that A is sufficiently similar to B for useful comparisons to be drawn, one has included all the relevant factors and excluded only the irrelevant – easier said than done.

Now we turn to the question of how we justify our causal explanations. What validates the connections we make between cause and effect?

First we should mention the laws of nature, or (preferably) the well established hypotheses of the natural sciences. These are, for the historian, almost beyond question. Unfortunately, while they can be tacitly assumed, they rarely function in historical explanation. To ask why Pompeii was destroyed in AD 69 and to be told that it was due to an eruption of Vesuvius is neither a historical question nor a historical answer. Both are scientific. Historical questions might be 'Why was the town built so near to the volcano?' or 'What effect did the destruction have upon the ideas of the Romans?' Nevertheless, this instance should remind historians that they must never overlook the importance of the natural environment to man in history.

Second we have the structures and theories of the social sciences. These are more useful, because, like history and unlike the natural sciences, they deal with human affairs. They are useful in explaining sequences of events: how food shortages lead to high prices; how unemployment leads to riots and crime; how political theory leads to political rhetoric; how political symbols give meaning and motive to action; how overseas trade leads to the amassing of capital and to greater cultural tolerance, and so on. They do much to enlarge the historian's understanding of how the world works and they facilitate the Mill-like approach (discussed above) to explanation. Their disadvantages are that they cannot easily account for exceptional cases (the very things that historians often need to explain) nor for the sort of conjunctures that Butterfield spoke of (see above, chapter 4, 2.10).

Third, and distinct from the natural and social sciences, we have the judgements of the historian. These judgements come into play when the sciences cannot help. These are judgements about probability. Of most of the past we have no direct evidence, but the well-informed historian has a shrewd idea of what is likely to have happened at a given time and place. To take a trivial example, she does not know precisely what Henry VIII had for breakfast on any particular day, but she can give the fairly restricted list from which the menu would have been drawn. Moreover, she is certain that almost all the items of our breakfast tables (fruit juice, muesli, croissants, margarine, tea, coffee) would not have appeared on his. Equally, as we have remarked, historians' judgements are the basis for counter-factuals. Many of our most important conclusions about historical causation and the significance of events rest on counter-factuals. 'If Germany had won the aerial Battle of Britain in the summer of 1940, invasion and defeat would have followed.' 'If Hitler had not delayed the attack on Russia in 1941 by first invading the Balkans, the German armies would have captured Moscow and Leningrad.' If these counter-factual statements are correct, then a few aerial combats and a comparatively small military operation played fateful parts in the history of Britain and of the USSR. Of course, no one can be sure whether they are correct or not, but such judgements are the very stuff of history. What is their foundation? It is nothing but the considered opinions of historians. These opinions do not rest directly upon theories of either kind of science, though they may be grounded in some such theories. Directly, they are a combination of the historian's wide, but largely second-hand, experience (possibly formulated in the light of various non-historical theories, such as Malthusianism, monetarism or Marxism) with his or her own metaphysical and moral outlook or *Weltanschauung*.

Fourth and lastly, we have the sort of explanation that virtually gives up on causation, allowing explanation why to dissolve into explanation how. Causes are not sought; events are merely narrated. A close and detailed account of *how* things occurred offers (on this theory, as Oakeshott suggests) an account of *why* they occurred. There are arguments for and against this method. Among its advantages is the fact that it avoids the theorizing and speculation of our first three kinds, and brings us close to the actions of the agents – what men and women actually thought and did at the time. It shows how these actions derive from the agents' perceptions of their situation. For example, a close narrative of the events in France will show how the generous hopes of 1789 and 1790 gave way to the hatreds and Terror of 1793–4. This will show why the Revolution changed its nature and, perhaps, why it failed. The detailed story here offers a better explanation than reams of theory about the Revolution. On the other hand, there are disadvantages. One is that this method makes it difficult to distinguish foreground from background. Which events are more, which less, important or relevant. Yet this distinction must be made in any meaningful historical account – whether theoretical or narrative. Another disadvantage is that the term 'close' can only be very relative; the historian cannot, in the nature of things, tell everything that happened. And, again, we must remember that action theory rests largely on the agents' own understanding of what they were doing. But, as Furet following Tocqueville insists, the customary accounts of the Revolution that are based on what the revolutionaries *thought* they were doing is very far from the truth. What the historian seeks is the correct interpretation of the events.

2.17.2   Interpretative explanation   At this point we turn to the second part of our summary; having considered causal explanation, we now look at meaningful explanation or interpretation.

A number of historiographical surveys have been entitled 'Interpreting the French Revolution' or 'Interpretations of the French Revolution'. What is it to interpret a historical phenomenon (an event or, less often, a person)? Surely, it is to explain its meaning. But in what sense can such things have meanings? Symbols and signs have meanings. Symbols (the cross, the crescent, the stars and stripes, a crown, a signature tune) have meanings by convention. Their meanings result from human intentions, so we may ask what is intended by the use of this convention, both on particular occasions and in general. Language can be regarded as a set of symbols. When we hear a speech or read a text we may ask both what is the intention of the speaker or writer and what does the speech or text itself *mean*. Signs are not conventional, but are naturally related to their meaning. Hence heavy clouds mean rain. A countryman may 'read' the signs of the weather; a surgeon may 'read' an X-ray. Thus signs, too, may be interpreted.[21]

The question is this: when a historical event is interpreted and its meaning is explained, is this the explanation of a sign or of a symbol? Are we interpreting reality (an exercise in metaphysics) or human ideas about reality (an exercise in epistemology)? We should be clear at this point that interpretation is an exercise of intelligence, though not necessarily of human intelligence. Many animals can 'read' the natural signs of weather, tide and so on. Some of the higher mammals (apes, dogs, dolphins) can interpret spoken symbols. However, the interpretation of historical meanings is exclusively human.

Anything that has meaning does so by virtue of indicating something else that is not itself. The symbol 'X' refers to the intersection of roads; the letters 'C-A-T' refer to a feline; the symbols are not themselves roads or animals. When we interpret a poem, say, we are explaining one or more of several meanings. We may be giving in our words the thoughts and feelings of the poet, thoughts and feelings that he expressed in the words of the poem. Or we may be expressing in our own words the thoughts and feelings that the poem aroused in us. Thus we have the meaning for the poet and the meaning for the reader. Third, some people maintain that a poem has a meaning in and for itself (a sort of objective meaning) that may (or, more probably, may not) be identical either with the poet's meaning or the reader's. If we agree that a poem can have an objective meaning of its own, distinct, in principle, from either the poet's or the readers' meanings, then we have something analogous to what the historian seeks when he asks 'What was the meaning of the French Revolution?' He is not asking 'What did it mean for its makers?' This is analogous to the poet's meaning. As we have seen, some historians reject this interpretation and declare (with Tocqueville) that the makers of the Revolution did not at all understand what they were doing. Nor is he asking 'What did this or that historian make of it?' The various authors cited in the historiographical surveys (Mignet, Taine, Lefebvre, Soboul and so on) are ana-logous to the poem's readers, each of whom gives his or her own particular 'reading' of it. But just as with a poem, such interpretations often tell us more about the interpreter than about the event itself. Most of them seem far too subjective. What the historian wants is the true, correct, objective meaning that the event has in and for itself. In short he wants a slice of reality, not a pot-pourri of half-baked ideas. Is this a vain or foolish quest?

Surely not. The historian, like the scientist, the theologian and the philosopher, seeks to understand reality; studying other people's ideas (however impressive) may be left to literary folk. On the other hand (as the literary folk will be quick to point out), ideas may soon turn into objective reality when they move men and women to vigorous action – in fact, to make history. Seen as a man, they may point out, Rousseau was little better than a moral and psychological disaster, but his ideas (it is small exaggeration to say) brought down the oldest monarchy in Europe. This power (that ideas have to move people) brings home the importance of historical interpretations. It is obvious that history is interpreted not only by historians, but by thinkers, politicians, publicists and preachers of all kinds who try (with varied success) to impose their ideas on the public. Not only Rousseau, but also Jefferson, Sieyès, Marx, Lenin, Hitler are among the successful practi-tioners of historical interpretation. These interpretations are probably some way from the considered judgements of the patient and industrious academic historian, but none can deny the importance of their consequences.

Ideally, there is a true account of history, where the role and significance of every event is nicely calculated and given its correct place in the causal sequence that we believe to constitute the reality of history. This interpretation would involve both true descriptions and a full understanding of the mysteries of causation, of determination, of counter-factuals and of contingency. We have seen in our discussions, the problems and difficulties raised by every one of these. Nevertheless, it is this (or the closest possible approximation to it) that the serious historian aims at.

In practice, many non-historians have other aims. They intend that their interpretations of history should move people – and they do. Sometimes the popular conception of an event's importance (as with the battles of Salamis [480 BC] or Britain [AD 1940]) may coincide with the historians' counter-factual judgements. More often it does not. Yet the popular conception may itself become a symbol and breed more symbols, like the Bastille in 1789. In this way a historical event (like a poem) may have strange and unlooked-for meanings. The negro spiritual 'Swing Low, Sweet Chariot' (a song of religious devotion) has become a national emblem for English followers of rugby football, sung to arouse their team to ever more vigorous action. Blake's 'Jerusalem' is part of a mystical poem of obscure imagery by an anti-Establishment radical. It too has become an English national emblem, often sung on occasions of light-hearted jingoism that would have appalled its author. Are these distortions of the 'real' meaning of the poems? Or are they part of their real meanings? The same question must be asked of historical interpretations. Perhaps the problems of meaning should lead us to take a closer look at language and at symbols in general.

Notes

1 Realists hold that true laws – invariant, incorrigible, necessary – are real features of the world, according to which things not merely *do* occur as they do, but *must* occur as they do. A Realist, believing that real laws exist, would distinguish them from the law-like statements that constitute the latest stage of scientific knowledge, but which can, in principle, always be amended. The problem is not that we cannot know the real laws of nature, but that we cannot know we know them.

2 For an example, see the remarks on the pendulum in Gleick (1988, pp. 39–45).

3 See chapter 1, 2, and chapter 2, 7. For further discussion, see Stanford (1986, pp. 7–25).

4 'cause-words are theory-loaded in relation to their effect-words' (Hanson, 1965, p. 62).

5 See Skinner (1990, pp. 3–20). In spite of the title it may be questioned whether all the themes discussed in this book qualify as 'grand theory'.

6 See especially Winch (1958), who follows ideas of Ludwig Wittgenstein.

7 A notorious example is Malinowski's work among the Trobriand Islanders. His accounts of their society – *Argonauts of the Western Pacific* (1922), or *The Sexual Life of Savages* (1929), among others – suggested that the islanders were permanently locked in a Stone Age culture. His perspective was quite ahistorical. He ignored both the conflicts within society, which brought about some changes, and the entry of other white men, which brought about more. Rather to his embarrassment, his subjects were to prove themselves capable of rapid adaptation to the impacts of the modern world.

8 For further discussion of this point, see chapter 4, 2.

9 For further discussion of time and change in social science, see chapter 1, 2.11–2.17.

10 For an attempt to combine structural explanation with action theory explanation, see Callinicos (1987).

11 It is better described as 'scientistic' See Popper (1972, p. 185); von Wright (1971, p. 171).

12 Comte in Gardiner (1959, p. 79). See chapter 4, 1.3.

13   I keep six honest serving-men
                          (They taught me all I knew);
                          Their names are What and Why and When
                          And How and Where and Who.

14 'The acceptance of rise and decline in the affairs of men and the idea that a rebirth or renaissance of the fine arts had taken place in Tuscany were both common currency in the intellectual world of Vasari's time. For the idea of a rebirth of the arts, however, Vasari gave compelling chapter and verse: the signs were first seen in such and such buildings, such and such works of sculpture.' See George Bull, Introduction, to Vasari (1965, p. 15).

15 Oakeshott (1933, p. 143. See also chapter 3, 1.9).

16 For further discussion see Stanford (1986).

17 See, for example, R. R. Palmer, *The Age of the Democratic Revolution* (1964), 2 vols; Barrington Moore, *Social Origins of Dictatorship and Democracy* (1966); Theda Skocpol, *States and Social Revolutions* (1979); J. G. A. Pocock (ed.) *Three British Revolutions, 1641, 1688, 1776* (1980).

18 One need mention only two: Georges Lefevbre's *Quatre-vingt-neuf* (1939) ET *The Coming of the French Revolution* (1947) and William Doyle's *Origins of the French Revolution* (2nd edn, 1988).

19 Hunt (1984, p. 14). Pre-eminent among these are the works of Richard Cobb (1970, 1972 and 1987); also Alan Forrest (1975) on Bordeaux; Martyn Lyons (1978) on the Gard; Hubert Johnson (1986) on the Midi; W. D. Edmonds (1990) on Lyon.

20 See Furet (1981); also Best (1988); and Mason and Doyle (eds) (1989). One should not not overlook Gérard (1970) or even the opening pages of Karl Marx's 'Eighteenth Brumaire' (1852).

21 Signs and symbols can be defined in more than one way. I prefer this way.

Suggested Reading

The Social Sciences

Fairly easy ways into the topic are von Wright (1971), as already mentioned, or Passmore (1962) in Nadel (1965). Ryan (1970) is sound. Ryan (1973) has a good introduction and a useful set of readings. Comte in Gardiner (1959) gives a clear and brief statement of the postivist case. Weber's views are important; see Weber (1964, part I) or Weber (1978, sections 1, 2, 4 and 5). Not to be overlooked is Winch (1958).

History

Von Wright (1971) and Passmore (1962) are again relevant here. Also Walsh (1967, chapter 3), Elton (1970, chapter 4), Atkinson (1978, chapter 4), McCullagh (1984, chapter 2). There are three useful articles (by Dray, Hempel, and Skinner) in Gardiner (1974). The great controversy over laws and explanations in history began with Hempel (1942) (printed in Gardiner (1959)) and Dray's reply, in Dray (1957). The whole of this section in Gardiner (1959, pp. 344–444), makes the main points clear. Gardiner's own contribution is Gardiner (1952). A thorough examination is Martin (1977).

5

Science, History and Historicism

1 Science and History

1.1 Preliminary remarks: applications of science to the past

It is the task of history, as it is of other arts and sciences, to bring certain objects before the mind. Yet there is one big difference between art and science. A masterpiece in the arts (the *Mona Lisa* or Bach's *St Matthew Passion*) is visible or audible; a masterpiece in the sciences (such as the theories of Newton, Darwin or Einstein) is apprehended by the mind, not the eye or ear. History is not an art, in the sense of creating particular sights or sounds. Like the sciences, it brings to the mind representations of an unseen reality. But whereas the unseen reality of the sciences is the laws of the universe, the unseen reality of history is simply the past. Since the objects of the studies are so different, it is not surprising that they often differ in procedure and method.

Here we should pause to recall the familiar but necessary distinction between history 1, which is roughly equivalent to all the happenings of the human past, and history 2, which is what we think, believe and write about that past. There is no obvious or necessary connection between history 1 and what historians do with it, any more than there is between flour and what bakers do with it. (After all, it has been used to whiten the hair of footmen.) The past is a field of possible study. It is as open to the practices of the scientist as it manifestly is to the painter or the novelist. Anyone is as free to use it for his own ends as he or she is with the present or the future. It is real, at least as real as the theories of the scientists, but (like those theories) it is not apprehensible by the senses, only by the mind. It is worth emphasizing that the past is a field open to all. The people most concerned with it are historians, and since they have worked in it more than anyone else, they have developed sound methods and procedures. Any non-historian working in that field would be well advised to pay attention to the practices of the historian. However, some of these practices are shaped by the historian's particular aims. As with bakers and flour, it must not be supposed that what historians do is the only thing to be done with the past.

We may note that science can be used in relation to the past in several ways. One way is for historians to use later scientific knowledge to discover what was going on at a particular time. The frequent plagues that are well reported in sources of early modern Europe were a puzzle to the sufferers. Historians have been able to bring current medical knowledge to gain a clearer understanding of the events. Because, in the sixteenth and seventeenth centuries, it was believed that plague was carried by putrid vapours whose atoms would stick to clothing or to the skin, doctors wore waxed tunics and hoods as protection. These proved to be quite effective – though not for the reason supposed. The plague was, in fact, carried by fleas which were unable to penetrate the waxed garments (Cipolla, 1991, p. 55). Similarly the science of vulcanology has illuminated reports of what happened at Pompeii in AD 69 or at Thera in 1470 BC. A third example is the light cast on the reign of George III by recent researches into the disease of porphyria. It should be pointed out that historico-scientific investigations of this kind usually employ the procedures and knowledge of scientists and historians together. The results may contribute to science or to history or (more commonly) to both.

Science may be applied to the past in a different (and perhaps more suspect) way when theories of history are elaborated on a supposedly scientific base. The best known of these is Marxism, which has many followers among historians who, while not regarding themselves as Marxists, still adopt a materialist approach. Other historians who use a supposedly science-based approach are the Annales school of France, especially the recent leader of that school, Fernand Braudel. From the structure of his master-work on the Mediterranean in the sixteenth century one might be forgiven for supposing that he regarded mountains as more important than men (see Braudel, 1975).

However, perhaps the most interesting application of science to the past comes when the past is used to provide material for present research. This may be done in two ways, in what can be described as the non-temporal and the temporal approaches. The first is when information recorded in the past is used in the formulation of present theories. An example is the earlier sightings of comets which enabled Edmund Halley correctly to predict the return of 'Halley's Comet' in 1758, long after his death in 1742. In such cases the scientist makes no distinction between old and new data (past or contemporary), because he believes that the nature of the phenomenon has not changed in the interval. The second approach, the temporal, is more relevant to our concerns, for here time and change are taken into account. It is very relevant to stock-breeding to have accurate records of animals over many generations. There was a great difference between an early eighteenth-century bullock and an early nineteenth-century bullock, as histories of farming show. Such records also helped Darwin to develop his theory of evolution. What happens in the short term on farms, he realized, could have happened in the long term in nature. Modern doctors wrestling with contemporary disease are much concerned with the evolutionary adaptations of viruses and bacilli. The records of history, of prehistory and of geology, are essential to the important science of evolutionary biology, with its myriad modern applications. So let us compare some of the methods of history and science.

1.2 Science and history – similarities

Science and history have much in common. Both try to show the unseen, both tackle problems, both seek the truth, both try to give accurate descriptions of the data before them, both look for the causes of things, both seek to explain the phenomena, both employ some sort of induction, both make use of the resulting generalizations. Finally, it may be argued that they both pursue simultaneously conjecture and refutation (see Popper, 1969, p. vii and (1972), p. 186). That is to say, that both make imaginative (but tolerably well-informed) guesses as to a possible solution of the problem before them. They then test out their conjectures against the evidence, but always seeking contrary as well as supporting evidence. The two things proceed in close alternation, if not entirely simultaneously; testing follows conjecture and improved conjecture the testing.

1.3 Science and history – differences (preliminary)

Where, then, do science and history differ? Perhaps the most important distinction lies in the sort of representation of unseen reality that they aim to bring before the mind. The one desires to reduce the number of facts; that is, to dispense as far as possible with particular true statements; the other can never have enough singular truths. A distinguished biologist says, 'The factual burden of a science varies inversely with its degree of maturity. As a science advances, particular facts are comprehended within, and therefore in a sense annihilated by, general statements of steadily increasing explanatory power and compass . . . In all sciences we are being progressively relieved of the burden of singular instances, the tyranny of the particular' (Medawar, 1984, p. 29). Whether all sciences can ever be free of the single instance seems doubtful, but certainly no historian would ever complain of the 'tyranny of the particular'. To be able to describe and to account for what exactly happened in all its multifarious detail is always the major part of his purpose, sometimes the whole part.[1]

Yet historians cannot hope, any more than scientists, to bring before the mind at any one time all the available facts. Even if they could, what would be the point? 'What's Hecuba to him, or he to Hecuba?' asked Hamlet. 'In making sense of the past, the historian not only tries to discover what happened – and all that those two brief words involve – but also how the things that happened were linked one with another: their meaningful relationship' (Elton, 1970, p. 112).

These remarks of Elton raise three more concerns in which there is a difference between the methods of the typical scientist and the typical historian. (That, in practice, historians and scientists frequently collaborate has already been pointed out.) These concerns are structure, time and meaning. Although we are here considering methodology, it is worth noting that the differences lie not so much in the different natures of the subject matter; for this applies only to the natural sciences – social sciences share much subject matter with history. A greater distinction lies in the different aims of the two disciplines – that is, in the ways they wish to represent unseen reality. We begin with structure.

2   Structure, Time and Meaning

2.1   Differences of structure

Medawar claims that the aim of science is to represent the universe by 'general statements of steadily increasing explanatory power and compass'. It may be that this approach is a little outdated. Since he wrote, chaos theory and complexity theory have shown that most natural phenomena are not fully describable by linear equations. Medawar's statement looks like reductionism. And 'if reductionism means that all explanations for complexity must be sought at a lower level . . . then reductionism is false' (Barrow, 1992, p. 140; see also pp. 124–5, 192; and Gleick, 1988, p. 6). But whether or not Medawar has correctly described the aims of science, we must ask what are the aims of history. The question has been answered in various ways. One of the first answers is also one of the best: 'It will be enough for me, however, if these words of mine are judged useful by those who want to understand clearly the events which happened in the past.' This aim would be acknowledged by virtually every historian today, nearly two and a half thousand years since Thucydides wrote. Less happily, his sentence continues: 'and which (human nature being what it is) will, at some time or other and in much the same ways, be repeated in the future'[2] This further remark gives credence to the common, but very doubtful, belief that history repeats itself and can, therefore, be a guide to present and future action.[3] 'History,' it was long ago said, 'is philosophy teaching by examples.' (Dionysius of Halicarnassus, 40–8 BC). But so-called 'exemplar history' (that is, history as a moral or practical tutor) was written until well into the nineteenth century (See Stoianovich, 1976, p. 25). Let us stick with the aim outlined above (and endorsed by Thucydides and von Ranke): namely, that of effecting for the mind a representation of the unseen world of the past, a representation to enable understanding.

All representations have to be structured in some way. To repeat an earlier analogy, a map is a two-dimensional representation of a terrain. Various conventions are used in the structure. The most important is the scale (for example, the familiar 1:50,000 of the Ordnance Survey) that links the two sets of dimensions. The third dimension of the terrain requires a different convention: either contour lines or shading. Types of roads are indicated by lines of different colours and thicknesses, and so on. History, however, is rarely able to achieve so clear a representation of its subject matter. Chronological tables or family trees are comparatively rare examples of similar simplicity. To be sure, crude diagrams in school textbooks or on blackboards may be used for instruction, but the pupils are hardly likely to suppose that the French Revolution looked like the diagram of circles, names and arrows that helps them to memorize its suggested causes. (One might suppose that the terrain does not resemble the map either, but one of the minor delights of air travel is to find that it often does.) With these few crude exceptions, history is a verbal representation of a 'field' (as we may describe the past) – a field that is populated by men and women, countries, institutions, nations, churches and so on. It is extended over four, not three dimensions. When one considers what problems a third dimension gives the cartographer, one cannot be surprised at the historian's difficulty with representing four. Nor is this all. Not only does he have to bear in mind the most important dimension of the four – that of time. He must also show other relationships. The commonest of these is concurrence – the coming together of various members of the field in a simultaneous conjunction that we call an 'event' or a 'happening'. Every event has a definite spatio-temporal location – for example, the decisive battle of the English Civil War was fought at Naseby in Leicestershire on 14 June 1645. But establishing the 'where' and the 'when' of the event is only the beginning. The historian must establish exactly what happened – '*wie es eigentlich gewesen*', as von Ranke said. And the very 'what' (the event) was extended over time. In those days a battle rarely lasted beyond one day; in 1916 the Battle of the Somme took four and a half months. Both battles would be marked on a map with the symbol of crossed swords with nothing to indicate their different temporal extensions, for the third and fourth dimensions cannot be shown on a map. One could analyse the 'what' further, by pointing out that these events (distinguished by a single term) were, in fact, made up of a number of smaller events. Any extension in time is almost infinitely divisible. But let us leave that aside and go on to the next questions, the 'how' and the 'why' of the event. Part of the 'how' can be dealt with by a detailed description of the micro-events just mentioned; another part of the 'how' must be a description of the circumstances, the surrounding conditions which helped to shape the course of the event. They all interacted to form the event. To give an accurate account of these interactions is to show *how* the battle of Naseby was fought. Problems of the 'why' have been discussed above, in chapter 4, 2.

2.2   Structure in explanation

There is a good deal to be said for this view. It is not unlike the situation in science, for here, too, the repetition of 'Why?' has to come to a stop. In science laws of increasing generality may be cited. 'Why did this cup break when I dropped it on a hard floor?' 'Because cups always do break when you drop them on hard floors.' 'But why do all cups break when...?' 'Because of the molecular structure of porcelain together with the mass of the cup and its acceleration in the fall.' And so on, until we come to the most fundamental properties of the universe – gravitation, nuclear forces and so on. In the end, however, the scientist is reduced to answering the last 'Why?' with a shrug of the shoulders and 'Well, the universe just is like this.' He can go no further. So should we expect more of the historian? Is it not enough for her to explain exactly how it happened; and if we still ask 'Why?' to reply, 'Well, that's just how things are.'?

No, in history we are not usually content with such an answer. And this for two reasons. The first is that, in explaining how things *were* on that particular occasion, she has not explained how things *are* in general. Her answer cannot satisfy a scientist unless she can show that the particular (how things were on that occasion) was an instance of the general (how things of that kind always are). And this requires her to cite a law or generalization independently established (like the molecular structure of porcelain in the above example). Now to do this in history is not at all easy, as we shall see when we discuss generalization. Even so, there remains the second reason for our dissatisfaction. History consists largely of the actions of human beings like ourselves. We know from our own experience that most things are done from a motive, preferably a rational one. That is to say, when we ask 'Why' about a human action we expect an answer in terms of motives and intentions. (We'll not bother at the moment about the definition of those terms.) Now this is quite a different sort of explanation from the scientific one that is given in terms of natural laws.[4] Rightly or wrongly, this is the sort of answer that we want in history because it is the one we want in life. Suppose I am black and the police beat me up. It is small satisfaction if my indignant 'Why?' is answered by 'Well, policemen just do these things. The world is like that.' Thus we have worked through our first concern, structure, to our second concern, meaning.

It turns out that we have found another difference between the scientific and historical ways of bringing unseen reality before the mind. History is primarily concerned with human actions (including human thinking) and human actions are fraught with meanings. The historian, therefore, must allow for meanings in his representations of the past. The natural scientist (though not the social scientist) is under no such necessity. In his law-based representations he can (and many believe he should) ignore meanings.

However much the above account has over-simplified the scientist's task, it may yet be true that the historian's is harder. Let us recapitulate. The scientist aims to bring to the mind an understanding of the natural universe – for the moment we leave aside the special problems of the social sciences. This is done by the formulation of laws and generalizations that are (1) mutually consistent, (2) partially interdependent and (3) of maximum explanatory power, so that myriads of particular facts are swallowed up in them. (I am paraphrasing Medawar.) The generalizations are established by the simultaneous practice of observation and experiment on the one hand and the testing of the generalization on the other. This is often done by the creation of models (mathematical, physical, symbolic or merely verbal) and their continuous refinement to bring them ever closer to the reality to be understood.

From this representation two things are normally omitted. One (as we have seen) is any consideration of meaning. The other is time. When scientific laws and generalizations are established they are not labelled with a date. One does not say that Newton's three laws of motion were true only for the seventeenth century or that the structure of the atom in terms of neutrons and protons is valid only on Sundays and bank holidays. Whatever is true in the physical sciences is held to be true at all times and places. This is not the case in all the biological or human sciences, but many workers in those fields would desire a similar universality. In general, however, I think we can say that most scientists would wish to establish laws or generalizations that are not limited by time or space.[5] The contrast with the work of historians, who are almost obsessed with spatio-temporal particulars, is almost too obvious to state.

2.3   The historians' preferred structure: narrative

Now to turn to the harder tasks of historians. Their concern with generalizations is small, though not negligible. Their concern with the exact plotting of events in the three dimensions of space and the one of time is considerable. Equally important are the differences of structure and of meaning. How is the historian to structure her representation of reality in such a way as to allow not only for fixed location in space and time, but also for extension through time (as in the case of the battles above)? In addition to this, how is she to allow for the important component of meaning – a component of many aspects? The short answer lies in one word – narrative. This is not to claim that all history is narrative history, but it is to claim with Paul Ricoeur that 'if history were to break every connection to *our basic competence for following a story* . . . it would . . . cease to be historical' (Ricoeur, 1984–5, p. 91). Telling a story is a very old skill. It long pre-dates history by unnumbered millennia. It may be adapted and improved upon in all sorts of ways, but there is, ultimately and basically, no better way than a narrative for representing the complex tapestry of human action and interaction over periods of time, while still giving full value to all the meanings involved.

After the maps of the geographer or the generalizations (hypotheses or laws) of the natural scientist, a narrative may seem a very queer sort of representation. In comparison with either of these it is noticeably lacking in breadth, dealing as it does with one thing at a time and progressing through its data in a continuous line without any of the range and sweep of the other two kinds of representation. Unlike them, however, it is capable of dealing with questions both of time and of meaning, possibly the two most important constituents of history – as they are of an individual human life. We shall have more to say about narrative in chapter 6. At the moment we will continue our discussion of the methods and procedures of science and history.

2.4   Time in Science

It might be supposed from the last few paragraphs that all sciences are blind to time, but this is not so. For in physics, and especially in cosmology, time does play an essential part. For one thing, there is the theory of special relativity, which claims that time is not an absolute but is always relative to the observer. (This is one corollary of the fact, or axiom, that the speed of light *is* an absolute or constant). Again, time plays a part in theories about the origin and subsequent expansion of the universe. The whole universe, including time itself, is believed to have begun in a 'big bang' some ten to twenty thousand million years ago, and expanded from something infinitely small and infinitely dense to something immeasurably large containing millions of mutually receding galaxies. Another question arises about the origin of the galaxies, for if the original material of the universe had spread outwards smoothly, then there would be no difference between one part of the universe and another. But clearly there is: some parts consist of planets, stars and galaxies; others of almost empty space. Whence the irregularity? One theory is that it is due to a perturbation of gravity itself. Cosmological theories are being recast, or at least modified, almost every year. We need not here try to keep pace with them. The essential point for us is that any account of the universe today has to envisage growth, change and development. We can no longer take as axiomatic that it is static and unchanging. Time itself has a history.

Nor is cosmology the only science that has to take time into account. Since Darwin published in 1859 his theory of evolution to explain the origin of species, biologists have developed and tested his basic theory in the light of further scientific advance. The evolution of living creatures over thousands of millions of years is accepted, though its course has recently been shown to be rather more chancy and contingent than many had supposed (see Gould, 1991, passim). Each stage is restricted in its possibilities by the previous stage. This does not mean that its course is determined, but it does mean that options are limited. A primeval ape forty million years ago was the ancestor of both chimpanzees and humans. Both options were then open. Its descendants thirty-five million years later had no such option. Some were set on the path towards humanity, others on that to chimpdom, while yet others were becoming gorillas or orang-utans, and so on. New possibilities were opened up at every stage, while others were closed off. As the door in front opens, so the one behind shuts. In evolution, as in history, there is little chance of going back. (At least, that seems to be true in natural evolution. Some recent experiments suggest that it is possible to reverse evolution in domesticated animals, so that, for example, forms of primitive, wild oxen can be back-bred from modern cattle. The same phenomenon is seen in a long-neglected garden where the roses have gone back to their wild form.) By and large, however, natural evolution is a cumulative process through time.

It should not be forgotten that most of the material for evolutionary biologists has come in fossil form from the ground. For its dating the science of palaeontology (that is, the study of past forms of life such as ammonites and brontosauruses) depends on a physical science – geology. This, sometimes romantically called 'the story of the rocks', is essential to fixing the relative chronologies of species: which came before which and which were contemporary. Here again, time is a necessary part of these sciences.

The parallels and analogies with human history, especially with various developmental theories of history, are now obvious. Among other things we may recall the attempts made in the late nineteenth and early twentieth centuries to apply Darwin's theory to society – 'Social Darwinism'[7] There remains the question for scientists of whether the laws of nature as found in physics and chemistry are adequate to explain biological and social phenomena, where time plays a central role. Can the latter be regarded simply as states of a system? For many scientists claim that all that is needed for explanation of a phenomenon are two statements: (1) of the relevant laws of nature; and (2) of the initial conditions of the system. Any other state of the system can be deduced from these. For such scientists the laws of nature have the timelessness of mathematics and, indeed, can in principle be expressed mathematically (see Barrow, 1992, p. 188; Davies, 1993, pp. 79–80). On the other hand, there seems to be a contingency about evolution (whether of the rocks – geology, or of life – palaeontology). This suggests (as in the famous cases of the Burgess Shale or the extinction of the dinosaurs) that chance plays a part as well as necessity, that there is randomness as well as regularity in the story. Indeed, the story of evolution is a mixture of chance and necessity – as Monod implied in the title of his great work.[8] But how much should be allotted to chance and how much to necessity is a debatable and possibly unending question.[9]

How important is time in the scientific account of the universe – that is, in the biological as well as the cosmological account? Time is obviously essential to history; but is history different from all sciences in this respect, or only from some of them? And if time should prove inessential to all science, would that mean that it is merely an illusion in history, too?[10]

So much for time in science. It is now time to turn to meaning.

2.5   Meaning

With meaning we leave all the natural sciences, for by common consent they have no place for this concept. Meaning is a concept that has meaning only for humans. Of course, the laws of nature and the problems of cosmology have meaning for the scientists who work on them, but meaning is not one of the phenomena they work on.

Meaning is a slippery concept. It can relate either to significance or to symbolism. In one sense we can say of an event that it is full of meaning (or meaningful) because it is perceived as significant. In another, and most common in philosophy, it connects with words or other symbols. This is the realm of semantics. The basic philosophical problem of meaning is that of how words relate to the world. What is clear for our purposes is that the ability to see the significance of some event or cultural construct (a ritual, for example), and the ability to understand a word, a sentence, a page or a book are all exclusively human attributes.

The fact that meaning belongs to humans alone has led to a great dispute in the methods of the human sciences, especially psychology. In dealing with non-human phenomena – stars and worms and thunder storms – scientists have to rely on observation. Even with an intelligent animal like a dog they cannot ask it what it is feeling or thinking, and what such an experience means to it. They can only observe its behaviour. With human beings, however, the simple and obvious way to find out these things is to ask. They can be questioned, 'How (or why) does that matter to you?' (significance); 'What do you mean by that statement?' or 'What do you understand by that phrase?' (semantics). The characteristic of a sign is that it conveys the idea of something other than itself. But it can only do so to a being capable of making the conscious connection between the sign and what it signifies – cloud and rain, word and reference. Whether or not a few highly intelligent animals or machines are also capable of making such connections, our concern here is with humans.

So far we have been comparing the methods and procedures of history with those of the natural sciences. It is clear that meaning raises a difficult question with the social sciences (or the sciences of man, as the French put it). If these sciences are to be worthy of the name, should they not model themselves on the far more advanced and successful natural sciences? In that case the methods to be adopted are observation and experiment, description, classification, generaliza-tion, and explanation by means of the generalizations (or 'laws') so arrived at. These may be applied to human as well as natural phenomena, as Durkheim demonstrated (see Durkheim, 1964; also Lukes, 1975; Giddens, 1978). But is this adequate? Are we not missing several essential aspects of humanity, especially meaning? If meaning has no place in the natural sciences, does that necessitate its exclusion from the human sciences? To exclude meaning from their study seems like studying fish only when they are out of water – methodologically defective. On the other hand, meaning is often very subjective, varying widely with whoever perceives them. Can an objective science deal with so much subjectivity? Social scientists with a positivist attitude answer, 'No'. Others, like Weber, have said in effect, 'It's difficult, but we have to.' (Meaning will be discussed in more detail in chapter 7.)

3 Historicism

I can see... only one safe rule for the historian: that he should recognize in the development of human destinies the play of the contingent and the unforeseen.

H. A. L. Fisher, *A History of Europe*

3.1   What is 'historicism'?

These words of Fisher (written in 1918) fully support Popper's condemnation of what he called 'historicism'; namely, the search for 'the "rhythms" or the "patterns", the "laws" or the "trends", that underlie the evolution of history' (Popper, 1961, p. 3). Ironically enough, Popper's use of the word 'historicism' is almost unique to him. Most people have used the term to designate almost the exact opposite: the recognition that all social and cultural phenomena are historically determined, and therefore have to be understood in terms of their own age. Each has its location in space and time; such phenomena therefore cannot be subsumed under laws or generalizations that transcend the limits of their age or their society. No one who accepts this kind of historicism can believe in the rhythms, patterns, laws and trends of history that Popper attacked under that very label. Confusing as it is, we must explore this concept a little further, for historicism springs from the most profound question: 'What is the nature of man?' Perhaps by giving some thought to 'What is historicism?', we may become clearer about the big question too. Historicism as an outlook, rather than a theory, began in the eighteenth century, and developed largely as a reaction to the Enlightenment.

3.2   What was the Enlightenment?

We must remind ourselves that the previous century, the seventeenth, had seen both the birth of modern science and the birth of modern historiography. (Both, of course, had originated with the Greeks and had been developed during the Middle Ages.) One characteristic in each justifies this claim for the seventeenth century: namely the realizations that mathematics is the key to the physical world and that the key to historical research is a grasp of the *original* meaning of historical documents (see Stanford, 1986, pp. 131 and 78). But mathematics is only applicable to the world if we ignore many differences. One apple plus one orange does not make two apples or two oranges; it makes two pieces of fruit, a general term. Thus the use of mathematics encourages generalization. Towards the end of that century Isaac Newton crowned his mathematical labours by the invention of the calculus and the discovery of the structure and forces of the solar system. The triumph of a mathematics-based science is proclaimed in the title of his great work – *Philosophiae Naturalis Principia Mathematica* – *The Mathematical Principles of Natural Philosophy* (that is, of science). As a historian of science puts it: 'The essential revolutionary element was that Newton had conceived a working universe wholly independent of the spiritual order' (Singer, 1962, p. 294). Such was increasingly taken to be the truth about Newton's achievement even though he did not think so himself. In the relief at finding truths about the universe that were not taught from the pulpit or subordinate to priestly dominance, it was perhaps not immediately noticed that Newton's version was also independent of meaning. The conflict between science and religion began and raged on for centuries. The more human point about meaning was largely overlooked. The scientific view was welcomed by unbelievers like Bayle and Voltaire, and the Enlightenment began. How strong a role was played by anti-clericalism in this great movement is a matter for debate. Here we simply note the attempt made to extend scientific methods from the physical world to the study of man. Hence the Encyclopaedists, the Physiocrats, the early Scottish sociologists (such as Ferguson and Millar) and the great figures of Montesquieu, Hume and Adam Smith. Man, they believed, was a part of nature and was to be studied as such. Human affairs could be as much a matter for science as celestial motions.[11]

3.3 The dawn of historicism and Vico

Yet questions of meaning and purpose, if now denied to God, were still important to some men – namely, lawyers. The intentions of a testator, the meaning of a document, the truth about a particular action are all central to their work. There is a greater affinity between law and history than between either and science. It is not surprising that the first steps in opposition to the Enlightenment view just outlined came from a lawyer, the Neapolitan, Giambattista Vico (1668–1744). Against the dogmas of rationalism (a belief in 'timeless truths ... clothed in universally intelligible symbols which anyone, at any time, in any circumstances, might be fortunate enough to perceive'), he urged that a true understanding of any knowledge is historical, that is, an understanding of how it arose (see Berlin, 1976, p. 11). As a corollary he insisted upon a clear distinction between the works of God (i.e. nature) and the works of man (i.e. language, society and culture). From this he concluded that we have a better chance of achieving a true grasp of the latter since they were made by men like us (Vico, 1970, pp. 52–3). Most of the subsequent notions of historicism are already to be found in Vico, though of course he is not be held responsible for the uses to which they were sometimes put. Isaiah Berlin summarized the tenets of Vico thus (I paraphrase for brevity):

1 The nature of man is not static, but mobile. It continually changes as his own actions transform him.
2 Those who make can understand in ways that mere observers cannot.
3 History, dealing with the works of man, and hence taking the 'inside' view, is superior to natural science, which must take the inferior 'outside' view.
4 Every society in all its aspects is characterized by its own particular pattern or style; and each successive stage of a society grows from its predecessors by human effort not natural causation. This involves both the concept of a culture and that of historical change.
5 The cultural creations of man (language, law, religion, art and so on) are forms of communication and of self-expression.
6 Works of art must be appreciated not by timeless standards, but in terms of what they meant to their own society. From this come comparative histories of art, religion, law, institutions and so on.

7   Traditional categories of knowledge – logical deducation or sense experi-
    ence – are insufficient. To these must be added a third, the reconstructive
    imagination or empathetic insight. (Berlin, 1976, pp. xvi–xix).

3.4   Historicism: Herder

If an Italian laid the foundations of historicism, its continuation was to be largely
(though not entirely) in German hands. One of its leading tenets, the uniqueness
of the individual, was the theme of a profound reaction to the Enlightenment: this
was most successfully advanced by Johann Gottfried Herder. Although Herder
was born in the year that Vico died (he himself died in 1803), he knew little of his
Neapolitan predecessor (Berlin, 1976, pp. 76n., 147, 193–4). He developed his
ideas in explicit opposition to the Enlightenment (which had hardly begun in
Vico's time). In contrast to the Enlightenment attempt to bring human affairs
under laws and generalizations (in emulation of Newton's triumph), Herder
insisted on the uniqueness of each human being and of every one of his or her
words and actions. As such, they cannot be brought under general principles. In
particular, he emphasized three things: (1) that in order to live as human beings
we need to be members of communities – (we remind ourselves of Aristotle's
saying that a solitary life belongs only to a beast or a god); (2) that creative
activities of all kinds are the individual expressions of a particular person's point
of view, his or her own 'voice' – (we can see how this foreshadows the Romantic
view of art); and, (3) that every civilization, or society with its own culture, must
be judged according to its own values and not by some universal, impersonal
standard (Berlin, 1976, p. xxii). Hence, in Herder's philosophy, the central role
played by nations.

Now the nation is not to be confused with the state. Herder praised the one and
hated the other. He had the cosmopolitan loyalties of a true man of the Enlightenment. 'He is interested, not in nationality, but in cultures... in the total
experience of peoples... personal relationships... ways in which truth, freedom
and happiness are pursued' (Berlin, 1976, pp. 182–3). The essence of nationality,
one might say, was language and literature, the voice of the people that spoke the
experiences of their life together. In this way, as well as being enlarged families
(the root of the word is the Latin *nasci* – to be born), nations are visible organic
entities that constitute the most important part of the world of experience. Thus
they are clearly superior both to mechanical constructions, like houses and
machines, and to national constructions, like reason, law and the state.

3.5   The impact of revolution and law

The subsequent development of historicism was less happy. The sunny hopes of
Enlightenment Europe ended in a full generation (1789–1815) of bloodshed,
revolution and war – just as 1914 was to shatter La Belle Époque. The

consequences for historicism were malign: a cultural view of nationality gave way to one of power – the nation-state; the emphasis on the individual was replaced by an emphasis on the collective – especially the state; and the notion that a community should be judged by its own standards was used to justify international immorality (the breaking of treaties, wars of aggression and so on) in the name of the higher morality of the state.

This latter view was firmly held by a number of distinguished German thinkers, including the philosopher, Johann Gottlieb Fichte (1762–1814), and the historian, Friedrich Meinecke (1862–1954). The former could assert in 1807 that in international relations 'there is neither law nor right except the right of the stronger'. Indeed he made the state (not the Church or the family) 'the moral and religious educator of the German nation' (Iggers, 1983, p. 42). Meinecke wrote the history of the origins of historicism (*Die Entstehung des Historismus* (1936) and devoted several other works of cultural history to the notions of *Realpolitik* – that is, politics without morality. The state, he believed, had its own ethical standards, within which it could do no wrong. 'For nothing can be immoral which derives from the profoundly individual nature of a being' (Iggers, 1983, p. 203). Only in his last years, after the disasters of Nazism and the destruction of the old Germany in the Second World War, did he reconsider his values. He gave up his veneration for power and the state, and returned to the values of high culture as exemplified in perhaps the greatest of all Germans, Goethe (see Meinecke, 1946; also Cannon et al., 1988, pp. 274–6).

Employing the concepts of social systems and sub-systems, we may conclude that the 'higher morality' of the state is an error arising from the confusion of smaller and larger systems. It is true that communities like families or clubs or regiments have many customs of their own – that is, systems of interpersonal behaviour. The norms that govern much of this behaviour are restricted to those communities only. But there are also wider communities, of national or international scope. Their numbers are bound by less exclusive rules and standards. For example, in London I must settle my bills in pounds; not so in Paris or New York. But the moral and legal obligation to pay my debts is equally binding in all cities. Honesty, like telling the truth, is part of a system as wide as the human race; morality does not, like currency, change at frontiers. Neither states nor individuals are exempt from its demands.

3.6   Hegel

The theoretical consequences for historicism in the nineteenth century were scarcely more fortunate. The greatest (in the sense of most influential) philosopher, Hegel, made extensive use of the concept of the *Zeitgeist* – the spirit of the age. 'Whatever happens, every individual is a child of his time; so philosophy too is its own time apprehended in thoughts', he wrote in his *Philosophy of Right* (Hegel, 1967, p. 11). The greatest historian of the time, Leopold von Ranke, placed a similar emphasis on the age: 'Every epoch is immediate to God, and its worth ... rests in its own existence, its own self' (Ranke, 1973, p. 53). Here again we see a well-founded belief about the human individual (the belief, common to the great religions as well as to secular humanism, of the inherent value of every man and woman) being illegitimately transferred to a notional construct – this time the age. In fact, Ranke did hold a similar (surely unjustified) belief about states, which are 'thoughts of God' (Iggers, 1983, p. 82). One can perceive here the contrast with the Enlightenment view. This was based on the belief, expressed by scientists in the late seventeenth century that, by discovering the laws of nature, they were 'thinking the thoughts of God after him'. That God created the reality that we experience is common to all Christian (and Judaic and Islamic) believers, but that that reality is constructed of nation-states is a far cry from the modern view that scientific laws provide the structure of the universe. Adumbrated here is the coming contrast between *Naturwissenschaften* – the natural sciences – and *Geisteswissenschaften* – the human disciplines.

Meanwhile a demon even yet unexorcised rears his head in Hegel's philosophy. This is the menace of relativism – the idea that knowledge is strictly limited by the nation and epoch of the knower. The absolute universal spirit, says Hegel, realizes itself in the consciousness of the nation. 'The individual *exists* within this substance ... No individual can transcend it', he wrote in 1830 in his *Lectures on the Philosophy of World History* (Hegel, 1980, p. 52). But nations, like individuals, grow old and die. 'The individual national spirit is subject to transience. It perishes' (p. 60). It is replaced by another national spirit. 'The fruit again becomes the seed, but the seed of another nation, which it brings to maturity in turn' p. 63). The progress of the world spirit in self-knowledge is accomplished 'in gradual stages rather than at a single step' (p. 6).

3.7   Was Hegel a relativist?

Does all this imply that Hegel was a relativist? The answer, as so often, depends on what we understand by the term. There is partial, or epistemological, relativism; there is also full, or metaphysical, relativism. First, partial relativism: it is arguable that we all need some conceptual framework in order to think and talk about reality. It is also fairly obvious that human ideas must at least sometimes be inadequate to reality. After all, they vary from time to time and place to place. Certainly there have been many conceptual frameworks for the interpretation of reality, and almost certainly no one of them is fully adequate to an understanding of reality. Yet these facts (if facts they are) do not rule out a steady growth of knowledge – a growth that at least in science and technology seems manifest over the course of history. That much of our knowledge and understanding is relative to where we happen to be living in history seems fairly uncontroversial. Much, for example, was hidden until both the telescope and the microscope were invented in the seventeenth century. The (fairly obvious) conclusion was drawn by Karl Popper:

> What we should do, I suggest, is to give up the idea of ultimate sources of knowledge, and admit that all knowledge is human; that it is mixed with our errors, our prejudices, our dreams, and our hopes; that all we can do is to grope for truth even though it be beyond our reach. (Popper, 1969, p. 30)

Clearly Hegel was a relativist in this partial or epistemological sense.

But what of the full or metaphysical sense of the term? A full relativism denies that there is a reality independent of our understanding or interpretation. This involves metaphysical beliefs about the nature of being; it implies some form' of idealist philosophy. This does not ask whether our ideas are adequate to an independent reality; it asserts that ideas *are* reality. Now whether Hegel was also a full relativist (in the sense just defined) is more debatable, but it seems probable that he was. 'The spirit in history ... is the nation in general ... the nations are the concepts which the spirit has formed of itself' (Hegel, 1980, p. 51). 'The spirit's own consciousness must realise itself in the world ... in ... the consciousness of the nation ... No individual can transcend it' (Popper, 1969, p. 52).

Two conclusions follow: one is that, if the individual's knowledge is confined to his nation and is limited by its spirit which he cannot transcend, what becomes of that international community of scholars which grew up in eleventh- and twelfth-century Europe, which brought to birth modern science in the seventeenth, provided the international and cosmopolitan ideals of the eighteenth, and is quite indispensable to the science of the twentieth century? Surely here the national spirit is transcended? One might, on these grounds, reject Hegel's idea.

But what of the second conclusion? If all thought advances step by step, so that (by a dialectical process) each idea is annihilated by its opposite to be replaced by a synthesis of the two, then all our knowledge is part ignorance, all truths are partly false. For Hegel, divine revelation (the basis of the most important knowledge from 1700 BC to about AD 1700) is only a 'moment' in human thought – true, but not wholly true, nor the whole truth.

Scientists might not have minded this. But their own position is equally attacked. No longer can one believe, as did the Greek and all subsequent scientists, that their discoveries related to the real world.[12] 'This is what our science is *about*: the discovery of explanations built into the logical structure of nature', writes a contemporary physicist, Steven Weinberg (Weinberg, 1993, p. 6). Hegel's philosophy implies that we have only a limited grasp of reality; so far, he is a partial relativist. But he also believes that our inadequate ideas are themselves part of reality – that is, part of the growing self-realization of Spirit. Does this not make him a full, metaphysical relativist? Worse still, without his faith in progress there is no guarantee that the later ideas *will* be better; they may be more inadequate. The spectre of relativism never ceases to haunt the domain of historicism.

3.8 Must historicism imply relativism?

Let us step back for a moment and see where we have come to. The great achievements of seventeenth-century science culminated in Newton. A combination of empirical experiment and observation with the rational structure of advanced mathematics had brought intoxicating success. Indeed, this is still the essential scientific approach. The intoxication had led men of the Enlightenment to believe that a similar method (science = empirical fact + rational thinking) could be applied to human affairs. This optimism had been opposed by Vico, Herder, Hamann and others on the grounds that there is an essential difference between man and nature, such that the methods and approaches suitable for one are quite inappropriate for the other. Both the use of mathematics and the search for laws underlying phenomena imply an erasing of differences, an assumption that many things are alike; entities become units. Further, though this was more implied than explicit in their criticisms, such laws can take no account of meanings. Since our different individualities and our meanings (both of word and action) are the most important things about us, the scientific approach, they argued, is manifestly wrong. Unfortunately, many went further; they denounced not only scientific method but reason itself. Hegel, of course, was not of these, but Hamann was, to whom Isaiah Berlin largely attributed the origin of modern irrationalism (Berlin 1993). Hamann cannot be blamed for all the follies of the Romantic Movement of the nineteenth century, either in art or in political philosophy and historiography, but most of their ideas were consistent with his.[13]

Let us return to more responsible thinkers. The very considerable intellectual achievements of the nineteenth century highlighted the problem. The irrational side of human nature has been celebrated not only by artists of the Romantic school, by poets like Shelley or Baudelaire, by novelists like Turgenev and Dostoevsky, but by a figure of even greater impact today – Friedrich Nietzsche. On the other hand, the Enlightenment ideal of applying science to human affairs had been carried much further by positivists (Comte), economists, (Ricardo), utilitarian philosophers (the Mills) and even historians (Buckle, Taine and Lecky). In passing we may note the heroic figure of Sigmund Freud who, at least initially, attempted to bridge the gap with scientific and rational accounts of highly irrational behaviour.

History flourished in the nineteenth century, but philosophy of history was at a low ebb. After Hegel and Marx no great over-arching structures held the field. The vision of history as one great meaningful process gave way to concern with the logic and epistemology of historical thinking (see Iggers, 1983, p. 125). In face of the challenge of scientific method as now embodied in positivist thinking, how could history and the social sciences be justified? Either historians must turn history into a positivistic science (as Buckle attempted), or they must find an intellectually respectable foundation for their over-riding concerns – that is, concern with meanings, with the individual, and with those moral, aesthetic and spiritual values that are so important in life and yet have no place in positivism. Among those who faced up to the challenge in various ways were Rickert, Windelband, Dilthey, Weber, Meinecke and Troeltsch. From the point of view of our study of historicism, the most interesting of these is Wilhelm Dilthey (1833–1911).

3.9   Wilhelm Dilthey

'Now we must ask if it is possible to study individual human beings and particular forms of human existence scientifically and how this can be done.' This was how Dilthey saw the problem towards the end of his working life in 1896 (Dilthey 1976, p. 247). He makes the distinction between the *Naturwissenschaften* and *Geisteswissenschaften* which was explained above. The difference of subject matter (nature and mind) entails different approaches. The problem for the latter was how to take account of individuals, meanings and values. These are the essential subject matter of human studies, but can find no place in the well-established method of the natural sciences. Physics, for example, can tell you how fast a man falls off a cliff, but not whether he is a good or a bad man. Yet in a book or a film it matters very much whether he is hero or villain. Unfortunately (as the scientist is quick to point out) there may be two opinions about the moral status, but only one about the rate of fall. Thus the natural sciences seem to have attained an objectivity and exactitude that is quite absent from history or the other human studies. How can these studies find a basis for knowledge as firm as that of the natural sciences?

Dilthey's answer was 'Interpretation'. In human studies we are dealing with human beings like ourselves. Indeed, we know ourselves largely in relation to others. As he said, understanding is 'the re-discovery of the I in the Thou' (Dilthey, 1976, p. 15). It is in language that we best express ourselves, he argues, 'The art of understanding therefore centres on the *interpretation of written records of human existence*.' There is, in fact, an art of interpretation, which has developed its own rules, methods and standards; it is hermeneutics, 'which is *the methodology of the interpretation of written records*' (p. 249). Dilthey took this to be the appropriate method for historical reality, as we shall see in chapter 7, 2, where we say more about hermeneutics and Dilthey.

History as it comes to us in the present seems to consist of memories, relics, monuments, documents, books. Memories excepted, these are objects; their existence is as objective as the natural objects of science. But they are solid lumps of lifeless matter. It is only when we bring our own interpretative understanding to them that they reveal their meanings and their values; then history comes alive. Similarly, my friend is not so much the mass of flesh, blood and bones that stands before me as the living person constituted by our friendship and by countless other human relationships. In one sense we can say, 'I am because you are.' The study of history, the bringing of our human understanding to the past, transforms these solid lumps, the dead weight of the past, into a flowing, living reality. As the past ceases to be a mere object and becomes part of experience, so it loses something of its objectivity. But this is inevitable and need not be a subject of reproach by philosophers of science. So do you and I, in the changing daily intercourse of our lives, lack complete objectivity. In a real sense, human beings living in a community are parts of each other; subjects and objects blend.

This I take to be the the the substance of Dilthey's argument. But does historicism so understood avoid the charge of relativism? Unfortunately it came, perhaps, too late in life for him completely to work out an answer. Unfortunately, too, he seems towards the end to have had doubts. On his seventieth birthday he reviewed his life work:

> The finitude of every historical phenomenon... hence the relativity of every sort of human conception about the connectedness of things, is the last word of the historical world view. All flows in process; nothing remains stable... where are the means for overcoming the anarchy of convictions which threatens to break in on us? (quoted in Iggers, 1983, pp. 143–4)

Surely he was needlessly worried about the relativity of conceptions. As we saw above, all knowledge needs to be articulated in some conceptual framework. Moreover, epistemological relativism does not imply metaphysical relativism.

3.10   Conclusions on historicism

Let us put this into perspective. Compare his doubts over human conceptions of the connectedness of things with a modern physicist's faith. 'Our present theories are only of limited validity, still tentative and incomplete. But behind them now and then we catch glimpses of a final theory, one that would be of unlimited validity and entirely satisfying in its completeness and consistency' (Weinberg, 1993, p. 3). Stephen Hawking concurs: 'I think that there is a good chance that the study of the early universe and the requirements of mathematical consistency will lead us to a complete unified theory within the lifetime of some of us who are around today' (Hawking, 1990, p. 167). Dilthey's phrase, 'All flows in process', takes us straight back to Heraclitus. And his fears of an 'anarchy of convictions' have been only too well justified in the subsequent century. Less than twenty years later the words of an Irish poet echo Dilthey:

> Things fall apart; the centre cannot hold;
> Mere anarchy is loosed upon the world,
> The blood-dimmed tide is loosed, and everywhere
> The ceremony of innocence is drowned;

> The best lack all conviction, while the worst
> Are full of passionate intensity.
> (from W. B. Yeats, 'The Second Coming')

Historicism rests on the historicity of human life – the fact that all we do must take place within the limits of time and humanity, with all the restrictions of knowledge that that implies. Are we, then, condemned to uncertainty? Are all the arguments of historicism from Vico to Dilthey quite invalidated by the taint of relativism? Are there no sound epistemological foundations for history? Must we after all rely on the scientists for our understanding of the world, both present and past?

The debate did not cease with Dilthey, but it has lost its ardour and many of the participants have just walked away. The late twentieth-century position is that, on the one hand, we have the positivistic (if not positivist) approach to history and the human sciences of people like Popper, Hempel and Ernest Nagel. On the other are the historicist philosophies of Croce and of Collingwood. Among philosophers perhaps only Heidegger is distinguished by a serious concern with historicity, and his impact is much diminished by both obscurity of style and the taint of Nazi sympathies. The present position is that the historicists are largely ignored, the scientists continue on their (only slightly less) triumphant way, and the historians keep their heads down, pursuing their studies with little regard for epistemology or any other philosophical concerns. The word 'historicism' is now rarely heard, except in the 'New Historicism', a largely literary movement (see chapter 9, 2). On the other hand, Dilthey's century-old suggestion (that the key to the problem is interpretation) has taken new life. 'Hermeneutics' is important not only to much modern German philosophy (Heidegger, Gadamer, Habermas), but also to serious historiographical conflict in the notorious *Historikerstreit* of the 1980s (see chapter 1, 4). Sadly, both the common man or woman and the philosopher seem to have lost sight of the underlying questions: 'What sort of creature is man? What is the nature of human existence?' To claim to have the answer to these would be overwhelming arrogance; to ignore them may be both cowardly and stupid. Surely the questions need to be brought into sharper focus.

Appendix for clarification

It may help to add a brief summary of the main points of Historicism:

1   the contrast of nature and history;
2   the uniqueness and incomparability of historical phenomena;
3   the importance of volition (or will) and of intention;
4   men, groups, institutions and, above all, nations seen as concrete centres of identity and stability;

5   the existence within these of inner forces and principles of development;
6   the vital unity of each age or epoch;
7   the belief that criteria of judgement are local and temporal rather than universal;
8   the conclusion that the methods and logic of the historian herself are likewise time-bound;
9   the need for understanding and insight rather than reasoning;
10 the insistence that all ranks and aspects of a society must be objects of study.

Note: These are typical historicist beliefs. It must not be assumed that every historicist holds all of them (taken from Stanford, 1994, p. 256).

Notes

1 The distinction is by no means new. It was made in the late nineteenth century by Windelband and Rickert. See, for example, MacRae (1974, pp. 63–4); also Iggers (1983, pp. 147–59), Hughes (1974, pp. 189–91).
2 Thucydides, *Peloponnesian War* (1954), I, 22, p. 24.
3 Much, of course, depends on how detailed a repetition we are looking for. For further discussion see Trompf (1979), passim and Stanford (1994, pp. 26–7).
4 For a fuller discussion of explanation, see chapter 3.
5 A modern physicist claims that the laws of nature are universal, absolute, eternal and omnipotent. See Paul Davies (1993, pp. 82–3).
6 For more on structure in history, see Munz (1977); Stanford (1986); Lloyd (1993).
7 See H. S. Hughes (1974, pp. 38–9); Philip Appleman 1970; Michael Ruse (1979 and 1986). A crude form of social Darwinism supplied many of the themes of Nazism.
8 Jacques Monod, *Le hasard et la nécessité* (1970), Paris. ET *Chance and Necessity* (1972).
9 In addition to Monod, see also Gould (1991); Mayr (1993); and Paul Davies (1995).
10 For further discussion, see Hawking (1990, pp. 166–9); Barrow (1992, pp. 193–7, 199–201); Davies (1993, pp. 152–60); also Le Poidevin and MacBeath (eds) (1993).
11 For another reaction to the Enlightenment, see Postmodernism in chapter 9.
12 Both Greeks and moderns believed this, though they disagreed about the definition of 'real'.
13 See Iggers (1983). For irrationalism, see Berlin (1979) and (1993); N. Cohn (1957); Jäckel (1981); J. P. Stern (1975).

Suggested Reading

Science

For a modern attempt at a scientific approach to history, the best example is the 'Annales' school of French historians. For this see Braudel (1980), Stoianovich (1976), Iggers (1975), Hunt (1986) and Clark in Skinner (1990). Another attempt to combine history and science can be found in Popper (1962), chapter 25.

Structure

For this see Stanford (1990, chapter 1, and Lloyd (1993). Perhaps also Giddens (1984).

Time

For this see Whitrow (1972) and (1980), Wilcox (1987) and Le Poidevin and MacBeath (1993).

Historicism

For this see Berlin (1980), Iggers (1983) and Meinecke (1972).

6

Mind

1 Mind and the Historian

1.1 The ability to use symbols

The previous chapter began with the assertion that it is the function of history (like science and art) to bring certain objects before the mind. What can this mean? A modern philosopher provides a clue. Anthony Kenny says that 'in its primary sense the mind is the capacity to acquire intellectual abilities . . . that is to say, abilities for intellectual activities'. Such intellectual activities, he holds, 'involve the creation and utilization of symbols' – as in mathematics, philosophy, portrait painting and poetry (Kenny, 1992, p. 123). It is a question whether intellectual activities *must* involve symbols, but certainly the most important activity of the intellect is the use of language. This involves concepts and conceptual thinking. Symbols are the means of doing so. Then let us consider symbols. For our knowledge of history is symbolic knowledge in two senses: (1) the symbols of the past (documents, seals, inscriptions and so on) have to be interpreted; (2) the present form of that knowledge (lectures, books, articles and so on) is couched in words. Largely, it is symbols that bring before the mind objects that are not present to the senses.

A great part (though by no means all) of our knowledge of the past rests on the interpretation of symbols. These symbols are mostly words and numbers contained in historical documents or texts, but other kinds are also important – e.g. armorial bearings, the crosses, crucifixes, crescents or candlesticks of the great religions, and all the motifs of medieval and Renaissance art (see Panofsky, 1970; Haskell, 1993, passim). We shall have more to say about these later. Here it is enough to notice that two kinds of meaning have normally to be interpreted. The first is the conventional meaning of a symbol – both the letters 'K I N G' and a crown are accepted as standing for a monarch. Conventions vary and change, however. The word 'king' does not mean exactly what it did in the sixteenth century, nor do armorial bearings have the same meaning that they did in the Middle Ages. Therefore, when we interpret a symbol we must take care that we attribute the meaning that it had at the time and place of usage. The second kind of meaning to be interpreted is the intention or purpose of the individual who used it on the particular occasion that produced the text or document or painting or map or monument or decoration. Here the question is not 'What did it mean?', but 'What did he (or she) mean by it?' There is more to be said later about symbols; here we will content ourselves with noting that both their use and their interpretation are definitely intellectual activities and so involve the mind.

We must also remember that our knowledge of the past does not rest exclusively on symbols. Human artefacts of all kinds, from lasers to flint tools, remain as evidence of their makers and users. So do larger artefacts – houses, castles, ships, bridges, villages and cities. So do human remains – especially teeth and bones. All these offer evidence of the past to be carefully interpreted by technologists, archaeologists, anthropologists, and historians. Surely such interpretations, though they are not of symbols, count as intellectual activities, for they involve language and concepts? Certainly they are exercises of the mind.

It becomes clear, then, that studying the many kinds of human activities employs the mind several times over. The persons who build the houses, paint the pictures or write the letters exhibit mental capacities in doing so. The historians, archaeologists, iconographers and other scholars who interpret the evidence of these earlier activities have to use *their* minds to understand the mental activities of the historical agents. Thus the Colosseum at Rome, for example, employed the Romans' minds and, in a different way, employs ours. The historian has to articulate this knowledge in linguistic form – lectures, essays, books. Finally the reader or student has to use his mind to grasp the meaning of her linguistic symbols (words) so that he can understand certain past events.

1.2   Capacity and exercise

Questions about the nature of mind are among the perennial (and possibly insoluble) problems of philosophy.[1] Fortunately these questions are of little significance to the philosophy of history. Here it is the function, rather than the nature, of the mind that concerns us. The important thing is to realize that for our purposes the mind can be defined as what people do and what they *can* do (or have the capacity to do.) We must distinguish a capacity from its exercise. Henry VIII had two good servants, Thomas Cromwell and Thomas Cranmer. He had the capacity (in this case, both mental and political) to condemn them to death. He exercised that in the case of Cromwell, not (to many people's surprise) in the case of Cranmer – who, in the end, held his dying hand. Similarly a man may have the intellectual ability to speak French, but he exercises it only on certain occasions. It is important when making historical judgements to know what the historical agents might have done (because they had the ability or capacity), but did not. Our judgements about why a person, P, did not do something, X, that seems to us the proper or probable thing to have done on a particular occasion partly depends on whether P had the ability to do X but refrained, or whether he simply was unable to do X. Again, if the mind is 'the capacity to acquire intellectual abilities', this does not apply equally to everyone. I doubt whether my mind includes the capacity to acquire the ability to compose an opera or do higher mathematics. Thus in history we may think it important to know what abilities P had the capacity to acquire, as well as to know what abilities he actually had acquired at a certain date.

1.3 Summary

I will conclude this section by listing the ways in which the mind comes into the philosophy of history. They are as follows:

(1) Both philosophy and history, like science, are largely intellectual activities, making considerable use of symbols and concepts. They are, in fact, more intellectual and less empirical than technology or common sense. Probably the practice of history is in many ways becoming closer to science and philosophy and less like everyday common sense. This may not be altogether desirable.

(2) Mind is very much the concern of philosophy. Reason, intellect, brain, consciousness, person and subject – also bulk large in contemporary philosophical thinking. So do the various problems of the self and of morality, of knowing and doing what is meaningful and what is right. These debates cannot but be relevant (in varying degrees) to the historian's task of establishing, understanding and evaluating the actions of people in the past.

(3) History is seen more and more nowadays as an activity of interpretation, of grasping meanings – not only the meanings of documents and texts, but also of human actions, both individual and collective. Nor can it fail to reflect the relevance of at least some of the past for our present – hence the apposite question 'What does this mean for us?' (This may not be the primary question in history, but without it much less history would be researched, written or read.)

(4) Historians tend to be more and more interested in the thinking as well as the doing of historical agents. Intellectual history, the histories of 'mentalités', of art, of politics, literature, theology or of philosophy itself are all seen as part of the history of ideas. To these should be explicitly added, as one historian believes, the history of meanings (see Bouwsma in Rabb and Rotberg, 1982). This is not to support the outdated mind–matter dichotomy. The intelligence of Napoleon, for example, is seen in the way he fought battles as much as in the composition of a code of laws. Such considerations of this kind make it difficult for historians of ideas to define their subject matter. Where do we draw the line between histories of mathematics, of witchcraft, of fashions, of cooking? All these are activities of the mind, involving more or less of physical activity. If the modern mathematician

uses more technology (computers and so on), than the chef, does this make his activity less intellectual, or less 'mental', than the latter's work in the kitchen?

(5) The historian's business is with relics – that is, with things left behind by former ages. These constitute her evidence, almost her only evidence, for the past. She tries to interpret this evidence to establish just what someone (perhaps a painter or a writer or a musician or a builder) was doing. No matter what he was doing, it was an exercise of his mind, expressed in the movements of eye and hand as in the cogitations of the brain. Her activity is also mental as she works her way through the physical relics to the mind (*not* just the brain) that created the works many years or centuries before. Minds thus come to comprehend minds, although separated by centuries.[2] Of course, in these activities both brains and other parts of the body are employed, but the parts of anatomy involved are usually irrelevant (though relevant in some cases like the affections of Monet's eyes or Renoir's arthritic hands). It is better to envisage the activities of both painter and scholar as actions of the whole person. Thus the historian tries to penetrate through the centuries to the minds of generals, criminals, politicians and other men of action in the same way as to the minds of 'thinkers', like poets or philosophers. In all cases, minds are constituted by capacities and abilities, and abilities are exercised in what people do. The mind is chiefly but not entirely the person in action. All this suggests that there may be something in Collingwood's well-known dictum that 'the historian must re-enact the past in his own mind' (Collingwood, 1961, p. 282). This is because he believed that 'all history is the history of thought' (p. 215). Perhaps he should have said that all history is the history of mind. This would have been rather more plausible, as we can now see. But would not any re-enactment involve the imagination? To this topic we must now turn.

2   Imagination and Understanding

If you do not expect the unexpected, you will not find it; for it is hard to be sought out, and difficult to compass.

Heraclitus, Fragments

There is an astonishing imagination even in the science of mathematics... There was far more imagination in the head of Archimedes than in that of Homer.

Voltaire, *Dictionnaire Philosophique*

2.1   Free-ranging thoughts

Great works of art are, it is generally acknowledged, great feats of the imagination. Theseus puts the common view in *A Midsummer Night's Dream*:

And as imagination bodies forth
The forms of things unknown, the poet's pen
Turns them to shapes, and gives to airy nothing
A local habitation, and a name.

Perception is reliable, but can be banal. Imagination is unrestricted by reality; it can bring before the mind mermaids and unicorns and all the wonders of the Arabian Nights. How boring would human life have been down the ages without our story-tellers and artists and poets! But what has their creative faculty to do with the pursuit of truth and accuracy in science and history?

The answer is suggested in the words of Heraclitus (quoted above). The great advances in science were totally unexpected. The Sun does *not* go round the Earth (Copernicus); planetary orbits are *not* circular (Kepler); the blood does *not* flow back and forth (Harvey); earthly and celestial motions are *not* different (Newton); species are *not* fixed (Darwin); time is *not* an absolute (Einstein); the present position and velocity of a particle *cannot* be separately measured – hence the future state of the universe *cannot* be exactly predicted (Heisenberg); biological evolution did *not* have to lead to man – it is highly contingent (Gould) (see also Wolpert, 1993, pp. 54–5; Gould, 1991, chapter 5). These are milestones in the history of science precisely because the new ideas were *not* variations on the old; they were previously almost unthinkable. In Kuhn's words, they were not developments in 'normal science'; they were 'paradigm shifts' (see Kuhn, 1970, passim). From time to time we have not just new ideas, but new frameworks of thought. These may be described as revolutionary. Nevertheless we always have to start with some sort of theory, even if the unexpected shows it to be wrong (see, for example, Popper, 1972, pp. 258–9).

2.2   Focused thought

Now history in many of its practitioners has always been as Fisher saw it – the realm of 'the contingent and the unforeseen'. As I remarked above, there is a tendency among modern historians, partly under pressure from the social sciences, to make history more theoretical. (This we saw in chapter 1.) There are many advantages for the historian in doing so, which have been pointed out by Lawrence Stone. He urged historians to follow social scientists in being more critical, more explicit about models and assumptions, and more precise; to define their terms more carefully; to use samples, comparisons and the definition of problems; to use quantitative methods wherever possible; and to formulate hypotheses to be tested against the evidence (Stone 1987, pp. 17–19). All excellent advice. He did not point out the disadvantages, however. The more attention the historian pays to his carefully chosen models, hypotheses, assumptions, theories, the less likely is he to spot the unexpected. The same consideration applies to the scientist, whether of the natural or the social variety. There seem to be only two possible remedies. One is trusting to luck. Many people believe that this lies at the basis of scientific advance, as in the well-known story of Fleming's discovery of penicillin. (*Can* this have been pure luck?) However, practising scientists are less ready to agree, but rather to stress that 'scientific research is based not on chance but on highly focused thoughts' (Wolpert, 1993, p. 79). The same goes for history.

2.3 Negative capability

The other possible remedy is imagination – expecting, or at least considering, the unexpected. Let us take a closer look at this word. The basic definition of 'imagination' in the *Shorter Oxford English Dictionary* is 'forming a mental concept of what is not actually present to the senses'. This is done in dreaming and in remembering, but these are not what we are after here. What we need is more like the creative imagination of the poet or story-teller of Theseus's speech. We can imagine what is not so – like at this moment sitting under the palms on an island in the South Seas. We can also imagine what could not be so, like climbing a golden mountain or flying like a bird. These are more properly described as fantasies. 'What has science to do with such rubbish?' you snort indignantly. Well, recall that any pre-Copernican scientist would have rated the chances of realizing fantasies as far greater than the truth of the heliocentric theory. And try stretching your intellectual imagination by answering Einstein's question: 'What would the world look like if I rode on a beam of light?'

What we need here is a quality that, perhaps surprisingly, severely tests our intellectual powers. It is what Keats called 'negative capability' – the ability simultaneously to hold a belief in the mind and also hold the possibility that it is or may be false.[3] At the very least, this is a kind of pretending; it is 'a more sophisticated operation than ingenuous thinking'. As Ryle says, 'The concept of make-believe is of a higher order than that of belief' (Ryle, 1963, pp. 249, 250). Three hundred and forty-five years ago, to the very day that I write this, Oliver Cromwell addressed the Commissioners of the Kirk of Scotland: 'I beseech you, in the bowels of Christ, think it possible you may be mistaken.' (They did not consider it, and Cromwell's victory at Dunbar a month later enforced his point.) Their inability marked no lack of intelligence; the more powerful a man's mind the more tenacious can be his hold on his beliefs. Yet even the greatest scholar, the most indefatigable researcher, must always think it possible he may be mistaken – and this not where he is already doubtful but in the places where he is most certain. The great breakthroughs are rare because, as a modern scientific writer points out, 'it is very, very hard to think of revolutionary ideas'[4] Of course, the ideas must not be merely revolutionary; they must also fit the facts better and possess greater explanatory power than their predecessors. Perhaps the main reason why it is so hard to think of revolutionary ideas is the scholar's very competence with the old ones. Gould stresses 'the most important message taught by the history of science: the subtle and inevitable hold that theory exerts upon data and observation... The greatest impediment to scientific innovation', he says, 'is usually a conceptual lock, not a factual lack' (Gould, 1991, p. 276). This puts it neatly.

2.4 Focus

We spoke above of the necessity for 'highly focused thoughts'. These are just the problem. The steady concentration of well-informed scholars of high intelligence sometimes produces a simultaneous solution: the coincidences of Leibniz and Newton over the calculus or Darwin and Wallace over the evolution of species are well-known examples. This suggests the value of the highly focused thoughts. At the same time, the fact that many good brains can work on a problem for years without seeing what later appears, with hindsight, to be the obvious solution suggests that there can be a danger in too close a focus.

Focus comes up in particular relation to history. It is sometimes remarked that a true historian is to be distinguished not so much by what he knows to be the case, as what he knows cannot be the case. He can spot an anachronism. For example, there is no evidence (literary, pictorial or archaeological) that the Roman cavalry had either stirrups or horse shoes. The Normans at the Battle of Hastings had both. Almost any good historian could therefore tell you that they must both have been introduced into the West between the fifth and eleventh centuries. Scholars who have researched the topic have narrowed the dates down to the early eighth century (stirrups) and the late ninth century (shoes). Nobody knows the exact dates. Much historical research consists of narrowing down the possibilities rather than identifying precise places, dates or persons. The scholar, in history as in science, is supposed to know where to draw the line beyond or outside which the answer is not to be sought. For that would be impossible, we say, and fantastic to suppose it. Dragons and mermaids and sea-serpents are out! Yet how often in the history of thought have we had to adjust our minds to notions quite as unthinkable? Widen the focus too far and it becomes fuzzy and we lose the benefits of previous scholarship. Narrow it too closely and we miss the essential point which lies just outside it.

Imagination, we conclude, must be allowed to roam freely, like a pig seeking truffles. Yet the pig must be on a leash, which in this case is the whole sum of previous scholarship. How long a leash shall we allow the pig? Too short, and we miss the truffles; too long and we risk losing both pig and truffles, leaving us only with the leash (the existing state of knowledge.) Is it any wonder that the great breakthroughs are so rare?

2.5 Understanding

Imagination also has an important part to play in one of the key functions of history – understanding. How can this be? For imagination, as we have seen, is 'forming a mental concept of what is not actually present to the senses'. One of the commonest occasions of understanding is functional. When we are confronted with a new piece of apparatus, we examine its parts, perhaps reading the handbook, and then exclaim, 'Now I understand how it works!' Similarly, when our car breaks down, we examine its parts until we understand why it didn't work. Our understanding flows from making things present to our senses – just the opposite of the definition of imagination. However, this not always so. There is the story of Thomas Hobbes, the seventeenth-century philosopher, that in a gentleman's library, he came upon a book of Euclid open at the 47th proposition. 'By God', said he, 'this is impossible!' So he read the proof, which directed him back to another proposition, and so on, right back to the axioms. Thus he was convinced. 'This made him in love with Geometry', adds Aubrey, who tells the tale (Aubrey, 1962, p. 230). Understanding mathematics like this is an analytical process, often aided by, but not dependent upon, figures present to the senses. Even mending the car is primarily an intellectual as well as a physical exercise.

Another kind of understanding altogether is involved in following a story. It is amazing at how early an age (two or three years) a child can both follow quite an intricate story and at the same time be perfectly clear that it is fiction, not truth. Here, in contrast to the other instances, we have an example of understanding something that is far from present to the senses. (Does this have any bearing upon the old adage, *Nihil in intellectu nisi prius in sensu* – There is nothing in the mind that was not first in the senses'?) This early ability of children illustrates a fictive power that is also illustrated in the 'make-believe' of children's games – 'mummies and daddies' or 'cowboys and Indians'. If the understanding of the natural sciences is like our examples of understanding machinery and mathematics, then understanding in history and the social sciences is like the understanding of 'Goldilocks and the Three Bears' or 'Snow White and the Seven Dwarfs'. Indeed, one philosopher has insisted that 'historical understanding is the exercise of the capacity to follow a story', while another, as we have already remarked, thinks that 'If history were to break every connection to *our basic competence for following a story* ... it would ... cease to be historical' (Gallie, 1964, p. 105; Ricoeur, 1984, p. 91; quoted above, chapter 5, 2.3).

2.6 Intentional flow

If we can describe the first kind of understanding (of machinery and mathematics) as analytical, how are we to describe the second? As narrative perhaps. Where, then, does it leave the social sciences, whose understanding I have compared to that of following a story? The answer, I think, is that the social sciences blend something of each type of understanding (analytical and narrative), though in varying proportions. What distinguishes the narrative type is not so much the grasp of a whole plot as following the actions and reactions, decisions and responses, of the characters in the story. The subjects of children's stories –

witches, fairies, talking animals, extra-terrestrials – may be quite outside their experience. This does not matter, so long as these exotic creations behave in a more or less predictable and accustomed way. If they do not, the intelligent child will interrupt the story-teller for clarification: 'Why did she do that?' Or sometimes will interrupt for confirmation: 'He climbed the tree because he wanted to see where his house was, didn't he?' A small child's comprehension of motives, reasons for acting, the constraint of circumstances, typical reactions and responses can show a very firm grasp of what we might call the 'intentional flow' of human actions and interactions. This grasp is acquired so early that one almost wonders whether there may not be an innate proclivity for it, similar to Noam Chomsky's theory of an innate universal grammar. Children have the ability to imagine themselves (or the story characters) in situations far from anything they could possibly have experienced, and yet they have a clear idea of what would be rational action in those often improbable circumstances. This can easily be tested by stopping the narrative and asking, 'What do you think she decided to do then?'

Now it is actions like these (though often at a more sophisticated level) that form most of the material of the social sciences. An individual action may be the selling of shares in a 'bull' market, the decision to marry, or the laying of a wager on a cock fight, but to the actor and his friends each seems the natural and proper thing to do in the circumstances. To understand it needs little more than the generalized knowledge of intentional human actions that a child brings to the stories. The social scientist then comes along and, imitating the procedures of the natural sciences, formulates hypotheses and theories on the basis of a number of similar observed actions. This gives the appearance of a law-based (or at least rule-based) field of study. Often, however, there is no law or rule about it. There is simply the fact that in similar circumstances people tend to act (quite sensibly) in similar ways. As Weber said of sociological generalizations customarily designated as laws: 'These are in fact typical probabilities confirmed by observation to the effect that under certain given conditions an expected course of social action will occur, which is understandable in terms of the typical motives and typical subjective intentions of the actors' (Weber, 1964, pp. 107–8). Of course I am not suggesting that that is all there is to the social sciences; they have developed much further. All I am doing is to point out that any science that has human beings for its subject matter must have as its basis the same sort of imaginative but rational understanding of sensible behaviour that a child brings to following a story. At this point it may well be objected that not all actions are rational; they fall short of rationality in various ways. This is true. Yet it does not alter the basic fact of their comprehensibility. Even children understand that people often do foolish things, make mistakes or are led into error. They also understand those apparently pointless actions by which we express our emotions – throwing our hats in the air with joy or tearing our hair or clothes with grief, for example. Some sociologists find such actions hard to analyse and categorize, but they afford little problem to the child listening to a story (Rex, 1970, pp. 84–5).

2.7 Empathy

It is sometimes claimed that empathy is a necessary attribute of the student of history. This is not the same as 'sympathy', which implies 'feeling with' another person – sharing his griefs and hopes. To be sure this is often present in the student (whether researcher or casual reader), and when it is, then history achieves one of its main aims – that of bringing us closer to the past. But nobody supposes it necessary. 'Empathy', however, is 'the power of projecting one's personality into, and so fully understanding, the object of contemplation.'[5] To be sure, one may not sympathize with Charles I's foolhardy attempt personally to arrest the Five Members in the House of Commons on 4 January 1642, but when he found his 'birds flown' one knows how he felt. We can empathize in many cases (though not in all), for there are diverse personality traits in each one of us. (Can we not declare with Walt Whitman, 'I am a multitude'?). Sometimes, however, we are brought up short by an action, perhaps of great heroism, of great sanctity, or of horrifying cruelty – the history of Nazi Germany yields examples of all three. Then our empathy fails us; we cannot fully understand the feelings.

Fortunately as we grow older our youthful understanding of human nature, human society and human actions is extended and deepened by experience – both directly in personal confrontations and indirectly in history, biography and literature. All that we need to follow the stories of history is that basic understanding of human actions that is so conspicuous in children – an understanding that is widened and deepened but never replaced in the ensuing years. We do not, as holders of the empathy theory require, have to project our personality into another. Is this possible even with contemporaries, let alone with people far in the past? Nor are we ever likely to attain 'full understanding' of another. For most purposes it suffices to have an acquaintance with the springs (mostly emotional) and the resourcefulness (mostly rational) of human action.

In all fairness, however, some modification is called for. Admittedly, in similar circumstances most people behave in similar ways. But not always. It furthers our understanding if we can account for the differences. First, there are physical limitations. When hungry most people eat – unless there is no food. To know the time most people look at a watch or clock – unless these happen not to have been invented. Much more significant are the norms and values of a society that may differ from our own. 'The past is a foreign country. They do things differently there' is the oft quoted opening of L. P. Hartley's novel, *The Go-Between*. This truth should not be exaggerated. If you make the effort to acknowledge the differences, it is not too difficult to adjust to life in a foreign country; millions do it every day. Similar efforts enable us to enjoy the literature of societies separated from us by hundreds, even thousands, of years and many thousand miles. One can stage Shakespeare four centuries later in modern dress and the plays come off very well in spite of many changes in the language. Greek and

Roman classics are still read with comprehension and enjoyment. The Old and New Testaments, from very remote ages, are largely clear in their messages. The Tale of Genji, set in tenth-century Japan, can still entertain us.

Other societies, both past and present, have languages, technologies, religions, political and economic systems different from our own. Historians and anthropologists may enjoy impressing us with how exotic they are. When every allowance is made for our ignorance and for the natural laziness and lack of imagination that makes it easier to assume that everyone else is like us, yet we can follow the accounts (both in history and in fiction) of human deeds with at least a workable degree of understanding. Empathy, as defined, is not necessary. Nevertheless, making the necessary allowances for a different society is a task of the imagination.

2.8   Counter-factuals

There is one more important task for the imagination in the study of history. We have already discussed the role of counter-factuals in helping us to make judgements about causes (see chapter 3, 1.6, above). That is the duty of trying to estimate what the subsequent state of affairs would be if a particular event had not occurred. To do this, I suggested, the historian needs a sixth sense – a 'feel' for the way things flow. This, too, is a form of imagination, though one that is remote from fantasy; it rests (or should rest) on rational arguments. Whenever I think of the Second World War I am haunted by the failure of the Generals' Plot against Hitler of July 1944. It was a well-thought out plan which, had it succeeded, would have ended the war in Europe. When one thinks of the destruction (of Dresden, for example), the massacres in the gas chambers, the subsequent toll of deaths in battle, the Russian incursion into Eastern Germany, one finds it hard to assess the misery that the world would have been spared without the last terrible ten months. The whole thing turned on the chance movement by a tidy-minded orderly of a brief-case from the proximity of the dictator. History is full of these 'might-have-beens.' Many people scoff at the sort of speculation I have just indulged in. 'What happened, happened,' they say. 'There is no point in concerning yourself with what never occurred.' To this hard-headed common sense, one must point out that it is the custom of historians, as of men and women in general, to attach significance, of greater or lesser degree, to certain events. Why do we commemorate wars and battles won and lost, the lives and achievements of statesmen, the passing of statutes, the introduction of reforms (votes for women in 1918, the 'aggiornamento' of the Catholic Church in the second Vatican Council), and so on? The only reason for marking any event as important or significant is that we believe it brought about changes; that is, that without that event the world would have taken (for better or worse) a different course. If we believe that the event made no difference, we should disregard it. But all these evaluations of significance rest on our belief in certain hypothetical events that would otherwise have occurred. ('If Hitler had won the war, then...!') Such hypotheses are, of course, contrary to the facts of what *did* occur, so they are called counter-factual hypotheses or suppositions. Supported as they are by reasoning, often with facts and figures and theories to lend plausibility, there is yet no question but that they ultimately rest on a basis of pure imagination. Nevertheless, one must insist that counter-factuals lie at the root of two important kinds of historical judgement – judgements of cause and judgements of significance.

3   Action

3.1   History in action

History, said Aristotle, is about 'what, say, Alcibiades did, or what happened to him'[6] Sometimes what happens to a person in history is the impact of impersonal forces, but more often it happens because he is on the receiving end of someone else's action. So, either way, most of history is about actions. And, according to one of the greatest sociologists, Max Weber, so is sociology. This he defines as 'a science which attempts the interpretive understanding of social action in order thereby to arrive at a causal explanation of its course and effects' (Weber, 1964, p.88). Perhaps with the omission of the word 'science', this is a definition which many historians would not find difficult to accept as a definition of their own subject. The relevance for our consideration of mind (the subject of this chapter) is that Weber defines 'action' as 'all human behaviour when and in so far as the acting individual attaches a subjective meaning to it'. Such action is social when its meaning 'takes account of the behaviour of others' (Weber, 1964, p.88). We recognize this on the occasions when, being on the receiving end of another's action, we desire an explanation. The sort of explanation we ask for is not usually of the law-like kind – 'Because all entrepreneurs/jealous husbands/witch-doctors/bureaucrats behave like that'. Instead we ask, 'What do you/does he/does she mean by that?' This almost instinctive response demands Weber's 'interpretive understanding of social action'.

For both the historian and the sociologist, social action is normally and typically rational. However, we all know (none better than children) that many actions are not rational at all. As far as their subjective meaning goes this is irrelevant. As Weber says, 'Sociological investigation attempts to include in its scope various irrational phenomena...formulated in terms of theoretical concepts which are adequate on the level of meaning' (Weber, 1964, p. 110). However foolish our action (for example, an outburst of rage or jealousy) may appear to us in our better moments, at the time it has a meaning for us. One recalls the epigram on a certain politician: 'Count not his broken pledges as a crime. / He *meant* them, *how* he meant them – at the time.'

3.2   A five-part analysis of action

There is, however, an important distinction between folly and ignorance. This has a bearing on history. If someone in the past did not act sensibly (as it appears to us), was he a fool or was he simply ignorant of what we know? This is important for the understanding both of the person and of the action. To see this, let us analyse action into its five constituent parts: (1) the end, aim or objective; (2) the drive or motive to attain the end; (3) the agent's assessment of the current situation; (4) the choice of means to the end; and (5) the context of the action. We consider each in turn. They can all be involved in the subjective meaning of the action, though in the fifth case the chief interest lies in any mismatch between the subjective meaning and objective reality.

(1) If the action is rational we may assume it has an *aim*. The aim may be pursued for its own sake – love, beauty, loyalty, duty, worship, and so on. Such things are often held to have intrinsic value, so there may be no need to ask why we pursue them. For a utilitarian, however, these things may be valued only instrumentally – that is, as means to the production of pleasure and the reduction of pain. Thus other aims may be valued not for their own sake, but because they lead on to those that are. For example, if you value beauty you may pursue money as a means to buying flowers for your garden or pictures for your room. Some people, however, pursue money for its own sake. Is this rational? With aims of this kind (which Weber calls '*zweckrational*' – roughly, expedient), there can be a conflict. In my pursuit of beauty, shall I work to make more money to buy flowers or shall I take the day off to work in the garden or walk in the country? On the other hand, some aims may be of little worth, like trying to get even with someone who has offended you or causing harm to a fellow-citizen on grounds of his race or culture. Lastly, what are we to make of spontaneous behaviour like singing, dancing or laughing – that is, when they are spontaneous, which is not always the case? If they have a purpose at all, it is surely expressive. Can this also be the case in artistic creation? The historian has to take all these possibilities into account when she is trying to understand the actions of people in the past. For the evidence before her is rarely of their intentions, but rather of the results. She knows the battles they fought, the letters they wrote, the voyages they made, the goods they sold, the marriages they contracted. From the results she hopes to deduce their intentions. Why did they do these things? As we shall see, she cannot leap to a conclusion; she must carefully consider each of the constituent parts.

(2) In order to attain any proposed end, one has to pay a price. It may be in money, or in time, or in mental or physical labour, or in nervous energy. Moreover, it nearly always entails foregoing something else desirable. So any action has to be driven by a *motive* – sometimes a pretty strong one. Otherwise one merely contemplates the good things without every summoning the energy to get them – like the Lotus-eaters of the *Odyssey*, lolling spinelessly in 'a land / In which it

seemed always afternoon' (Tennyson). How strongly motivated, asks the historian, was the historical agent? Would he have settled for anything else? What price was he paying, what other good was he forgoing, in order to do what he did? What was driving him?

(3) 'Can you tell me the way to London?' 'If I were going to London, I wouldn't start from here.' So runs the old joke. Every action has to begin where we are. Yet it is not always easy to determine exactly where we do stand at the moment. What is our *assessment* of the economic or political or social situation around us? In these circumstances is it sensible to try to achieve this aim? Very often the historian, with the advantage of hindsight, is better placed to answer this than the agent was. When the first troops of the allied expeditionary force disembarked on the shores of the Gallipoli Peninsula in April 1915 they had an advantage in numbers and in surprise. Confusion of command reigned on some beaches, where a vigorous advance would have captured the heights (Liddell Hart, 1972, p. 176). The advantage of surprise was lost and never recovered. As so often in warfare, a failure properly to assess the situation proved fatal to the enterprise. On many other historical occasions, however, it is still unclear to the historian just how the situation did appear to the agent. Certainly Bismarck's cunning bamboozled Napoleon III in 1870 over the Ems telegram. But did the Emperor really believe that the situation, even as he saw it, warranted a declaration of war? Many such puzzles remain, in spite of much historical argument.

(4) This last element (assessment) runs on into the next one, choice of *means*. 'Who chooses the end chooses the means' is an old saying. Behind it is the implication that an attractive end may exact an unattractive price. Certainly one of the first considerations in this choice is effectiveness. Should we not select the means that is most likely to bring the desired result? But what if that involves telling a lie, betraying a friend, injuring an innocent person? And if there are no moral objections to the likeliest road to success, what about the financial, nervous or physical price to pay? All these and other things have to be considered in the choice of means. Again, the historian brings a different viewpoint with attendant questions. How many possible means to this end did the agent envisage? Did he notice this one, or this one? Did he fail to perceive them, or did he reject them as unsuitable? And if the latter, then on what grounds? Were there no other means for the US government to end the war against Japan than annihilating two cities with atomic bombs? The assessment and the means together betray the world-picture of the agent. Sometimes these beliefs (that he is threatened by witches or communists or Jews or that the federal government contains a conspiracy against the people of the United States) may appear to us bizarre in the extreme. Nevertheless, the historian has to stretch her imagination to conceive that these improbabilities may have seemed matters of fact to the agent, however irrational. Again, we have to remember that the difficulty for the historian is that often she has only the results of the action before her. The improbable beliefs of the agent need

separate empirical evidence, for they might not occur to a rational person. The choice of means is revealing of the agent's mind in other ways. First, his acceptance or rejection of ethically dubious methods furnish clues to his morality; hence to his possible or probable behaviour on other occasions. Second, his belief in the efficacy of this or that means shows both his judgement of human nature (a corrupt person believes that every man has his price), and, still more interestingly, his belief in how the world runs, what are the efficient causes of things. This, as we remarked above (chapter 3, 1.6), is also an important quality of the historian herself. In her case, however, it is often made explicit: for example, that history has a basis in materialism if she is a Marxist; or that truth will overcome in the end if she is a liberal; or that the world is under the judgement of God if she is religious in the Christian, Islamic or Jewish traditions.

(5) Finally we have the *context* of the action. Unlike the other four elements, this one is objective. As such it forms no part of the subjective meaning which defines an action. Nevertheless (as the very words 'agent' and 'action' imply) we are concerned not merely with subjective imaginings but with deeds performed in and on the real world. History being largely concerned with what men and women do, action is the realm of history *par excellence*. Every action has its consequences, intended and unintended. If it had none history could ignore it; indeed, history could not know of it. Just what the consequences are is largely due to the context of the action. For full understanding, then, the historian needs not only the subjective meaning of the action (that is, the agent's aim, motive, assessment and choice of means), but also the objective historical situation in which the action took place. There is much to be said about this. Here we must restrict ourselves to one consideration: the context of the action should be seen as the intersection of two axes. The horizontal axis consists of all the relevant events and situations contemporary with the action: that is, in a broad sense, the conditions – war or peace, plenty or famine, dictatorship or democracy, and so on. The vertical axis consists of the relevant events and situations before and after the action: that is, in a broad sense, the possible causes and effects of the action. Both these have to be thoroughly understood by the historian if she is to grasp the historical significance of the action. Here, once again, in a chapter about mind, we see that to grasp historical significance is a considerable mental exercise. We also see how much that exercise involves an understanding of the minds of the people whose actions constitute the history of our past.[7]

3.3   Consistency

The above analysis of ends and means accords with the opening sentences of Aristotle's *Nicomachean Ethics*. But, as the development of that book illustrates, we are not always clear at the beginning of an action exactly what it is that we are aiming at. We start off in what we hope is the right direction, but can only define our goal as we come nearer. This is perhaps best seen in artistic creation, but it can also be seen in moral and religious experience. Indeed it may be that to live wisely is just to learn by experience how to distinguish the gold from the dross, to discover what are the most worthwhile aims in life. The analysis of practical action given above is a simple one, based on the short term as in 'I intend to catch that plane. What is the quickest way to the airport?' Historians often have to ask whether a politician has a consistent aim, whether he learns by experience to define better (or other) aims, or, third, whether he has only very short-term aims and veers with every wind that blows. Of Stalin a modern historian writes: 'There is no doubt about Stalin's remarkable gifts as a politician, but it is a mistake to suppose that he (any more than Hitler) was following a carefully worked-out plan' (Bullock, 1993, p. 199). It is possible that the successful careers of Cromwell, Washington, Napoleon or Lincoln were as surprising to them as to their contemporaries.

Notes

1 For insolubility, see McGinn (1993), especially chapters 1 and 2.
2 This is to make no metaphysical assertion about the nature of mind. Even a physicalist may surely accept this explanation of the historian's activity.
3 See Keats's letter of 22 December 1817 to his brothers.
4 Wolpert (1993, p. 78). Heraclitus would have agreed.
5 *Shorter Oxford English Dictionary*.
6 *Poetics*, 9. See Aristotle (1965, p. 44).
7 For the analysis of a historical event in terms of these five elements of action, see my discussion of the 'Velvet Revolution' in Prague of November–December 1989 in Stanford (1994, pp. 24–7).

Suggested Reading

The basis for this is Kenny (1992). Also relevant are Weber (1964, section 1), Trevor-Roper (1980) in Lloyd-Jones (1981), Bouwsma in Rabb and Rotberg (1982) and perhaps a reconsideration of Collingwood (1961, part V). Priest (1991) may be a help.

7

Meaning

1 Language

1.1 History and the sieve of language

What has language to do with the philosophy of history? Quite a lot. To begin
with, here are two sets of considerations.

One set is concerned with the practice of history, what we have called history 2.
The other belongs to history 1, the endless flow of events which we inhabit. The
first set of considerations turns on the obvious but important fact that most of the
evidence before the historian and most of the products of the historian are
couched in language, usually written. If you are interested in any question about
the past you will probably read what historians have written about it – the so-
called secondary sources. If you wish to go further you will read the evidence
produced at the time (as well as consulting memories if the events in question are
fairly recent. These, too, will come in linguistic form, though not written.) These
are the primary sources. Thus nearly all of your and my knowledge of the past
comes filtered (usually several times) through the sieve of language. Let us take for
example the Battle of Hastings in 1066 – said to be the one memorable date in
English history. You may read of it in any number of history books written in
English (and a few in French). If they are scholarly works they will be based
directly on primary sources. It is more likely, however, that you have read a
popular work, a guidebook, or a school textbook. These are derived from the
scholarly works. Your knowledge has gone through two filters already. Then
where do the scholars get their knowledge? They will have relied chiefly upon
the *Anglo-Saxon Chronicle* (a contemporary but laconic record written in English),
the *Carmen de Hastingae Proelio* – the *Song of the Battle of Hastings* (written by a
French bishop in 1067), the *Gesta Guillielmi* – the *Deeds of William* (written about
1072 by Duke William's chaplain), and the Bayeux Tapestry, an illustrated
documentary with Latin text made at the order of the Duke's half-brother.
Since these were written in obsolete languages (Anglo-Saxon and medieval
Latin), the English account has to be translated – another filter. But of course

even a contemporary text is not the battle itself – which is after all the object of your interest. The events of the day were written down, but not all from direct observation. Many (perhaps most) of them must have come to the writer at second hand. Thus the events of the battle were transformed into words by the observer, into other words by the writer, into English by the translation (probably done by the scholar), into his own words by that same scholar, and yet again by the popularizer. Thus your simple knowledge of a well-known event in history has been filtered through language four or five times. Is it any wonder that both the student of history and the philosopher of history have to pay serious attention to the medium through which their knowledge has passed so many times? To view a landscape through even one pane of glass can be restricting and distorting. Our view of the past normally goes through several such 'panes'. Should we not examine the glass very carefully if we want to be sure of the features of the landscape?

A word more about the Bayeux Tapestry. Here the information comes not only in verbal form (the Latin text above the pictures), but chiefly in pictorial form. The pictures speak directly to us, avoiding the filter of language. But it is not to be supposed that the (probably English) needlewomen who sewed it were themselves observers of the scenes they recorded. By the time the instructions came to them those scenes had probably been through two or three filters already. A further point is that the pictures (being in needlework) are stylized and conventionalized. They cannot be absorbed directly like a photograph; they too have to be understood, rather than registered as by a camera in the mind. Although not linguistic, they must yet be interpreted.

1.2 Future and past

The second set of considerations concerns history 1, the course of things. Our moments of consciousness are set in the brief present between past and future. Language links us to both of these. A fully active human being confronts the future – an unknown into which we are ceaselessly travelling. I cannot know what the future holds, but I can know who I am, what values and perspectives I shall take into the future. I know I shall be me, not nobody, nor somebody else. This sense of the self, this definite orientation to the future rests (both for the individual and for society) on an orientation to the past. This entails not just knowing what I did and what happened to me and my society, but also having a definite stance towards it – a stance again, as with the future, made up of values, experiences and memories – in short, my total outlook on life, what in sum I make of it. The question, 'What does the future mean to you?' can only be answered in relation to the question, 'What does the past mean to you?'. Those who have only a weak orientation to the past can have only an equally weak orientation to the future. They are permanently like post-operative patients in that bewildered moment of waking – 'disorientated', as we say. They show the futility of the maxim: 'Live only in the present'.[1]

English is a living language, alive on our tongues today, that relates us directly to the past – to Joyce and Yeats, Keats and Wordsworth, Milton and Pope, Shakespeare and Chaucer. The same goes, of course, for other literatures. This is a common theme, too well known to need exposition here.

If language joins us to our past, it also relates us to our future. This is because it enables us to speak of that which is not: 'the grammars of the future tense, of conditionality, of imaginary open-endedness are essential to the sanity of consciousness and to the intuitions of forward motion which animate history' (Steiner, 1976, p. 227).

1.3   Semiotics

It is becoming apparent that the relations between thought and language are both vitally important and bafflingly unclear. Part of the difficulty is obvious: it is the problem of using our only available tools to investigate those same tools. One of the tools to dissect this relationship is semiotics – the science of signs. The name, derived from the Greek *'semeion'* – a 'sign', was given by its founder, the American philosopher Charles S. Peirce (1839–1914). He believed signs to be vehicles of our thinking. He put it thus: 'The only thought, then, which can possibly be cognized is thought in signs. But thought which cannot be cognized does not exist. All thought, therefore, must necessarily be in signs' (Peirce, 1960, vol. 5, # 251, p. 151). It is important to remember here both that the signs most commonly used are words, and also that many other things that are not single words (including sentences) or not words at all (like symbols) are to be understood as signs. (see, for example, Barthes, 1973). It is worth our while to look briefly into this science of signs, for words are essential to our understanding of history in each sense of that word.

We start with Peirce's simple observation that the function of a sign involves three things – the sign, the object signified or referred to, and the idea or thought that connects them; this third element Peirce calls the interpretant. (If you are ignorant of Russian there is no thought in your mind to connect the word 'DOM' with 'house': for a Russian the thought is there.) The function of a sign is, therefore, a three-term relationship. The third term (Peirce's 'interpretant') is the crux of interest here; it is the idea or thought that links the first two elements. Let us note that the connection can be rigid or variable. To take our example, if the word 'DOM' is rigidly connected to the thing, house, then the two are always connected in the same way by the same idea. But the connection has to be made by a human mind. There is nothing in the word itself to suggest the object, nor in the object to suggest the word: a house is not DOM-shaped. In fact, as we shall see (Chapter 7, 2.2), this lies at the root of a very influential theory of language, that of Saussure.

To say that word and object are connected by the same idea implies that the connection is nearly always made in the same way; the word 'idea' suggests some

permanence. But if we say that they are connected by a thought, the connection seems less rigid. For a thought is an act of thinking, and every act of thinking is subtly different from every other – for such acts are performed by different people on different occasions. Thus you and I may be said to have the same idea (of Paris as the capital of France, for example), but every time you or I entertain that idea our action is slightly different. Thus 'red light = Stop' and 'DOM = house' are not automatic or mechanical links. They appear so in a driving handbook or in a dictionary, but in fact the connection is only made by a particular mind thinking the appropriate thought on a particular occasion. Now that act of thinking is rarely confined simply to 'stop' or 'house'. Very often it includes other thoughts, like 'That is a main road' or 'That is where my father lives'. In short, the effect of a sign upon a living mind is rarely confined to its conventional object; it extends to other thoughts. This ongoing capacity of signs was named by Peirce 'unlimited semiosis'. In mathematics and symbolic logic great efforts are made to restrict the signs to exactly the same meaning on every occasion. The mind, necessarily active in making the connection between sign and concept, is yet forbidden to go beyond the strictly defined meaning of the symbol. This may be one reason why many people find maths and logic difficult. On most occasions we allow our minds to wander. Thus the function of a sign is not a fixed process like the meshing of cogs in a machine; it is open-ended and capable of almost infinite development. This 'unlimited semiosis' is a characteristic of signs (or, more accurately, of the using of signs) to which Peirce first drew attention. It has been developed by the contemporary semiologist and novelist, Umberto Eco.

1.4 Unlimited semiosis

Now this open-endedness of sign function is not a drawback or weakness; it is healthy and desirable. It makes possible creativity and progress both in language and in literature. A living language, alive on the lips of countless speakers today, like Italian or English, is constantly changing, in spite of being recognizably the same as the tongue of Dante or Chaucer. People enjoy using it, finding new uses to match the fresh experiences of living. Continuity must be there or their speech would be unintelligible; but a boring repetition of usage would be as deadly dull as a schoolboy's Latin exercises – and for the same reason.

Look at literature. One of the joys of studying one's own (or, for a few people, another) literature is exploring the different and ever-new uses of the same language. Another, even richer delight, is to read a great work at several stages in life and to find that it has more to say on each occasion. (This could almost be the definition of a literary classic.) If it were not for unlimited semiosis the cogs would grind round on every reading and we should repeat exactly the same experience. Fortunately, as we all know, this is not the case: the good books become better on re-reading, the bad books more boring. But does 'unlimited semiosis' imply that a word or text can mean anything that the hearer or reader wants it to mean? Should we not insist that semiosis is unlimited in theory, but cannot be so in practice? I am theoretically free to travel the world, but in fact if I am in England I cannot be in Australia. Similarly, we *could* use 'black' for the colour of snow, but if so we cannot use it to describe coal. A neglect of this fact underlies one of the key claims of postmodernism. That words or texts lack a definite meaning is quite subversive of history, a discipline that is said by post-modernists to be as susceptible to 'deconstruction' as any literary text. As one writer on history puts it, 'What is clear is therefore the utter contingency of readings and the recognition that interpretations at (say) the "centre" of our culture are not there because they are true or methodologically correct...but because they are aligned to the dominant discursive practices: again power/ knowledge.'[2] There is no question but that history (at least as traditionally conceived) is under attack – an attack that can for a time be ignored, but that in the end must be met face to face. That is why historians have to understand the nature of the linguistic challenge of postmodernism.

2   Hermeneutics

2.1   Truth and meaning

There is a painting by Titian (or one of his school) that is an allegory of Truth and Falsehood. Truth is a maiden naked and unadorned, Falsehood is clad in all the luxury of the day. The implication is that falsehood would not prevail were it not made more attractive than truth by various additions and embellishments. To a modern eye the allegory is less cogent: the clean lines of the well-formed body have not less but more appeal than the huddle of silks and velvets, pearls and jewels on a rather over-weight lady. This raises a profound question for both historians and philosophers. Granted that their very *raison d'être* is to pursue what is true, how is it that they are so often seduced by what is not? Why do they not always prefer the bare facts of the case? (Notice that even the austere science of mathematics often praises a solution as 'beautiful'.) Granted again that scholars are not intentionally misled, what are the silks and pearls that mislead them by obscuring the truth?

The answer in many cases would seem to be 'meaning'. When we are con-fronted by the unfamiliar – be it object, text or theory – we try to make sense of it. But what we make of it can be a distortion or misperception of what it actually is. Children are amused by pictures of optical illusions, psychologists are familiar with the processes of perception involved in, for example, trying to decide whether we are looking at the staircase from above or below. The artist M. C. Escher has a lot of fun with this. The same applies to our meetings with new mental objects – ideas, sentences, documents, books. We have to use our mental powers to get some sort of grasp of them. Only after that can we begin to consider whether or not they are true. The question, 'What is it saying?' comes before the question, 'Is it true?' In short, meaning comes before truth, nor is it less important. Yet it would not be far wrong to say that for two centuries after the Enlightenment (roughly mid-eighteenth to mid-twentieth centuries) both philosophy and history were more concerned with truth than with meaning. In the second half of the twentieth century questions of interpretation have challenged, and in some cases displaced questions of knowledge: epistemology yielding to hermeneutics. Yet we must not forget the allegory: the meaning that appeals to us may be other than the truth.

At this point we should be clear that 'meaning' is used in a broad and inclusive sense in this chapter. It can, as here, imply 'making sense' of something. It can also be seen as conveying (or attempting to convey) an idea – as in 'What do you mean by that?' It can mean grasping the significance – as in 'I see what that means.' It can even be the constitutive relations with other events that characterize a particular event – for example, 'The meaning of the assassination at Sarajevo is that it led to the First World War.' All four (at least) senses of the word are used in history. Since they often overlap, a broad interpretation has advantages. Nevertheless, a recognition that the term 'meaning' has several uses may help to avoid misunderstandings.

Put simply: we need both truth and meaning; even if truth is our aim, we may yet have to deal with meaning first. Speaking philosophically (rather than psychologically), there can be no question of primacy between truth and meaning; they are equally important. Unfortunately, while truth may be single, interpretations can be multiple. Hence the conflict. 'There is only one truth about the matter. Hermeneutics is all poppycock', one lot harrumph through their moustaches. The other side wind you round with weasel words: 'It all depends on what interpretation you give it. As you will see, when we have deconstructed the text there can be no question of truth; only of various readings.'

2.2 The advantages of science

The problem comes to a head in history and the social sciences. On the one hand, these disciplines are rightly concerned with objective truth; on the other hand, the things that they deal with seem not to be solid and stable like stones, but changing and fleeting, like mercury or water; for they are thoughts, ideas, schemes, concepts, theories, perceptions – all apprehensible only by the mind. (One recalls Dr Johnson's attempt to refute Berkeley's idealism: he kicked a large stone.) Now the natural sciences have made great advances in the apprehension of objective truths. This is partly due to the nature of their material; an anthropologist may wonder whether a raised arm is a threat or a greeting, but the zoologist does not mistake an elephant for a giraffe. More subtly, some of their success is due to their procedures: when there seems inadequate evidence they tend to defer the problem.[3] Science, as Medawar says, is 'the art of the soluble'. Quantum theory, chaos theory and complexity theory, with the attendant non-linear equations, are recent attempts to tackle (if not to solve) the apparently insoluble. Perhaps a third advantage of the natural sciences is that (at least in many cases) they can more easily isolate the phenomenon under study. The fact that many scientific experiments can be repeated (at least, in principle) supports their claim to objectivity. These four advantages, though not unknown, are much less common in history and the social sciences. Early in the Enlightenment it was expected that the methods of the natural sciences would prove equally successful in the study of human affairs. For most of the nineteenth century positivism was powerful. Although as we have seen it was challenged in the eighteenth century by people like Vico and Herder, the strongest criticisms were not made until Wilhelm Dilthey (1833–1911).

2.3   Dilthey and life-experiences

Dilthey's ambition was to do what Kant did not – write a Critique of Historical Reason.[4] His ultimate failure to do so was perhaps due to the fact that he held two apparently incompatible beliefs. One was the belief that knowledge is a highly personal affair: our cognition is subjective, being a direct relationship with the known object – one might almost say that for him all knowledge is '*connaître*' never '*savoir*'. This is because one re-discovers 'the I in the Thou' (Dilthey, 1976, p. 208). Thus the human sciences deal with human relationships and symbolic structures of all kinds – actions, social practices, norms and values. We understand these things because, as Vico said, we made them. Hence Dilthey coined the phrase '*Geisteswissenschaften*' for these scientific disciplines of the mind as against the natural sciences – the *Naturwissenschaften*. But here comes his other (and opposing) belief. He believed that history and society can be studied scientifically by the establishment of objective facts. Thus 'a very disturbing contradiction runs through all of Dilthey's writing, as if he wanted to have his cake and eat it, too' (Iggers, 1983, p. 134).

The difficulty comes in the leap from being conscious of our own experiences to understanding those of others. It has sometimes been claimed (for example, by the neo-Kantians Windelband and Rickert) that history differs from science in the nature of its objects: that science deals with classes of things while history deals with individuals and specific events. But this distinction is often disputed, for science sometimes deals with single cases, while historians often deal with classes of events or of people. On the other hand, it may be argued that scientists do not deal with the individual as an individual, but only as a possibly unique case of its kind. And how many of the generalizations used by historians are purely historical? In any case, as Dilthey saw, the difference between the human and the natural sciences lies rather in the modes of experience than in the objects. A surgeon experiences a patient on the operating table as a medical 'case', but his wife experiences the same individual as a person. It is not simply that, for the surgeon, the patient is just one more example of a strangulated hernia, while for the woman he is the most important man in her life. It is that the experiences that a man and wife have of each other are rich, fully human, at once emotional, physical and rational; each experience, moreover, is situated, and only to be understood, in the complex context of a particular time and place. Two things are to be noted about these 'life-experiences' (Dilthey's *Erlebnisse*). One is the contrast with scientific procedure which, ignoring such things as emotional and social contexts, simply abstracts from a situation the one element that is of relevance (for example, the acceleration of a glass falling from a table or the clotting of blood from a wound), links it with other similar abstractions, joins causes with effects, and proceeds (usually with the help of mathematical analysis) to build up a theoretical structure. This is what a particular event may mean for a scientist. The other thing to note about life-experiences is their inter-dependence. The meaning that an experience has for us depends partly on our earlier experiences; by the same token it helps to shape our future experiences. Nevertheless, we are not totally dependent on our prejudices. We do learn (sometimes with difficulty) from experiences. And we act accordingly. Learning and acting shape each other. Thus, what we make of life in general (whether we are prone to be optimistic or pessimistic, for example) helps to shape each experience; while the meaning for us of each single experience (what we make of it and how we deal with it) helps to build up the total meaning of life. This mutual reinforcement of meanings is known as 'the hermeneutic circle'. Moreover, understanding of meaning, or interpretation, extends beyond personal relations to all aspects of social life – language, literature, society, law, politics, art, and so on. These human creations, which make up culture, all rest largely on symbols – hence the importance of semiotics. We understand these things, as Vico said, just because they are of human construction and we are human. Acting and understanding make other circles of mutual reinforcement, as do the individual and society.

2.4 Being objective about the subjective

It is here that the crunch comes for Dilthey. How does one move from the life-experiences of oneself to those of others? It is difficult enough to grasp the way life looks even to our nearest and dearest. How many can claim a full understanding of their spouse, sibling or child? How much greater is the problem for the social scientist or historian dealing with people she has never met. Nevertheless, he insists that the human sciences can have objectivity and truth-values just like the natural sciences. 'Only by reacting to life and society do the human studies achieve their highest significance . . . But the road to such effectiveness must pass through the objectivity of scientific knowledge' (Dilthey, 1976, p. 183). Here again we meet the pervasive tension between meaning and truth. To secure the one does not guarantee the other.

This is Dilthey's dilemma. On the one hand 'it is in the life actually lived that the reality known in the human studies lies' (Dilthey, 1976, p. 210). This is the emphasis on personal life-experience. But on the other hand he has to ask 'if it is possible to study individual human beings and particular forms of human existence scientifically and how this can be done'. He believes that the human sciences 'like history, depend for their certainty on the possibility of giving general validity to the understanding of the unique' (p. 247). The possibility lies in our understanding of the 'mind-constructed world' – that is all the creations, material and ideal, of man in society – houses, laws, tools, songs and so on. These constitute the 'objectification of life'. Our insights into these can be expressed by generalizations – 'ever new general truths' (pp. 190, 192, 221). But how do we test the validity of these insights?

The answer, he believes, lies in the practice of the science of hermeneutics – the established methods hitherto used chiefly on Biblical and classical texts for determining their meanings (p. 249). Defining hermeneutics as 'the methodology of the interpretation of written records', he insists that correct understanding depends on their valid interpretation (p. 249). Thus hermeneutics is the key, and 'the theory of interpretation becomes a vital link between philosophy and the historical disciplines' (pp. 249 and 260). Has Dilthey squared the circle? As we have noted, he ended in some despair (see chapter 5, 3.9, above).

2.5   'Reading' is Dilthey's solution

For Dilthey, then, the answer to the problem of relativity is to 'read' the whole historico-social situation as a text. Since any period in history, past or present, is largely delineated by linguistic processes and products (spoken or written), these products can be interpreted as texts by the recognized methods of hermeneutics and so their general validity can be established. By putting these 'readings' together, the history of the whole age can be 'read'.

There are a number of difficulties here. The first that springs to mind is the modern (or post-modern) denial of the possibility of one firm meaning to any text. This we shall look at later. Another is the doubt whether linguistic texts supply the whole of the evidence for an age. The many other sources (in the arts or in economics or demography, for example) that recent historians have used to good effect suggest that Dilthey is wrong here. The problem will come up again with postmodernism – see Chapter IX below. Such other sources would be particularly relevant if we suspected that the age might be in the grip of a collective illusion, such as the Marxist 'false consciousness', or the racist beliefs of an imperialist age. The conflicting evidence would then at least open up a debate. A third doubt is about the possibility of agreeing on the interpretation of a whole age or society solely as a sum of particular interpretations. Is there any sense in which an epoch is more than the sum of its parts? Hegel certainly thought so, and though few would follow him in every detail about the Spirit of the Age (Zeitgeist), yet many sociologists follow Durkheim in insisting on societal facts as well as individual facts.[5] Another German philosopher, Hans-Georg Gadamer (b. 1900) had a more subtle, more interesting and perhaps more important criticism of Dilthey and his use of hermeneutics.

'Hermeneutics', Gadamer says, 'is the art of understanding the opinion of another'. Hence it is the art of 'being able to be wrong'.[6]

2.6   Gadamer

Gadamer published his chief work, *Wahrheit und Methode* (*Truth and Method*), in 1960, some sixty or more years after Dilthey laid down his pen. In the interval two world wars and several dictatorships had plagued the world. In both Europe and America positivism had had a new lease of life; Husserl and phenomenology, Heidegger and historicity, Sartre and existentialism, Wittgenstein and problems of language, had all made their impact on the philosophical scene. Gadamer resumed the discussion of hermeneutics – in a form which he called 'philosophical hermeneutics'. His work had far-reaching effects upon the social sciences, theology and law, and upon the arts and literary studies; less so far upon philosophy and history. Yet he must not be ignored, for in all these disciplines some of the chief questions centre upon meaning. It is probable that some of our ideas about truth also need to be re-thought in the light of what Gadamer has to say.

We may start with the point already made: that when we meet something unfamiliar (whether an object or an idea) our first instinctive reaction is to try to make sense of it. This is to fit it into the context of the familiar. In this sense, experience is always 'knowledge of the known' (Gadamer, 1985, p. 181). Meaning comes before truth. So far we are at the level of animals; they, too, try to make sense of a strange object, and if they cannot they leave it alone. Our instinct, like theirs, when confronted by the totally incomprehensible is to take avoiding action. In the majority of cases, however, we make *some* sense of it and act accordingly. Further experience, however, often compels us to revise our first opinion. The obvious example is meeting a stranger. It can happen that that stranger becomes an acquaintance, a friend, and even a lover. During the course of the growing relationship both partners will make many alterations of their first reactions. In philosophy we are concerned chiefly with ideas, but the same sort of process of learning by experience takes place as strangeness turns into familiarity. Thus philosophy is usually best done through dialogue – as Plato demonstrated. Two and a half thousand years later it was still true. On a train shortly after the Second World War I met a young soldier who was in the Pioneer Corps – the lowest form of military life, devoted entirely to hard physical labour. He was on his way to Oxford to sit for a scholarship in philosophy at one of the colleges. He told me he had learned philosophy in the evenings in a bar, arguing with an ex-priest, a scholar of Thomism (medieval philosophy centred on Thomas Aquinas). When I asked what philosophers he had read, he told me none. He borrowed my handkerchief and asked my address to return it. A week or two later the clean handkerchief was returned together with the news that he had won the scholarship. The dons, I thought, knew their business.

2.7   The process of learning

Plato also believed that this is the way to pursue wisdom. 'It is not something that can be put into words like other branches of learning', he says in the Seventh Letter; 'only after long partnership in a common life devoted to this very thing does truth flash upon the soul, like a flame kindled by a leaping spark, and once it is born there it nourishes itself thereafter' (Plato, 1973, p. 136). It can be argued that the learning process is never the simple acquisition of facts or ideas. Popper says it is 'an activity with an aim (to find, or to check, some regularity which is *at least* vaguely conjectured); an activity guided by problems, and by the context of expectations (the "horizon of expectations" as I later called it). There is no such thing as passive experience' (Popper, 1976, pp. 51–2). Plato, in fact, was so impressed by the superiority of personal conversation (like the Thomist in the bar) that he – half-seriously, one assumes – deprecated the writing of books. 'Then it shows great folly' says Socrates in the *Phaedrus* 'to suppose that one can transmit or acquire clear and certain knowledge of an art through the medium of writing, or that written words can do more than remind the reader of what he already knows on any given subject'. Written words are dumb. 'If you ask them what they mean by anything they simply return the same answer over and over again' (Plato, 1973, p. 97).

Nevertheless, one does learn from the written word. Doing so involves a sort of dialogue with the text. When this dialogue is proceeding, one does *not* find that the words 'simply return the same answer'. Hard thinking as one reads makes the text yield up its message – perhaps only at the third or fourth reading. (By speaking of 'its message' I have begged the question of whether a text can have more than one meaning. This we shall discuss later.) It can also be argued that historians and scientists act in the same way; they hold dialogues with their evidence or data. 'The relation between a historian and his facts', wrote the historian E. H. Carr, 'is one of equality, of give-and-take. As any working historian knows ... the historian is engaged in a continuous process of moulding his facts to his interpretation and his interpretation to his facts'.[7]

Gadamer's simple point in *Truth and Method* is that our apprehension of a fact or an idea is never a single act, but rather a process. To resume the analogy of personal acquaintance, although a relationship may grow from one of strangers to one of lovers, yet mutual learning never comes to an end. There is always more to be known of the other even in the most intimate relationship. What sense we make of a new person, object, notion, text or set of scientific or social phenomena is an interpretation. Where Gadamer goes beyond Dilthey is in pointing out that any understanding begins with 'prejudices' – that is, with pre-judgements. Just as a journey to any destination whatever must begin from where we are, so must any interpretation begin from our initial understanding. Much of the interest of Gadamer's ideas lies in his tracing the predecessors and successors of that first impact of the new – what go before and come after it. The second part of the word 'dialogue' reminds us that it is a matter of language; conversation is any exchange of words. Gadamer recognizes that the linguisticality of understanding cannot possibly mean that all experiencing of the world takes place only as language and in language. Circumstances, like hunger and love, work and domination, circumscribe the space for conversation.[8] Nevertheless, 'the communality that we call human rests on the linguistic constitution of our life-world' (Gadamer, 1985, p. 180). Hence hermeneutics comes in almost everywhere. For our use of language can be both an interpretation of our (and the world's) situation at any given moment, and also (like every other symbolic structure) stands itself in need of interpretation. We live in society. The interpretation that we give to any personal or social phenomenon is likely to spring from, and hence conform to, the norms, values and conventions of our society. For this reason we normally have little difficulty in understanding one another – that is, in interpreting one another's speech and actions. Nor does this apply only to society in general. It is equally true of the specialized societies of law, medicine, the natural sciences, history, theology or social science. Each of these has its own norms, conventions, history and specialized language. These form its tradition, within which the practitioners do most of their thinking. Thus we all tend to bring judgements already formed (hence 'pre-judices') to a new situation. Indeed, these pre-formed judgements are not, for the most part, consciously our own; they are embedded in the very language that we use. This is the importance of tradition. To be sure, Gadamer acknowledges that it 'is part of the nature of man to be able to break with tradition, to criticize and dissolve it' (Gadamer, 1979, p. xxv). Yet he feels that an emphasis on the weight of the past is necessary in an age that is all too happy to forget it. The modern philosopher is too ready 'to make radical inferences from everything'. He should be more aware of his historicity, of his situatedness in particular circumstances, of the inevitable limits of human life and thought. 'Experience is experience of human finitude', Gadamer, 1979, p. 320). 'What man needs', says Gadamer, 'is not only a persistent asking of ultimate questions, but the sense of what is feasible, what is possible, what is correct, here and now' (p. xxv). From all this it has been concluded that Gadamer's preferred outlook is conservative rather than radical, practical rather than idealistic.

2.8   The art of being wrong

But this is not all: he traces not only what we bring to our acts of understanding, but also what flows from them. He is concerned with the future as well as the past. This brings in the partner in the dialogue. The very question of interpretation does not arise until we meet something – a text, an argument, an experience, an idea, a theory – that needs understanding. To understand it we have to engage with it; preferably to meet its proponent in a dialogue (as with Plato), but in any case to enter into some sort of debate – even with a silent text. We bring our own perspective (for which Gadamer uses the term 'horizon'); the other meets us with his. If we try, each can grasp something of the other's point of view. In Gadamer's phrase, we fuse our horizons. The result is that each has a larger perspective, a broader understanding. This is reason in action. Now we can see the point of Gadamer's remark (quoted above on p. 192) that hermeneutics is the art of being able to be wrong. This is how civilized people advance to greater wisdom. 'a person who is called "experienced" has become such not only through experiences, but is also open to new experiences . . . [He] proves to be . . . someone who is radically undogmatic' (p. 319). In this respect Gadamer is by no means as conservative as he seems; he is progressive. (One is reminded of Popper's belief that in a civilized community we let our hypotheses die in our stead.)

2.9   Loosening the ties of history

It will now, perhaps, be apparent why history is so important for Gadamer and he for history. The main emphasis is on historicity – the fact that we are all beings located at particular spatio-temporal points in the unending flow of things that we call 'history'. Archimedes said that given a fixed point to stand and a long enough lever he could move the world. But how could he get outside the world (or the universe, as we should now say) to find a place to stand? Similarly, where can the historian stand in order to get an objective perspective upon history from the outside?[9] The historian, as much as the people he studies, is immersed in history. From this historicity of our understanding of history several conclusions follow for Gadamer.

The first is that hermeneutics (the study of meanings) can free us from the local prejudices that we bring to every judgement. Hermeneutics does this by revealing that any symbolic structure – be it text, social or economic institution or practice, or historical narrative – has not one meaning but a large number of possible meanings. This is because every such structure has not one single determinate meaning, but can possess as many meanings as there are occasions of understanding and interpretation. Take something whose nature and existence is as indisputable as a national government. It enforces laws, exacts taxes and wields armed force. Yet we each see it in slightly different ways, and have attitudes towards it that differ not only between individuals but in the same individual at different times. Think of the uncertainty of public opinion polls. 'Government' means different things on different occasions. So can political labels: is anarchism (the absence of government) a position of the extreme right or the extreme left? It is of the nature of meaning not to be a fixed, inherent quality but to be a relationship between the sign and the percipient (who is also the interpreter), as well as between the sign and the (often indeterminate) signified. 'The true historical object is not an object at all, but the unity of the one and the other, a relationship in which exist both the reality of history and the reality of historical understanding' (Gadamer, 1979, p. 267). Meanings are, therefore, partly constituted by the percipient and his or her historicity. But, it is important to note, only in part. Meanings are also in part constituted by the symbols and what they stand for, by words or concepts and their references. Meanings, though plural, are never random. The simple words 'I love you' have been used a countless number of times by a large number of people in a wide variety of contexts. It could be argued that each separate occasion has a meaning for the participants that is never exactly repeated. But the possible meanings are at least circumscribed. Presumably they can never include 'It is raining' or 'Germany won the World Cup.' This obvious point needs to be made to avoid the excesses of some postmodernists who have extended the argument for plurality of meanings to an assertion that a given sentence or text can have no ascertainable meaning at all. But what can mean anything must mean nothing.

2.10   The historicity of meaning

The stress on historicity is particularly valuable in the understanding of history. For in viewing the past we view it from a temporal distance. This distance gives us different perspectives. Undoubtedly perspectives can obscure what at other times is plain, but equally they can reveal what has been hidden. Looking at the past is rather like standing in a dense crowd to watch a spectacle. One never has a clear, uninterrupted view, but as the heads in the crowd in front move, so one sees different parts of the scene. Gadamer has been accused by his critics of imprisoning our interpretations in tradition, hence in this or that ideology. His reply is that hermeneutics, by searching out every meaning, is just the thing to free us from bondage to ideology. This does not, of course, solve questions of truth and objectivity, but at least it clears the ground.

There is an important point about meaning here. What is the meaning of an event, a historical process, or an epoch? Viewing it as a text, we might suppose that its meaning is to be discerned within it, as we discern the meaning of an utterance as that which the speaker intended to convey. But that is certainly not the case with a period of history. Ranke, in a famous phrase, asserted that all epochs are equidistant from God. By this he implied two things: one, that ultimately all ages are of equal value, and, two, that all of history is laid out (as it were, on a flat surface) before God, who can see each epoch for what it is.[10] Whatever may be true of the first (for this is a religious statement about spiritual worth), the second is manifestly untrue of the human understanding of history. In no way can we see each epoch for what it is. There would seem to be a logical distinction between the meaning of an event consisting in its relation to other events, and the meaning consisting of the significance found by later historians. In practice, however, the distinction can be as elusive as the reality – appearance distinction in other contexts. Here we touch on one of the central problems of epistemology.

The modern philosopher, A. C. Danto, has pointed out that the meaning of an event is only to be discerned by its relation to other events. (That I am a brother is not inherent in me; it depends on my relation to someone else.) Two men being thrown out of the windows of a castle in Prague in 1618 was a matter of some interest to contemporaries. But no one at that time could possibly have seen (as we can) its significance as the beginning of the Thirty Years War. Following this argument through, we can say that the meaning of an event can never be fully grasped until we have a complete description of it. Danto says, 'Completely to describe an event is to locate it in all the right stories, and this we cannot do. We cannot because we are temporally provincial with regard to the future.' And again, 'To be alive to the historical significance of events as they happen, one has to know to which later events these will be related, in narrative sentences, by historians of the future. It will then not be enough simply to be able to predict future events. It will be necessary to know *which* future events are relevant, and this requires predicting the *interests* of future historians' (Danto, 1965, pp. 142 and 169).

Now that we see that the meaning of an event is not inherent in it, but lies rather in its relation to other events, what conclusions can we draw? One is that it derives its meaning from its place in narratives. And narratives are stories that we tell about the significances that we find in history. Hence the importance of narratives, which will be discussed below in chapter 8. Another conclusion from both Danto and Gadamer is that we can never see history as a whole. If we could, that would be the end of history, for to do so we should have to stand outside history (like Archimedes standing outside the world). Hegel believed that we *can* grasp the end of history. In that case it was not illogical for him to believe it possible to see the historical significance of events as they happen. But hardly any historian is a Hegelian. Certainly both Dilthey and Gadamer rejected Hegel's views. We are left, then, with the conclusion that historical understanding can never be single and objective for the simple reason that it can never be complete; it must always be partial and perspectival. The historian, let us never forget, is herself situated in history – and always will be.

2.11   Historical knowledge is practical

The historian, dealing with human beings and being herself human, has to understand them from a human point of view. This particular insight was valued by R. G. Collingwood. He believed that 'all history is the history of thought', and can only be the history of thought (Collingwood, 1944, p. 75). 'The historian must re-enact the past in his own mind', he insisted (Collingwood, 1961, p. 282). In particular, he applied the logic of question and answer. Gadamer found Colling-wood one of the few philosophers to understand this. 'The historical method requires that the logic of question and answer be applied to historical tradition'

(Gadamer, 1979, p. 334). Collingwood's point is that one cannot understand a speech, a text or an action unless one first understands the question or problem to which this was the answer (see Collingwood, 1961, p. 283). One must, however, avoid the temptation to read back the plans of the agent from the subsequent events. There are two questions to be asked, says Gadamer: 'the question of meaning in the course of a great event and the question of whether this event went according to plan' (Gadamer, 1979, p. 334). If the answer to the second is in the negative (as probably happens more often than not), then one cannot deduce the agent's intentions from the events. It is interesting that Gadamer accuses Collingwood of doing just this with the battle of Trafalgar and Nelson's plans for it (p. 334 and n. 275). It does not appear from Collingwood's *Autobiography* that he *did* make this mistake. Collingwood was discussing a different question – whether or not Nelson should have worn the medals that brought about his death. (Collingwood, 1944, p. 77–8).

It is partly for this reason that Gadamer insists that history cannot be theorized. As he points out, people make plans and then are frustrated. They try again, and again partially fail. Thus the historian has to take into account *both* the moral and rational ideals incorporated in the plans *and* the contingency of their fates. Historical knowledge is, therefore, practical, rather than theoretical. Of course, one might try another approach and theorize about the frustrations. This is done when the ruling forces in history are declared to be impersonal or inhuman – that is, material or divine. In such cases the moral and rational efforts of humanity are mere bubbles on the surface of a rushing stream. But this is quite at variance with the views both of nearly all working historians and of Gadamer himself.

2.12 History is effective

More to the point is Gadamer's reminder to us that historical understanding is located in the historical agent himself. He, like the historian, is situated in a particular time and place. His understanding of his own historicity is a factor in those very actions that constitute the subject of the historian's interest. There is thus a double role for hermeneutics – first, in the agent's interpretation of his own situation, and, second, in the historian's bifocal interpretation of that interpretation and of that situation.[11]

Finally, Gadamer has a warning for those who, like Collingwood, believe that historical understanding consists in the reconstruction of some idea or thought or scheme or plan held by people in the past. However careful our reconstruction may be, it is almost impossible for it to be exact. Repeating exact reproductions is the method of science, not of history, he maintains. The modern mind that does the reconstructing is itself the product of the (often unfelt) influence of the past.

This is because of what Gadamer calls 'effective-history'. All past events have some effect on subsequent ones. Some of these chains of consequence run from the historical phenomenon to the historian. In studying the phenomenon, even when she is trying to put herself into the minds of the historical agents, her thinking is partly influenced by the effects of that phenomenon. These include whatever aroused her interest to make this study in the first place. This is required, says Gadamer, 'every time that a work of art or an element of the tradition is led from the twilight region between tradition and history to be seen clearly and openly in terms of its own meaning'. Normally our effort to see the past objectively 'conceals the involvement of the historical consciousness itself in effective-history'. Here, indeed, is the main task of philosophical hermeneutics: 'to move back along the path...until we discover in all that is subjective the substantiality that determines it' (Gadamer, 1979, pp. 267, 268, 269). In this way we see that it is the effects of history that largely constitute our present mind. Thus even our most empathetic reconstruction is likely to be itself partial and biased. This is because of all that has happened between the phenomenon to be reconstructed and the present. History, in short, is always effective.

2.13 The way out

After all this one might be forgiven for supposing that Gadamer's ideas have enmired us in total relativism. Must the historian give up all hope, all pretence, of truth or objectivity? Gadamer does not think so. His position is that our prejudices (often unexamined) bind us into a tradition. This confines us to one road, as it were. Hermeneutics causes us to search out every nook and cranny of interpretation, even in the most deep-seated of judgements or pre-judgements. Since all rests on interpretation and since there are many interpretations, then we now see that there are many roads. This is an advance on seeing only one road. It does not, however, tell us which is the right direction. We now come from the critical to the constructive side of Gadamer. It consists in his notion of the 'fusing of horizons' by dialogue. In this (as we saw above, chapter 7, 2.8) both participants can expand their understandings. It is sometimes objected at this point that two such thinkers could expand their points of view to embrace each other's and yet still both could be wrong. Can this be rectified? There may be a number of roads to knowledge, but at least we should know which are more and which less likely to lead there. Whether or not Gadamer explicitly states this, the answer is implicit in his thinking.

The solution is to apply the notion of dialectic to research. We have seen above that the work of both the scientist and the historian can be seen as a dialogue between data and theory, each modifying the other. Historian and scientist (whether natural or social) are in dialogue with reality. It is this contact that prevents them from losing themselves in a world of dreams. It also justifies them against postmodernist attacks as we shall see. Scientists and historians are aware that they deal with hard, unexpected facts – the realm of 'the contingent and the unforeseen'. Here, as they well know, historical truth has none of the simplifications suggested by some philosophers – Hegel, for example, on the role of reason or of the state, and sometimes Marx.[12] There is no knowledge of the future, no way to anticipate what our successors will think.[13] In the pursuit of truth there are no substitutes for hard work and an open mind. On the way, scientists and historians have to make, and to deal with, many interpretations. Gadamer's case is that philosophical hermeneutics performs a necessary role in this. Hermeneutics does not reveal the truth (to which there are no shortcuts), but it does help us on our way.

In conclusion, we may add that Gadamer is worth the reading. He is not an easy philosopher, but, unlike some of his compatriots, he is a practical philosopher. He does not set before us elaborate theoretical constructions, but tries to come to terms with life as we meet it in our intellectual activities. That is why he has had an impact on so many disciplines.

3   Political Correctness

3.1   The need for confidence

In recent years a claim has been made that history is predominantly written by white male heterosexuals and that, as a consequence, the legitimate place in history of blacks, women and homosexuals has been ignored or under-played through the prejudices of historians. This claim breaks down into four possible accusations. One is that (male and so on) historians omit important parts of history; another is that they distort their conclusions, usually by under-valuing the neglected groups. (Many people would argue that these boil down to the same thing since, in history, to omit relevant facts *is* to distort. For the sake of clarity we keep them separate.) A different question is whether these omissions and distortions are deliberate or unavoidable, perhaps for psychological reasons, but more probably for lack of evidence in most cases (see chapter 2, 2.8). This applies to both the omission and the distortion accusations, thus making four lines of attack. In the ensuing discussion it is worth bearing these distinctions in mind. The previous section on hermeneutics will, perhaps, throw some light on these vexed questions.

Vico believed that we understand history (like the other human sciences) because we made it. Gadamer's view is that we understand history because history made us. If this were the whole truth there would be little hope of correcting the distortions of white male heterosexual history. The only way open to the excluded groups would be for them to build up equally powerful counter-traditions of their own. Sometimes it seems that the more militant members are trying to do just this.

Is there a case for such counter-traditions of history? At first sight there is. Any individual or group that feels oppressed will also lack self-confidence. There is ample evidence that self-confidence is a valuable asset in action (think of men and women who climb the peaks of the Himalayas, for example), and also that it is much strengthened by membership of a self-confident group. Examples that spring to mind are Spartans in ancient Greece, Romans of the Republic, Normans in the eleventh and twelfth centuries, Puritans in seventeenth- and eighteenth-century America, Prussians in nineteenth-century Germany, and the English in nineteenth-century India, China and Africa. The morality of their deeds is debatable; their vigour and confidence are not. It has been remarked that a strong sense of group identity is partly the product of traditions and histories cast in the heroic mould. History has often been written deliberately to create a proud sense of nationality. Examples are legion, but one may point to the writings of Macaulay for the English, Michelet for the French, Treitschke for the Germans, Palacky for the Czechs, and Bancroft for the Americans. It is hardly surprising that groups feeling oppressed should desire similar historiographical support for their self-esteem. Books that have attempted this for black people include Arthur Haley's *Roots*, Eric Williams's various histories of the West Indies, Martin Bernal's *Black Athene*. The writers of feminist history are too numerous to list.

3.2 Are counter-traditions the answer?

Another advantage of building up counter-traditions in history is that it forces both the general public and historians to pay attention to the just claims of the oppressed. So, with these advantages, what might be said against such counter-traditions? The answer is: just that which can be urged against traditions – they can easily become ideologies or products of false consciousness. If we only build up counter-traditions against traditions we shall have a conflict of ideologies. Both peace and truth will suffer.

Let us be fair to tradition. In confronting the world we all have to begin somewhere. Tradition is where we begin. As we discussed in the previous section, any perception, however brief, brings with it some interpretation of the object. Further experience may well alter our understanding of it; the point is that we never see things as crude, simple sense-data. We see them as *things*.[14] Gadamer's concern is rather with symbolic systems (texts, rituals, theories, works of art and so on) than with natural objects. The point is the same. We always bring to them our own pre-judgements before (if at all) we make our considered judgements. Our tradition is what we have already learned from life – from our family, our schooling, our society and, above all, our language. It is not only that these things give us our roots, our place of standing. In a certain sense, they *are* us.

'In fact,' says Gadamer, 'history does not belong to us, but we belong to it. Long before we understand ourselves through the process of self-examination, we understand ourselves in a self-evident way in the family, society and state in which we live... That is why the prejudices of the individual, far more than his judge-ments, constitute the historical reality of his being' (Gadamer, 1979, p. 245). If that were all there is to Gadamer's philosophy, then his notion of tradition would genuinely be what it is often taken to be: a belief that each of us is so determined by history that we can never change our minds, open our eyes to new truths. The theory would deny us our freedom.

If this were true, then there would be a strong case for national and group histories so that members of those groups could determine who, in reality, they are. Often there have been deliberate attempts to establish national traditions and national identity through such cultural movements as the Celtic Revival in nine-teenth- and early twentieth-century Ireland (associated with Yeats, Synge and the Abbey Theatre) or the Arya Samaj and the Theosophical Society (associated with Annie Besant and the Swami Vivekananda) in India at the same period. Both of these were reactions to English hegemony. On the continent of Europe the dominance of the Russian and Austro-Hungarian Empires produced similar reactions among subject peoples. The remnants of Native American tribes in both North and South America are making similar efforts today.

3.3   The danger of traditions

There is little doubt that such movements help to build up both self-esteem and respect from others for these peoples. In a revival confined to the arts little harm and much good is done. There is ample room for differences in poetry, song or textiles. It is when cultural differences extend to the moral sphere that difficulties arise. It is easy to be tolerant of other people's arts; less easy to tolerate such practices as female circumcision, enforced temple prostitution, the ill-treatment of prisoners of war or the subjugation of women, even when defended on moral and religious grounds. Similar problems arise with history. An important part of the culture of any nation or other self-conscious grouping is the myths and legends of a heroic past, which play a large part in the (usually harmless) poems, plays, songs, dramas, paintings of any cultural revival. These legends might remain harmless if everyone were always aware that they are fictitious. But it is not so simple. Legends blend with history: such figures as Bluff King Hal, Good Queen Bess or the Merry Monarch (Charles II) are both legendary and historical. The same goes for Jeanne d'Arc, Henri IV and Napoleon in France. In the US the figures of George Washington, Abraham Lincoln and Robert E. Lee bring legend into almost contemporary history. The sarcophagus of Lenin, a place of pilgrimage in Moscow for nearly seventy years, was a particularly blatant example of turning history into legend. Thus traditions not only exist; they are deliberately created to fashion our personalities. Remember Gadamer's saying of history that 'we belong to it'. (For further discussion, see, for example, Hobsbawm and Ranger (eds.) (1984).) It becomes more and more clear that in the modern world many and vigorous attempts are made to ensure that not only our immediate pre-judgements but even our later considered judgements are shaped to this or that political end.[15] The phrase at the head of this section ('political correctness') reminds us that among women, blacks and homosexuals today there is a tendency to jump aboard this old but still mobile bandwagon.

There is then a strong case for tradition. Gadamer is right to insist that to a large extent we cannot avoid it. The restorers of tradition are also right to believe in the benefits of a proud group tradition. The Celtic Revival, for example, not only gave the Irish people more self-respect; its cultural products made them more worthy of respect. National pride can be part of our self-confidence. So is the pride in other groups and institutions of which we may be members. The question for historians, however, is whether this strong case for tradition conflicts with objective truth – or, at least, with our best efforts to attain it. There is a further question for any serious person: does the existence of traditions and counter-traditions work against the harmony and peace of the human race?

3.4   Overcoming traditions

If we suspect that the answer to either of these questions is 'Yes', then we must consider what can be done about it. Perhaps the best solution lies in the one word, 'dialogue'. Upholders of tradition and of counter-tradition should enter into dialogue with each other. It is important, however, to specify this dialogue more exactly. For 'dialogue' does not mean 'debate' or 'conflict'. It is not the task of the participants to justify their own points of view. It is not a political occasion where rhetoric is used to arouse the hearers to a particular persuasion – like Pitt in the Commons, Lincoln in Congress or Mark Antony in the Forum. Nor is it an academic occasion for the defence of a thesis. The scene is more like that of the *agora* in Athens with Socrates sitting down to search out philosophical truths in discussion with his friends. The participants must, in Gadamer's phrase, 'know how to be wrong'. Their aims will be not so much to advance their own ideas as to understand the others'. The result is unlikely to be the wholesale conversion of one party to another's views (as in Plato), but a broadening of the understanding of each, with a modification in the direction of the other. They are likely to end up less far apart than when they began. Even when each remains convinced of the substantial correctness of his or her opinion, that opinion will have a broader and more rational base simply because it now takes account of the other. When such a dialogue is successful there is mutual understanding, if not always mutual agreement. Both possess wider horizons; each is in a position to acquire better (because more comprehensive) norms and values. Taste and judgement can be improved. Then the plurality of histories presents less of a problem, rationality is furthered, concord is promoted and truth, if not wholly possessed, is less remote than before.[16] Some thinkers (Rorty, Foucault, Derrida) have used the insight of historicity to overthrow reason and to relativize values. Gadamer, by contrast, shows how rational thinking can be advanced, together with at least the possibility of sounder norms and values.

For historians, as for scientists, there remains a further resource for attaining these desirable ends. We have already remarked that scholars are not only in dialogue with each other; they are also always in dialogue with the evidence. No scientist (of whatever kind) and no historian (of whatever persuasion) carries weight in serious discussion until he is fully seised of all the relevant evidence. Those historians who wish to make a strong case for the traditions of a particular nation or grouping can be very selective in the evidence they adduce. Omitting important and relevant material is either ignorance or dishonesty. These are reprehensible in scholarly discussion. We have to ask: are either the 'politically correct' or their opponents always quite innocent in these respects? If they are not, Gadamer (like Plato) shows how they may strengthen their positions.

Notes

1 See also Oliver Sacks, *Awakenings* (1982) and *The Man Who Mistook His Wife for a Hat* (1985).
2 Jenkins (1991, p. 66). For similar attacks on science, see Wolpert (1993, pp. 110–23).
3 For example, the centuries-long debate in embryology between the believers in pre-formation and those in epigenesis had to wait until the late nineteenth century for decisive evidence. See Wolpert (1993, pp. 125–9).
4 Dilthey (1976, p. 207). For another aspect of Dilthey, see chapter 5, 3.9.
5 See, for example, the discussion in Ryan (ed.) (1973), and Durkheim (1938). For Dilthey's agreements and differences with Hegel, see Dilthey (1976, pp. 193–5).
6 Interview with H.-G. Gadamer in *Cogito*, (1994), vol. 8, no. 3, p. 216.
7 Carr (1964, p. 29). It should be pointed out that Carr has a somewhat idiosyncratic understanding of 'fact' – (pp. 10–12). For discussion of this, see Stanford (1986, pp. 71–4)
8 See his essay 'To What Extent Does Language Preform Thought?', in Gadamer (1979, pp. 491–8).
9 For a reasoned critique of this notion of objectivity, see the arguments of Thomas Nagel in *The View from Nowhere* (1986) and 'Subjective and Objective' in Nagel (1979).
10 'I imagine the Deity . . . as seeing the whole of historical humanity in its totality (since no time lies before the Deity), and finding it all equally valuable.' Ranke, quoted in Gadamer (1979, p. 185).
11 For further discussion see Stanford (1986, pp. 5–6, 172–9), and Stanford (1994, pp. 22–42).
12 'The state is absolutely rational' *Philosophy of Right* # 258; Hegel (1967, p. 155). Or 'The history of all hitherto existing society is the history of class struggles' *The Communist Manifesto*; Marx (1977, p. 222).
13 See, for example, Popper's arguments in *The Poverty of Historicism*.
14 See, for example, the arguments of J. L. Austin (1962) and J. J. Gibson and Vernon – quoted in chapter 2, 7.2.
15 Edward Said (1993) offers abundant examples.

16 For some further discussion on these lines, see Warnke (1987, pp. 168–74); also Lionel Rubinoff's argument that 'historicity and objectivity are not incompatible' – 'Historicity and Objectivity' in Van der Dussen and Rubinoff (eds) (1991).

Suggested Reading

Language

On language the best is Pinker (1995). Otherwise there are Crystal (1971) Culler (1976), Saussure (1980) (especially 'Principes Généraux').

Hermeneutics

Iggers (1983) especially chapter 6, and Gadamer (1985) make the important points. Bauman (1978) is useful here. Gadamer (1979) is fundamental, but too indigestible to begin with.

Political Correctness

Hobsbawm and Ranger (1984) are good on tradition. For types of history, see Burke (1991). For women's history see Perrot (1992) and the journal, *Gender and History*, Blackwell, (1989–).

8

'Only Connect'

> For whatever else a science may be, it is also a practice that must be as critical about the way it describes its objects of study as it is about the way it explains their structures and processes.
>
> Hayden White, *The Content of the Form*

1 Communication and Culture

1.1 The need for history

History is a concern with the whole of the human past. It is also the concern of all humans present. We all need history. Any such common concern requires some common understanding, and common understanding requires communication. Most, though by no means all, communication is carried on through language. For these reasons alone (there are others) language is a primary concern of the historian and of the philosopher of history.

The way things work with history can be symbolized by a large capital Z. Let the upper bar stand for the community of the present – all the people who are now in communication with each other. Let the lower bar stand for any given community of the past – say, fifth-century Athens or Tudor England or colonial North America. The oblique line of the Z represents the connection that the present makes with the past. This connection is history – but it is not only history. It consists also of manners, language, ways of thought, values, works of art, building styles, ideas and institutions of law and government, philosophical and religious theories and practices, and so on – all the ways in which our predecessors affect and influence us, the routes of Gadamer's 'effective history'. Part of the task of the historian is to trace the connections between past and present (along the oblique stroke) and to make them explicit. Then we may be clearer about what we inherit from the past and be in a position to decide what to reject, what to retain, and what to modify. By revealing the influences of the past we weaken its power over us, as J. H. Plumb pointed out long ago in *The Death of the Past* (1969). This is not the least of the services that historians can render to their society. Another of the historians' tasks is to concentrate upon the lower bar and to strive for an ever fuller understanding of that community and of the men and women who made it up. In order to do this they have to examine not only the apparent survivals from the past that I have just listed, but also those not apparent because they are hidden in the ground or in repositories of documents or in odd corners of the mind. For of course we can know nothing of the past except through the evidence that survives in the present.

Communications (chiefly linguistic) play vital parts in each of the three strokes of the Z. Much of the connection in the oblique stroke consists of language. We understand (fairly well, though not perfectly) the languages of past communities. Where we do not (as in the cases of Linear A in Crete or the Indus Valley civilization, for example) history proper is at a loss; we have to rely solely on the skills of the archaeologist. Deprived of language, historians are largely, though not completely, frustrated in their task of understanding societies of the past.

Now let us take the lower bar. That past community was itself largely constituted by language. No human society can hold together if people do not talk to one another, though of course there are non-linguistic bonds also. As well as habits and customs, it is important, then, to consider the role of the non-linguistic symbols. Language is the primary means of communication because of its flexibility and almost limitless capacity. But anthropologists in particular are very aware of the communicative powers of symbols and rituals – of things whose significance is not proclaimed in their appearance. A sword, a castle, a gun or a tank actually *is* power. A double-headed eagle, a crown, a fasces, a crossed hammer and sickle are only symbols of power, but were sometimes little less feared. The writings of Clifford Geertz or Roland Barthes, for example, are luminous with the importance of symbolic meanings (see Geertz, 1975; Barthes, 1973, 1984). Since every community, then or now, is held together by a common language – a language of symbols both verbal and non-verbal – it follows that the historian has to acquire a grasp of the language (verbal and non-verbal) of the community that he is studying.

1.2 Culture and language

Yet, strictly, it was not the symbols that held that community together, but the meanings of those symbols. For man is a 'creator of meanings' (Bouwsma in Rabb and Rotberg, 1982, p. 288). It is to some extent through language that he makes sense of the initially chaotic world in which he finds himself.[1] For although his first notions of it may be vague and incoherent, he can and must put that world into words (or other symbols – mathematical or musical, for example) if he is going to make it manageable. And he can best make it manageable by rendering it communicable. That involves articulating his experiences and ideas in a common language.[2] Such articulation is not to be taken for granted. Contrary to what some people have supposed, our words do not immediately match our thoughts. The philosopher, like the poet, is especially aware of the problem. For both, the expression of a new idea is 'a raid on the inarticulate / With shabby equipment always deteriorating / In the general mess of imprecision of feeling' (T. S. Eliot, 'East Coker').

Nevertheless, it is roughly true that the common language of a society embodies that society's understandings of its world and its intentions for that world, in spite of some necessary qualifications and exceptions. Such are the meanings that its language and other symbols hold for it. This social world 'might therefore be described as a vast rhetorical production'.[3] In attempting to come to terms with a social world of the past, historians do well to learn from their colleagues in anthropology.[4] One of these argues that the analysis of culture is 'not an experimental science in search of law but an interpretive one in search of meaning'.[5] This is because 'culture is the fabric of meaning in terms of which human beings interpret their experience and guide their action' (Geertz 1975, p. 145). Geertz regards man as an animal 'suspended in webs of significance he himself has spun' (p. 5). Bouwsma comments that we spin 'these webs primarily from – or with the help of – language.' (Bouwsma, in Rabb and Rotberg, 1982, p. 289). It would be small exaggeration to say that for human beings language is not only the vehicle of social action; it also fixes in place and gives meaning to all the elements of the world in which we live.[6]

1.3   Multi-cultural persons

When we turn to the upper bar of the Z, that is, to the contemporary world, we find that words and other symbols play no less a part. There is one significant difference, however. Most of the communities of the past were comparatively self-contained. This meant that the languages of word and symbol in daily use by the people were also the languages that held in place the world-picture of that society. This world-picture was the culture, the 'fabric of meaning' peculiar to that society, in terms of which its members could 'interpret their experience'. Today, by contrast, few communities are so self-contained. In the Europe of the 1990s most nation-states have their own distinct language; indeed, partly submerged nations that are not states (like Wales, Brittany, Catalonia) struggle to retain other languages than the national one as a mark of their distinct identity. Thus one might suppose that the world-picture of a Breton is markedly different from a Frenchman's, a Welsh woman's from an English woman's, and so on. But this is not the case. National television systems, American films, the products and advertising of multi-national corporations (think of the ubiquity of the red-and-white of Coca-cola or the golden arches of McDonald's) combine with other influences to break down local cultures. One language has already become the sole medium of communication for air traffic worldwide. It is the first language not only of Great Britain, but also of North America, much of the Caribbean, and of Australasia. It is also widely understood as a second language over much of Europe and Asia, so that books published in English have a ready market in the Far East as in the far West.

All this means that for most of the modern world language is no longer co-terminous with culture. For culture is now experienced at several layers; any one person today is likely to find the meanings of life expressed at more than one level. There is the culture of the locality: family, school, clubs, church, pubs or cafés. There is the culture of the nation: news media, government, economy. Third, there is the international culture of television, films, cars, radios, computers, pop music, multi-national products and advertisements, the European Union and the United Nations. Sometimes another stage is interposed between the first and the second in the cases of submerged nations already mentioned. That makes four layers of culture. It is not impossible that for immigrants and their descendants (West Indians or Pakistanis settled in Britain, North Africans in France or Turks in Germany) there is a fifth layer. The words and symbols that any one individual uses and understands may be restricted to his or her locality, or region, or nation, but an increasing number are international, some covering the whole Earth. It may be that the microchip with its offspring of electronic communication is already rapidly extending a worldwide culture. Perhaps we should no longer speak of a person's culture to characterize him or her. We shall soon have to use the plural and speak of an individual's *cultures*. Thus the term 'multi-cultural society' will change its meaning. At present it is taken to mean a society in which several cultures live side by side: Christian with Jew, Muslim with Hindu, Orthodox with Catholic, and so on. Soon, however, it will come to mean a society in which each member has several cultures.

1.4   The interpretation of cultures

What is the significance of this cultural plurality for the historian and the philosopher of history? For many reasons neither of them can afford to ignore the contemporary changes going on in the world about them. Marc Bloch tells the story of visiting Stockholm with Henri Pirenne, who insisted on seeing first the new city hall. 'If I were an antiquarian,' he said, 'I would have eyes only for the old stuff, but I am a historian, therefore I love life' (Bloch, 1954, p. 43). Pirenne's point is sharper in a world changing even more rapidly than his. This, we now see, is a world of multi-cultured individuals, as well as of multi-cultural societies. Moreover, both cultures and communications need to be interpreted. Historians have a manifold task of interpretation and communication which, making use of our device of the capital Z, may be analysed like this.

One part of the task is to concentrate upon a particular historic community. This community is to be envisaged as existing not only at the bottom of the oblique stroke of the Z – the point where historians first come into contact with it – but also right along the bottom bar. Therefore, in order to understand even the data immediately in front of them (that is, at the point where the oblique stroke meets the bottom bar), they have to move horizontally to take in the whole of that community, or they are liable to misunderstand even what seems most obvious. For the data before them is likely to be in linguistic, that is, symbolic form. But even if it is not written the historical evidence still consists largely or entirely of human artefacts – buildings, ships, tools, paintings and other products of common crafts and fine arts. Virtually every human product embodies meaning in one or more ways. It contains the intentions of the maker; like a church bell or a plough it has its place in a social activity; and it will often convey a message to the beholder or hearer, like the contents of a church or the details of a painting – details that afford so much scope for the ingenious discernment of the iconographer. All these meanings are there for the enlightenment of historians, who ignore them at their peril. This sub-section bears the title of Clifford Geertz's book. It reminds us that historians have a similar task to that of anthropologists but one even harder to execute. The difficulties of historical interpretation are not to be under-estimated. It is obvious that for a thousand years the symbol of a crown has meant 'king' or 'kingship'. Yet it is doubtful whether anyone alive today thinks and feels about monarchy as the subjects of Henry VIII or Louis XIV did. To get a proper grasp of what the symbol of a crown meant to them may call for a lot of hard work and deep thinking by historians. Ideally, a knowledge of the whole of Tudor England or of early Bourbon France is required. The good historian never forgets that this degree of comprehension is as desirable as it is impossible. Nevertheless, some notable advances have been made by the historians mentioned in Chapter 8, 1.2, above.

1.5 A network of meanings

These considerations may suggest to the philosopher another application of the Quine thesis that a body of knowledge consists of a network of meanings. Thus a statement in the natural sciences cannot be verified or falsified without reference to other scientific statements. 'The totality of our so-called knowledge or beliefs, from the most casual matters of geography and history to the profoundest laws of atomic physics or even of pure mathematics and logic, is a man-made fabric which impinges upon experience only at the edges' (Quine, 1980, p. 42).

From this one may conclude that the great historians are not those who know all the facts of their period – which is anyhow impossible – but those who can think like Tudor Englishmen or seventeenth-century Frenchmen. Even here, however, the concept of culture is not simple. In comparison with our societies, those of early modern Europe may seem culturally homogeneous, as we have remarked above. But an educated Englishman or Frenchman of those days bore more than one culture. As well as his local and national cultures he was likely to have been educated in the classics. His language (whether English or French) was being greatly enriched in his day by Greek and Latin – evidence that his best thinking was shaped by ancient as well as contemporary cultures. Thus the educated subject of Elizabeth I or Louis XIII was multi-cultured to the extent of at least three cultures – something that the historian must not neglect. Students of the history of literature or of ideas are likely to be aware of this; others (one may suggest historians of international relations or of economies, for example, who are more concerned with power or wealth than with ideas or texts) may well be less alert to such complexities of culture. All this shows that the historian, having descended the oblique stroke of the Z, must move along the length of the lower bar properly to comprehend even what lies at the foot of the descent. This may be because, as Saussure has argued, language and meaning are interlocked in a synchronic network of mutual support and mutual limitation. Concepts are 'defined negatively by their relations with the other terms of the system. Their most precise characteristic is in being what the others are not' (Saussure, 1980, p. 162; my translation).

1.6   The problem of languages

Before leaving the lower bar we must not overlook another problem. Many historians need a mastery of several languages besides their own. Turning to my bookshelves I find that Steven Runciman's *History of the Crusades* was based largely on texts in English, French, German, Italian, Latin and Greek – that is, in the medieval forms of these languages. In addition he used texts in Arabic, Persian, Armenian, Syriac, Hebrew, Georgian and Ethiopic – texts which had been translated into some convenient modern European language. Modern works on translation (for example, George Steiner's *After Babel*) draw attention to the almost superhuman skills needed to effect a good translation. Here we see a twentieth-century historian struggling with six medieval languages at once. As if this were not enough he has to rely on other people's translations for seven other languages. In doing so he is well aware that he is giving hostages to fortune, for even if the translators are as skilled as he, it is unlikely that they were looking out for the particular hints and nuances that he needed. Second-hand work never satisfies the scholar, but beyond six or seven medieval languages he has to acknowledge his limitations. When we are discussing texts and meanings (here and elsewhere in the book) we must remember that for the historian those considerations frequently apply to texts in languages not his own. Nor is Runciman unique. Many historians of Europe (particularly those dealing with international affairs or the lands of former empires like those of a Charles V, a Philip II, a Ferdinand II, a Maria Theresa, a Catherine of Russia or a Napoleon Bonaparte) have to master a handful of languages. The chances of error inevitably increase with the complexity; all the more praiseworthy then are the successes.[7]

1.7   Bunk is now history

The historian's second task with communication lies in the upper bar. Having completed his researches in the lower bar, he has to regain his starting point in the upper bar and then move sideways to convey to us, his contemporaries, the profound interpretations and understandings of what he has found. This is not merely a matter of translating the data of the lower bar into a language acceptable in the upper bar. Any competent linguist could do that. It is rather a question of articulating his own thoughtful comprehensions of a past society into such language as will have the same meanings for other people as it does for him. That means getting a grasp of what Gadamer calls 'the linguistic constitution of our life-world' (see above, chapter 7, 2.7).

This is not so simple as it may appear. Gadamer's phrase implies (as many have held) that our world-picture is constituted by our language. But surely it is not formed by language alone, but rather by our culture as a whole. It is culture, not just language, that forms the webs of significance in which our lives (according to Geertz) are suspended. This would matter less if we lived in the sort of primitive society where language and culture were coterminous. But, as we have just seen, this is not true of the contemporary world. The average man in the street, (whether the street be Broadway, Piccadilly, the Champs Elysees, the Unter den Linden, the Via Vittoria Veneto or the Castellana) is likely to speak only one language but to be a bearer of several cultures or sub-cultures; language and culture for him do not share the same limits. Now if anyone (be he historian, teacher, journalist, advertiser, politician or TV producer) wishes to speak about the past to the common man he must communicate his ideas (to repeat) in such language as will have the same meaning for the recipient as for him. In considering the role of communication in history we have concentrated on the work of the professional historian. But now that we are looking at the dissemination of historical knowledge – or, rather, the dissemination of ideas, true or false, about the past – we are concerned less with the writings of professional historians (who are read by comparatively few people) than with the various informers, popularizers, entertainers and persuaders who somewhat irresponsibly convey their notions about the past while ostensibly doing something else. It is they, rather than the serious and responsible historians, who speak the language of the man in the street. It is they who are largely heard and read. It is not difficult to point to a number of advertisements, films and television programmes that are seen by audiences of millions or tens of millions and which convey palpably distorted or simply false views of the past. (One may cite the misrepresentations of Columbus's first voyage or of the story of Pocahontas). Of this proliferation it has been remarked that history used to be bunk (a reference to Henry Ford's famous dictum); now bunk is history. This is to be set against the sale of serious historical works which run only into thousands or tens of thousands. This would matter less if the alternative to historical knowledge were complete historical ignorance. But this is not so. Virtually no one can escape having some ideas about the past. The only remedy for bad history is good history: no history (however desirable) is not an option. No more is to be said here, since I have discussed the matter at greater length elsewhere (see Stanford, 1986, chapters 10 and 11; 1994, chapter 3). Before we go on to look at the most distinctive manner of conveying historical knowledge – that of narrative – let us sum up this section.

1.8 Meeting the need

To see the fundamental importance of language for history in every meaning of that word (whether it refers to events of the past, scholarly researches or public opinions), it is necessary only to consider its importance in each stroke of that Z. For the communities of the upper and lower bars it acts both as a medium of communication and as a shaper of their life-worlds or, put another way, of their cultures. In addition, and no less essentially, it acts as the chief connecting medium of understanding between the communities of the past and the present. Yet the gap between what the present *ought* to know about the past and what it thinks it knows remains too wide. The understanding of medieval France, for example, requires more than the ability to read medieval Franch, but that is certainly the indispensable starting-point. How many people make casual pronouncements about the Middle Ages who have never been able to read a single sentence in medieval Latin, medieval English, or medieval French? Similarly, there are many who pontificate about science without ever having been inside a laboratory. With history as with science the gap is too wide between academic knowledge and popular belief. There is no shortage of scholars on the one hand and professional communicators on the other. What we need is scholars who can communicate.

2 Narrative

2.1 Grasping reality

The close link between history and narrative is clear from the fact that many languages use the same, or nearly the same, words for them – 'histoire', 'Geschichte', for example. While it is obvious that there are plenty of stories that are fictitious and therefore not history, and plenty of histories written in other than narrative form, nevertheless there seems to be more than a chance connection between history and narrative. The latter is certainly the traditional form of history, and many people claim that it is still the most appropriate form. Narrative history, they believe, constitutes an autonomous mode of understanding; that is, a way of understanding the world according to its own rules and standards, owing nothing to the methods and criteria of other disciplines, scientific or philosophical.

Valid or not, such a claim alerts us to the possibility that a story gives us a grasp upon reality that is not available in other ways. Of course, stories enchant us all – from fairy tales to Dostoevsky and Proust. But what is the nature of the hold they have upon us? They represent reality – but so do photographs. They stretch the imagination – but so do books on travel or science. They investigate character – but so does psychology. They portray social interaction – but so does sociology. They demonstrate cause and effect, but so do all the sciences. They enable us to escape into another world, but so do dreams, drugs, art and religion. They relax our tensions, but so do tobacco and physical exercise. Stories can do each of these things, yet all of them taken together do not quite explain the hold that good stories have.

2.2   Art and meaning

Before turning to narrative history let us look at narrative in general. In his discussion of tragedy Aristotle says that the chief requirement is plot. And this, surely, is true of any good story. But what exactly is 'plot'? It is 'the ordering of incidents', says he: an ordering of the incidents into a whole, a unity. This is the unity of 'a single action', which has a beginning – 'that which does not necessarily come after something else', and an end – 'that which naturally follows something else'. For well constructed plots 'must neither begin nor end in a haphazard way'. A plot, then, is an arrangement of incidents in a necessary or probable sequence from a clear beginning to a demonstrable end; the whole constitutes a recognizable and satisfying aesthetic unity.

All this is sound enough, but there is one thing that Aristotle does not mention: that is, meaning. Can it be that Greeks in his day were not so conscious as we are of the need to find meaning in life? The meanings of life, of history, of the universe-not surprisingly-elude us. But it is characteristically human to seek them – to find, to grasp, if not all then at least some meaning in existence. And, if we judge correctly, this was never more true in the history of the world than it is today. Now it may be argued that a work of art, almost any work, offers a meaning. The meaning may seem profound or trivial, good or bad, satisfying or unsatisfying; reactions vary. Science and philosophy today have little to say about the mysteries of life. In the past most people have found that religion helped to come to terms with these. It is another characteristic of the modern world that many people no longer find answers in religion. But art in all its forms is perhaps today more practised and valued and discussed than ever before. Is this because works of art offer some meaningful comment on existence and its mysteries? And that in so doing they take the place, for many people, of religion?

In this connection we may recall Plato's distrust of art. Most of us have encountered this in the *Republic* where he describes how, in his ideal common-wealth, the greatest poets will be honoured and then expelled (Book III, # 397). The work concludes (Book X) with a wholesale attack on all forms of art. His reasons in the *Republic* are metaphysical and moral; metaphysical because art is reality only at third hand, and moral because the behaviour of gods and heroes (the normal subjects of art) offers, at best, highly questionable models for young people. It has always seemed anomalous that what is one of the greatest works of European literature, the product of a comsummate artist, should contain such attacks. In her reading of another of his works, the *Phaedrus*, a modern philo-sopher suggests a more subtle reason. The *Phaedrus* and Plato's *Seventh Letter* reveal his unease about the nature of language – a worry that has surfaced again in our own day. He doubts whether the written word can convey fundamental ideas; the interplay of minds that marks a spoken discussion is absent. The written word is at the mercy of knaves and fools, apt to be twisted or misunderstood. Thus art corrupts because 'it apes a sort of insight, a unified vision, which in its true form is a spiritual achievement.' The work of art can mislead us because we think it has 'a unity, a perfection, which is not really there'. It is 'a spurious short-cut to "instant wisdom"' (Murdoch, 1993, p. 19). This leads to the startling conclusion that good art can be even more corrupting than bad art. In an age when works of art are often regarded with an almost religious reverence, these doubts are worth remembering.

2.3 Telling stories

Such speculations are not irrelevant to our question about the special attraction of a story. Without using the word, Aristotle seemed to be talking about meaning when discussing tragedy in the *Poetics*. Much of what he was saying about tragedy seems to apply to stories in general. Is it not an important, even a defining, quality of a narrative that it has a meaning; that it is not just a recital of random events – 'one damn thing after another'? It has been pointed out by some psychologists and philosophers that people often see their own lives as ongoing narratives; they tell themselves stories about themselves as they go on. 'Our world is full of things and persons and stories. We constantly weave our experience into limited wholes (art works).'[8] Surely this familiar practice is an attempt to give meaning, both to our own lives and to the world about us. One may not see the meaning of one's own life as a whole, but one can find a meaning in this or that episode of the day's experiences. A person with a gift for narrative can make a good story out of quite commonplace material. Duller people go through life without noticing the humorous, the significant, the ironic, the contradictory, the extraordinary or the pathetic. Each of these is grist to the mill for the entertaining story-teller.

  Almost everyone numbers among their acquaintance at least one good story-teller. How does he do it? His first consideration is to make a point: that is, to convey the humour, irony, pathos and so on of the cluster of events narrated. His second is to hold the attention of his audience so that they take the point. This is done by the use of various skills employed in fashioning plot, character, dialogue, setting, logical development, suspense and conclusion. The last is most important. The ending of the story should be significant, succinctly making the desired point; it should be seen as the necessary or probable consequence of the preceding events and so, in a way, summarize them; above all, it should be unforeseen. It is the neatness and unexpectedness of a good ending that arouses the audience's appreciation – gasps of surprise or bursts of laughter. Moreover, a good story is pared to a minimum; no more details are given than are strictly necessary for the audience's comprehension. You can learn a lot about the art of narrative by listening to conversations in bars or at dinner-tables where stories flow freely. Almost everyone has one or more tales to tell and is keen to do so. But some tellers are much more effective than others. Examples of good and bad narratives are there for analysis. Keep a clear head and see how the best is done.

2.4 Narratives in history

So much for narrative in general. What is to be said about historical narratives? The first requirement is truth. In amusing one's fellow diners one is not upon oath. A good story is often rightly suspected of exaggeration. Some details are enlarged, others omitted to make a better story. In writing history this consideration imposes a great burden. A good historical narrative, like any other kind, should hold the attention of its audience – or, more commonly, readers. In pure fiction the teller can invent his own details. In history none must be invented. But even in narrating a true story the teller may highlight some details, diminishing others, for the sake of effect. This is permissible in the social circle; but is it allowed in serious history?

If we are clear about truth, what about balance? Clearly the historian cannot put in all the details, not even all the details that he knows. He puts in the details that are significant for his story. Take the battle of Poitiers (or Tours) in 732.[9] The religion of Islam had exploded on the world in Arabia a century before. Within a few decades its warriors had conquered much of the Middle East and advanced triumphantly across North Africa to the Atlantic. In 711 they crossed the Straits of Gibraltar and swept north through Spain and across the Pyrenees. In a famous passage Gibbon speculated on the possible consequences:

> A victorious line of march had been prolonged above a thousand miles from the rock of Gibraltar to the banks of the Loire; the repetition of an equal space would have carried the Saracens to the confines of Poland and the Highlands of Scotland . . . Perhaps the interpretation of the Koran would now be taught in the schools of Oxford, and her pulpits might demonstrate to a circumcised people the sanctity and truth of the revelation of Mohammed.[10]

Having shown us the high stakes at issue, Gibbon proceeds: 'From such calamities was Christendom delivered by the genius and fortune of one man.' The drama of Charles Martel's victory is the point of the story. Would not Gibbon's point be ruined and our enjoyment shattered if attention were drawn to other details suggesting that the invaders could, in any case, have penetrated little further, and that they might indeed be ready to retreat? Gibbon was not only a great historian; he was also a great artist. After two centuries his massive work is still read with pleasure. The pleasure comes not from the spectacle of a slowly crumbling empire, but from the appreciation of the historian's intellectual grasp coupled with wit, irony, pathos, drama, urbanity, yet also with deep conviction.

Many other historians have told the story, or part of it, but they are all dull in comparison with Edward Gibbon.

Here is the narrative historian's dilemma. As a narrator, is he to bring out the drama, significance, irony, pathos and so on, that (as we have seen) are the making of any good story? Or is he scrupulously to balance all his details with their opposites, larding his paragraphs with: 'On the other hand...', 'Nevertheless, it must be remembered that...' and so on? Is not this the death of a good story? If you are condemned to dullness and boredom, why be a narrative historian at all? Should narration be given up and history be written in other modes altogether – more truthful but also more boring? (Let us not forget the heavy penalties of being dull. The dinner-table narrator loses his audience's attention; the historian is simply not read.)

2.5   Why not narrative chemistry?

Narrative history is not so easily dismissed. There is no question of the universal popularity of stories. As Barthes points out, they are found in every mode (myth, novella, tragedy, painting, conversation) and in every age, place and society. 'Narrative is international, transhistorical, transcultural: it is simply there, like life itself' (Barthes, 1966, in Barthes, 1984, p. 79). This ubiquity, however, does not mean that narratives do not have a recognizable form or structure; we have just seen that they do. The great problem for the historian is whether the phenomena of history are best dealt with in narrative form. After all, the life of societies around us is dealt with by economists and sociologists in quite other ways. Why should yesterday's similar phenomena require wholly different treatment? In short, while nobody doubts the value of narrative, why should we have narrative history any more than, say, narrative chemistry?

What is it about human affairs – whether on the individual or the social level – that encourages us to see them and to tell them as stories? It is not just that they are human rather than natural, for, as we have just remarked, human affairs can be dealt with by the methods of the social sciences. It is the dimension of time that marks the difference. Though time is not altogether absent from the natural and the social sciences, it is not fundamental to them. But time is fundamental to history in two senses. First it is fundamental because history deals with an age (however recent, however remote) that is not the present; the period that the historian studies is removed in time from the action of studying. This temporal gap brings both benefits and difficulties to the student – benefits and difficulties unknown to the student of present society. Second, and even more important, time is fundamental to history because traditionally it deals with a number of events extended over time. It is true that nowadays many historical works deal with one point in time. They concentrate on describing the state of affairs at that point with little consideration of what came before or after. An example is Namier's *The Structure of Politics at the Accession of George III*. Time is fundamental to this kind of work only in the first sense. To use a useful term from linguistics, this is a *synchronic* study – that is, concerned with things happening together, simultaneously. But the familiar form of history (that which accounts for the similarity of words for 'story' and for 'history') is *diachronic* – that is, it is about events extended through time, or along the dimension of time. To this kind of history, time is fundamental in both senses, and it is this diachronic arrangement of events that lends itself to narrative form. Thucydides and Tacitus offer classic examples.

2.6 Annals

Before we examine narrative history, we should look at those works that also arrange events diachronically but are not regarded as works of history proper. These are annals and chronicles. Annals, as the name implies, are calendars of events listed year by year. Medieval annals originated from the need to calculate the date of Easter. (It is confusing that the word is also used as a synonym for history, as in the *Annals* of Tacitus, one of the greatest works of ancient historiography, or in the journal *Annales: économies, sociétés, civilisations* of our own day.) Perhaps the most familiar example is the early pages of the *Anglo-Saxon Chronicle*. One of the simplest, however, is the *Annals of St Gall*. It is quoted by Charles Haskins in *The Renaissance of the Twelfth Century*. Some of it reads:

720   Charles fought against the Saracens
721   Theudo drove the Saracens out of Aquitaine
722   Great crops
725   The Saracens came for the first time
731   The blessed Bede the presbiter died
732   Charles fought against the Saracens at Poitiers on Saturday.[11]

What, then, are the characteristics of annals? First, there is a sense of chronology in the succession of fixed dates. But it is not a continuous succession; the annalist is obviously not concerned that a list of events worth recording should leave large gaps. From this we can draw our second conclusion; the annalist clearly has no intention of telling a story or he would close the gaps and link the events. Third, and again unlike a story, there is no beginning and no ending. The fourth characteristic is the most striking of all: there is no central subject and no background, two essential narrative elements.[12] The events recorded are not the actions of any person (except possibly of God) or of any collective organization. As far as the annalist is concerned they are what men suffer rather than what they do. Nor is the setting of the events made clear. What is the political, religious or social system that is disturbed by them? If these annals were presented to us as a history, we should ask: 'A history of what?'

2.7 Chronicles

It is in this that chronicles differ from annals, for it is the mark of a chronicle that it has both a central subject and a setting. Some of the best known of medieval examples were the chronicles of great cities – London, Paris, Cologne, Genoa, Florence. Some covered a whole country or kingdom, like the *Anglo-Saxon Chronicle*; others attempted all history, like the universal chronicles of Otto of Freising or Matthew Paris. Chronicles were often compiled from a collection of annals; therefore, unlike the former, they were not wholly written as things happened (like a diary), but also recorded the past. Indeed, many of them, like the *Anglo-Saxon Chronicle*, attempted to go back to the beginning – either the beginning of the country or the birth of Christ. Unlike a narrative, however, they did not have a conclusion but were added to year by year. Nor did they have a plot. What they did do, however (and this made them much more like a narrative than an annal), was to trace the connection (usually causal) between successive events. Finally, there is the question of meaning. Did the chronicler (in any particular case, for there must be more than one answer to this question) – did the chronicler impose his own meaning on the events he recorded, or did he think that their meaning revealed itself, or lastly, was he totally unconcerned with any question of the meaning of the whole? On the third supposition we have a clear differentiation from a work of history, for surely every historian believes that there is a meaning in what he has to tell us, whether he uses narrative, social analysis or any other form of historical discourse.

2.8 An objective narrative?

It is clear then that there are other ways than narrative of recording the past in chronological order. An examination of these shows up more clearly the characteristics of narrative. It also leaves open the question of whether narrative history *is* the best way of recording and understanding the past, even if (unlike analytic historians) we do insist on maintaining chronological order. After all, events happen one after another; why should they not be recorded and studied sequentially? One answer might be found in the old *Cambridge Modern History*, produced at the beginning of the the the century, where we have pages of 'dead-pan recapitulation' (as Butterfield put it). He could see no purpose in these 'forms of itemization which are neither story nor explanation' (see Butterfield, 1968, pp. 172–3). Of course, a story *can* be an explanation in itself.[13] Like Butterfield I cannot see the purpose, but I can see the reason: the authors were attempting to write the purely objective history that Acton required of them in his famous Letter to the Contributors.[14] Some of the pages of the original *Cambridge Modern History* are so boring that they are virtually unreadable. Like annals, they show how meaningless is a mere sequential record of events without plot, causal links, central subject, recognizable characterization, or identifiable point of view.

Medieval chroniclers produced much more interesting texts. 'Perhaps so,' might reply one of Acton's contributors, 'but our knowledge is more extensive than theirs, our standards of criticism more searching, our statements more careful, our criteria more exacting. In short, our history is more truthful.'

This imaginary exchange highlights the distinction between truth and meaning in narrative history. They are not at all the same thing, but a good work of history cannot do without either. (It is worth remarking here that non-narrative history usually makes its meaning more explicit. There is little doubt about the meaning of Burckhardt's *The Civilization of the Renaissance in Italy* or Le Roy Ladurie's *The Peasants of Languedoc*.) An important question about any work of history (as of any other representative art) is whether its meaning is found in the reality that it reveals, or is imposed by the artist.

Let us consider painting and photography. A portrait or landscape appears to reveal, or represent, what is before the painter. Nevertheless, it is almost impossible that the painter, in composing the picture, will not give it some meaning. Usually this is his intention, rather than a neutral and objective mirroring of his subject. Sometimes, however, the viewer can discern a meaning that was *not* the painter's intention. Is the meaning then 'in the eye of the beholder'? A camera, however, in so far as it is a mechanical device, can have no intention. The apparatus does neutrally record what is before the lens. There is, however, an art of photography, which art lies not in the machine but in the photographer. It is he who gives meaning, as we can all recognize, to the photograph. The more successfully he does so, the better photographer he is considered to be. Now let us return to history. Let us suppose that a gigantic cine camera is set up to run ceaselessly through the centuries and to record, objectively and neutrally, whatever passes before it. Let us suppose that we then arbitrarily cut off a length of the film and project it. Would we consider that a good history? Yes, in the sense that it is accurate and unbiased. No, in that it has no marked beginning, no conclusion, no explanation of how or why one event follows another, no subject, no setting of a social, moral or political system, no plot and, above all, no meaning. Is it, or is it not, a narrative?

2.9   Narrating and narrativizing

If we are not sure whether to answer, Yes or No, that may be because of the ambiguity in the word 'narrative'. To narrate, as the dictionary tells us, is to relate or recount; its basic meaning is simply to say what happened. It is only in the secondary and derivative sense that narrating is understood to be making a story. Often an investigator (for example, a parent, a teacher, a policeman, a barrister) will say to the witness: 'Now please don't make a story out of it. Just tell me clearly and simply what happened.' Many unsophisticated people find it difficult to relate or recount events neutrally; things tend to shape themselves in their minds as a story. 'Don't make a drama out of a crisis', as the insurance advertisers tell us.

People therefore invented another word, to 'narrativize'. This covers the secondary sense of 'narrate'; it means 'to make a story' (or a narrative in the second sense). To make the distinction clearer, we can say that the imaginary automatic camera in the previous paragraph was narrating. But a film-maker (an Eisenstein, a Spielberg) narrativizes with his camera. Much of the discussion of narrative history is led into difficulties by neglecting this ambiguity. Every historian, we can say, narrates, for he tells what happened. But only some historians narrativize, for only some (Gibbon, Michelet, Macaulay, Motley, Mattingly for example) make a story out of what they are relating. If their stories lack the perfect narrative form of a good novel, that is because their faithfulness to fact sometimes gets in the way.

2.10   Is history story-shaped?

This raises the question of how far the course of history is inherently 'story-shaped'. There seem to be at least three possible ways of answering this question. The first is to assert that history is itself a story. Thus one has only to relate the significant events in a roughly chronological order and the result is a story. Works of history have often been (rather naively) entitled 'The Story of...' such as, 'The Story of Ireland' or 'The Story of Flying'. The assumption here is that 'history' and 'story' are equivalent – an assumption that underlies the similarity (already noted) of the words in many languages. Hence there is no distinction between 'narrating' and 'narrativizing', for (in this view) to tell what happened (that is, to narrate) is to make a story (that is, to narrativize the events). At least one philosopher has made this equation. W. B. Gallie equates understanding history with following a story, 'where the story is known to be based on evidence and is put forward as a sincere effort to get at *the* story so far as the evidence and the writer's general knowledge and intelligence allow' (Gallie, 1964, p. 105). Gallie's reference to getting at '*the* story' (as far as circumstances permit) surely implies that he believes there lies one correct story behind (or within) the evidence, and that story is the true history: there is only one story to be told. This identification of story with history may appear uncritical, but it is probably a common assumption that has been widely held for a long time. Moreover it is not necessarily uncritical, as we have seen from Ricoeur's remarks quoted above – chapters 5, 2.3, and 6, 2.5 – and few have given more thought to narrative theory than he (Ricoeur, 1984, p. 91). Hayden White comments: 'Ricoeur's is surely the strongest claim for the adequacy of narrative to realize the aims of historical studies' (H. White, 1990, p. 54).

2.11   The same facts, many stories

This claim has been challenged by White himself. In a remarkable book, *Meta-history*, published in 1973, he argued that our understanding of history depends upon how it is told. As he put it, in any non-scientific study 'thought remains the captive of the linguistic mode in which it seeks to grasp the outline of objects inhabiting its field of perception' (H. White, 1973, p. xi). This fails to convince working historians, who know that their thinking is *not* the captive of any one linguistic mode; they know this because the objects of their study (people, institutions, events and so on) have been represented to them in many different modes in the many primary and secondary sources that they have used. There is no need here to follow the intricate details.[15] It is sufficient to note White's belief that historical narratives are 'verbal fictions, the contents of which are as much invented as found and the forms of which have more in common with their counterparts in literature than they have with those in the sciences' (H. White in Canary and Kozicki, 1978, p. 42). It is clear that for White the story is far from identical with the history; rather the story of the events can be told in many different ways according to the taste of the historian. This is not to say that the historian tells untruths; he does not falsify the evidence. It is simply that the evidence supplies only story-elements at most, elements which can be put together in various ways.

When one considers the many different stories that have been told of, say, the French Revolution or the peace settlement of Versailles, one finds the salient facts in each account, yet one also finds that different stories with very different meanings have been made of them. The Dutch historian, Pieter Geyl, wrote a very readable survey of lives of Napoleon.[16] It was an admirable critique of the Napoleonic Legend. François Furet more recently offered a valuable critique of the Revolutionary Legend.[17] These and similar historiographical surveys lend some support to White's claim that historians can narrativize the same set of events in different ways without doing violence to the evidence. Similar views can be found in E. H. Carr, Paul Veyne and Louis O. Mink. Carr insists that the basic facts are the same for all historians, but they do not speak for themselves; 'the facts speak only when the historian calls on them: it is he who decides to which facts to give the floor, and in what order or context . . . a fact is like a sack – it won't stand up till you've put something in it' (E. H. Carr, 1964, p. 11). Veyne also insists on the facts: 'The field of history is thus completely undetermined, with one exception: everything in it must really have taken place.' Since the field is undetermined, says Veyne, the facts must be ordered into a plot by the narrator. The plot is a 'mixture of material causes, aims, and chances – a slice of life, in short, that the historian cuts as he wills' (Veyne, 1984, pp. 15 and 32). Mink, on the other hand, sees the historian taking a synoptic (or bird's-eye) view of the events of the field of history and 'comprehending them in an act of judgment which manages to hold them together' (Mink in Dray, 1966, p. 178). This is roughly what W. H. Walsh, writing on the philosophy of history, calls 'colligation' (see W. H. Walsh, 1967, pp. 24–5, 59–63). Common to all these is the notion that historians may agree on the facts but differ in their conclusions about 'what it all adds up to'; events may be legitimately narrativized in more than one way and history and story are not, therefore, identical. Such a view, though perhaps a little one-sided, is not unreasonable. It does, however, arouse opposition among some more traditional historians, as can be seen in the late G. R. Elton's attack on Hayden White in the Cook Lectures of 1990, where, after four pages of condemnation, he dismisses White's case as 'meaningless verbiage, testifying only to general lack of experience in trying actually to write serious history' (Elton, 1991, p. 34). While there is force in the argument that those who give their opinions on the writing of history should have some experience of writing history, this accusation cannot be levied against Paul Veyne or E. H. Carr, historians of repute in their own fields.

2.12 The structure of action

One is not compelled, however, to choose between these two views. There is a third possible answer to our question. One need not believe, like Gallie, that the events constitute one and only one story (speaking for themselves, as it were), nor that historians are free to make up stories in any form provided they are true to the evidence. A third view is perhaps more convincing than either. This is that history (that is, the sequence of events) takes on something like narrative form, but that there is more than one story that can be made of it. Both stories (true or fictional) and history rest on human experience and human action. As Frederick A. Olafson puts it: 'In this temporal form the rational structure of action is the structure of narrative' (Olafson, 1979, p. 151). History consists largely of the doings of men and women. Such doings do not have to be recorded in narrative form. They may be treated analytically, as they are in economics or sociology; the latter, however, do not attach importance to particular deeds. Now it is the essence of history to select certain individual events (clusters of deeds), to show their significance, and to trace the connections between them. Bearing in mind that these events occur in temporal order we may have here something of the structure of action: that is, one thing leads to another – to put it over-simply. But it is important to note that the sequence (the 'leading') is much less one of natural causation (like a stone falling under gravity) than of human action and response, of motivation and deed. The structure of action is familiar to us all. We experience it in our lives, we recognize it in narratives. It matters not whether the narrative is fictional (as in the novel or drama) or whether it purports to portray actual historical events; both fiction and history (at least, narrative history) have a common familiar structure: the structure of human lives. 'And it is the success of historiography in narrativizing sets of historical events that attests to the "realism" of narrative itself... There is, then, a certain necessity in the relationship between the narrative... and the representation of specifically historical events. This necessity arises from the fact that human events are or were products of human actions' (H. White, 1990, p. 54).

2.13 Living a story

Indeed, life experience is often like a story, as we have mentioned above (Chapter 8, 2.3). As one philosopher has put it: 'It is because we all live out narratives in our lives, and because we understand our own lives in terms of the narratives that we live out, that the form of narrative is appropriate for understanding the actions of others' (MacIntyre, 1981, p. 197). Another goes even further. David Carr argues that we see our lives as stories not merely after the events but while they are actually occurring. 'Narrative', he says, 'is not merely a possibly successful way of describing events; its structure inheres in the events themselves. Far from being a formal distortion of the events it relates, a narrative account is an extension of their primary features' (D. Carr, 1986a, p. 117). Of course, any account can be a distortion of the events if the narrator has got the facts wrong, but narratives do retain the primary features if the narrative (as normally is the case) relates to human actions. This is especially true of political history, for here individual human choice is much more in evidence than in economic and social histories which tend to deal with movements of masses of people over long periods. The 'primary features' to which Carr refers are the structure of action. Action has its costs in time, thought, energy and often money. We undertake it either because our present situation is distasteful or because we are attracted to a different state of affairs. Motivation follows hard upon the assessment of present and possible future situations; thought is often required to choose the means of moving from one to the other. The pattern, we have seen, is situation – motivation – means – goal (see chapter 6, 3.2). Of course, this pattern may be broken at any stage: we may find no means of leaving our situation; the means may prove ineffective; our plans may be frustrated by some unforeseen occurrence. Nevertheless, the basic structure of action is there, and this provides the framework for a story. As we are acting, says Carr, we 'throw ourselves forward' in thought into the future to the point of the completed action and imagine ourselves looking back on it. This he calls a 'future retrospective point of view on the present' (D. Carr, 1986a, p. 125). It is not necessary to agree with Carr that this is what most people do. His point is made if we acknowledge that our lives, in part or in whole, can be told in story form.

It may be that narration is fundamental to human nature. Yet another philosopher writing on 'The Philosophical Problems of Consciousness' says: 'Our fundamental tactic of self-protection, self-control, and self-definition is ... telling stories, and more particularly concocting and controlling the story we tell others – and ourselves – about who we are. These strings or streams of narrative,' he continues, 'issue forth as *if* from a single source ... *a center of narrative gravity*' (Dennett, 1991, p. 418). Such notions, derived not from historiography but from biology, in fact, from Richard Dawkins's theory of *memes*, serves to confirm Carr's suggestions.[18]

2.14 Narrative structure, narrative form

All these ideas lend support to Carr's further suggestion that group identity as much as personal identity is reinforced (if not actually created) by the stories we tell of ourselves. It is almost a commonplace that national histories were written in the nineteenth century largely to bolster the sense of nationhood. Macaulay, Michelet, Bancroft, Treitschke and many others may spring to mind. This is not news. What is more surprising is to realize that we are often aware of possible future stories and histories at the very time of action. I remember thinking in the eventful summer of 1940: 'What wonderful stories future historians will have to tell of all this!' Indeed we were encouraged to think in historical perspective by Churchill's own words: 'Let us therefore brace ourselves to our duties, and so bear ourselves that, if the British Empire and its Commonwealth last for a thousand years, men will still say: "This was their finest hour."'' The Empire was not to last much longer, but after half a century (not yet a thousand years) I believe it was indeed Britain's finest hour.

Carr's conclusion (and perhaps ours also) is that the events of history do not inevitably occur in the natural shape of a story, nor (on the other hand) is the historian free to shape them into any form that he wishes; the truth is that narrative form is inherent in many sequences of events because they have narrative structure – the structure of human action: situation – motivation – intention.[19] Since much of human life (i.e. history 1) lends itself to narrative form it is not difficult to make narratives out of it. This leaves open, however, the most important question about any particular narrative: how accurately does it represent the course of events that it claims to portray? Fascinated by theories of narratology we may be, but we must never forget that the historian is concerned with a real past, with events that actually occurred (just as they are occurring now), and that his primary duty is to the truth. And truth is the requirement not just of scholars, but, more importantly, of the public at large.

Notes

1 The part which language plays in the development of human intelligence is a large and controversial subject. But the enquirer could do worse than start with the works of the Swiss psychologist, Jean Piaget.

2 Wittgenstein has demonstrated pretty conclusively the impossibility of a purely private language. See Wittgenstein (1968). Nevertheless, his arguments have given rise to an extended philosophical debate.

3 Bouwsma in Rabb and Rotberg (1982, p. 290). See also Gadamer, quoted in chapter 7, 2.

4 Among those historians influenced by anthropology are Marc Bloch, Emmanuel Le Roy Ladurie, Georges Duby or Michel Foucault in France with others of the Annales school, as well as Natalie Zemon Davis or Carlo Ginzburg in America and Keith Thomas or Peter Burke in Britain.

5 Geertz (1975, p. 5. Cf. Wittgenstein's approval of Freud's *The Interpretation of Dreams*: 'What was wanted was not an explanation but an interpretation.' See Monk (1990, p. 448).

6 For theories of the structure of the social world, see among others, Weber (1964); Schutz (1972); Berger and Luckmann (1971).

7 For some of the philosophical problems of translation, see Quine (1960).

8 Murdoch (1993, p. 37); see also chapter 8, 2.13 and 2.14.

9 It is known by either name since it took place between the two towns.

10 *The Decline and Fall of the Roman Empire*, chapter LII.

11 Haskins (1957, p. 231). The monastery of St Gall is in Switzerland, some 500 or 600 kilometres from Poitiers and Aquitaine. The 'Charles' is Charles Martel, effective ruler of the Franks and grandfather of Charlemagne.

12 For a list of narrative elements, see Stanford (1994, pp. 87–92).

13 'History . . . is the narration of a course of events which, in so far as it is without serious interruption, explains itself.' Oakeshott (1933, p. 143). See also Dray (1964, p. 30).

14 It is printed in Stern (1970, pp. 247–9).

15 They are laid out in White's introduction to his book, and are discussed in Stanford (1986, pp. 133–7), as well as in *History and Theory* (1980), vol. 19, Beiheft 19: 'Six Critiques of *Metahistory*'. See also chapter 9, 1.4 and 1.5.

16 *Napoleon: For and Against* (1949).

17 Furet, *Penser la revolution française* (1978) ET *Interpreting the French Revolution* (1981).

18 For memes, see Dennett (1990, p. 201) and Dawkins (1976, p. 206) or (1991, p. 158).

19 If the terms 'form' and 'structure' seem confusing here, we may remind ourselves that the human form is the body, the human structure is the skeleton, musculature, neural system and so on which shape and sustain the body.

Suggested Reading

Culture

See Burke (1991) and (1992). Also Barthes (1973) and (1984). For the influence of anthropology, see Novick (1988), chapter 15), and Appleby et al (1994), chapter 6). Also the introduction to Geertz (1975). One of the first and best examples is K. Thomas (1978).

Narrative

One may begin with Stone's essay in Stone (1987). Gallie's is a clear statement of the case for narrative (Gallie, 1964). The essays of Mink (1965) and (1978), D. Carr (1986a), Carroll (1990) and Norman (1991) are good starting points. Olafson (1979), Chatman (1980) and H. White (1990) are book-length discussions.

9

The End of History?

History is bunk
Henry Ford

1 The Linguistic Turn in History

1.1 The antithesis of objectivity

The title of this chapter is deliberately ambiguous. There has been a good deal
of debate stimulated by Francis Fukuyama's notorious article 'The End of
History?' (1989) and his subsequent book *The End of History and the Last Man*
(1992). But this is not our concern here. Again, the phrase might refer to
the purpose of the historical enterprise. That we have never been far from
in the course of this book and we shall return to the theme. But at the
moment we need to glance at another kind of demise that threatens our subject –
this is the belief that there is no past reality to be the object of historical
studies.

We began this book with the search for objectivity. By this we understand the
notion that the nature of the object should determine whatever is said about it and
that no part of that discourse should stem from the thinking or knowing subject.
We now come to the opposite view of history: that there is no historical object. All
that is said, all discourse, is held to derive only from the brains of those who have
thought, spoken or written about it. (Ironically enough, other postmodernist
themes claim to have abolished the subject also; the name of Michel Foucault is
especially associated with this abolition. But let us stick to the historical object.)
We were able to show in earlier chapters how difficult it is for objectivity thus
defined to be achieved in history. We saw what obstacles lie in the way of speaking
or writing about a part of the past in such a way that our words exactly fit their
object: 'simply to tell it as it happened'. The opposite notion – that historical
language has no historical reference – is expressed by a postmodern writer thus:
'To put it in a nutshell, we no longer have any texts, any past, but just interpretations of them' (Ankersmit, 1989, p. 137).

What has happened?

1.2 A 'scientific' interlude

First, we should remind ourselves that until about the beginning of the nineteenth century (and often after that date) history was seen as a department of literature. That does not mean that its sole function was to amuse. Quite the contrary; it was intended to be useful. In the England of Edward Gibbon, 'History-writing claimed, and perhaps earned, its keep precisely by presenting itself as useful, capable of teaching by example or of providing ammunition for the political and religious controversies ceaselessly waged in Stuart and Hanoverian England' (Porter, 1988, p. 17). Most important was the fact that historians had to earn their keep – apart from a very few who were supported by highly placed patrons or, like Gibbon, had a substantial private income. In order to live historians had to sell their books, and this meant that they had to be readable. Few historians could afford to neglect public appeal until history became a professional discipline in universities in the second half of the nineteenth century. Other factors also influenced the ways in which history was written, but this weighed most. Thus the literary aspect of historiography was in the forefront of historians' minds from Herodotus to Macaulay or Michelet. Their use of rhetoric – that is, planning the effect upon hearer or reader – was nothing to be ashamed of. Considerations of clarity, order, presentation, style were (and are) essential to historical discourse.

The professionalization just referred to occurred at a time when the natural sciences were making great advances. Thus it is not altogether surprising that, against this background and under the influence of the prevailing philosophy of positivism, many historians claimed the status of a science for their discipline. In what for long remained a standard guide for historians, C.-V. Langlois and Charles Seignobos's *Introduction to the Study of History* (1898), the authors condemned 'the romantic historians' for 'a concern which is certainly not a scientific one. It is a literary concern' (Langlois and Seignobos, 1898, p. 261). They also claimed, in a famous remark, that history relies entirely on written sources: 'For there is no substitute for documents: no documents, no history' (p. 17). Although Trevelyan, an avowedly literary historian, argued that history is not a science, an attempt to write objective history was made by the publication of the *Cambridge Modern History* (1902–12) (followed by the volumes of the *Cambridge Ancient* and *Medieval Histories*.) It was not till after the Second World War that the impossibility of achieving Bury's and Acton's aim was acknowledged by the appearance in 1957 of the first volume of the *New Cambridge Modern History*. For this the General Editor, Sir George Clark, wrote an introduction which provided a wide and clear conspectus of the condition of historical studies. (It is still worth reading, for its twenty pages contain more good sense than many a lengthy book.) The nineteenth century had seen a 'cult of facts' by historians, of whom few enquired 'what facts are'. Acton's attempt to publish 'a definitive history' was now seen to be impossible of achievement. 'Historians of a later generation do not look forward to any such prospect. They expect their work to be superseded again and again.'[1] Historians today would almost all agree that history is not a fixed text but an unending debate.[2] Moreover it not only is, but should be, a debate. There is no foreseeable end to the appearance of fresh evidence, there is no closure to various methods of interpretation, there is no guarantee that one perspective (for all history must be perspectival – as Nietzsche noted) is superior to all others. But if a final, definitive history is impossible, this does not justify relativism – a point that we shall return to.

1.3   A 'linguistic turn'

Nevertheless, the realization that history is always a matter for debate does seem to shake the belief in the possibility of historical objectivity. One attempted way out of this difficulty was Collingwood's argument that the historian has to re-think the thoughts of the historical agent. This, if at all a possibility, would guarantee some objectivity for the historian, since what she is writing about is not only the past but also the present – that is, the same thoughts. On the whole, however, the drift of questions in the philosophy of history continued to centre around fact and explanation; in short, to be orientated towards questions of epistemology. However, it was perhaps almost inevitable that, sooner or later, in this era of questions about the historical enterprise, someone would recall the pre-positivist attitude of literary historians (the great figures of eighteenth- and early nineteenth-century historiography) for whom considerations of style and presentation ran a close second to questions of truth. (Think what Gibbon gained by his sly wit, and enjoy Clive's essays on 'Why read the great historians?') (Clive, 1989). At this point (approximately the 1960s) epistemological problems of history (never satisfactorily solved for those who want history to be a science) combined with a revival of interest in the literary and interpretative aspects of historiography. Put simply, questions of what we know and how we know it began to give way to questions of what we tell and how we tell it. Some people call this history's 'linguistic turn'.

1.4   Metahistory

A landmark in this development was the appearance in 1973 of Hayden White's *Metahistory*. This was an attempt to subsume the historiographical enterprise under the canons of literature. The details of what he did are less important than the fact that he did it at all, but this, roughly, is what he did. The historian, he argued, has to represent to himself the story of the events contained in the relevant documents. These events he has to 'prefigure' to himself as one of the four main literary tropes of Metaphor, Metonymy, Synecdoche and Irony. To these there correspond four literary modes of 'emplotment' – Romance, Comedy, Tragedy and Satire. The whole schema is based on that put forward by the Canadian literary critic, Northrop Frye, in his *Anatomy of Criticism* (1957). Taking four nineteenth-century historians and four philosophers of history, White attempted to show how these varied tropes and types of emplotment could be used in the representation of the past. Whether or not he succeeded must be left to the judgement of readers, but there is a full critical discussion of the work in *History and Theory*, (1980), Beiheft 19. The important point for us is that White believed that the literary mode adopted by the historian provided both the meaning and the explanation of the events. 'Providing the "meaning" of a story by identifying *the kind of story* that has been told is called explanation by emplotment' (White, 1973, p. 7). It is worth considering this claim in the light of the discussions in chapters 4 and 7.

At first sight we may be inclined to agree with White that ' "history", as a plenum of documents that attest to the occurrence of events, can be put together in a number of different and equally plausible narrative accounts of "what happened in the past" . . .' (White, 1973, p. 283). After all there exist a number of historiographical surveys that discuss the many very different accounts of the same events.[3] But history, as we shall see, is more than 'a plenum of documents'. Whether or not such varying accounts are put together in accordance with Frye's canon of tropes and modes is perhaps beside the point for historians, being rather a matter for literary critics. I think we may conclude that White's main achievement was to draw attention to the fact that a work of historiography has an important aesthetic aspect as a work of art, as well as an epistemological aspect as a contribution to knowledge. But aesthetics must not infringe upon the superior claims of epistemology.

1.5 Form and Content

Of course, as we have seen, there was nothing new about seeing the aesthetic or rhetorical aspects of history writing; traditional historians have always been aware of it. It is just that it was rather forgotten between the mid-nineteenth and mid-twentieth centuries and so comes as something of a shock to the older generation of historians. One of these has accused White of treating 'historical exposition as a form of literary discourse and no more'.[4] He is further accused of believing 'that the work of the historian depended on the historians rather than the work, so that its study should be reduced to a study of the manner in which historians accounted for the past' (Elton, 1991, p. 33). Such criticisms are rather unfair. It is not clear that White wishes to reduce historiography to a purely literary exercise unconcerned with questions of truth about a real past. It is more charitable to suppose that he desires merely to emphasize the aesthetic aspect of history writing while not denying its epistemological importance. However, he does give ammunition to his critics with some later claims. Historical narratives are 'verbal fictions, the contents of which are as much invented as found, and the forms of which have more in common with their counterparts in literature than they have with those in the sciences.' Or again, he sees the historical narrative as 'a verbal artifact that purports to be a model of structures and processes that are long past and cannot therefore be subjected to either experimental or observational controls'

(White in Canary and Kosicki, 1978, p. 42). Such remarks indicate something less than a full understanding of the nature of history, as we shall argue later. Nevertheless White shows a keen awareness of the problems of narrative discourse as a mode of historical representation. His later essays in *The Content of the Form* (1987), which centre around these problems, are introduced by this notion: 'the realization that narrative is not merely a neutral discursive form that may or may not be used to represent real events in their aspect as developmental processes but rather entails ontological and epistemic choices with distinct ideological and even specifically political implications' (White, 1990, p. ix). In other words, narrative cannot but contain a hidden message – even the form has a content.

1.6 Rhetoric – and beyond

It is true that representation of the past is not as simple a matter as many historians have assumed. Therefore nothing but good should come from an open and critical discussion of how this has been, can be and, perhaps, should be done. It is equally true that the rhetoric of the historian may (though it may not) distort the knowledge of a real past that it purports to convey. Nevertheless, it must not be hastily assumed that a recognition of these problems implies the impossibility of historical knowledge. Although, as we shall see, too great a concentration on the literary aspect can lead to a denial of the epistemological function of history, yet it is well to remember that there are literary theorists who explicitly recognize the primary function of history – to tell the truth about the past. One such is Ann Rigney, an expert on literary theory, whose study of three French writers on the Revolution is a valuable exposé of how historians work – still relevant in spite of the fact that the three works examined (by Lamartine, Michelet and Louis Blanc) appeared in the middle of the nineteenth century before the professionalization of history. As she rightly says:

> It seems necessary to consider the discursive dimension of the historian's work more closely in the light of its specifically historiographical function, that is to say, its function in representing and explaining real events of collective significance.
>
> (Rigney, 1990, p. xi)

Another valuable contribution to the contemporary debate has been made by three American historians, Joyce Appleby, Lynn Hunt and Margaret Jacob. On this same point of representation they state firmly:

> We see no reason to conclude that because there is a gap between reality and its narration (its representation), the narration in some fundamental sense is inherently invalid.
>
> (Appleby et al., 1994, p. 235)

They are arguing against the attacks on truth, objectivity and history made by postmodernist writers. This is not the place to go into the blind alley of postmodernism, nor to trace the faulty reasoning behind many postmodernist pronouncements.[5] Yet by way of illustration of how literary theory can be carried too far in respect of the writing of history, it may be useful to cite one or two examples – examples that do deserve Elton's accusation of regarding historiography as 'a form of literary discourse and no more'.

2   The Loss of the Object

HISTORY UNDER ATTACK (SUBSECTIONS 2.1–2.5)

2.1   History nothing but representation?

Put briefly, what happened in the philosophy of history was that the linguistic turn led to the claim that history is nothing more than language. Some people moved from the recognition that the historical past must be spoken about to the belief that the historical past is nothing other than that speaking. To put it another way, words that exist to speak *about* reality *become* that reality. This line of thought as applied to history may be traced in an article by F. R. Ankersmit that appeared in 1988. The writer identified three moves in the philosophy of history of the previous four decades. These were, in turn, a concern with explanation, with interpretation and, finally, with representation.[6] These views appear to be a development of a useful article on Western historiography that Ankersmit published two years earlier.[7] He argued that true history is not the past, but the present representation – as it might be the history book or the historical painting. Our concern then becomes aesthetic (that is, neither epistemological nor interpretative); we look *at* the representation itself, not *through* it to a further reality. As examples of 'postmodernist' history he cited such well-known works as Le Roy Ladurie's *Montaillou*, Ginzburg's *The Cheese and the Worms*, and Natalie Z. Davis's *The Return of Martin Guerre*. Such 'micro-stories' as these were the reality of history itself: 'Instead of constructing a representation of the past in the alien medium of narrative discourse' (that is, normal historical practice), 'these "micro-stories" themselves take on a reality that had previously only been attributed to the past we saw through the historical representations.'[8] A historical text then becomes like a stained-glass window where our concern is not with the sky or landscape to be seen through it, but with the glass itself. Ankersmit goes on to speak of *Montaillou* and others:

> The effect of these 'micro-stories' is thus to make historiography representative only of itself; they possess a self-referential capacity very similar to the means of expression used by the relevant modern painters. Just as in a modern painting,

the aim is no longer to hint at a 'reality' behind the representation, but to absorb 'reality' into the representation itself.[9]

Now the stained-glass window looks out on to a blank wall. There is no landscape; only the coloured glass.

The following year another article by Ankersmit reinforced his conclusion with a different argument – one taken this time from interpretation not representation. He pointed out that some writings (he instanced Hobbes's *Leviathan*) have been interpreted in different ways. He concluded from the varying understandings that 'naïve faith in the text itself being able to offer a solution to our interpretation problems became just as absurd as the faith in a signpost attached to a weather vane . . . To put it in a nutshell,' he goes on, 'we no longer have any texts, any past, but just interpretations of them.'[10] Later he used another image – that of a tree – to illustrate his point. Traditional historiography focused on the trunk of the tree of history. For postmodern history 'the essence is not situated in the branches nor in the trunk, but in the leaves of the historical tree.'[11] We have come to the autumn of historiography, where our task is to collect the leaves, not to see where they were on the tree, but to see what pattern we can form from them now.[12]

2.2   The claims of postmodernism

After some forceful criticism in an article by Zagorin, 'Historiography and Post-modernism: Reconsiderations', Ankersmit replied in 1990 with a list of the chief tenets of postmodernism which must be taken into account. These included the claims that 'narrative language has the ontological status of being an object, that it is opaque; that it is self-referential; that it is intensional . . . that as far as narrative meaning is concerned the text refers but not to a reality outside itself; that criteria of truth and falsehood do not apply to historical representation of the past'.[13] These conclusions would be denied by most, if not all, historians. It is unfortunate that in arguing for a constructivist case (that is, that 'narrative substances do not refer to the past'), Ankersmit cited the present author in support: 'As construct-ivists like Oakeshott, Goldstein or Stanford have successfully shown, there is no past that is given to us'[14] It is doubtful whether Oakeshott was a constructivist and I certainly am not. What all three of us pointed out was the obvious fact that the past is not present and therefore cannot be directly apprehended through the senses. This certainly does not imply (as Ankersmit appears to think) that it cannot be known at all. Indeed, my whole book, *The Nature of Historical Know-ledge* (1986) was written to show how such knowledge is not only possible but is actually achieved.

By way of footnote, we may mention another article of the following year, written by Patrick Joyce in reply to an attack by Lawrence Stone on postmodern-ism.[15] Joyce makes the same constructivist point as Ankersmit: namely, that the past that historians purport to describe is solely a product of their and our brains.

He writes: 'The major advance of "postmodernism" needs to be registered by historians: namely, that the events, structures and processes of the past are indistinguishable from the forms of documentary representation, the conceptual and political appropriations, and the historical discourses that constitute them.'[16]

2.3 The annihilation of history

Although the argument dwindled away in these journals, some ideas of post-modernism still have a certain vogue – all the more, perhaps, because of their vagueness, for many people are undecided exactly what they are or how to apply them. It is, then, worthwhile noting what at least some people claim for post-modernism in relation to history and to see what should be said about these claims.

Let us sum up the points made by Ankersmit and Joyce. We can identify six.

1 That in historiography the representation is the reality. Texts are self-referential; they do not refer to anything else.

2 That to such texts only aesthetic criteria are relevant, not epistemological norms or standards.

3 That we have no established texts and no past, but only (more or less plausible) interpretations.

4 That criteria of truth and falsehood are inapplicable to historiography.

5 That historical accounts are both opaque and intensional. (To make this clearer, let us remember that these attributes are more proper to poetry than to history. A poem is, or may be, a thing in itself, not a window on reality – hence it is opaque. A poem exists in the original words – it cannot properly be paraphrased; hence intensional. Neither of these is ordinarily held to be true of a historical account.)

6 That the historical past is only the creation of present historians, rather than existing in its own right – this is 'constructivism'.

It is pretty clear that all this adds up to an annihilating attack upon the whole historical enterprise. Before we sum up our conclusions about that enterprise it will be fitting to take a look at this matter of postmodernism. Primarily it is a literary and linguistic phenomenon. It is of concern to historians only in so far as they are concerned with the use of language in history (the 'linguistic turn') or in so far as postmodernists make direct attacks upon history, as in the examples of Ankersmit and Joyce quoted above. There is, however, another postmodernist belief which is of far greater importance to historians. This is the claim that the period of modernity has come to an end and that we are now living in the period of 'postmodernity'. Since this is a claim about history itself (history 1) rather than about the way we think and talk and write about history (history 2), it is of more direct concern to historians. We shall pursue this at greater length below.

2.4   A real past

A French critic, Alain Touraine, has described postmodernism as, above all, post-historicism (Touraine, 1995, p. 178). For post-historicism denies that history has an ordered course, that we know roughly what that course is, that we are moving towards greater rationality, greater prosperity and greater freedom (the three being interlinked), and that social and political events can be located in their proper place in that sequence. Postmodernism does not believe that, and so does not believe that history has any relevance to our lives. Thus not only is historicism irrelevant to our lives nowadays; history itself has no role. On the contrary, the remains of the past (old books, old tools, old houses, old styles) are only an assembly of disparate and unrelated objects, like the flotsam on a beach or the contents of a long-neglected drawer. Hence the widespread use of pastiche in contemporary architectural and decorative styles.[17] In Touraine's words, post-modernists are 'replacing a sequence of cultural forms with a simultaneity of forms'.[18] This 'aesthetics of diversity' is the demolition of history.

Although history is epistemologically vulnerable in that its objects are not present to the senses and although it relies a great deal upon written texts for both sources and products, yet it is not constituted solely by words. It is not a 'verbal existent' as a poem is. For example, as we chatted in a cathedral in the Kremlin in 1988, a Russian friend explained to me how historical knowledge was acquired in the USSR in defiance of all the efforts of the Soviet authorities to distort or suppress it. This would have been impossible if history is made up by the historians. And the Czech Revolution of 1989 was largely inspired by histor-ical memories (see Stanford, 1994, pp. 23–7). This is not the first time that both our knowledge of the past and, indeed, the very existence of the past have been challenged by sceptics and conclusively answered. 'How do we know,' Bertrand Russell once asked, 'that the world did not come into existence five minutes ago furnished with all that we take to be evidence for the past?' Such evidence would have to include fossils and fruits, cars and computers, books and babies. It would also have to include ideas and theories, stories and memories. The key to the answer is our awareness of the passage of time. The phrase 'five minutes ago' assumes time and our knowledge of its passage. 'Take to be evidence' implies this knowledge. Even if all that evidence of past events had been created only a few moments ago, how should we know to interpret it, how should we know what it was *evidence of*, unless we were aware of the various processes that bring the evidence about? Indeed, how could we have any sense of time? However fast I type, there is a minute time interval between typing one letter in a word and the next. I am aware that the chronological order of the actions of my fingers has to correspond to the order of the letters in a word. Is this awareness solely a matter of memory, or could it be said that one item of consciousness (a sort of *Gestalt*) covers the chronological ordering? What of motion? When I experience rapid movement (on a horse, on skis or on a bicycle, say), is that experience one of a succession of memory items such that at each point I remember being at a point half a centimetre back? Do you remember each centimetre as you flash through it? It seems unlikely. If, in whatever way, we are aware of a passage of time, that is enough to guarantee the reality of the past. As for knowledge of the past, that depends first upon memory, and then upon knowledge of various processes. When we see a field of wheat, a fried egg or a new-born baby we know what successions of past events brought them about. So with castles, earthworks, incunabula, acts of parliament, military uniforms, moon rockets and satellites. Thus the deconstructionist arguments of intertextuality have little purchase upon history; we know the real past, not merely writings about the past.

2.5 A message from Kant

So why should historians bother about postmodernism? The short answer is: because of postmodernity. The achievement of postmodernists is to have detected and highlighted some of the tendencies and possibilities of the contemporary world. The importance of postmodernism is not that it is all true, but that some of it could become true if we do not take action to prevent it.

It can be said in defence of postmodernists that many of them are moved by a justified fear of the tyrannical (or, as they prefer, totalitarian) tendencies of the twentieth century. These are most familiar in the form of fascist or communist dictatorships, but they are still to be found in the contemporary practice of even the most respected of states and in that of the powerful trans-national corporations. These were and are, and will for the foreseeable future remain, serious threats to what, in any age, must be understood as civilized life. The coercion of one human being by another is an affront to human dignity. It may have justification in other terms, but in itself it is immoral. Men and women, as Kant reminds us, constitute a kingdom of ends.

Another message coming firmly across the centuries from that same Immanuel Kant is that our thinking must never cease to criticize itself. Indeed, this is implied in the titles of his three great works. Such criticism must, however, be constructive as well as purgative. Postmodernists undertake criticism of the Enlightenment project almost wholly in destructive terms, while at the same time they remain remarkably uncritical of their own theories.

It is ironic that some postmodernists make much of the philosophy of Kant (see, for example, Norris, 1993, pp. 66ff, 245ff). What appeals to them is the hint of irrationality in his account of the sublime in the *Critique of Judgment*. Would they not do better to re-read his *Critique of Pure Reason*, probably the greatest philosophical work since the Enlightenment began? It is not only a critique of reason or metaphysics; perhaps its basic message is that we can go wildly astray if our speculations are not controlled and limited by empirical knowledge of the spatio-temporal world. It is true that he thought that we apprehend this world in accordance with our own nature; we do not perceive it as it is in itself. But he insisted that our ideas must conform to our perceptions of reality: 'The thought of an object . . . can become knowledge for us only in so far as the concept is related to objects of the senses.' And again, 'This extension of concepts beyond *our* sensible intuition is of no advantage to us' (Kant, 1963, pp. 162–3, B. 146 and 148). Few phrases are a better description of some contemporary errors than an 'extension of concepts beyond sensible intuition'. Our knowledge of history, like concepts in general, has an empirical basis in our experience of the world.

THE NEW HISTORICISM (SUBSECTIONS 2.6–2.8)

2.6 Cultural Poetics

Before exploring the notion of postmodernity, we may glance at another literary movement which, though no part of postmodernism, is linked to it by an emphasis on intertextuality and is concerned with history: namely, the 'New Historicism'. This, though good in itself, has less to offer history than might be supposed from the title. Indeed, as its progenitors remark, it is better described as 'cultural poetics'. The basic idea seems to be a recognition that a literary text (for example, a play, a poem or a novel) is not to be studied simply as a self-contained work of art (like the *Venus de Milo* or the *Mona Lisa*), but that we should also examine the circumstances of its production and its impact upon contemporaries. In short, its meaning is not to be found by reading or contemplating it in isolation, but by putting it in its cultural and historical context (see, for example, Montrose in Veeser, 1994, p. 89). This has been done very effectively by Stephen Greenblatt in particular. He explains that 'cultural poetics' is a 'study of the collective making of different cultural practices and inquiry into the relations among these practices'. Thus he intends to do more than the conventional historian's 'putting into context' of works of art. He aims to demonstrate the circulation of social energy, a circulation modelled on the exchanges of gain and loss in a market. It is, however, the energies of rhetoric rather than of physical energy whose social and historical significance Greenblatt investigates. The moral, spiritual and intellectual energies of Shakespeare still make a powerful impact, but their existence in our age depends upon 'an irregular chain of historical transactions that leads back to the late sixteenth and early seventeenth centuries'. Greenblatt does not trace these links over four centuries but (quite understandably) concentrates on the Renaissance world.[19] Such work illuminates both the plays and the age that produced them; thus it is profitably read by lovers of literature and of history. Some of the best New Historicist writings leave one inspired and keen to read more of, for example, sixteenth-century literature and about sixteenth-century life. This 'testing on the pulses' (to use Keats's phrase) may appear merely subjective, but there is a searching question to be asked about any piece of writing: 'After reading that, did you feel that life was more worth living, or less?'.

2.7 Historicism not so 'New'

What is to be said on the other side? Two things make the New Historicism of less value to historians than to students of literature. The first is that, not surprisingly, most of the contextual evidence that is used to illuminate a text comes from similar (more or less literary) texts; its practitioners tend not to use other (typically historical) sources – demographic or economic, for example. Understandably, being literary scholars, they do not see it their duty to spend hours in dusty archives, struggling with crabbed handwriting, as do historians. Nor do they spend as much time on those aspects of life (like trade or agriculture) that leave little in the way of readable texts; they give more emphasis to ideas and less to deeds than do most historians. The second point is that there is little in their approach that is new for historians. These have long known that any piece of writing, whether a Shakespeare play or an entry in a merchant's account book, has to be subjected to searching questions. These include: Who wrote it? When was it written? What were the intentions of the writer? What were the circumstances of its production? What pressures were brought to bear and what interests were being pursued in these circumstances? Who may be expected to have seen it? What effect is it likely to have had upon its readers? What ideas, memories, subconscious influences or recollections may have shaped the writing? What ideas, recollections, associations might it have produced in its readers? How does it fit in with other evidence from the period? How far does it challenge, how far confirm, the accepted general picture? – And so on. There is no doubt that the results of New Historicist scholarship can be of great benefit to historians in furthering their understanding of the period in question, but there is probably little fresh for historians to learn about how to use a text.

2.8 The uses of new historicism

Before leaving the subject it is only fair list the characteristics of the New Historicism as put forward by one of its chief supporters and publicists. Aram Veeser defines New Historicism as making the following assumptions (see Veeser, 1994, p. 2):

1 'that every expressive act is embedded in a network of material practices'. (That is to say that every speaker and writer, painter and composer lives in the real world of material objects, of material needs and satisfactions. His art is not apart from, but a part of, that world.)

2 'that every act of unmasking, critique and opposition uses the tools it condemns and risks falling prey to the practice it exposes'. (That is to say that an enemy is usually fought on his own ground and most effectively fought with his own weapons. There is, however, a danger that in doing so the fighter takes on some of the enemy's characteristics. The historian can bear witness that this is true of human conflict in all ages. Nevertheless, it is not inevitable. Buddhists,

Quakers, pacifists have borne effective witness against violence, as have persistent truth-tellers against systematized falsehood. Critics do not have to fall prey to the errors they expose).

3 'that literary and non-literary "texts" circulate inseparably'. (It is not clear to the uninitiated what is meant by the oxymoron 'non-literary text'; it sounds as confusing as the notion of a married bachelor. However, we may guess that Veeser is referring to habits, customs, systems, sets of ideas, institutions and established practices that may be questioned and criticized as if they were written texts. If so, this seems to be only another version of the first point – art is a part of life.)

4 'that no discourse, imaginative or archival, gives access to unchanging truths or expresses unalterable human nature'. (For historians this is a truism. With their experience of the almost infinite variety of human behaviour and the fallibility of even the most sacred documents – like the Bible, they are the least likely people to suppose anything of the sort. The warning is not necessary for them.)

5 'that a critical method and a language adequate to describe culture under capitalism participate in the economy they describe'. (This again looks at first like a version of point (1). However, the warning is worth noting. It is difficult for either literary critics or historians to distance themselves from the ideas, the values, the perspectives and the unconscious assumptions of the society and culture within which they grew, they live and they work. It has some bearing on point (2). It is, however, no new discovery. The case was argued explicitly in Collingwood's *Essay on Metaphysics* (1940) and has been taken up by a number of philosophers, including Stephan Körner, Alasdair MacIntyre and Michael Oakeshott. The roots of the idea can be found in Hegel and, strangely enough (because it has a conservative slant), in Marx.

From Veeser we can see that many New Historicists are concerned to ask what bearing their work has, not only on literary problems, but also on such contemporary issues as capitalism, racism, colonialism, feminism and so on. These, though important in themselves, are not immediately relevant to our concern here, which is the philosophy of history.[20]

A NEW AGE? (SUBSECTIONS 2.9–2.10)

2.9 A clarification of terms

'The word *postmodern* . . .,' writes Lyotard at the beginning of his seminal work, *The Postmodern Condition: a Report on Knowledge*, 'designates the state of our culture following the transformations which, since the end of the nineteenth century, have altered the game rules for science, literature and the arts' (Lyotard, 1984, p. xxiii). But what *is* the state of our culture? What were those transformations? What are the game rules? Above all, what does all this have to do with the philosophy of history?

This last question is the only one with an easy answer. The postmodern is a matter for history in both senses of that term. History 1 is affected because there are questions about what exactly is happening in the present age, about what course events are now taking. History 2 is equally affected, because there are questions about how we understand the course of events over the last two and a half centuries. This familiar distinction between the two meanings of 'history' enables us to draw the similar distinction between 'postmodernity' and 'postmodernism'.

'Postmodernity' claims to be a description of the present state of affairs. It can be recognized by a number of contemporary phenomena that are new and in many cases unforeseen. These include the power and wealth of trans-national corporations; the rise of the non-European world to equal status, and in some cases equal power and wealth with Europe; the revolution in communication and information resultant upon the microchip and the satellite; the ubiquity of television and the impact upon the viewers; the widespread use of and dealings in drugs, mass tourism; the urbanization of most people's lives; the predominance of advertising and mass forms of entertainment where the sign increasingly replaces the substance; the challenging advances in biology and medicine, especially in genetic knowledge and genetic technology; the exploration of space; and the new ideas in physical science, including quantum theory, catastrophe theory, chaos theory and complexity theory, together with such notions as non-linear equations and fractals in mathematics. These are only some of the indications that we are living in a different age from our fathers and that many of their assumptions have lost validity. The very word 'postmodernity' implies that this age succeeds and replaces the age of modernity. If 'postmodernity' names where we are now, then 'modernity' names where we have recently been. 'Modernity' stands for the phenomena that characterized a period of European (or, rather, Western) history, stretching from the eighteenth to the twentieth century; more specifically, from the second quarter of the one to the third quarter of the other. Postmodernity, then, is the term that designates an age and so belongs to the vocabulary of history 1.

'Postmodernism' (as the '-ism' implies) is a more or less coherent set of ideas that attempts to understand and interpret what is going on in postmodernity, especially in the world of thought. (Note that Lyotard calls his book 'a report on knowledge'). Again the prefix 'post-' implies that this set of ideas replaces a former set of dominant ideas called 'modernism'. Postmodernist writings contain many critiques or denials of established assumptions about rational speech and behaviour; in particular, of truth, reason, knowledge and meaning. Along with this goes a questioning of customary moral and aesthetic values: justice, honesty, proportion, balance, beauty, and so on. Thus postmodernism belongs to the vocabulary of history 2, to our thinking about historical phenomena.

2.10 'Making the world anew'

The greatest work of history in the English language is still Edward Gibbon's *Decline and Fall of the Roman Empire* (1776–88). It ran to six large volumes, but Gibbons's explanation of that fall is contained in one pregnant phrase: 'The triumph of barbarism and religion'.[21] Yet in Gibbon's day the course of history was still seen (in England at least) as the unfolding of a divine drama. Moreover it was felt that the past, in the shape either of tradition or of extant legal documents (for example, Magna Carta), gave authority to existing arrangements. This was particularly the case with precedent-based English common law. 'The past seemed to hold the key to the present through having laid down positive (albeit fiercely contested) and binding title-deeds of legitimacy: political, legal and ecclesiastical' (Porter, 1988, p. 26). It was against this attitude that the Enlightenment revolted. Reason, not tradition or precedent or God, was to rule the affairs of men from henceforth. Such was the Enlightenment project.

If the eighteenth century was the age of reason the nineteenth was surely the age of history. History, in the sense of scholarly research into the past, dominated men's minds as science was to do in the twentieth. Massive works of historiography loaded the bookshelves, departments of history were founded in the universities, and the greatest intellectual achievements of the age (namely, the theories of Marx, Darwin and Freud) were all based on the notion of development over time. The same century was also the great age of the narrative novel. It is little exaggeration to affirm that the achievement of those years was both history (the investigation of the past) and historicity (the sense of living in a continuing temporal sequence). 'The moment when we begin to think of ourselves in purely historical terms is a central moment in our history' (Touraine, 1995, p. 64).

Although this sort of outlook seems to contrast with that of the Enlightenment (for the eighteenth-century view was universal and 'horizontal', while the nineteenth-century view tended to be national and 'vertical' in time), yet a belief in progress, or at least in a meaningful development of human affairs, was common to both. Marx, who had his intellectual roots in both centuries (his father was a devotee of the Enlightenment), believed in reason, in history and in progress; his theories blend all three.

One of the abiding questions about Marxism is that of how far it is a deterministic system and how far a voluntarist. The usual compromise answer has been that the dictatorship of the proletariat will come about inevitably but will happen all the sooner if we support the Communist Party. This close association between great political transformations and the efforts of the individual was most marked in the French Revolution. Quite unprecedented, it fell like an electrical storm upon the French scene. Modern historians, like François Furet, Mona Ozouf, Lynn Hunt and Pierre Nora, have shown the importance of popular belief and popular will in these events. Robespierre, with his insistence on Virtue as the very heart of the Revolution, understood it very well. Furet points out, indeed, that the 'people's will' was an ideal rather than a social fact. 'The people was not a datum or a concept that reflected existing society. Rather it was the Revolution's claim to legitimacy, its very definition, as it were; for henceforth all power, all political endeavour revolved around that founding principle, which it was nonetheless impossible to embody' (Furet, 1981, p. 51). From now on until 1917 and beyond, revolutions were commonly held to legitimize themselves – a far cry from the legitimacy of monarchies and priesthoods in the *ancien régime*. Thomas Paine's phrase, 'We are making the world anew' admirably captures the spirit of it all. The nineteenth century was not only the age of history; it was also the age of historicism – the period of modernism when men not only saw themselves as part of a continuing history, but also as participants in the Enlightenment project of progress, a project planned by reason and executed by the peoples.

Unfortunately historicism had one great flaw – it made the nation-state the agent of historical change. With the growth of the state came the growth of bureaucracy, and that phenomenon, shrewdly analysed by Weber, was to deprive the individual man and woman even of the small part they had been able to play in the French Revolution. Bureaucracy made the modern state possible. It also made mass armies, mechanized genocides and totalitarian dictatorships possible. This is the triumph of Weber's 'instrumental reason'. It is in part against this dark side of modernism, this perversion of the Enlightenment enterprise, that postmodernism is reacting. That is also partly the reason why in postmodernity the idea of society has been replaced by the idea of the market. If modernity subordinated society to the state, and if the state is responsible for the horrors of twentieth-century wars and dictatorships, then perhaps the market is the lesser evil. Our present predicament is described by Touraine thus: 'We no longer explain social facts in terms of their place in a history which supposedly has a direction or meaning. Spontaneous social thought, ideologies and the mood of the times have jettisoned all reference to history. That is the primary meaning of the theme of postmodernism, which is above all a post-historicism' (Touraine, 1995, p. 178). If this is the end of historicism, is it (to use a now notorious phrase) also the end of history?

The answer may be that the end of the Cold War was not (as Fukuyama suggested) the end of history, but rather the end of that Utopian philosophy of history which, argues Koselleck, has dominated the thinking of both liberal capitalism and illiberal communism. In order to see where we stand now, at the turn of the millennium, let us briefly trace the course of modernity and of modernism – those offspring of the Enlightenment which may, or may not, have come to an end today.[22]

3 From the Enlightenment to Postmodernity

3.1 The Enlightenment

To the question 'What was the Enlightenment of the eighteenth century?' the best answer was given by Immanuel Kant: 'Enlightenment is man's emergence from his *self-incurred* immaturity . . . The motto of enlightenment is therefore: *Sapere aude!* Have courage to use your own understanding!'[23] The Latin quotation is from Horace and can be translated, 'Dare to be wise!' Scientists and philosophers were persuaded that they could discover the purpose of nature and the rights and duties of man by the unaided light of human reason. Their greatest (and very typical) achievement was the compilation in France of a compendium of universal knowledge, the *Encyclopédie*, a work of twenty-four volumes published under the editorship of Denis Diderot, the first volume appearing in 1751. Faith in reason was sustained throughout the turmoils of the French Revolution by a leading *philosophe*, the Marquis de Condorcet, who wrote while in hiding (1793–4) his *Sketch for an Historical Picture of the Progress of the Human Mind*. The title alone is an Enlightenment manifesto, to which may be added two extracts from the work. One is the statement of his theme: 'We have watched man's reason being slowly formed by the natural progress of civilization.' The other is his picture of the unceasing struggle of the *philosophes* of France and England against the 'two scourges' of religion and despotism – 'never ceasing to demand the independence of reason and the freedom of the press as the right and the salvation of mankind ... invoking the name of nature to bid kings, captains, magistrates and priests to show respect for human life ... and, finally, taking for their battle cry – *reason, tolerance, humanity*' (see Cahoone, 1996, pp. 72 and 82). By rejecting dogmas of religion and metaphysics they believed they could work in harmony with nature guided by reason alone. Thus the way lay open to progress, peace and universal brotherhood. Sure foundations of knowledge would be laid, and mankind needed only the courage and determination of Kant's *Sapere aude!* to bring mankind to a rational and universal happiness. 'In this bright springtime of the modern world ...', wrote the American historian of ideas, Carl Becker, 'the words without which no enlightened person could reach a restful conclusion were nature, natural law, first cause, reason, sentiment, humanity, perfectibility' (Becker, 1932, pp. 40, 47). This 'heavenly city of the philosophers' (Becker's title) was to be gained by laying aside all prejudice and following only empirical methods guided and justified by reason. Such were the aims which postmodernists call the 'Enlightenment project'. Most postmodernists attack them – Lyotard, for instance, sees the project as the source of two modern scourges, totalitarianism and ecological destruction. Perhaps their most distinguished defender today is the German philosopher, Jürgen Habermas, who continues to believe that the Enlightenment project can be fulfilled. On the whole, however, the confidence and optimism of the Enlightenment contrasts sadly with the disillusionment and despair characteristic of many postmodernists.

MODERNITY AND ITS CRITICS (SUBSECTIONS 3.2–3.4)

3.2 Hopes confounded

The Enlightenment, then, can be taken as the beginning of modernity. How can we, in a short sentence, summarize the history of the modern world in the last three centuries? It is a story of growth and of revolutions, of increasingly rapid change and of ever more destructive conflicts, of alternations of hope and of despair. One conclusion is certain: after all that we have done and suffered for so long, we have still not fulfilled the Enlightenment project of a harmonious, peaceful and prosperous world basking in the benevolent light of reason. If we are still far from that goal, from the philosophers' heavenly city upon earth, is it because we have not tried hard enough, or because the road thither is longer than we thought? Or is it (as postmodernists nearly all agree) because the vision was only a mirage, no more than a cruel or foolish delusion? Worse still, were the lamps of the Enlightenment mere will-o'-the-wisps, the treacherous lights that can appear at night over bogs and swamps and lead the hapless traveller away from the safe path down to destruction? These are very real, very serious questions with which postmodernists confront us. If we reject some of their answers, we must not ignore the questions.

Looking back at the course that modernity, the modern world, has taken since the early eighteenth century, we can see much to justify Enlightenment hopes. If the greatest advances have been made in the physical sciences and in technology, the extension of our knowledge of the living world – whether through biology, the social sciences, archaeology or history – has been hardly less revolutionary. It would seem that the combination of empirical investigation with rational modes of thought has brought hitherto unimaginable extensions of knowledge. So far the Enlightenment project has succeeded – surely beyond the wildest dreams of its proponents. And yet, as the twenty-first century dawns, we are far from content. We stand at the end of the most murderous and destructive century the world has ever known. The very worst has not happened, but we risk the completion of that murderous destruction either through nuclear war or by exhaustion of the planet's natural resources. The eighteenth-century dream of steadily advancing peace and happiness has already for millions of people become a nightmare – of war, of torture, of genocide; of bitter hatred and inhuman cruelties.

What went wrong?

3.3   Early opposition

Postmodernists to a man (and a woman) are virtually unanimous in finding the fault in the Enlightenment project itself. But we must not forget that they were by no means the first to do so. Almost since the inception of the modern world modernity has been criticizing itself. Well before the end of the century of Enlightenment Herder had launched the assault of historicism in his *Also a Philosophy of History* (1774). This attacked two Enlightenment axioms: the notion that man is a part of nature, and the belief that truth is to be found in universals. (The latter lies at the root of many other things, nineteenth-century positivism and twentieth-century structural history, by the way.) Historicists (largely a

German trend of thought) argue that the laws of nature do not apply, or do not apply in the same way, to human beings. They also emphasize the reality of the individual, rather than of the general or universal.[24]

Equally opposed to the Enlightenment project was the whole phenomenon of Romanticism. Some of the roots of the Romantic outlook are to be found in Rousseau, with his belief in the natural goodness of human beings and their subsequent corruption by society. Whether Rousseau was a true son of the Enlightenment or was one of its most trenchant opponents is still a matter of debate. Without suggesting any other connection between them we may remark that Hegel, Wagner, Pope Pius IX, Nietzsche and Hitler were all, in their various ways, vigorous opponents of the Enlightenment. Among philosophers of history we may note Croce and Collingwood.

3.4 Devastating criticism

But perhaps the strongest critique before postmodernism came from the Frankfurt School in Horkheimer and Adorno's *Dialectic of Enlightenment* (1944). Writing at the time of a fascist-dominated Europe, they found the cause of the failure of the Enlightenment's best hopes in that very Reason that lay at its heart. By rejecting the individual for the universal, by discarding emotion and exalting intellect, by abolishing metaphysics and religion as sources of values and grounds for meaning, the men of the Enlightenment reduced reason to a system of bloodless calculating.

'For enlightenment', they said, 'is as totalitarian as any system. Its untruth does not consist in what its romantic enemies have always reproached it for ... but instead in the fact that for enlightenment the process is always decided from the start.' It becomes mathematical: 'In the anticipatory identification of the wholly conceived and mathematized world with truth, enlightenment intends to secure itself against the return of the mythic. It confounds thought and mathematics.' In a remarkable, pre-Turing prophecy of the computer age, they go on to complain: 'Thinking objectifies itself to become an automatic, self-activating process: an impersonation of the machine that it produces itself so that ultimately the machine can replace it' (quoted from Cahoone, 1996, pp. 244–5). Half a century later machines not only *can*, but *do*, replace our thinking. After the purging of reason by Kant's first *Critique*, they claim that it (Enlightenment reason) is incapable of finding any values. With religion and metaphysics (or any other myth) abolished, reason is at the disposal of evil as much as of good. This was already foreshadowed, as they show, in the writings of the eighteenth-century Marquis de Sade. The twentieth century was to see reason equally employed at Auschwitz or Hiroshima or in the 'Gulag Archipelago' as in hospitals and schools. Thus, they argue, the aims of the Enlightenment were self-contradictory (hence the use of the term 'dialectic'); the movement for greater light eventually plunged mankind into deeper darkness.[25] Power and self-interest became the only goals.

MODERNISM (SUBSECTIONS 3.5–3.9)

3.5 Failure of success?

In attempting to answer the question 'What went wrong?' we have not yet decided whether the fault lies in mankind's failure to carry out the Enlightenment project or, conversely, in that project itself. The criticisms just cited, those of historicists, romantics or critical theorists, all place the blame on the project itself. It may be, however, that, while a large number of people were striving over those two and a half centuries to bring about the reign of reason, they could never overcome the forces of unreason – forces that in pre-Enlightenment terms could be described as forces of evil. There is no need here to trace the history of the last few centuries, but when one looks at the unnecessary wars – Napoleonic, Crimean, American Civil, Franco-Prussian, First and Second World Wars, Vietnam, Falklands, the Gulf, the Balkans – together with the attendant retributions, persecutions and massacres, one is compelled to ask, 'Why?' Were these disasters the fruits of sin (notably the deadly sins of greed, anger and pride) or of sheer stupidity (as seems often the case when men adopt counter-productive means to their ends)? Surely they could not all be due to bad luck – as politicians would have us believe; could not all be unforeseeable misfortunes befalling men and women of excellent intentions? Were these disasters (for disasters they were, despite politicians' attempts to justify them – disasters in terms not only of death, suffering and destruction, but also in their frustration of so many good intentions) – were they the consequences of the Enlightenment project? If a few believed so, it is probable, nevertheless, that most thinking people over these years still had faith in reason, empirical knowledge and at least the possibility of universal mutual understanding and harmony. Such was to be the history of modernism.

Indeed, in spite of all the catastrophes just referred to, these centuries of the modern world were by no means wholly disastrous. They saw many great achievements. Modernism, then, arose historically in the context not only of the Enlightenment but also of great political events – the American and French Revolutions, followed by the nationalist revolutions of the succeeding century. The economic and social changes brought about by the growth of capitalism, the industrial revolution and the growth of cities all transformed the European context from that of the original Enlightenment project. How did the project fare in these changed conditions?

One central legacy of the Enlightenment was to remain at the heart of Western history over these centuries: that legacy was hope. It was not the hope in God that formed part of St Paul's famous trio of faith, hope and charity. Rather, was it the secular hope that mankind, rejecting all religion and metaphysics, could, by its own endeavours and in the light of reason, bring about an elysium of peace, prosperity and brotherhood. Man, it was believed, could fashion society anew according to his wishes, and in so doing could remake himself. It is this centuries-old inspiration that postmodernism has finally rejected.

3.6 Re-arranging society

The social sciences, as we know, emerged from the Enlightenment and grew rapidly in the modern world. In doing so they took two directions:

1 That of the thinkers who accepted the modern world as 'progress' and who saw capitalism and industrialism and élites and bureaucracy as the way ahead.

2 That of those who criticized the modern world, and who believed that a proper understanding of society would go along with a proper re-arrangement of society – good theory leading to good practice. Thus description gives place to prescription. Marx is foremost in this group, but Durkheim and Weber also both understood the failures of modernity and had a belief that a more scientific approach (at least Marx and Durkheim did) would set it right. As Crook puts it:

> Marx's historical materialism and Durkheim's sociology are *radical* projects which set out to revolutionise both social theory and social practice, and which insist on the necessary unity of these twin revolutions. They are *modernist* projects to the extent that they insist that only through the twin revolutions which they accomplish can social modernity be understood and completed.[26]

But what is a 'proper' understanding or re-arrangement of society? Here we come up against the old problem of apperance and reality. Is the world just as it appears to be? Or are reality and truth concealed behind appearances? The debate goes back at least as far as Plato. Religion and metaphysics, whatever their differences, agree that reality is not on the surface of things, but lies deeper. It is important, however, to note that science has always held this view also. Newton's law of gravity, Darwin's theory of evolution, Einstein's relativity were far from evident to the naked eye. They were believed to be truths behind the appearances which were only arrived at by a great deal of hard thinking. Now Marx, Durkheim and other theorists of society on the one hand deliberately rejected religion and metaphysics, but on the other still believed that they were revealing hidden truths; they believed that they were discovering what society is 'really' like. It is just such modernist assumptions that postmodernists condemn as equally metaphysical. Postmodernists do not believe that there is one reality behind the multiplicity of appearances. They believe that there is simply the multiplicity of appearances. It is these, if anything does, that constitute 'reality'.

What about the 'proper' re-arrangement of society? Modernists strove for this also. In fact it is a characteristic of modernist thinking that theoretical and practical change must proceed together. Hence Marx's *Theses on Feuerbach*, with such remarks as 'Man must prove the truth . . . in practice' (II); 'All social life is essentially practical' (VIII); and 'Philosophers have only interpreted the world, in various ways; the point is to change it' (XI). These are typically modernist precepts. Indeed, modernism can be defined as the visions and ideas for making men and women the subjects as well as the objects of modernization. None of this fits the postmodernist outlook: for many thinkers the subject is dissolved away, and even if it were not, men and women have no power to change the world that is changing them.

3.7 Bringing in the subject

This attempt to bring men and women as subjects into the modern world is fairly familiar in the political sphere with the growing nineteenth-century demands for a share in government. It is worth recalling that no longer than eight years after Marx jotted down the *Theses*, Charles Dickens (who had probably never heard of Marx) described Mrs Jellyby, the philanthropist in *Bleak House*, as taking up the cause of women in parliament. One recalls also the reformist characters in the great Russian novels of Turgenev, Dostoevsky and Tolstoy. It took rather longer for modernism to affect the style and method of the arts. Thus the typical modernist novelists included Henry James, Joyce and Kafka; the poets included Mallarmé, Eliot, Pound and Rilke; the playwrights Strindberg and Pirandello; the painters Matisse, Picasso and Kandinsky; the musicians Stravinsky, Debussy and Schoenberg. (These, of course, came considerably later than Dickens or Dostoevsky.) In their works four common themes may be discerned:

1 *self-reflexiveness*: that is, methods and procedures often incorporated in the art-objects themselves;
2 *juxtaposition or montage*: that is, the simultaneous presentation of differing perspectives;
3 *ambiguity or paradox*: that is, the sort of multiple perceptions typical of a Kafka novel; and
4 *loss of the integrated subject*: that is, the presence of psychic conflicts.

These themes or characteristics are perhaps most familiar in the paintings of Picasso or the poetry of T. S. Eliot. It is possible to see in these typically modern works both the modernist enterprise of bringing the subject into an active role and the roots of the postmodernist dissolutions of both subject and meaning. Nevertheless, these artists were definitely modern and not postmodern in their beliefs that underlying realities do exist and are attainable.

A good museum of modern art makes at least one thing clear. Traditional representational art is rejected because it relies too much on appearance. The aim of modern art is to reveal *what is really there*. This is not normally on the surface, so modern art aims to bring it to the surface and there to show it. Here again we have the old appearance–reality conflict. The problem for modern art was that when the underlying reality had been brought to the surface and revealed there, this revealed reality still had an appearance – just because it was on the surface. One cannot get rid of appearances. Thus modern art is difficult for the common man, because he expects to be shown a representation. But what he sees (or hears) is not a representation; it is a revelation of reality. Postmodernism undercuts all this, not only by negating the intention of the artist and denying any stable meaning to the work, but also by ignoring the reality problem. In the current phrase, 'It's all up front. What you see is what you get.' There is nothing else. In the remark of Ankersmit quoted above we can see how this applies to our subject: the writing of history totally displaces the reality of the past or any possible knowledge of it.

3.8 A counter-Enlightenment

This digression into the arts is justified for two reasons. One is that much postmodernism tends to put aesthetic concerns in place of epistemological or ethical ones. The other is that modern arts vigorously demonstrate in their various ways the basic modernist theme of 'man making himself'. It may be put like this: in the traditional world the rules of reality, the logical structures of the universe, were laid down by religion and philosophy; in the eighteenth century the Enlightenment dethroned religion and philosophy and handed over the description and understanding of the universe to science. Then, around 1800, emerged a counter-Enlightenment which was to insist that the point is no longer to show how the world is, but to create the world anew, either in politics (revolution) or in imagination (art, literature and social theory). Thus Shelley said that poets are 'the unacknowledged legislators of the world'. This would only make sense to a generation that could see the connection between imagination and politics – a conceit probably impossible to anyone before the American and French Revolutions.

One has to acknowledge that, almost from the beginning, the Enlightenment project aroused opposition. This opposition was at first merely conservative. The vigorous counter-revolutionary movements in France over the 1790s may be seen as counter-Enlightenment, but they looked back to the past. However, contemporary movements of thought, historicism and Romanticism, while aware of many attractions in the past, were themselves essentially modern (though perhaps not modernist) because they looked to the future. Historicism saw the importance of cultural traditions and of the particular and individual.[27] Romanticism sees art no longer as an imitation of the world but as a means of self-creation and self-expression. This was the beginning of the task of 'bringing the subject in', which was to be carried to greater lengths a century later in modernist art, as we have noted above.

The almost parallel existence of the Enlightenment project with the counter-Enlightenment does not make it easy to locate them in the postmodernist context. Was that the birth of modernism? Or, if one equates modernism with the Enlightenment project (roughly the position of most postmodernist critiques), was this early opposition the remote birth of postmodernism? Our decision depends on how we see modernism. If we see it as the attempt to carry out the Enlightenment project (that is, to make dominant science, reason, universality and impersonal objectivity – a somewhat bleak and mathematical view of life), then the opposed movements of historicism and Romanticism can be seen as postmodernism in embryo. Without doubt, the move to 'bring the subject in' (both in politics – democracy or Marxism, and in art – Shelley or Picasso) is characteristic of the period of modernity. Was it also part of modernism? It seems not to belong to the Enlightenment project. Thus we have to define 'modernism' before we can decide whether postmodernism is a contradiction of modernism or a continuation of it.

3.9 What was Modernism?

Can we obtain a clearer view of the question if we take a brief look at movements of thought and art in the chronological period I have called 'modernity'? One good place to start is with the poet Baudelaire. What he says is important – though it is confusing that when he says 'modernity' he does not designate a chronological period; he is referring to the state of the arts in his day. 'Modernity,' he wrote in 1863, 'is the transient, the fleeting, the contingent; it is the one half of art, the other being the eternal and the immutable' (quoted in Harvey, 1990, p. 10). As a rough generalization, we could say that up to the middle of the nineteenth century art was largely representational, science and philosophy sought clear and firm truths. (We may recall Descartes' first precept in the *Discourse on Method*: 'To embrace in my judgment only what presented itself to my mind so clearly and distinctly that I had no occasion to doubt it') (Descartes, 1954, p. 20). Up to then Enlightenment thinkers – from Voltaire via Hume and Kant to Comte and John Stuart Mill, and even Karl Marx – believed there was only one answer to a question, only one view of the truth. Then, for various reasons, both art and science saw that there could be more than one answer, more than one perspective, more than one way to see the truth. As the century advanced, as Marx, Darwin and Freud overthrew accepted beliefs; as hitherto unthinkable advances were made in communications and transport; as Nietzsche mocked traditional philosophy, so modernism grew until early in the next century it reached its peak in the artists listed above – to whom we might add Bartok, Braque, Klee, Lawrence and Proust. Like Marx and Freud, they sought to reveal the truth behind appearances. Absorbed with 'the transient, the fleeting and the contingent', they had yet not forgotten 'the eternal and the immutable'. It was just that the latter was not where we thought it was; it was concealed or, perhaps, still somewhere ahead. Hence the importance in those years of the concept of the 'avant-garde'. Nobody believes in that importance who does not also believe in progress.

In the troubled years after the First World War modern art offered increasing evidence of a concern with 'the transient and the fleeting', but where were 'the eternal and the immutable'? One answer was the starkness of the Bauhaus school of architecture; another was the grandiose spectacles of Mussolini's Rome, of Stalinist Moscow or of the Nuremberg rallies. These demonstrated 'the aestheticization of politics', not any of the eternal verities. But the modern world was still serious, still earnest in its search for the right outcome. One aspect of this was the growth after the Second World War of bureaucratic planning – whether in the layout of towns or the organization of public welfare, especially in health and education. These post-war years saw a modernism that was 'positivistic, technocratic and rationalistic' (Harvey, 1990, p. 35). Milton Keynes can be seen as a triumph of the spirit of the Enlightenment.

Was modernism so bad after all? Putting our disasters behind us, can we agree with Habermas that the Enlightenment project still holds out the best hopes for our future? Can we accept Touraine's belief that modernity is based upon both Reason and Subject, that either without the other has been unfortunate for modernity, but that it may now be possible 'for both figures of modernity, which have either fought or ignored one another, to begin to speak to one another and to learn to live together'? (Touraine, 1995, p. 6). Perhaps it takes postmodernism to put modernism into perspective. And perhaps we are now seeing postmodernism more clearly as we pass beyond it. But before we go, what is (or was) it? Perhaps then we shall be able to bring postmodernism, too, into historical perspective.

> There are signs, these days, that the cultural hegemony of postmodernism is weakening in the West . . . In a sense it does not matter whether postmodernism is or is not on the way out since much can be learned from a historical enquiry into the roots of what has been a quite unsettling phase in economic, political, and cultural development. (Harvey, 1990, p. ix)

POSTMODERNITY BUT NOT POSTMODERNISM (SUBSECTIONS 3.10–3.13)

3.10 A period or a movement?

So can we now clarify our ideas about postmodernity? Some writers use the two terms 'postmodernism' and 'postmodernity' almost interchangeably, making no discrimination. This I take to be unhelpful. Nevertheless, we are still faced with the question of whether the term 'postmodernity' is an objective description of a chronological period of history, or whether it designates only those thinkers and movements of thought that believe we no longer live in the modern era. My own preference is for the objective description. After all, many people lived in the

Renaissance or the Reformation and contributed to those great movements without being aware of doing so. If we decide that postmodernity is a chronological period, the question naturally arises about its limits – its beginning and end. The 'counter-culture' of the 1960s culminated in the rebellions of 1968. In 1972 a prize-winning modernist housing development in St Louis, Missouri, was deliberately blown up as uninhabitable. Here, according to Charles Jencks, was the clean break between modernist and postmodernist architecture (see Jencks in Cahoone, 1996, p. 472; also Harvey, 1990, p. 39). Perhaps we may accept the judgement: 'Somewhere between 1968 and 1972, therefore, we see postmodernism emerge as a full-blown though still incoherent movement out of the chrysalis of the anti-modern movement of the 1960's' (Harvey, 1990, p. 38). If postmodernism thus began c.1970, let us suppose that was also the beginning of postmodernity. What of the end?

3.11 A diagnosis, but no prescription

It is possible, as we have just seen, to argue that postmodernism may be ending. The decision whether postmodernity is also ending must rest on how we define it. We should note two things: one, is that there occurred a great and decisive break in world affairs with the collapse of the Soviet Empire and the end of the Cold War in 1989; the other is that most of the characteristics of the contemporary world that I sketched above are still very much with us. The following description of postmodernity does not seem at all out of date, but rather fully applicable to today's world:

> The experience of time and space has changed, the confidence in the association between scientific and moral judgements has collapsed, aesthetics has triumphed over ethics as a prime focus of social and intellectual concern, images dominate narratives, ephemerality and fragmentation take precedence over eternal truths and unified politics, and explanations have shifted from the realm of material and political-economic groundings towards a consideration of autonomous cultural and political practices.[28]

In addition to all these, however, it is desirable to draw attention to one of the most worrying aspects of the age: that is, the increasing power of trans-national corporations, especially those that control communications. For here power is not subject to the votes of an electorate – hence there is no way of removing it from the hands of those who abuse it. Nor has it any legitimation (as traditional rulers had in previous ages) beyond that of market success.

3.12 Where are we?

Where do we stand now at the end of the second millennium? Can history help us to identify our position? As we have observed, history can be seen as a reliable record of the past; it can be a form of understanding, of coming to terms with, a peculiar (because not present) form of existence; it can be an account of our present experience; or it can be the equivalent of historicity – a sequence of meaning in which that experience finds a place. It may even be the case that postmodernity is not, after all, a sequel to modernity. It may be that they co-exist, as Harvey suggests may be the case with modernism and postmodernism. Perhaps we should 'dissolve the categories of both modernism and postmodernism into a complex of oppositions expressive of the cultural contradictions of capitalism. We then get to see the categories of both modernism and postmodernism as static reifications imposed upon the fluid interpenetration of dynamic oppositions' (Harvey, 1990, p. 339).

But however we choose to confront our present situation, it is almost impossible not to see it in historical terms. It is tempting, for example, to say that up to the eighteenth century man saw himself occupying an appointed place in a divinely ordered cosmos. He worshipped God for many reasons, but above all because the Deity was not only the creator but also the continuing sustainer of the universe by his laws and his mercy. Thus he gave meaning both to the whole and to the individual life. With the onset of the Enlightenment man was portrayed as a part of nature, subject to the laws of nature and of reason rather than to the authority of a personal God. In contemporary debates between scientists and Christians that is the point of view that scientists still put forward. The reason is that ever since the eighteenth century Western man has been engaged in the Enlightenment project which still teaches him to see himself in that way: namely, as a part of nature subject to nature's laws. The postmodernists tell us that the period of the Enlightenment project, the age of modernity, has come to an end and that we now find ourselves in the condition of postmodernity. The gods of the Enlightenment are thus as outmoded as the traditional Biblical God that they were thought to have displaced.[29]

As we have seen, postmodernists have invested a good deal of energy in demonstrating that the old ideals will no longer do. At least to their own satisfaction, they have demonstrated that we can no longer believe in truth, objective knowledge, reason, stable meanings in language, or enduring ethical values. After all this deconstruction, fragmentation, devastation and liquidation, what have they put in place of the former gods? Nothing at all, answer their critics. If we look around us today we see many people of good will trying to support the collapsing project, to uphold the collapsing values and to help the poor, the sick, the orphaned, the oppressed and other unfortunates. Thank Heaven that such people are still around. But what seem to be the dominant forces in the world, the forces acknowledged by politicians and other men of power? Is not capitalism dominant? Capitalism, the economic system that has become also a political and social system? Capitalism that, as Marx showed, tries to turn everything into a commodity? Is not society nowadays largely replaced by the market, where consumer choice is held to reign supreme? Are not the acknowledged aims self-fulfilment, self-satisfaction and self-expression?

Of course, this won't do. Human society cannot last long if these are its leading aims and its dominant social forces. What has become of such Enlightenment ideals as mutual understanding, justice and universal harmony? Admittedly a society of the market is far better than a society of bureaucratic dictatorship like Stalin's USSR or Orwell's *1984*. Nevertheless, many people, including not a few postmodernists, are deeply dissatisfied with this state of affairs. Perhaps it is little wonder that they want to deny or dismiss history, rather than face the thought that the world of the supermarket, guided by the precepts of Thatcherism, is the consummation of five thousand years of civilized endeavour.

3.13   Help from history?

We may reject much of postmodernism, for its arguments are often fallacious, its facts often inaccurate and is creative suggestions virtually nil. But we cannot deny much of its criticism of the contemporary world, nor can we escape the conclusion that the Enlightenment project – so far, at least – has been a failure. If the gods of the Enlightenment have failed us, as the 'religion' of Leninist Communism has failed the former USSR, then where do we turn for inspiration? It is not that we are facing great and palpable evils, as we were in the 1930s and 1940s, nor (we hope) are we daily threatened by nuclear destruction, as we were from the 1950s to the 1980s. But the Western world at least (for other areas have other problems) needs to be brought out of the mean-spirited and self-centred condition of consumerism and 'Me first'. I dare not offer a solution, but I firmly believe that we owe it to our ancestors over five millennia of history to search for something to lift us out of the warm and squelchy swamp of postmodernity. Perhaps historians (who are after all those most familiar with the five millennia) will be able to recover from the past men and women, ideas and achievements, to give us better hopes for the future.

4   An Unceasing Conversation

MISUNDERSTANDING HISTORY (SUBSECTIONS 4.1–4.4)

4.1   Is history fiction?

If history is to be of genuine assistance in our present predicament, we need to be clear about what it is. The views hostile to normal history that we have expounded in this chapter are persuasively argued by Hayden White and his followers, by constructivists and by postmodernists. Roughly they concur with White's statement that historical narratives are 'verbal fictions, the contents of which are as much invented as found' (White in Canary and Kosicki, 1978, p. 42). The conclusion drawn by some people, as we have seen, is that historical accounts have no basis in fact, but are inventions of the historians. As Ankersmit puts it: 'There is no past that is given to us . . . So narrative substances do not refer to the past' (Ankersmit, 1990, p. 281). This is not the place to show how these claims rest upon literary and linguistic theories, for our concern is with history. (In passing one might note that many of those who deny history are making a self-contradictory assertion of the reality of history by use of the prefix 'post' in 'postmodernism', 'postmodernity', 'post-structuralism'. This implies that the present state of affairs was preceded by an earlier state, and that *we know what that state was*. The same applies to postmodernist assaults upon that historical phenomenon, the Enlightenment.)

In respect of history, however plausible the arguments, surely (we think) it cannot be that we have no knowledge of the past and that all historical accounts are fictitious? Again we ask, 'What has gone wrong?'

4.2   The roots of error

The chief root of the error lies not in the linguistic and literary theories of postmodernism, but somewhere deeper. It lies in the attempt to see history as a linguistic activity. Poetry is a wholly linguistic and literary activity; it is self-referential. History is not wholly or even primarily such an activity, for it refers to objects outside or beyond itself.[30] It is an activity, of many modes and media, that helps us to understand human existence in relation to the dimension of time. No doubt words play an important part in this activity, just as they do in most other human affairs – think of war, politics, diplomacy, commerce, love and friendship, chess, cricket, science or religion. But none of these is wholly or even primarily a verbal matter, like poetry or the novel. The so-called 'linguistic turn' in history must therefore be judged as largely an error. It is not erroneous to draw attention to the part that words play in that activity – any more than it is wrong to look at the part that language plays in baseball or advertising. In all those cases listed above it may be useful to make just such a linguistic enquiry. It would be a serious fault, however, to suppose that, say, a grandmaster contest or a pontifical high mass is no more than a linguistic activity. They are about something quite other.

The basic misunderstanding of the nature of history that I have just outlined is compounded in much contemporary thought by two further errors. One is to suppose that a historical account rests entirely upon other texts (as postmodernists say) – or entirely upon documentary evidence (to use the language of historians). A moment's thought will remind us that castles, cannonballs, hedges and houses are among the non-linguistic evidence for the past, not to speak of many kinds of works of art that bring us closer to that world.

The other is to suppose that a historical world arises Athene-like – new and fully formed – from the pages of Michelet or Burckhardt (two of Hayden White's examples), just as a vivid, fictitious world aries from the pages of *Don Quixote* or

Anna Karenina. Ann Rigney ends a scrupulously intelligent study of the writings of three historians of the French Revolution with these words:

> For words to bring a world immediately into being in the act of pronouncing them, the speaker can indeed only be 'on the first day of creation' – a possible image for the fiction-writer, but the very antithesis of the historian. (Rigney, 1990, p. 176)

The historical world – that is, the world in which humanity enjoys an existence extended over space and time – did not begin when we started to read a book (as is the case with a poem or novel). It had its beginning no later than the time when man evolved from the ape. When the tadpole becomes a frog, climbs out of the water and fills its new-made lungs, it must seem to have found a freshly created world. Not so: the world had been there a long time. In fact it had included the pond and the spawn and the tadpole. Similarly, neither the historian nor her reader is creating or discovering a new world. They are, on the contrary, continuing the 'conversation of mankind'. In the words of Michael Oakeshott:

> As civilized human beings, we are the inheritors ... of a conversation, begun in the primeval forests and extended and made more articulate in the course of centuries. It is a conversation which goes on both in public and within each of ourselves. (Oakeshott, 1967, p. 199)

In this essay Oakeshott was actually speaking about poetry, but his point is even more true of history. In short, the historian's work is not an art-object, minted anew, but just another contribution to a conversation about what we already have before us – humanity in the dimension of time. This is why a good historian makes a careful study of the secondary, as well as the primary, sources for her subject. Herbert Butterfield showed this in an important essay, and pointed out that 'it is possible for retrogression to take place in historical science if students lose touch with the work that their predecessors have done' (Butterfield, 1960, p. 170).

4.3   Figuration inevitable

It is sometimes argued that the historian can never be impartial because his evidence comes to him already biased; that is to say that the events he is describing have already been prefigured in the texts that form the evidence. He can never 'get behind' someone's view of the matter. This is true, but it is only half the truth. In respect of prefiguring one can go further than the critics. For every human action – every thought, every word, every deed – is partly a response to the situation as the agent conceives it. Unceasingly we 'prefigure', or figure, the world as we find it. But the world never exactly accords with any figuration; it cannot, because every figuration is perspectival. This is none other than the ancient and ever-lasting problem of knowledge and belief.

Perfect knowledge, if possible at all, is possible only to God. But we can all strive towards greater knowledge. In human affairs this can be done by bringing together different perspectives on the same matter and then, through comparison and discussion, arriving at something like Gadamer's 'fusion of horizons' – that is, a description or statement with which all parties can agree. This is best exemplified in the history of science. Paradoxically, science also offers the best illustration of the limits of this approach. The fusing of horizons may be achieved in human affairs, but what of the universe? Do we know, shall we ever know, what our galaxy looks like from the other side? Can we compare and discuss our views with one who dwells a billion light-years away? In this respect, historians and scientists are in the same boat. Neither the positivist demand for infallible science nor the objectivist demand for infallible history are capable of being satisfied. The most that either scientist or historian can offer is the agreed (though doubtless temporary) judgements of those who are, at the moment, the best informed.

4.4 An unbroken process

I said above that the figuring inevitable in any historical report is only half the truth. A famous sentence of Marx reminds us of the other half: 'Men make their own history, but not of their own free will; not under circumstances they themselves have chosen but under the given and inherited circumstances with which they are directly confronted.'[31] The world is not as we would choose it to be; often it is not even as we believe it to be. So how does the historian get away from the inevitable prefigurings of his witnesses and their contemporaries? By paying attention to those factors in the situation which do not contain prefigurings – to non-documentary, even non-verbal, evidence. The great error of many recent theorists of historiography is to suppose (to quote Hayden White) that history is a 'plenum of documents... that can be put together in a number of ways' (White, 1973, p. 283). It is not.

In a devastating review Nancy Struever shows the errors of Hayden White's approach to history and herself evinces a greater understanding of the subject.[32] She accuses White of being anti-historical because he focuses on the products, not the process. She accuses him of the 'extreme nominalist position that texts are, in fact, all that we have, that "history" is simply a group of texts, and that the only commitment of the historian is to his product, the finished text in its textuality'.[33] The structure of the discipline, she rightly points out, is argument. It is the duty of the more active historian to 'argue narratives, not simply narrate arguments'.[34] She concludes that a neglect of argumentative discipline in 'scientific' history can, in spite of its pretentious, technical prose, make it seem rustic and unsophisticated in contrast with, say, the urbane Tacitus.[35]

Thus, if a historical text is more like an argument, or (as I should prefer to see it) a contribution to an ongoing discussion, then it is possible to see the whole activity as a continuing conversation – spoken and written mainly, but also couched in other media like paint or stone or music, a conversation about what strike us as the more noteworthy things of life. Talk about the French Revolution did not begin with the historians; it did not begin with Burke's contemporaneous *Reflections on the Revolution in France*; it did not begin with the Tennis Court Oath; it began several decades in advance in the conversation of French intellectuals. Nor has the discussion ever ceased. (It will be a sad day when it does.)

But the continuing flow is not confined to words. As is well known, the Revolution changed manners, clothing styles, furniture, buildings, street plans, military tactics, methods of execution, crockery, music and many other non-verbal objects or actions. All things of this sort furnish non-documentary evidence to the historian, but, more significantly, they constituted part of the contemporary world for the people of France – a world on which they worked to express their intentions, but also a world that altered or frustrated those intentions. These were the 'given and inherited circumstances' with which they were confronted.

The world we inhabit is a continuity in time. Each life is a strand in that unbroken rope. Other strands are the material and immaterial accompaniments of our lives – like pets, furniture, factories, customs or governments. These things last for longer or shorter periods of time and thus form connecting links between lives and between generations. To take an example close at hand, I inherited many books and some furniture from my grandfather. I well remember him reading the books and sitting in the chairs. Perhaps my grandchildren will inherit the books and the furniture and recall my using them. Such is the continuity of life.[36] The world of the past is not created anew when we open a history book or enter a heritage museum; it is more like a moving platform on to which we step at our birth and on which we travel for only a limited time. Our perceptions of that journey will differ more or less from those of other travellers; hence the interest of the conversation. But no one should suppose that the journey and the other travellers are figments of imagination. Did other travellers build Stonehenge and the Taj Mahal? Or were they put there by fairies or Walt Disney Inc.? The fact that we know little about the architects, and may have different opinions about them, does not imply that they did not exist.

So let us take a final look at the historical enterprise.

THE HISTORICAL ENTERPRISE (SUBSECTIONS 4.5–4.7)

4.5   Memories

Over the last two hundred years the Western mind has built itself largely around historical structures. These, as we have remarked, include both a knowledge of the past and a sense of living in a temporal continuum – one where we recall pasts and look to futures that will be different both from each other and from the present. This sense is amply reinforced by our enjoyment and appreciation of the arts together with the contexts in which the works were produced. The sense of history gives a shape and a meaning not only to our individual lives, but also to our common life – to our shared experiences. Can we do without it?

To begin with, we must be clear that history is not one thing but several things. There is history as it happens and there is what we make of it in memory. The first is what we like to believe to be a series of objective events or situations, identifiable and recognizable entities that occurred at a definite time and place. The second is our storage and recall, our re-living and re-understanding of those events and, finally, their influence on the way we deal with present events and situations. Loosely, all this can be called the realm of memory. Now memory comes in various forms – personal memory, collective memory, official memory, sectarian or party memory, academic memory, and perhaps others.

Let us start with personal memory. George Steiner speaks of memory of a poem or piece of music:

> Accurate recollection and resort in remembrance not only deepen our grasp of the work: they generate a shaping reciprocity between ourselves and that which the heart knows. As we change, so does the informing context of the internalized poem or sonata. In turn, remembrance becomes recognition and discovery (to re-cognize is to know again) . . . it safeguards the core of individuality. What is committed to memory and susceptible of recall constitutes the ballast of the self. (Steiner, 1989, pp. 9–10)

Does not that ring equally true of our memory of significant events – the birth or death of one very much loved, knowing an outstanding person, or visiting an exotic land? Are they not some of the 'ballast of the self'? It is surely no accident that many of the literary masterpieces of modernism – Joyce's *Ulysses*, Proust's *A la Recherche du Temps Perdu*, Eliot's *The Waste Land* – should all be explorations of memory.

With the advent of computers we have become familiar with another kind of memory – the mechanical memory of a data bank. This remains fixed in electronic form, apart from human intervention. In this respect it is unlike human memory. There is no 'shaping reciprocity between ourselves and that which the heart knows.' That is the purpose of data banks; they do not change. We look to them for information, not imagination. However, they are increasingly useful to historians, whose function it is to supply the imaginative content.

Another kind of memory is that of the genes. Here are stored traces of all earlier stages of evolution. However, like computers, they are rigid archives of information, not flexible sources of imagination constituted by neural memory.

Somewhere between the rich idiosyncrasies of personal memory and the reliable but boring samenesses of the computer and the genes, we have collective memory.

This comes in several forms: the spontaneous shared memory of one village, family, city, military unit or ship's crew; the traditional memory of non-literate peoples which is handed on by tribal poets and remembrancers; the official histories approved (and sometimes written) by governmental or military authorities; propaganda history manufactured to further religious or political ends; the cool, objective history of the academics; and entertainment history, which includes films, TV and radio programmes, novels and popular histories, and the 'heritage' history of preservation and restoration. The aim of all this last class is not the personal enrichment of which Steiner speaks, nor the 'correct' attitudes produced by official histories nor the convictions of ideological history, nor the unbiased truth of academic aims, but simply (or at least primarily) the amusement of the public. (It is hardly necessary to point out that these categories overlap in various ways.) Sometimes occurrences can slip from one category to another. This seems to have happened in 1989 when advertising agencies in France were put in charge of the celebrations to mark the bicentenary of the French Revolution. Alain Touraine rather gloomily thought that this indicated that the Republic's founding event had 'lost all meaning and become a piece of kitsch' (Touraine, 1995, p. 191). Of all these forms we may say, with Jacques Le Goff, 'Memory is an essential element of . . . individual or collective identity, the feverish and anxious quest for which is today one of the fundamental activities of individuals and societies' (Le Goff, 1992, p. 98). Again, Robert Gildea writers: 'It will be my contention that what defines a political culture above all is not some sociological factor such as race or class or creed but collective memory, that is, the collective construction of the past by a given community.' His work is a comprehensive survey of the part that French history has played in French life (Gildea, 1994, p. 10 and passim).

4.6   Academic history

From all these forms of memory it is worth picking out the kind that the readers of this book are most likely to be familiar with – academic history. I have referred to it as 'cool' and 'objective' and said that its aim is unbiased truth. These are the acknowledged desiderata of scholarship, though few historians are bold enough to claim that they are often achieved. Another characteristic is that of inclusiveness. Memory, whether mental, oral or written, is the raw material of history and is inescapably selective. We all, singly or collectively, remember what we cannot or do not wish to forget. (In the latter case we make special efforts not to forget. Sometimes, though, as Geary illustrates in a fascinating book on eleventh-century society, special efforts were made to forget (see Geary, 1994). But for modern historians it seems that all is grist that comes to their mill. There appears to be no human activity that nowadays lacks its own history. And if there remain any such, we can be confident that the lack will soon be remedied. Everything possible must be remembered. Naturally when at work on a particular project the historian will have to be selective; one cannot at the same time talk about everything. But there is almost nothing that historians will rule out *in principle* as irrelevant to some possible work of historiography. This can be partly accounted for in terms of a genuine curiosity about every aspect of human life – as the Roman playwright said, 'I am a man; I count nothing human indifferent to me.' Partly, also, it is due to the interrelatedness of all human affairs. The more widely historians throw their nets the more of this interrelatedness they discover, so that it becomes increasingly difficult to be sure that one has not omitted some possibly relevant factor. A third explanation is the banal one that some seams of history (especially political) are getting worked out, and the many budding historians have to look further to make new diggings. Hence the proliferation of fresh journals dealing with new types of history.

In so far as history is a system of knowledge or a discipline (like science), then it is open to theories about 'language games' (to use Wittgenstein's pregnant phrase), about their rules, and about the authority or legitimation of those rules. In so far as history is an activity or discipline that claims to represent reality, it is open to aesthetic problems about what we take reality to be and how or whether it can be represented. Finally, since history claims not only to tell the truth but also to exhibit the meaning of what it tells, then history is susceptible to contemporary worries about loss of meaning (in life, in philosophy, in literature and the arts) and to doubts and questions about the meaning of meaning – that is, what is it?

4.7 In the spirit of Collingwood

All these are problems for discussion by historians and philosophers. The historian A. F. Fell offers the following challenge: surely 'the discipline of philosophy is strong enough in its traditions to accommodate and benefit from the new impetus from hermeneutics, the new pragmatism, literary theory, and critical theory without giving up the task of comprehending history's cognitive claims' (Fell in van der Dussen and Rubinoff, 1991, p. 84). It is precisely this challenge that the present book is trying to meet. R. G. Collingwood described his life's work as 'an attempt to bring about a *rapprochement* between philosophy and history' (Collingwood, 1944, p. 54). He opined in 1939 'that we might very well be standing on the threshold of an age in which history would be as important for the world as natural science had been between 1600 and 1900' (p. 61). If that prophecy has, in any sense, been justified it is not only because of the shattering events of the rest of the century, but also because the practice and thinking involved in history can throw valuable light on our present perplexities. In the subsequent six decades the philosophy of history has been dominated by two distractions: first, the attempt to see history as a kind of science; then the attempt to see it as a kind of fiction. This book has attempted to expose both errors. Surely it is now time to see history as an activity of its own kind, an activity (as we have described it) that, in the form of unceasing conversation and debate, helps us to understand human existence in relation to the dimension of time. It is on this (to echo Collingwood's autobiography) that the wise philosopher will concentrate with all his might, 'and so do his share in laying the foundations of the future' (p. 62).

Notes

1 *New Cambridge Modern History*, (1957), vol. 1, pp. xxiv–xxv.
2 'History is indeed an argument without end.' P. Geyl (1965, p. 18).
3 One may mention McManners's Chapter XXII of the *New Cambridge Modern History* (1965), vol. 8; Geyl (1949); A. G. Dickens and J. Tonkin (1985); Richardson (1977); Bosworth (1993).
4 See Elton's outraged diatribe against White, in Elton (1991, p. 31).
5 On postmodernism there is a vast literature. A few of the more useful books are listed at the end of this chapter. Appleby and her colleagues have said much of what historians need to say. See Appleby et al. (1994 pp. 198–237).
6 Ankersmit, 'Historical Representation', in *History and Theory* (1988), vol. 27, pp. 205–28.
7 See *History and Theory*, (1986), Beiheft 25.
8 *History and Theory*, (1988), vol. 27, p. 226.
9 Ibid., pp. 227–9.
10 Ankersmit, 'Historiography and Postmodernism' in *History and Theory*, (1989), vol. 28 p. 137.
11 Ibid., p. 149.
12 Ibid., p. 150.
13 Ankersmit, *History and Theory*, (1990), vol. 29, pp. 295–6. For P. Zagorin, see ibid. pp. 263–74.
14 Ibid. p. 281.
15 *Past and Present*, no. 133, pp. 204–13.
16 Joyce, ibid., p. 208.
17 See Harvey (1990, chapter 4, 'Postmodernism in the City'.)
18 Ibid., p. 189.
19 Greenblatt (1990, pp. 5–6. See also his *Renaissance Self-fashioning* (1980) and *Marvelous Possessions* (1991).
20 For one historian's critique of New Historicism, see Lawrence Stone in *Past and Present* (1991), no. 131, pp. 217–18. See also Gabrielle Spiegel in *Speculum* (1990), vol. 65, pp. 59–96.
21 The fatal step was the incorporation of the Goths into the defence of the Empire (AD 382). Again Gibbon's explanation is brief: 'while the republic was guarded or threatened by the doubtful sword of the barbarians, the last sparks of the military flame were finally extinguished in the minds of the Romans'. Gibbon (1910) chapter XXVI, vol. 3, p. 63.
22 Koselleck (1988) was first published, in German, in 1959.
23 Kant (1977, p. 54).
24 For more on historicism, see chapter 5, 3. Also Stanford (1994, pp. 251–7); Meinecke, *Historism* (1972); Iggers, *The German Conception of History* (1983).
25 One recalls the words often attributed to the dying Goethe – '*Mehr Licht!*'.

26 Stephen Crook, 'Radicalism, Modernism and Postmodernism' in Boyne and Rattansi (1990, p. 50).
27 For more on this, see above, chapter 5, 3, and Stanford (1994, pp. 251–7).
28 'Postmodernity as a Historical Condition': Harvey (1990, p. 328).
29 For a trenchant critique of the Enlightenment as a flight from political reality in favour of Utopian dreams, see Koselleck (1988, 1959).
30 Roland Barthes is quite wrong to deny this. See above, chapter 2, 4.3.
31 'The Eighteenth Brumaire of Louis Napoleon' in Marx (1973, p. 146).
32 See *History and Theory*, (1980), Beiheft 19.
33 Ibid., pp. 66–7.
34 Ibid., p. 74.
35 Ibid., p. 76.
36 For more on this theme, see Raphael Samuel (1994) and Kevin Walsh (1992).

Suggested Reading

The Linguistic Turn

You may begin with Appleby et al. (1994, chapter 6) and Novick (1988, chapter 15). Elton (1991) affords some relief. Canary and Kosicki (1978) and H. White (1973, Introduction only), and H. White (1990) are indicative.

Loss of Object

This is best seen in Jenkins (1991), following Lyotard (1984). For Foucault, see Rabinow (1986), Merquior (1985) and Goldstein (1994). For Derrida, see Norris (1987). For Structuralism, see Sturrock (1979). Lechte (1994) is a good, brief guide to current fashions. LaCapra and Kaplan (1982) is not for beginners.

From Enlightenment to Modernity

Start with Kant's brief essay (1784b) and then Harvey (1990, chapters 2 and 5). Crook in Boyne and Rattansi (1990) is clear. Extracts with useful introductions are found in Cahoone (1996).

No End – No Beginning

Oakeshott (1983) and Samuel (1994) express this view. Above all, see Collingwood (1944).

Bibliography

The date given before the title is that of the edition consulted. The date of first publication (if different) follows in brackets.

Achinstein, Peter 1983. *The Nature of Explanation*, Oxford University Press, New York.

Acton, Lord 1970. Letter to the contributors to the *Cambridge Modern History*, 1898. Printed (n.d.) in Fritz Stern, *The Varieties of History*, 2nd edn.

Ankersmit, F. R. 1986. 'The Dilemma of Contemporary Anglo-Saxon Philosophy of History', *History and Theory*, vol. 25, Beiheft 25.

Ankersmit, F. R. 1988. 'Historical Representation', *History and Theory*, vol. 27.

Ankersmit, F. R. 1989. 'Historiography and Postmodernism', *History and Theory*, vol. 28.

Ankersmit, F. R. 1990. 'Reply to Professor Zagorin', *History and Theory*, vol. 29.

Appleby, Joyce, Hunt, Lynn, and Jacob, Margaret, 1994. *Telling the Truth about History*, W. W. Norton.

Appleman, Philip (ed.) 1970. *Darwin*, W. W. Norton.

Aristotle 1952. *Aristotle's Metaphysics*, tr. Richard Hope, Columbia University Press.

Aristotle 1961. *Metaphysics*, ed. and tr. Sir David Ross, Everyman, J. M. Dent.

Aristotle 1965. 'On the Art of Poetry' in *Classical Literary Criticism*, tr. T. S. Dorsch, Penguin.

Aristotle 1976. *The Ethics of Aristotle: the Nicomachean Ethics*, tr. J. A. K. Thomson, Penguin.

Aron, Raymond 1961. *Introduction to the Philosophy of History: an Essay on the Limits of Historical Objectivity*, tr. George J. Irwin, Beacon Press (1938).

Atkinson, R. F. 1978. *Knowledge and Explanation in History: an Introduction to the Philosophy of History*, Macmillan.

Aubrey, John 1962. *Brief Lives*, ed. Oliver Lawson Dick, Penguin.

Austin, J. L. 1964. *Sense and Sensibilia*, Oxford University Press (1962).

Austin, J. L. 1970. *Philosophical Papers*, Oxford University Press (1961).

Ayer, A. J. 1964. *The Foundations of Empirical Knowledge*, Macmillan (1940).

Ayer, A. J. 1971. *Language, Truth and Logic*, Penguin (1936).

Bann, Stephen 1981. 'Towards a Critical Historiography: Recent Work in Philosophy of History', *Philosophy*, vol. 56, no. 217.

Barnes, Jonathan (ed.) 1995. *The Cambridge Companion to Aristotle*, Cambridge University Press.

Barrow, John 1992. *Theories of Everything: the Quest for Ultimate Explanation*, Vintage (1990).

Barthes, Roland 1970. 'Historical Discourse', in Lane, M., *Structuralism*, Jonathan Cape.

Barthes, Roland 1973. *Mythologies*, tr. Annette Lavers, Paladin.

Barthes, Roland 1984. *Image – Music – Text*, tr. Stephen Heath, Fontana/Flamingo (1977).

Bauman, Zygmunt 1978. *Hermeneutics and Social Science: Approaches to Understanding*, Hutchinson.

Becker, Carl L. 1932. *The Heavenly City of the Eighteenth-Century Philosophers*, Yale University Press.

Benson, Lee and Strout, Cushing 1960. 'Causation and the American Civil war: Two Appraisals', in Nadel, 1965.

Berger, Peter L. and Luckmann, Thomas 1971. *The Social Construction of Reality: a Treatise in the Sociology of Knowledge*, Penguin (1966).

Berlin, Isaiah 1979. *Against the Current: Essays in the History of Ideas* ed. H. Hardy, Hogarth Press.

Berlin, Isaiah 1980. *Vico and Herder: Two Studies in the History of Ideas*, Hogarth Press (1976).

Berlin, Isaiah 1993. *The Magus of the North: J. G. Hamman and the Origins of Modern Irrationalism*, ed. H. Hardy, John Murray.

Bernstein, Richard J. (ed.) 1985. *Habermas and Modernity*, Polity Press.

Bernstein, Richard J. 1991. *The New Constellation: the Ethical-Political Horizons of Modernity/Postmodernity*, Polity Press.

Best, Geoffrey (ed.) 1988. *The Permanent Revolution: the French Revolution and Its Legacy 1789–1989*, Fontana.

Bloch, Marc 1954. *The Historian's Craft*, tr. Peter Putnam, Manchester University Press.

Bosworth, R. J. B. 1994. *Explaining Auschwitz and Hiroshima: History Writing and the Second World War 1945–1990*, Routledge (1993).

Bottomore, T. B. 1971. *Sociology: A Guide to Problems and Literature*, rev. edn, G. Allen & Unwin.

Bottomore, Tom, and Nisbet, Robert (eds) 1979. *A History of Sociological Analysis*, Heinemann.

Bouwsma, William J. 1982. 'Intellectual History in the 1980s: from History of Ideas to History of Meaning' in Rabb and Rotberg, 1982.

Boyne, Roy and Rattansi, Ali (eds) 1990. *Postmodernism and Society*, Macmillan.

Braudel, Fernand 1975. *The Mediterranean and the Mediterranean World in the Age of Philip II*, tr. Sian Reynolds, rev. edn, Fontana/Collins (1949).

Braudel, Fernand 1980. *On History*, tr. Sarah Matthews, Weidenfeld & Nicolson.

Brown, Peter 1991. *The World of Late Antiquity AD 150–750*, Thames & Hudson, (1971).

Bullock, Alan 1993. *Hitler and Stalin: Parallel Lives*, Fontana/Collins (1991).

Burke, Peter (ed.) 1973. *A New Kind of History – from the Writings of Febvre*, Routledge & Kegan Paul.

Burke, Peter, 1974. *Tradition and Innovation in Renaissance Italy: a Sociological Approach*, Fontana (1972).

Burke, Peter (ed.) 1991. *New Perspectives on Historical Writing*, Polity Press.

Burke, Peter 1992. *History and Social Theory*, Polity Press.

Buruma, Ian 1994. *Wages of Guilt: Memories of War in Germany and Japan* Jonathan Cape.

Butterfield, Herbert 1960. *Man on his Past: the Study of the History of Historical Scholarship*, Beacon Press, (1955).

Butterfield, Herbert 1968. 'Narrative History and the Spade-work behind It', *History*, vol. 53, no. 178.

Cahoone, Lawrence (ed.) 1996. *From Modernism to Postmodernism: an Anthology*, Blackwell.

Callinicos, Alex 1988. *Making History: Agency, Structure and Change in Social Theory*, Polity Press (1987).

Callinicos, Alex 1995. *Theories and Narratives: Reflections on the Philosophy of History*, Polity Press.

Canary, Robert H. and Kozicki, Henry (eds) 1978. *The Writing of History: Literary Form and Historical Understanding*, University of Wisconsin Press.

Cannon, John (ed.) 1980. *The Historian at Work*, G. Allen & Unwin.

Cannon, John, Davis, R. H. C, Doyle, William and Greene, Jack P. (eds) 1988. *The Blackwell Dictionary of Historians*, Blackwell.

Carey, John (ed.) 1995. *The Faber Book of Science*, Faber.

Carr, David 1986a. 'Narrative and the Real World', *History and Theory*, vol. 25.

Carr, David 1986b. *Time, Narrative and History*, Indiana University Press.

Carr, E. H. 1964. *What is History?*, Penguin (1961).

Carroll, Noël 1990. 'Interpretation, History and Narrative', *The Monist*, vol. 73, no. 2.

Chatman, Seymour 1980. *Story and Discourse: Narrative Structure in Fiction and Film*, Cornell University Press.

Cipolla, Carlo M. 1991. *Between History and Economics: an Introduction to Economic History*, Blackwell.

Clark, Sir George 1964. General Introduction 'History and the Modern Historian', in *New Cambridge Modern History*, vol. 1 (1957).

Clark, G. Kitson 1967. *The Critical Historian*, Heinemann.

Clark, Stuart 1985. 'The "Annales" Historians' in Skinner, 1990.

Clive, John 1990. *Not by Fact Alone: Essays on the Writing and Reading of History*, Collins Harvill (1989).

Cohn, Norman 1962. *The Pursuit of the Millennium*, Heinemann/Mercury (1957).

Collingwood, R. G. 1940. *An Essay on Metaphysics*, Clarendon Press.

Collingwood, R. G. 1944. *An Autobiography*, Penguin (1939).

Collingwood, R. G. 1961. *The Idea of History*, Oxford University Press (1946).

Collingwood, R. G. 1965. *Essays in the Philosophy of History*, ed. William Debbins, University of Texas Press.

Comte, Auguste 1959. Extracts from *The Positive Philosophy of Auguste Comte*, in Gardiner, P. (ed.) 1959.

Connerton, Paul (ed.) 1976. *Critical Sociology: Selected Readings*, Penguin.

Crook, Stephen 1990. 'Radicalism, Modernism and Postmodernism', in Boyne and Rattansi (eds) 1990.

Crystal, David 1971. *Linguistics*, Penguin

Culler, Jonathan 1976. *Saussure*, Fontana/Collins.

Dancy, Jonathan 1985. *Introduction to Contemporary Epistemology*, Blackwell.

Danto, Arthur C. 1965. *Analytical Philosophy of History*, Cambridge University Press.

Davies, Paul 1993. *The Mind of God: Science and the Search for Ultimate Meaning*, Penguin (1992).

Davies, Paul 1995. *Are We Alone? Philosophical Implications of the Discovery of Extraterrestrial Life*, Penguin (1993).

Dawkins, Richard 1991. *The Blind Watchmaker*, Penguin (1976).

Davis, Natalie Zemon 1975. *Society and Culture in Early Modern France*, Duckworth.

Dennett, Daniel C. 1991. *Consciousness Explained*, Little, Brown & Co.

Descartes, René 1970. *Philosophical Writings*, tr. and ed. G. E. M. Anscombe and P. T. Geach, Nelson (1954).

Dickens, A. G. 1976. *The German Nation and Martin Luther*, Fontana/Collins (1974).

Dickens, A. G. and Tonkin, John 1985. *The Reformation in Historical Thought*, Blackwell.

Dilthey, Wilhelm 1976. *Selected Writings*, ed. H. P. Rickman, Cambridge University Press.

Doyle, William 1988. *Origins of the French Revolution*, Oxford University Press (1980).

Doyle, William 1989. *The Oxford History of the French Revolution*, Clarendon Press.

Dray, William H. 1957. *Laws and Explanations in History*, Oxford University Press.

Dray, William H. 1964. *Philosophy of History*, Prentice-Hall

Dray, William H. (ed.) 1966. *Philosophical Analysis and History*, Harper & Row.

Dray, William H. 1980. *Perspectives on History*, Routledge & Kegan Paul.

Dunn, John 1978. 'Practising History and Social Science on "Realist" Assumptions' in Hookway and Pettit, 1980.

Durkheim, Emile 1964. *The Rules of Sociological Method*, tr. S. A. Solovay and J. H. Mueller, Free Press (1938).

Eckstein, Harry 1965. 'On the Etiology of Internal Wars', in Nadel, 1965.

Eliot, T. S. 1934. *The Sacred Wood: Essays on Poetry and Criticism*, Methuen (1920).

Elster, Jon 1989. *Nuts and Bolts for the Social Sciences*, Cambridge University Press.

Elton, G. R. 1969. *The Practice of History*, Fontana/Collins (1967).

Elton, G. R. 1970. *Political History: Principles and Practice*, Allen Lane, Penguin Press.

Elton, G. R. 1991. *Return to Essentials: Some Reflections on the Present State of Historical Study*, Cambridge University Press.

Emmet, Dorothy 1994. *The Role of the Unrealisable: a Study in Regulative Ideals*, Macmillan/St Martin's Press.

Fisher, H. A. L. 1936. *A History of Europe*, Edward Arnold.

Floud, Roderick (ed.) 1974. *Essays in Quantitative Economic History*, Clarendon Press.

Floud, Roderick 1979. *An Introduction to Quantitative Methods for Historians*, Methuen (1973).

Fogel, R. W. and Elton, G. R. 1983. *Which Road to the Past? Two Views of History*, Yale University Press.

Fukuyama, Francis 1992. *The End of History and the Last Man*, Penguin.

Furet, François 1981. *Interpreting the French Revolution*. tr. Elborg Forster, Cambridge University Press.

Gadamer, Hans-Georg 1979. *Truth and Method*, tr. William Glen-Doepel, Sheed and Ward (1965, 2nd German edn).

Gadamer, Hans-Georg 1985. *Philosophical Apprenticeships*, tr. Robert R. Sullivan, MIT Press (in German 1977).

Gadamer, Hans-Georg 1994. 'The Art of Getting it Wrong', an interview in *Cogito*, vol. 8, no. 3.

Gallie, W. B. 1964. *Philosophy and the Historical Understanding*, Chatto & Windus.

Gardiner, Patrick 1952. *The Nature of Historical Explanation*, Oxford University Press.

Gardiner, Patrick (ed.) 1959. *Theories of History*, The Free Press.

Gardiner, Patrick (ed.) 1974. *The Philosophy of History*, Oxford University Press.

Geary, Patrick J. 1994. *Phantoms of Remembrance: Memory and Oblivion at the End of the First Millennium*, Princeton University Press.

Geertz, Clifford 1975. *The Interpretation of Cultures*, Hutchinson (1973).

Gender and History, 1989–. Blackwell

Geyl, Pieter 1965. *Napoleon: For and Against*, tr. Olive Renier, (1949).

Gibbon, Edward 1910. *The Decline and Fall of the Roman Empire*, Dent (1776–88).

Gibson, J. J. 1968. *The Senses Considered as Perceptual Systems*, G. Allen & Unwin (1966)

Giddens, Anthony 1976. *New Rules of Sociological Method: a Positive Critique of Interpretative Sociologies*, Hutchinson.

Giddens, Anthony 1978. *Durkheim*, Fontana/Collins.

Giddens, Anthony 1984. *The Constitution of Society: Outline of the Theory of Structuration*, Polity Press.

Gilbert, Felix, and Graubard, S. R. (eds) 1972. *Historical Studies Today*, W. W. Norton.

Gildea, Robert 1994. *The Past in French History*, Yale University Press.

Gleick, James 1988. *Chaos: Making a New Science*, Cardinal/Sphere.

Goldstein, Jan (ed.) 1994. *Foucault and the Writing of History*, Blackwell.

Goldstein, Leon J. 1976. *Historical Knowing*, University of Texas Press.

Gould, Stephen Jay 1991. *Wonderful Life: the Burgess Shale and the Nature of History*, Penguin (1989).

Greenblatt, Stephen 1990. *Shakespearean Negotiations: the Circulation of Social Energy in Renaissance England*, Clarendon Press (1988).

Greene, Thomas M. 1982. *The Light in Troy: Imitation and Discovery in Renaissance Poetry*, Yale University Press.

Habermas, Jürgen 1972. *Knowledge and Human Interests*, tr. Jeremy J. Shapiro, Heinemann (1968).

Habermas, Jürgen 1979. *Communication and the Evolution of Society*, Heinemann (1976).

Habermas, Jürgen 1987. *The Philosophical Discourse of Modernity*, tr. Frederick Lawrence, Polity Press.

Halévy, Élie 1937–8. *A History of the English People in 1815*, 3 vols, Penguin (1924).

Hampson, Norman 1968. *The Enlightenment*, Penguin.

Hanson, Norwood Russell 1965. *Patterns of Discovery: an Enquiry into the Conceptual Foundations of Science*, Cambridge University Press (1958).

Harman, Gilbert 1973. *Thought*, Princeton University Press.

Hart, H. L. A. and Honoré, A. M. (eds) 1959. 'Causal Judgment in History and in the Law', in Dray (ed.) 1966.

Harvey, David 1990. *The Condition of Postmodernity*, Blackwell.

Haskell, Francis 1993. *History and Its Images: Art and the Interpretation of the Past*, Yale University Press.

Haskins, Charles H. 1957. *The Renaissance of the Twelfth Century*, Meridian Books (1927).

Hawking, Stephen 1990. *A Brief History of Time: from the Big Bang to Black Holes*, Bantam Books (1988).

Hawking, Stephen 1993. *Black Holes and Baby Universes and Other Essays*, Bantam.

Hay, Denis 1977. *Annalists and Historians: Western Historiography from the VIIIth to the XVIIIth Century*, Methuen.

Hegel, G. W. F. 1956. *The Philosophy of History*, tr. J. Sibree, Dover Publications.

Hegel, G. W. F. 1967. *Philosophy of Right*, tr. T. M. Knox, Oxford University Press (1952).

Hegel, G. W. F. 1980. *Lectures on the Philosophy of World History, Introduction: Reason in History*, tr. H. Nisbet, Cambridge University Press (1975).

Hempel, Carl Gustav 1942. 'The Function of General Laws in History' in Gardiner (ed.) 1959.

Hexter, J. H. 1971. *Doing History*, Indiana University Press.

Hexter, J. H. 1972. *The History Primer*, Allen Lane, Penguin Press (1971).

Hill, Christopher 1962. *Puritanism and Revolution: Studies in Interpretation of the English Revolution of the 17th Century*, Mercury/Heinemann (1958).

Hobbes, Thomas 1914. *Leviathan*, Dent/Everyman (1651).

Hobsbawm, Eric and Ranger, Terence (eds) 1984. *The Invention of Tradition* Cambridge University Press (1983).

Hollis, Martin 1987. *The Cunning of Reason*, Cambridge University Press.

Hollis, Martin 1994. *The Philosophy of Social Science: an Introduction*, Cambridge University Press.

Hollis, Martin and Lukes, Steven (eds) 1982. *Rationality and Relativism*, Blackwell.

Hookway, Christopher, and Pettit, Philip (eds) 1980. *Action and Interpretation: Studies in the Philosophy of the Social Sciences*, Cambridge University Press (1978).

Hospers, John 1967. *An Introduction to Philosophical Analysis*, Routledge & Kegan Paul (1956).

Hoy, David Couzens and McCarthy, Thomas 1994. *Critical Theory*, Blackwell.

Hughes, H. Stuart 1974. *Consciousness and Society: the Reorientation of European Social Thought 1890–1930*, MacGibbon & Kee (1959).

Hume, David 1975. *An Enquiry Concerning Human Understanding*, Clarendon Press, (1777).

Hunt, Lynn 1984. *Politics, Culture and Class in the French Revolution*, University of California Press.

Hunt, Lynn 1986. 'French History in the Last Twenty Years: the Rise and Fall of the "Annales" Paradigm', *Journal of Contemporary History*, vol. 21.

Hunt, Lynn 1992. *The Family Romance of the French Revolution*, Routledge.

Hutton, Ronald 1987. *The Restoration: a Political and Religious History of England and Wales 1658–1667*, Oxford University Press (1985).

Iggers, Georg G. 1975. *New Directions in European Historiography*, Wesleyan University Press.

Iggers, Georg G. 1983. *The German Conception of History: the National Tradition of Historical Thought from Herder to the Present*, Wesleyan University Press (1968).

Jäckel, Eberhard 1981. *Hitler's World View: a Blueprint for Power*, tr. Herbert Arnold, Harvard University Press (1969).

James, William 1907. *Pragmatism* in Olin, Doris (ed.) *Pragmatism in Focus*, Routledge (1992).

Jay, Martin 1973. *The Dialectical Imagination: a History of the Frankfurt School and the Institute of Social Research 1923–1950*, Heinemann.

Jay, Martin 1989. 'Review essay on J. Habermas – *The Philosophical Discourse of Modernity*', *History and Theory*, vol. 28.

Jenkins, Keith 1991. *Re-thinking History*, Routledge.

Joyce, P. 1991. 'History and Post-Modernism', *Past and Present*, 133.

Kant, Immanuel 1784a. 'Idea for a Universal History with a Cosmopolitan Purpose', reprinted in Reiss, 1977.

Kant, Immanuel 1784b. 'An Answer to the Question: "What is Enlightenment?"', in Reiss, 1977.

Kant, Immanuel 1963. *Critique of Pure Reason*, tr. Norman Kemp Smith, Macmillan.

Kant, Immanuel 1991. *Political Writings*, ed. Hans Reiss, tr. H. B. Nisbet, Cambridge University Press (1977).

Kennedy, Paul 1994. *Preparing for the Twenty-first Century*, Fontana/Collins (1993).

Kenny, Anthony 1992. *The Metaphysics of Mind*, Oxford University Press (1989).

King, Preston and Parekh, B. C. (eds) 1968. *Politics and Experience: Essays Presented to Professor Michael Oakeshott*, Cambridge University Press.

Körner, Stephan 1970. *Categorial Frameworks*, Blackwell.

Koselleck, Reinhardt, 1988. *Critique and Crisis: Enlightenment and the Pathogenesis of Modern Society*, Berg (1959).

Kuhn, Thomas 1970. *The Structure of Scientific Revolutions*, University of Chicago Press (1962).

LaCapra, Dominic and Kaplan, S. L. (eds) 1982. *Modern European Intellectual History: Reappraisals and New Perspectives*, Cambridge University Press.

Lane, Michael (ed.) 1970. *Structuralism*, Jonathan Cape.

Langlois, C. V. and Seignobos, C. 1898. *Introduction to the Study of History*, tr. G. G. Berry, Duckworth.

Lechte, John 1994. *Fifty Key Contemporary Thinkers: from Structuralism to Postmodernity*, Routledge.

Leech, Geoffrey 1981. *Semantics: the Study of Meaning*, Penguin (1974).

Lefebvre, Georges 1947. *The Coming of the French Revolution*, tr. R. R. Palmer, Princeton University Press (1939).

Leff, Gordon 1969. *History and Social Theory*, Merlin Press.

Le Goff, Jacques 1992. *History and Memory*, tr. Steven Rendall and Elizabeth Claman, Columbia University Press (1977–82).

Le Poidevin, Robin and MacBeath, Murray (eds) 1993. *The Philosophy of Time*, Oxford University Press.

Le Roy Ladurie, Emmanuel 1978. *Montaillou: Cathars and Catholics in a French Village 1294–1324*, tr. Barbara Bray, Scolar Press (1975).

Le Roy Ladurie, Emmanuel 1979. *The Territory of the Historian*, tr. Ben and Sian Reynolds, Harvester Press (1973).

Le Roy Ladurie, Emmanuel 1980. *Carnival: a People's Uprising at Romans 1579–1580*, tr. Mary Feeney, Scolar Press (1979).

Le Roy Ladurie, Emmanuel 1981. *The Mind and Method of the Historian*, tr. Sian and Ben Reynolds, Harvester Press (1978).

Levi, Carlo 1982. *Christ Stopped at Eboli*, Penguin (1947).

Liddell Hart, B. H. 1972. *History of the First World War*, Pan (1930).

Lipton, Peter 1991. *Inference to the Best Explanation*, Routledge.

Lloyd, Christopher 1993. *The Structures of History*, Blackwell.

Lloyd-Jones, Hugh Pearl, Valerie and Worden, Blair (eds) 1981. *History and Imagination: Essays in Honour of H. R. Trevor-Roper*, Duckworth.

Lukes, Steven 1975. *Emile Durkheim – His Life and Work: a Historical and Critical Study*, Peregrine (1973).

Lyotard, Jean-François 1984. *The Postmodern Condition: a Report on Knowledge*, Manchester University Press.

McCullagh, C. Behan 1984. *Justifying Historical Descriptions*, Cambridge University Press.

McGinn, Colin 1993. *Problems in Philosophy: the Limits of Inquiry*, Blackwell.

McIntire, C. T. (ed.) 1977. *God, History and the Historians: an Anthology of Modern Christian Views of History*, Oxford University Press.

MacIntyre, Alasdair 1985. *After Virtue: A Study in Moral Theory*, Duckworth (1981).

MacIntyre, Alasdair 1988. *Whose Justice? Which Rationality?*, Duckworth.

Mackie, J. L. 1974. *The Cement of the Universe*, Clarendon Press.

McManners, J., 1965. 'The Historiography of the French Revolution' in *New Cambridge Modern History*, vol. 8.

MacRae, Donald G. 1974. *Weber*, Fontana/Collins.

Maier, Charles S. 1988. *The Unmasterable Past: History, Holocaust and German National Identity*, Harvard University Press.

Mandelbaum, Maurice 1977. *The Anatomy of Historical Knowledge*, John Hopkins University Press.

Martin, Rex 1977. *Historical Explanation: Re-enactment and Practical Inference*, Cornell University Press.

Marwick, Arthur 1990. *The Nature of History*, Macmillan (1970).

Marx, Karl 1973a. *The Revolutions of 1848*, ed. David Fernbach, Penguin.

Marx, Karl 1973b. *Surveys from Exile*, ed. David Fernbach, Penguin.

Marx, Karl 1975. *Early Writings*, Penguin.

Marx, Karl 1976. *Capital: a Critique of Political Economy*, vol. 1. tr. Ben Fowkes, Penguin.

Marx, Karl 1977. *Selected Writings*, ed. David McLellan, Oxford University Press.

Mason, H. T. and Doyle, William (eds) 1989. *The Impact of the French Revolution on European Consciousness*, Alan Sutton.

Mayr, Ernst 1993. *One Long Argument: Charles Darwin and the Genesis of Modern Evolutionary Thought*, Penguin (1991).

Medawar, Peter 1984. *Pluto's Republic*, Oxford University Press.

Meiland, Jack W. 1965. *Scepticism and Historical Knowledge*, Random House.

Meinecke, Friedrich 1963. *The German Catastrophe*, Beacon Press (1946).

Meinecke, Friedrich 1972. *Historism: the Rise of a New Historical Outlook*, tr. J. E. Anderson, Routledge & Kegan Paul.

Merquior, J. G. 1985. *Foucault*, Fontana/Collins.

Meyerhoff, Hans (ed.) 1959. *The Philosophy of History in our Time*, Doubleday.

Mill, John Stuart 1973. *A System of Logic in Collected Works of John Stuart Mill*, vol. 7, University of Toronto Press (1843).

Mill, John Stuart 1988. *The Logic of the Moral Sciences*, the Sixth Book of *A System of Logic*, Open Court (1843).

Mills, C. Wright 1970. *The Sociological Imagination*, Penguin (1959).

Mink, Louis O. 1965. 'The Autonomy of Historical Understanding' in W. H. Dray (ed.) *Philosophical Analysis and History* (1966).

Mink, Louis O. 1978. 'Narrative Form as a Cognitive Instrument', in Canary, R. H. and Kozicki, H. (eds) 1978.

Monk, Ray 1990. *Ludwig Wittgenstein: the Duty of Genius*, Jonathan Cape.

Monod, Jacques 1974. *Chance and Necessity: an Essay on the National Philosophy of Modern Biology*, Fontana/Collins (1970).

Moore, Barrington 1969. *Social Origins of Dictatorship and Democracy: Lord and Peasant in the Making of the Modern World*, Peregrine (1966).

Munz, Peter 1977. *The Shapes of Time. A New Look at the Philosophy of History*, Wesleyan University Press.

Murdoch, Iris 1993. *Metaphysics as a Guide to Morals*, Penguin (1992).

Nadel, George H. (ed.) 1965. Studies in the Philosophy of History: *Selected Essays from 'History and Theory'*, vols. 1–4, Harper & Row.

Nagel, Thomas 1989. *The View from Nowhere*. Oxford University Press (1986).

Nagel, Thomas 1991. *Mortal Questions*, Cambridge University Press (1979).

Namier, Sir Lewis 1965. *The Structure of Politics at the Accession of George III*, Macmillan (1929).

Nietzsche, Friedrich 1957. *The Use and Abuse of History*, tr. Adrian Collins, Bobbs Merrill (1874).

Nisbet, Robert A. 1970. *Social Change and History: Aspects of the Western Theory of Development*, Oxford University Press (1969).

Norman, Andrew 1991. 'Telling it Like it Was: Historical Narratives on their Own Terms' *History and Theory*, vol. 30, 2.

Norris, Christopher 1987. *Derrida*, Fontana/Collins.

Norris, Christopher 1993. *The Truth about Postmodernism*, Blackwell.

Novick, Peter, 1988. *That Noble Dream: The 'Objectivity Question' and the American Historical Profession*, Cambridge University Press.

Nozick, Robert 1981. *Philosophical Explanations*, Clarendon Press.

Oakeshott, Michael 1933. *Experience and Its Modes*, Cambridge University Press.

Oakeshott, Michael 1967. *Rationalism in Politics, and Other Essays*, Methuen (1962).

Oakeshott, Michael 1983. *On History and Other Essays*, Blackwell.

Olafson, Frederick A., 1979. *The Dialectic of Action: a Philosophical Interpretation of History and the Humanities*, University of Chicago Press.

Palmer, R. R. 1964. *The Age of the Democratic Revolution: A Political History of Europe and America 1760–1800*, Princeton University Press.

Panotsky, Erwin 1970. *Meaning in the Visual Arts*, Penguin, (1955).

Passmore, John 1962. 'Explanation in Everyday Life, in Science and in History' in Nadel (ed.) 1965.

Peirce, Charles Sanders 1960. *The Collected Papers of Charles Sanders Peirce*, vol. 5, ed. Charles Hartshorne and Paul Weiss, Harvard University Press.

Penrose, Roger 1990. *The Emperor's New Mind: Concerning Computers, Minds and the Laws of Physics*, Vintage (1989)

Perrot, Michelle (ed.) 1992. *Writing Women's History*, tr. Felicia Pheasant, Blackwell.

Pinker, Steven 1995. *The Language Instinct: The New Science of Language and Mind*, Penguin (1994).

Pitcher, G. (ed.) 1964. *Truth*, Prentice-Hall.

Plato 1941. *The Republic of Plato*, tr. Francis Cornford, Clarendon Press.

Plato 1965. *Timaeus*, tr. H. D. P. Lee, Penguin.

Plato 1973. *Phaedrus and Letters VII and VIII*, tr. Walter Hamilton, Penguin.

Pocock, J. G. A. 1967. *The Ancient Constitution and the Feudal Law: a Study of English Historical Thought in the Seventeenth Century*, W. W. Norton (1957). ˘

Pocock, J. G. A. 1968. 'Time, Institutions and Actions: an Essay on Traditions and their Understanding', in King and Parekh (eds) 1968.

Pocock, J. G. A. 1972. *Politics, Language and Time: Essays on Political Thought and History*, Methuen.

Pocock, J. G. A. 1975. *The Machiavellian Moment: Florentine Political Thought and the Atlantic Republican Tradition*, Princeton University Press.

Pocock, J. G. A. (ed.) 1980. *Three British Revolutions: 1641, 1688, 1776*, Princeton University Press.

Pocock, J. G. A. 1985. *Virtue, Commerce and History: Essays on Political Thought and History, Chiefly in the Eighteenth Century*, Cambridge University Press.

Popper, Karl R. 1961. *The Poverty of Historicism*, Routledge & Kegan Paul, (1944–5).

Popper, Karl R. 1962. *The Open Society and Its Enemies*, Routledge and Kegan Paul (1945).

Popper, Karl R. 1969. *Conjectures and Refutations: the Growth of Scientific Knowledge*, Routledge & Kegan Paul (1963).

Popper, Karl R. 1972. *Objective Knowledge: an Evolutionary Approach*, Clarendon Press.

Popper, Karl 1976. *Unended Quest: an Intellectual Autobiography*, Fontana/Collins (1974).

Porter, Roy 1988. *Edward Gibbon: Making History*, Weidenfeld & Nicolson.

Pressly, Thomas J. 1965. *Americans Interpret Their Civil War*, Free Press.

Priest, Stephen 1991. *Theories of the Mind*, Penguin.

Putnam, Hilary 1979. *Meaning and the Moral Sciences*, Routledge & Kegan Paul (1978).

Putnam, Hilary 1989. Interview in *Cogito*, vol. 3, no. 2.

Quine, Willard Van Orman 1960. *Word and Object*, MIT Press.

Quine, Willard Van Orman 1980. *From a Logical Point of View: Nine Logico-Philosophical Essays*, Harvard University Press (1953).

Rabb, Theodore K. and Rotberg, Robert (eds) 1982. *The New History: The 1980s and Beyond*, Princeton University Press.

Rabinow, Paul (ed.) 1986. *The Foucault Reader: an Introduction to Foucault's Thought*, Penguin.

Ranke, Leopold von 1973. *The Theory and Practice of History*, tr. Wilma A. Iggers and Konrad von Moltke, Bobbs-Merrill.

Reiss, Hans (ed.) 1977. *Kant's Political Writings*, Cambridge University Press (1970).

Renier, G. J. 1965. *History: Its Purpose and Method*, Harper (1950).

Rex, John, 1970. *Key Problems of Sociological Theory*, Routledge & Kegan Paul, (1961).

Richardson, Roger C. 1977. *The Debate on the English Revolution*, Methuen.

Ricoeur, Paul 1984–5. *Time and Narrative*, tr. K. McLaughlin and D. Pellauer, 2 vols, University of Chicago Press (1983–4).

Rigney, Ann 1990. *The Rhetoric of Historical Representation: Three Narrative Histories of the French Revolution*, Cambridge University Press.

Rorty, Richard 1982. *Consequences of Pragmatism (Essays 1972–1980)*, University of Minnesota Press.

Rorty, Richard 1989. *Contingency, Irony and Solidarity*, Cambridge University Press.

Ruben, David-Hillel 1990. *Explaining Explanation*, Routledge.

Ruben, David-Hillel (ed.) 1993. *Explanation*, Oxford University Press.

Ruse, Michael 1979. *The Darwinian Revolution*, University of Chicago Press.

Ruse, Michael 1986. *Taking Darwin Seriously*, Blackwell.

Ryan, Alan 1970. *The Philosophy of the Social Sciences*, Macmillan.

Ryan, Alan (ed.) 1973. *The Philosophy of Social Explanation*, Oxford University Press.

Ryle, Gilbert 1963. *The Concept of Mind*, Penguin (1949).

Said, Edward 1994. *Culture and Imperialism*, Vintage (1993).

Salmon, Wesley C. 1971. *Statistical Explanation and Statistical Relevance*, University of Pittsburgh Press.

Samuel, Raphael 1994. *Theatres of Memory*, vol. 1, Verso.

Saussure, Ferdinand de 1966. *Course in General Linguistics*, tr. Wade Baskin, McGraw-Hill.

Saussure, Ferdinand de 1980. *Cours de Linguistique Générale*, ed. Charles Bally and Albert Sechehaye, Payot (1915).

Schutz, Alfred 1972. *The Phenomenology of the Social World*, tr. George Walsh and Frederick Lehnert, Heinemann (1932).

Scriven, Michael 1966. 'Causes, Connections and Conditions in History' in Dray (ed.) 1966.

Seddon Keith 1987 *Time: a Philosophical Treatment*, Croom Helm.

Singer, Charles 1962. *A Short History of Scientific Ideas to 1900*, Oxford University Press, (1959).

Skinner, Quentin (ed.) 1990. *The Return of Grand Theory in the Human Sciences*, Cambridge University Press (1985).

Skocpol, Theda 1979. *States and Social Revolutions: a Comparative Analysis of France, Russia and China*, Cambridge University Press.

Skocpol, Theda (ed.) 1984. *Vision and Method in Historical Sociology*, Cambridge University Press.

Southern, R. W. 1967. *The Making of the Middle Ages*, Hutchinson (1953).

Spiegel, G. M. 1990. 'History, Historicism and the Social Logic of the Text in the Middle Ages', *Speculum*, vol. 65.

Stanford, Michael 1990. *The Nature of Historical Knowledge*, Blackwell (1986).

Stanford, Michael 1994. *A Companion to the Study of History*, Blackwell.

Steiner, George 1976. *After Babel: Aspects of Language and Translation*, Oxford University Press (1975).

Steiner, George 1989. *Real Presences: Is There Anything In What We Say?*, Faber.

Stern, Fritz (ed.) 1970. *The Varieties of History: from Voltaire to the Present*, Macmillan (1956).

Stern, J. P. 1975. *Hitler: the Führer and the People*, Fontana/Collins.

Stoianovich, Traian 1976. *French Historical Method: the 'Annales' Paradigm*, Cornell University Press.

Stone, Lawrence 1972. *The Causes of the English Revolution, 1529–1642* Routledge & Kegan Paul.

Stone, Lawrence 1981. *The Past and the Present*, Routledge & Kegan Paul.

Stone, Lawrence 1987. *The Past and the Present Revisited*, Routledge & Kegan Paul.

Stone, Lawrence 1991. 'History and Post-Modernism', *Past and Present*, 131.

Strawson, Peter 1985. 'Causation and Explanation', in Vermazen, B. and Hintikka, J. (eds) 1985.

Strout, Cushing and Benson, Lee 1960. 'Causation and the American Civil War: Two Appraisals' in Nadel, 1965.

Struever, Nancy S. 1980. 'Topics in History', *History and Theory*, vol. 29, Beiheft 19.

Stubbs, William 1906. *Lectures on Early English History*, ed. Arthur Hassall, Longmans Green.

Sturrock, John (ed.) 1979. *Structuralism and Since: From Levi-Strauss to Derrida*, Oxford University Press.

Temin, Peter (ed.) 1973. *New Economic History: Selected Readings* Penguin.

Thomas, Keith 1978. *Religion and the Decline of Magic: Studies in Popular Beliefs in Sixteenth- and Seventeenth-century England*, Peregrine (1971).

Thompson, E. P. 1993. *Customs in Common*, Penguin, (1991).

Thucydides 1954. *History of the Peloponnesian War*, tr. Rex Warner, Penguin.

Tosh, John 1984. *The Pursuit of History: Aims, Methods and New Directions in the Study of Modern History*, Longman.

Touraine, Alan 1995. *Critique of Modernity*, tr. David Macey, Blackwell, (1992).

Trevor-Roper H. R. 1980. 'History and Imagination' in Lloyd-Jones et al. (eds) 1981.

Trompf, G. W. 1979. *The Idea of Historical Recurrence in Western Thought: from Antiquity to the Reformation*, University of California Press.

Van der Dussen W. J. and Rubinoff, L. (eds) 1991. *Objectivity, Method and Point of View: Essays in the Philosophy of History*, E. J. Brill.

Vasari, Giorgio 1965. *The Lives of the Artists*, tr. George Bull, Penguin.

Veeser, H. Aram (ed.) 1989. *The New Historicism*, Routledge.

Veeser, H. Aram (ed.) 1994. *The New Historicism Reader*, Routledge.

Vermazen, Bruce and Hintikka, Merrill B. (eds) 1985, *Essays on Davidson: Actions and Events*, Clarendon Press.

Vernon, M. D. 1962. *The Psychology of Perception*, Penguin.

Veyne, Paul, 1984. *Writing History: an Essay on Epistemology*, tr. Mina Moore-Rinvolucri, Wesleyan University Press (1971).

Vico, Giambattista 1970. *The New Science of Giambattista Vico*, abridged tr. by T. H. Bergin and M. H. Fisch of 1744 edn, Cornell University Press (1961).

Vincent, John 1995. *An Intelligent Person's Guide to History*, Duckworth.

Walsh, Kevin 1992. *The Representation of the Past: Museums and Heritage in the Post-Modern World*, Routledge.

Walsh, W. H. 1967. *An Introduction to Philosophy of History*, 3rd edn, Hutchinson.

Warnke, Georgia 1987. *Gadamer: Hermeneutics, Tradition and Reason*, Polity Press.

Weber, Max 1964. *The Theory of Social and Economic Organization*, tr. A. M. Henderson and Talcott Parsons, Free Press (1947).

Weber, Max 1978. *Selections in Translation*, tr. Eric Matthews, Cambridge University Press.

Weinberg, Steven 1993. *Dreams of a Final Theory: the Search for the Fundamental Laws of Nature*, Vintage.

White, Hayden 1973. *Metahistory: the Historical Imagination in Nineteenth-Century Europe*, John Hopkins University Press.

White, Hayden 1978. 'The Historical Text as Literary Artifact' in Canary, R. H. and Kozicki, H. (eds) 1978.

White, Hayden 1990. *The Content of the Form: Narrative Discourse and Historical Representation*, John Hopkins University Press (1987).

Whitrow, G. J. 1972. *What is Time?*, Thames & Hudson.

Whitrow, G. J. 1980. *The Natural Philosophy of Time*, Clarendon Press.

Wilcox, Donald J., 1987. *The Measure of Times Past: Pre-Newtonian Chronologies and the Rhetoric of Relative Time*, University of Chicago Press.

Winch, Peter 1958. *The Idea of a Social Science and Its Relation to Philosophy*, Routledge & Kegan Paul.

Winter, Denis 1991. *Haig's Command: a Reassessment*, Viking.

Wittgenstein, Ludwig 1968. *Philosophical Investigations*, tr. G. E. M. Anscombe, Blackwell (1953).

Wittgenstein, Ludwig 1974: *Tractatus Logico-Philosophicus*, tr. D. F. Pears and S. F. McGuiness, Routledge & Kegan Paul (1922).

Wohl, Robert 1994. *A Passion for Wings: Aviation and Western Imagination 1908–1918*, Yale University Press.

Wolpert, Lewis 1993. *The Unnatural Nature of Science*, Faber (1992).

von Wright, Georg Henrik 1971. *Explanation and Understanding*, Routledge & Kegan Paul.

Young, J. Z. 1971. *An Introduction to the Study of Man*, Clarendon Press.

Zagorin, P. 1990. 'Historiography and Post-Modernism: Some Reconsideration', in *History and Theory*, vol. 39.

Index

Pages where the term is defined are indicated thus: *def.*